Altogether Lovely

Altogether Lovely

A Thematic and Intertextual Reading of the Song of Songs

HAVILAH DHARAMRAJ

FORTRESS PRESS
MINNEAPOLIS

For
Pandu Dharamraj

Contents

Part II. In Praise of the Beloved

Part III. Gardens

Part IV. Love-and-Its-Jealousy

Acknowledgments

I am especially grateful to Langham Partnership International (LPI) for encouraging me in this project through its International Research and Training Seminar, which made possible a sabbatical at Wycliffe College, Oxford.

1.

Introduction

"I am my beloved's and he is mine," we bellowed in unison as children in Sunday school. "And his banner over me is love!" This was accompanied by hand motions, which could get furious depending on the accompanist. The next verse went: "He brought me to his banqueting-table (and his banner over me is love)," and was followed curiously enough by "He lifted me up from the miry clay (and his banner over me is love)."[1] For the last stanza, the songwriter shuffled back to: "Now, I am his and he is mine." If the children knew their Song of Songs well enough—as they sometimes did for motivations other than piety—the third verse should have struck them as a detour. That realization would have been their first experience of an intertextual reading of the Song. In retrospect, that experience is mine.

While reading the Song intertextually with the Psalter (as the Sunday school song does) is less usual, the Song has traditionally been one of the voices in the choral ensemble of texts[2] such as Ezekiel 16 and 23, Isaiah 5, and Hosea 1–3. In other words, it is heard within the canonical spread of the divine-human conjugal metaphor in which YHWH is the husband, and Israel is his wife.[3] Of course, the problem here is that while

---

1. A half generation later, I found that this verse had morphed to "He lifts me up into-heavenly-places."

2. Examples of both Jewish and Christian readings are, respectively, Shalom Carmy, "Perfect Harmony," *First Things* (2010): 34–36; Hector Patmore, "'The Plain and Literal Sense': On Contemporary Assumptions about the Song of Songs," *Vetus Testamentum* 56, no. 2 (2006): 239–50.

3. For treatment of how metaphor works in the divine marriage imagery, see Gerlinde Baumann, *Love and Violence: Marriage as Metaphor for the Relationship between YHWH and Israel in the Prophetic Books*, trans. Linda M. Maloney (Collegeville, MN: Liturgical, 2003), 27–37; Julie Galambush, *Jerusalem in the Book of Ezekiel: City as Yahweh's Wife*, SBLDS 130

the prophetic texts lay out the equivalences between signifier and signified, the Song itself does not invite figurative reading.[4] If we wished to read the Song intertextually with the aforementioned prophets, on what hermeneutical basis would we do that?

HISTORY OF RECEPTION

The first appeal might be to the history of the reception of the Song within Judaism and Christianity:[5] The fact that in the Hebrew canon the Song of Songs opens the Megilloth (compared to the LXX, where it comes after Ecclesiastes) and is read at Passover, signals that as far back as the point of its canonization it was treated allegorically, with the human protagonists transposed to YHWH and Israel.[6] In 4 Ezra 5:23–26, dated to the end of the first century CE, appears the first documentation of

(Atlanta: Scholars, 1992); Nelly Stienstra, *YHWH Is the Husband of His People: Analysis of a Biblical Metaphor with Special Reference to Translation* (Kampen: Pharos, 1993); Renita J. Weems, *Battered Love: Marriage, Sex and Violence in the Hebrew Prophets* (Minneapolis: Fortress Press, 1995); Brigitte Seifert, *Metaphorisches Reden von Gott in Hoseabuch*, FRLANT 166 (Göttingen: Vandenhoeck & Ruprecht, 1996); Rut Törnkvist, *The Use and Abuse of Female Sexual Imagery in the Book of Hosea: A Feminist Critical Approach to Hos 1–3*, Uppsala Women's Studies: Women in Religion 7 (Uppsala: Academia Ubsaliensis, 1998).

For the vocabulary of the YHWH-Israel marriage in the prophets including "adultery" and "whoring," see: Baumann, *Love and Violence*, 39–55; Phyllis Bird, "The Harlot as Heroine: Narrative Art and Social Presupposition in Three Old Testament Texts," *Semeia* 46 (1989): 119–39; Phyllis Bird, "'To Play the Harlot': An Inquiry into Old Testament Metaphor," in *Gender and Difference in Ancient Israel*, ed. Peggy L. Day (Minneapolis: Fortress Press, 1989), 75–94; Törnkvist, *Use and Abuse* , 95–115; Irene E. Riegner, *The Vanishing Hebrew Harlot: The Adventures of the Hebrew Stem ZNH*, SBL 73 (New York: Lang, 2003).

4. Jewish exegesis worked by the concentric unity of the Scripture: the Torah formed the hermeneutical core circled by the Prophets and then the Writings. Thus, the Song, which is in the Writings, would be interpreted vis-à-vis the Torah and the Prophets, to arrive at a YHWH-Israel conjugal relationship. Jonneke Bekkenkamp and Fokkelien van Dijk-Hemmes, "Canon and Cultural Traditions," in *A Feminist Companion to the Song of Songs*, ed. Athalya Brenner (Sheffield: Sheffield Academic, 1993), 81.

Similarly, Christian hermeneutics views the Old Testament through the prism of the New. Thus, when the New Testament's Jewish writers import the metaphor into their writings (Eph 5:23–32; 2 Cor 11:2; Rev 19:7–9; 21:2), the Christian exegete readily accords the Song's protagonists a Christ-church equivalence.

5. For a detailed overview of the history of reception, see Marvin H. Pope, *Song of Songs: A New Translation with Introduction and Commentary*, Anchor Bible 7C (New Haven: Yale University Press, 1977), 89–229. For a shorter and handier review, see J. Paul Tanner, "The History of Interpretation of the Song of Songs," *Bibliotheca Sacra* 154 (1997): 23–46.

For the influence Jewish and Christian allegorists may have had on each other, see Raphael Loewe, "Apologetic Motifs in the Targum to the Song of Songs," in *Biblical Motifs: Origins and Transformations*, ed. Alexander Altmann (Cambridge: Harvard University Press, 1966), 173–93; Richard Tuttle Loring, "The Christian Historical Exegesis of the Song of Songs and Its Possible Jewish Antecedents," (doctoral diss., General Theological Seminary, New York, 1967).

6. Bekkenkamp and van Dijk-Hemmes, "Canon and Cultural Traditions," 80.

Israel's self-identification as a "lily" and a "dove," both familiar images in the Song.[7] The earliest traces of allegorical reading are in the Mishnah (*Taanit* 4.8), which, though committed to writing around 200 CE, represents thought dating back several centuries.[8] The *Targum*, the Aramaic rendering of the Song composed in Palestine between the fifth and eighth centuries CE, is an early and influential historical allegory[9] standing at the head of a long interpretive trajectory that correlates the text of the Song with Israel's national history. It starts with the exodus from Egypt, the giving of the law at Sinai, and the wilderness wanderings and the conquest of the land (*Tg Song* 1.4–3.6); it moves on to the establishment of the Temple in Jerusalem (*Tg Song* 3.7–5.1); and finishes with the Babylonian exile, the restoration, and the period of the Hasmonean rule (*Tg Song* 7.12–8.14). The *Targum*'s superimposition of providential history over heterosexual love lyrics sits easily with the marriage imagery in the prophets.[10] Indeed, the Song perfectly satisfies the emotional range the prophetic texts employ—frustration, disappointment, longing, desire, consummation, delight.

Medieval Jewish commentaries perpetuate the allegorical tradition, providing two models, both casting YHWH as the male character. Typically, the female beloved continues to be cast as corporate Israel, featured in various phases of her history (Rashi, Ibn Ezra). Less popularly, she is the individual devotee (Maimonides).

7. 4 Ezra 5:23–27: "'My Lord, my Master,' I said, 'out of all the forests of the earth, and all their trees, you have chosen one vine; from all the lands in the whole world you have chosen one plot; and out of all the flowers in the whole world you have chosen one lily. From all the depths of the sea you have filled one stream for yourself, and of all the cities ever built you have set Zion apart as your own. From all the birds that were created you have named one dove, and from all the animals that were fashioned you have taken one sheep." Translated by Jeremy Kapp, https://tinyurl.com/ycs6yrfe.

8. Tanner, "The History of Interpretation of the Song of Songs," 26. *Mishnah Taanit* 4:8: "Rabbi Simeon ben Gamaliel said . . . 'And thus it is said [in allusion to this custom]: "Go out, maidens of Jerusalem, and look on King Solomon, and on the crown wherewith his mother has encircled [his head] on the day of his espousals, and on the day of the gladness of his heart" (Song 3:11); "the day of his espousals" alludes to the day of the gift of the law, and "the day of the gladness of his heart" was that when the building of the Temple was completed.' May it soon be rebuilt in our days. Amen!" https://tinyurl.com/y73y6ku4.

9. Philip S. Alexander, "The Song of Songs as Historical Allegory: Notes on the Development of an Exegetical Tradition," in *Targumic and Cognate Studies in Honour of Martin McNamara*, ed. Kevin J. Cathcart and Michael Maher, JSOTSup 230 (Sheffield: Sheffield Academic, 1996), 14–29.

10. For a discussion of the *Targum*'s development of prophetic marital imagery, see Gerson D. Cohen, "The Song of Songs and the Jewish Religious Mentality," in *Studies in the Variety of Rabbinic Cultures* (Philadelphia: Jewish Publication Society, 1991), 3–17. For an interaction of the targumic treatment of the marital metaphor in the Isaiah, Hosea, and Ezekiel texts and Song of Songs, see Johannes C. de Moor, "The Love of God in the Targum to the Prophets," *Journal for the Study of Judaism* 24, no. 2 (1993): 257–65.

Early Christian exegetes followed the rabbinic traditions with variations on the typological theme of Christ and his bride—the bride being either the church or the individual Christian. Earliest evidence of an allegorical salvation-history type approach is Hippolytus (ca. 200 CE),[11] who, along with Jewish allegorists, influenced Origen's ten-volume work (240–245 CE). Origen's long legacy of Christian allegorical exegesis[12] resulted in another *magnum opus*, Bernard of Clairvaux's eighty-six sermons (1090–1153).

Meanwhile, the call to read the Song as an expression of human romantic love gained increasing audibility in the second half of the twentieth century, as studies began to show correspondence between the Song and secular love poetry in Egypt and ancient West Asia.[13] Picking up from early voices such as that of Theodore of Mopsuestia (fourth to

---

11. Roland E. Murphy, "Patristic and Medieval Exegesis—Help or Hindrance?" *CBQ* 43 (1981): 507.

12. Tanner, "History of Interpretation," 27.

13. Samples of scholarship on Egyptian parallels: G. Gerleman, *Ruth, Das Hohelied*, BKAT 18 (Neukirchen-Vluyn: Neukirchener, 1965), 63–72; John Bradley White, *A Study of the Language of Love in the Song of Songs and Ancient Egyptian Poetry*, SBLDS 38 (Missoula, MT: Scholars, 1978); Michael V. Fox, *Song of Songs and the Ancient Egyptian Love Songs* (Madison: University of Wisconsin Press, 1985); Michael V. Fox, "The Entertainment Song Genre in Egyptian Literature," in *Egyptological Studies*, ed. Sarah Israelit Groll, ScrHier 28 (Jerusalem: Magnes, 1982), 268–316; Michael V. Fox, "Love, Passion and Perception in Israelite and Egyptian Love Poetry," *JBL* 102, no. 2 (1983): 219–28; Othmar Keel, *The Song of Songs: A Continental Commentary*, trans. Frederick J. Gaiser (Minneapolis: Augsburg Fortress, 1994); Duane Garrett, "Song of Songs," in *Song of Songs, Lamentations*, by Duane Garrett and Paul R House, Word Biblical Commentary 23B (Nashville: Thomas Nelson, 2004), 1–265, esp. 49–57; Antonio Loprieno, "Searching for a Common Background: Egyptian Love Poetry and the Biblical Song of Songs," in *Perspectives on the Song of Songs*, ed. Anselm C. Hagedorn (Berlin: de Gruyter, 2005), 105–35.

For resistance specifically to Fox's championing of a human-literal reading of the Song, and a preference to read it within the prophetic marital metaphor, see Patmore, "The Plain and Literal Sense," 239–50.

Samples of scholarship on Mesopotamian parallels: Jerrold S. Cooper, "New Cuneiform Parallels to the Song of Songs," *JBL* 90 (1971): 157–62; Jack M. Sasson, "A Further Cuneiform Parallel to the Song of Songs?" *ZAW* 85 (1973): 359–60; Martti Nissinen, "Love Lyrics of Nabû and Tašmetu: An Assyrian Song of Songs?" in *"Und Mose schrieb dieses Lied auf": Studien zum Alten Testamentum und zum Alten Orient—Festschrift für Oswald Loretz*, ed. Manfried Dietrich and Ingo Kottsieper, AOAT 250 (Münster: Ugarit-Verlag, 1998), 285–634.

Samples of scholarship on Ugaritic parallels: Pope, *Song of Songs*.

Samples of scholarship on Greek parallels: Anselm C. Hagedorn, "Of Foxes and Vineyards: Greek Perspectives on the Song of Songs," *VT* 53, no. 3 (2003): 337–52; Anselm C. Hagedorn, "Jealousy and Desire at Night: *Fragmentum Grenfellianum* and Song of Songs," in *Perspectives on the Song of Songs*, ed. Anselm C. Hagedorn (Berlin: de Gruyter, 2005), 206–27; Joan B. Burton, "Themes of Female Desire and Self-Assertion in the Song of Songs and Hellenistic Poetry," in *Perspectives on the Song of Songs*, ed. Anselm C Hagedorn (Berlin: de Gruyter, 2005), 181–205; Richard Hunter, "'Sweet Talk': *Song of Songs* and the Traditions of Greek Poetry," in *Perspectives on the Song of Songs*, ed. Anselm C. Hagedorn (Berlin: de Gruyter, 2005), 228–44.

fifth century CE)[14] came a slew of human-literal readings.[15] More moderately, current scholarship allows for "both-and."[16]

The allegorical reading is clearly here to stay. But, other than the appeal to reception history, there may be another approach to examining the legitimacy of including the Song in the prophetic conjugal metaphor—a consideration of genderization within the divine-human hierarchy as it may have operated in the ancient world, including in Israel.

GENDERIZATION OF POWER

Carr posits that in the ancient world, humans and deity take on the gender "male" or the gender "female" depending on their position in the hierarchy relative to each other—that is, the higher-placed partner in any given pair assumes the "male" gender. So, in a human-human pair, the man is the "male" and the woman is the "female." In a God-human pairing, deity assumes "maleness" and the human becomes the "female."[17]

Carr explains that this assignment of genders goes back to the role and function of human genders within society, as prescribed in the legal canon.[18] The man is associated with the guardianship of the reproductive potential of both his wife and his daughter, while he himself is sexually autonomous—that is, he has the freedom to have sexual relations with prostitutes, slaves, and prisoners of war, but not with another man's wife or unmarried daughter, because that would interfere with the guardianship role of another man. Such a system requires that the woman should

14. In a climate dominated by the allegorical reading, his *Against the Allegorists* was pronounced as heresy by the Second Council of Constantinople in 553 CE. Rowan A. Greer, *Theodore of Mopsuestia: Exegete and Theologian* (Westminster, UK: Faith, 1961), 86–131.

15. E.g., Garrett, "Song of Songs," 97–121 (here 82): "There is no suggestion in the Song that it is a religious text or that the sexuality it celebrates has sacred significance." Similarly, André LaCocque, *Romance She Wrote: A Hermeneutical Essay on Song of Songs* (Harrisburg, PA: Trinity, 1998), esp. 49; Roland E. Murphy, *The Song of Songs*, Hermeneia (Minneapolis: Augsburg Fortress, 1990), 91–105, who has an occasional appreciation for ancient church allegory; Tremper Longman III, *Song of Songs* (Grand Rapids: Eerdmans, 2001), 58–62.

16. E.g., Richard S. Hess, *Song of Songs*, Baker Commentary on the Old Testament (Grand Rapids: Baker, 2005); Robert W. Jenson, *Song of Songs*, Interpretation (Louisville: John Knox, 2005); Iain Provan, *Ecclesiastes, Song of Songs*, NIVAC (Grand Rapids: Zondervan, 2001).

17. David M. Carr, "Gender and the Shaping of Desire in the Song of Songs and Its Interpretation," *JBL* 119. no. 2 (2000): 233–48.

18. David M. Carr and Colleen M. Conway, "The Divine-Human Marriage Matrix and Construction of Gender and 'Bodies' in the Christian Bible," in *Sacred Marriages: The Divine-Human Sexual Metaphor from Sumer to Early Christianity*, ed. Martti Nissinen and Risto Uro (Winona Lake, IN: Eisenbrauns, 2008), 278–80, argue their case from the Laws of Eshnunna and Old Testament texts.

be contained within these circles of guardianship—as a sexually non-autonomous individual. As such, she is allowed neither premarital nor extramarital sexual liaisons. Thus, the stereotype of undesirable female behavior is the proverbial Strange Woman who entertains herself in the absence of her husband by seducing incautious bachelors (Proverbs 7). In this social hierarchy of gender, the sexual initiatives of women like Tamar (Genesis 38) and Ruth (Ruth 3) are positive exceptions because their actions direct their reproductive potential into the custody of the rightful guardian.[19]

In such a scenario, "the category *marriage* . . . is not primarily about relations of heterosexual desire but about relations of power and *restricted female desire*."[20] Thus, the category "marriage" could be readily transposed into the arena of international politics to organize the power dynamic of the signatories of ancient Mesopotamian suzerain-vassal treaties. For example, Aššur-nirari makes this pronouncement over a disloyal vassal: "May the aforesaid indeed become a prostitute and his warriors women. May they receive their hire like a prostitute in the square of their city. May land after land draw near to them."[21] More explicitly, the vassal that violates its "wifely" fealty to its political lord is condemned to repeated rape by "land after land," that is, "male" invaders.[22]

This brings us to the language of war, which genders the victor and the vanquished, demonstrating again the role of power relations in the assigning of male-ness and female-ness. An army incapable of victory is dismissed as one made up of "women" (Isa 19:16; Jer 51:30, 50:37; Nah 3:13); a fearful one is like a "woman in labor" (Ps 48:7 [48:6]; Isa 13:8; Jer 6:24, 50:43; cf. Jer 22:23; Mic 4:9–10). Such language seems common across ancient West Asia in speaking of defeated armies.[23] A related

19. Carr, "Gender and the Shaping of Desire," 233–48. This fluidity within the gender hierarchy is evident in everyday South Asian culture. A "male" is expected to maintain and defend his autonomy (sexual and otherwise). Thus, for example, a house-husband with a working wife loses economic autonomy, and a cowardly man who cannot stand up for his rights loses social autonomy. In such cases, the man may be said to behave "like a woman" or may be spoken of as being one. Conversely, an individual who demonstrates autonomy—for example, by heroic conduct in war, which is a display of political autonomy—is thought of as "manly," irrespective of the biological sex. Behavior and virtues that reinforce autonomy decide who is "male" and who is "female."

20. Carr and Conway, "Divine-Human Marriage Matrix," 276.

21. Translation from Delbert Hillers, *Treaty Curses and the Old Testament Prophets* (Rome: Pontifical Biblical Institute, 1964), 58.

22. See F. Rachel Magdalene, "Ancient Near Eastern Treaty-Curses and the Ultimate Texts of Terror: A Study of the Language of Divine Sexual Abuse in the Prophetic Corpus," in *A Feminist Companion to the Latter Prophets*, ed. Athalya Brenner, FCB (Sheffield: Sheffield Academic, 1995), 326–52, esp. 341–46.

23. Cynthia R. Chapman, "Sculpted Warriors: Sexuality and the Sacred in the Depiction of Warfare in the Assyrian Palace Reliefs and in Ezekiel 23:14–17," in *The Aesthetics of Violence in*

example comes from loyalty oaths taken by Hittite soldiers. Renegades are castigated by genderization: "Let these oaths change him from a man into a woman! Let them change his troops into women, let them dress them in the fashion of women and put on their heads the kureššar [i.e., women's] headdress! Let them break the bows, arrows [and] weapons in their hands and let them put in their hands distaff and mirror [i.e., symbols of femininity]."[24]

Deity gets drawn into this hierarchy of genderized power relations through the tradition of sacred marriage, which is, strictly speaking, the ritual enactment of the marriage of a deity to either a human or divine partner.[25] The tradition covers a time span of some five thousand years, from the legendary King Enmerkar of Uruk (ca. 2700 BCE) to present day rituals such as the yearly celebration of the marriage of the Hindu deities Sundareshwara and Meenakshi[26] in the south Indian temple town of Madurai. Among these, the case of hierogamy, where a human king is legitimated and empowered by his marriage to a deity, is germane to our discussion of gender. This is the "classical sacred marriage"[27] seen in ancient West Asia.

Here, the human king, referred to as the antediluvian king Dumuzi/Tammuz, is ritually married to his divine wife, Inanna/Ishtar.[28] How the gender hierarchy responds to this pairing—which demands the allotment

the Prophets, ed. Claudia V. Camp and Andrew Mein, LHBOTS 517 (New York: T&T Clark, 2010), 1–17. See also the treatment in Pamela Gordon and Harold C. Washington, "Rape as a Military Metaphor in the Hebrew Bible," in A Feminist Companion to the Latter Prophets, ed. Athalya Brenner, FCB (Sheffield: Sheffield Academic, 1995), 308–25.

24. Harry H. Hoffner, "Symbols for Masculinity and Feminity," JBL 85 (1966): 326–34, esp. 332n33.

25. For the term itself, see for example, Kees W. Bolle, "Hieros gamos," ER 6:317–22. See for helpful samples across periods and regions, Martti Nissinen and Risto Uro, eds., Sacred Marriages: The Divine-Human Sexual Metaphor from Sumer to Early Christianity (Winona Lake, IN: Eisenbrauns, 2008).

26. Pirjo Lapinkivi, "The Sumerian Sacred Marriage and Its Aftermath in Later Sources," in Nissinen and Uro, Sacred Marriages, 7–41, esp. 14–15.

27. Jerrold S. Cooper, "Sacred Marriage and Popular Cult in Early Mesopotamia," in Official Cult and Popular Religion in the Ancient Near East: Papers of the First Colloquium on the Ancient Near East—The City and Its Life, Held at the Middle Eastern Culture Centre in Japan (Mitaya, Tokyo), March 20–22, 1992, ed. Eiko Matsushima (Heidelberg: Winter, 1993), 84–87.

28. The earliest scholarship (1960s and early 1970s) presents this union as a fertility rite, following the influence of Theophile James Meek, "Babylonian Parallels to the Song of Songs," JBL 43 (1924): 245–52; Theophile James Meek, "The Song of Songs and the Fertility Cult," in A Symposium on the Song of Songs, ed. Wilfred H. Schoff (Philadelphia: Commercial Museum, 1924), 48–79. See Samuel Noah Kramer, The Sacred Marriage Rite: Aspects of Faith, Myth and Ritual in Ancient Sumer (Bloomington: Indiana University Press, 1969); Thorkild Jacobsen, Toward the Image of Tammuz and Other Essays on Mesopotamian History and Culture (Cambridge: Harvard University Press, 1970); Thorkild Jakobsen, The Treasures of Darkness: A History of Mesopotamian Religion (New Haven: Yale University Press, 1976).

of femaleness to a hierarchic superior—is interesting. Inanna is invested with sexual liminality so as to protect any erosion of her position of power.[29] Her self-description is a bewildering assortment of genders: "I am a hierodule in Uruk, I have heavy breasts in Daduni, I have a beard in Babylon."[30] The paradox extends to other markers of her identity: "She was a heavenly queen, a virgin and a prostitute, pure and impure, a wife and an unmarried maiden . . . a bloodthirsty warrior and a protector, merciful and merciless, a goddess of light and a goddess of darkness, a good spirit and a demon."[31] Her nature at once encompasses order and disorder, structure and antistructure, kindness and cruelty.[32] Inanna descends from the heavenly realm into the netherworld, is captured by death, and is rescued by Dumuzi to be restored to her heavenly abode.[33]

Dumuzi, meanwhile, takes on inflections of liminality in a way that compensates for his disadvantaged power status. Though human, he assumes divine associations, he is both a shepherd and a god, an earthly king and Inanna's savior-bridegroom.[34] Dumuzi's divinity and guardian-like act of valor allows him to keep his human "maleness" when he marries Inanna. The myth (and associated rituals, if any) "allows the human royal patrons to participate in and intersect with the divine world, thus securing their place in the cosmos"[35]—as evidenced by their appropriation of maleness in the cosmic-human hierarchy.

In contrast to the king, whose maleness was carefully protected, when Inanna's male cult devotees figuratively sought union with her, they were first rendered "gender-ambivalent." In cultic performances, they carried spindles as well as swords, wore makeup, and processed before the goddess wearing women's clothing on their left sides and men's on their right.[36] They were "men who were changed into women"[37] so that

---

29. Tikvah Frymer-Kensky, "The Ideology of Gender in the Bible and the Ancient Near East," in *DUMU-E2-DUB-BA-A: Studies in Honour of Åke W Sköberg*, ed. Herman Behrens et al. (Philadelphia: Samuel Noah Kramer Fund, 1989), 185–91, esp. 190.

30. Erica Reiner, "A Sumero-Akkadian Hymn of Nanā," *JNES* 33 (1974): 221–36, lines 3–4.

31. Lapinkivi, "Sumerian Sacred Marriage," 34.

32. Rivkah Harris, "Inanna-Ishtar as Paradox and a Coincidence of Opposites," *HR* 30 (1991): 261–78.

33. See Lapinkivi, "Sumerian Sacred Marriage," 35n102, for a bibliography of references to the various ancient Mesopotamian versions.

34. Lapinkivi, "Sumerian Sacred Marriage," 35–36.

35. Mark S. Smith, "Sacred Marriage in the Ugaritic Texts? The Case of KTU/CAT 1.23 (Rituals and Myths of the Goodly Gods)," in Nissinen and Uro, *Sacred Marriages*, 113. Similarly, Beate Pongratz-Leisten, "Sacred Marriage and the Transfer of Divine Knowledge: Alliances between the Gods and Kings in Ancient Mesopotamia," in Nissinen and Uro, *Sacred Marriages*, 43–73.

36. Saana Teppo, "Sacred Marriage and the Devotees of Ištar," in Nissinen and Uro, *Sacred Marriages*, 78–79.

37. A Sumerian hymn sings of Innana's special ability: "to turn a man into a woman and a

they could achieve union with the goddess "on a level that no ordinary man could have achieved."[38] The goddess had unequivocally assumed "maleness."[39]

The gender hierarchy plays out similarly in the Hebrew canon, starting perhaps with the Pentateuch and coming into full force in the Prophets. Deuteronomy's treaty language, it has been argued, overlaps the language of marital love,[40] so much so that the *Shema*[41] could be read as an expression of metaphoric divine–human marriage.[42] Typically, YHWH assumes "maleness" and becomes the divine husband, and Israel, as the human wife, is necessarily "female." The relationship mirrors the social situation in that the female's sexual desire is restricted. That is, just as the institution of marriage required that the woman should devote her love exclusively to her husband, Israel was required to focus her unswerving loyalty toward God. Any misdirection of this affection was ruled as adultery—whether it was a wayward human wife or Israel casting her eyes at other gods—and attracted male "jealousy" whether from a human or divine husband (e.g., Num 5:11–39; Deut 4:24; 5:9; 6:15). The husband, whose guardian role was challenged by a wanton wife, was empowered to take punitive action on her—as depicted by the prophetic texts that correlate God with Israel on the gender hierarchy.[43] Such

woman into a man are yours, Innana." Åke W. Sjöerg, "in.nin šà.gur4.ra: A Hymn to the Goddess Innana by the en-Priestess Enḥeduanna," *ZA* 65 (1975): 161–253, esp. 190–91, line 120.

38. Teppo, "Sacred Marriage and the Devotees of Ištar," 75–76.

39. Alternately, the male devotees, by rendering their sexuality ambivalent, "are likely to have identified themselves with the androgynous goddess, the model for their souls, and thus they were able to take part in her union with the divine savior, the king" (Lapinkivi, "Sumerian Sacred Marriage," 41). Again, this supports Carr's argument that gender was determined by power rather than by physiology. David M. Carr, *The Erotic Word: Sexuality, Spirituality, and the Bible* (Oxford: Oxford University Press, 2003), 56.

40. First observed by William Moran, "The Ancient Near Eastern Background for the Love of God in Deuteronomy," *CBQ* 25 (1963): 77–87, esp. 78–80.

41. Deut 6:4–5, and also 10:12, 20; 11:1, 13, 22; 13:5; 19:9; 30:6, 16, 20. Carr points out that Deut 7:7 describes God's love for Israel with חשׁק, the same verb that is used elsewhere in the Hebrew Bible to describe "a man's passionate desire for a woman" (Carr, *Erotic Word*, 70).

42. Contra, for example, Moshe Weinfeld, *Deuteronomy and the Deuteronomic School* (Oxford: Clarendon, 1972), 82–83; Frymer-Kensky, *In the Wake*, 146.

43. The prophetic marital metaphor texts that carry at length the idea of "gender terror" are: Hosea 2, Ezekiel 16 and 23, Jeremiah 2–5, and Isaiah 47. A short bibliography on work done on these texts is as follows:

On Jeremiah: Athalya Brenner, "On Prophetic Propaganda and the Politics of 'Love': The Case of Jeremiah," in *A Feminist Companion to the Latter Prophets*, ed. Athalya Brenner, FCB (Sheffield: Sheffield Academic, 1995), 256–74; Athalya Brenner, "Pornoprophetics Revisited: Some Additional Reflections," *JSOT* 70 (1996): 63–86.

On Hosea 1–3: T. Drorah Setel, "Prophets and Pornography: Female Sexual Imagery in Hosea," in *Feminist Interpretation of the Bible*, ed. Letty M. Russell (Oxford: Blackwell, 1985), 86–95; Bird, "To Play the Harlot," 75–94; Fokkelien van Dijk-Hemmes, "The Imagination of Power and the Power of Imagination: An Intertextual Analysis of Two Biblical Love Songs:

action—however violent—was then seen as appropriate because the aberrant woman caused a breach in the hierarchy. Israel's offense of idolatry was then seen as even more grievous, because she was challenging a hierarchy that was extrapolated into a cosmic dimension.[44] For this postulation to work, we must conclude that ancient Israel understood divine-human love as "*governed by much the same principles as male-female love on the human level.*"[45] This is what would have given the marriage metaphor its razor-sharp rhetorical edge.[46]

We may summarize the discussion above in Carr's words: in the ancient world, "sexual identity would not be first and foremost about having a male or female body, but about having or not having male-like power over others."[47] If so, it would not have been an unwarranted interpretive leap for the Song to be read within the same divine-human, male-female gender hierarchy that underlies the oracles of Jeremiah, Isa-

The Song of Songs and Hosea 2," *JSOT* 44 (1989): 75–88; Andreas Weider, *Ehemetaphorik in prophetischer Verkündigung: Hos 1–3 und seine Wirkungsgeschichte im Jeremiabuch: Ein Beitrag zum alttestamentlichen Gottes-Bild*, FzB 71 (Würzburg: Echter, 1993); Stienstra, *YHWH Is the Husband*; Seifert, *Metaphorisches Reden von Gott in Hoseabuch*; Martin Schulz-Rauch, *Hosea und Jeremia: Zur Wirkungsgeschichte des Hoseabuchs*, CThM 16 (Stuttgart: Calver, 1996); Yvonne Sherwood, *The Prostitute and the Prophet: Hosea's Marriage in Literary-Theoretical Perspective*, JSOTSup 212, Gender, Culture, Theory 2 (Sheffield: Sheffield Academic, 1996); Marie-Theres Wacker, *Figurationen des Weiblichen im Hosea-Buch*, HBS 8 (Freiberg: Herder, 1996); Törnkvist, *Use and Abuse*.

On Ezekiel: Galambush, *Jerusalem in the Book of Ezekiel*; Fokkelien van Dijk-Hemmes, "The Metaphorization of Woman in Prophetic Speech: An Analysis of Ezekiel 23," *VT* 43, no. 2 (1993): 162–70.

On Hosea, Jeremiah, Ezekiel: Weems, *Battered Love*.

Across the Hebrew Bible: Raymond C. Ortlund Jr., *Whoredom: God's Unfaithful Wife in Biblical Theology* (Grand Rapids: Eerdmans, 1996); J. Cheryl Exum, *Plotted, Shot and Painted: Cultural Representations of Biblical Women*, JSOTSup 215 (Sheffield: Sheffield Academic, 1996).

44. Carr, "Gender and the Shaping of Desire," 237–40.

45. Carr, "Gender and the Shaping of Desire," 244. This would contrast sharply with the simplest present-day concept of gender, which is nearly inextricably linked to physical bodies. Thus, for Stephen D. Moore, a love relationship between a (anthropomorphically male) God and (biologically male) medieval allegorists such as Bernard of Clairvaux, "the Song . . . becomes an ecclesiastically sanctioned space . . . for an ordinarily prohibited homoeroticism." "The Song of Songs in the History of Sexuality," *Church History* 69, no. 2 (2000): 344.

46. The difficulty for present-day readers is, of course, the characterization of YHWH as an abusive husband in these prophetic texts. We have provided references to alternate approaches to reading these texts in the chapters that deal with Hosea 2 and Ezekiel 16 and 23.

47. David M. Carr, "Ancient Sexuality and Divine Eros: Rereading the Bible through the Lens of the Song of Songs," *Union Seminary Quarterly Review* 54, no. 3–4 (2000): 8.

iah, Hosea, and Ezekiel,[48] or possibly the orations of Deuteronomy.[49] In a culture where the less powerful and non-autonomous "marriage" partner is female, Israel naturally would have identified with the female protagonist in the Song of Songs.[50] However, the intriguing twist is that this literary construct, as wildly disruptive as she is, bears little resemblance to her domesticated social counterpart.[51]

Brenner proposes that allegorical readings of the Song were possibly a logical outcome of reading it "as an intertext for the prophetic 'love story' between the divine husband and his wayward 'wife'" specifically motivated by "the force of analogic difference" between the Song and the prophetic versions as seen in Hosea 1–3, Ezekiel 16 and 23, and Jeremiah 2–5: "faithfulness versus faithlessness, joy versus despair, exclusivity versus inclusivity"—all these making it "a therapeutic antidote for the grim prophetic metaphor."[52] Beyond this, if the tidy demarcations some twenty-first-century readers tend to make between the human-human and the divine-human readings of the Song are allowed to dissolve, then the Song is more than just a "therapeutic antidote." For Carr, it is a pointed "theological critique" of the world since Eden. "In our broken world, not only are women terrorized by men, but the suffering ancient people of Israel sometimes felt like a 'woman' terrorized by God,

48. See Martti Nissinen, "Song of Songs and Sacred Marriage," in Nissinen and Uro, *Sacred Marriages*, 210–12, 214–15, who argues similarly with reference to the cultural context (use of this hierarchy-dependent gendering from the Sumerian through to the Hellenistic periods), and with reference to the canonical context (of the Hebrew Bible and Hellenistic Jewish literature such as Wis 8:2–21 and Sir 51:13–19 [Hebrew]).

49. See David M. Carr, "Passion for God: A Center in Biblical Theology," *HBT* 23 (2001): 1–24.

50. Contra, e.g., Fox, *Ancient Egyptian Love Songs*, 237.

51. Contra, e.g., Christopher Meredith, "The Lattice and the Looking Glass: Gendered Space in Song of Songs 2:8–14," *JAAR* 80, no. 2 (2012): 365–86; Donald C. Polaski, "What Will Ye See in the Shulammite? Women, Power and Panopticism in the Song of Songs," *BibInt* 5, no. 1 (1997): 64–81.

52. Brenner's larger argument is that the Song's intrinsic gynocentrism and non-theocentrism were "falsified" in the process of allegorization—starting with the Jewish versions—for political and ideological ends. Athalya Brenner, "To See Is to Assume: Whose Love Is Celebrated in the Song of Songs?" *BibInt* 1, no. 3 (1993): 282–84. Samples of less adversarial positions that see the Song as a compensation or countertext to the prophetic marriage texts are: Ellen F. Davis, who posits that without the allegorical reading of the Song of Songs, we would have to "accept the sad fact that there is at the heart of the Bible a cosmic loneliness that finds no relief" (*Getting Involved with God: Rediscovering the Old Testament* [Cambridge, MA: Cowley, 2001], 66–67). Richard W. Corney surveys the history of Christian allegorical reading of the Song of Songs, identifying the various kinds of "literal" interpretations. He concludes: "throughout these centuries . . . there has been on the whole a reluctance to rest on the surface appearance of the text as a song or a collection of songs celebrating human love solely and simply" because "in its canonical context" the Song "will always call for something more." "What Does 'Literal Meaning' Mean? Some Commentaries on the Song of Songs," *Anglican Theological Review* 4 (1998): 516.

a God now experienced as the ultimate 'male.'"[53] This "gender terror" that patriarchy perpetuates is depicted in the prophetic divine marriage equation and in the gendered relationships that direct political and military language. Indeed, "patriarchy—*whether on a human or divine level*—is revealed as a post-garden tragedy by the imagery of Genesis 2 on the one hand and the Song of Songs on the other."[54] Carr thinks this multivalency within the canon does not simply throw up compensating images of love and sexuality. Rather, multivalency allows the Song of Songs to present "an alternative to both human *and* divine patriarchy, both male possession of women and images of divine genderized power over Israel." In so doing, the Song of Songs provides a response "not only to the human tragedy imagined in the Garden of Eden, but also to the cosmic tragedy of the garden of Isaiah and other prophetic gender texts."[55] We shall return to review this in the concluding chapter.

At the very least, the Song would have been seen as a radical reimagining of the prophetic depiction of Israel as the whoring, punishment-deserving wife.[56] Where the prophetic texts dramatize the breakdown of human–divine marriage, the Song enacts the satisfaction of it; if the other texts present the ferocity of a thwarted deity, the Song pictures one who delights in his beloved; if in the other texts the human remains sullenly silent, in the Song, the human voice is the first and last we hear.

INTERTEXTUALITY

Before we engage in an intertextual reading, we must set out our employment of this term. In current use, *intertextuality* has as many meanings as there are users of the term, embracing both text production and text reception.[57] The premise governing intertextuality is that within

53. Carr, *Erotic Word*, 56.

54. Carr, "Ancient Sexuality," 14.

55. Carr, "Ancient Sexuality," 16.

56. Carr, "Gender and the Shaping of Desire," 244–48.

57. For a survey of methods in use see B. J. Oropeza, "Intertextuality," in *The Oxford Encyclopedia of Biblical Interpretation*, ed. Steven L. McKenzie (Oxford: Oxford University Press, 2013), 1:453–63. For a comprehensive and up-to-date bibliography of reading on intertextuality, see B. J. Oropeza and Steve Moyise, *Exploring Intertextuality: Diverse Strategies for New Testament Interpretation of Texts* (Eugene, OR: Cascade, 2016), xviii–xix.

The concept is usually traced back to M. Bakhtin, *The Formal Method in Literary Scholarship*, trans. A. Wehrle (Baltimore: Johns Hopkins University Press, 1978); *The Dialogic Imagination*, ed. M. Holquist, trans. C. Emerson and M. Holquist (Austin: University of Texas Press, 1981); *Problems of Dostoevsky's Poetics*, ed. and trans. C. Emerson (Manchester: Manchester University Press, 1963); *The Bakhtin Reader: Selected Writings of Bakhtin, Medvedev and Voloshmov*, ed. P. Morris (London: Arnold, 1994). Bakhtin's idea is still author-centered, proposing that authors write in dialogue with two entities, existing texts and current reality.

a literary culture, texts grow out of a shared linguistic, aesthetic, and ideological substratum. So, what the intertextual critic maximizes is the "larger system of signification"[58] within which the authors and readers of the text operate, a system through which associations and relationships between texts become possible.

Ellen van Wolde helpfully tabulates the difference between the two domains of intertextuality as it existed around the turn of the millennium.[59] Where intertextuality concerns itself with the process of text production, its interests are author-centered, diachronic, and historical. The reader looks for *causality* between texts, where words in the (later) phenotext are indexed against words in the (earlier) genotext. It is understood that this relationship between texts exists because it was intentionally written in. Therefore, "the reader must discover them, because they formed the very foundation of the genesis of the text."[60] Discovering the *purpose* of the intertextual relationship becomes the interest, as in inner-biblical exegesis[61] and inner-biblical allusion[62] (or literary influence).

Intertextuality in the sense of text *reception*, in contrast, is reader-centered, synchronic, and literary. Being synchronic, it intentionally

Julia Kristeva ("Word, Dialogue and Novel," in *Desire in language: A Semiotic Approach to Language and Art*, ed. L. S. Roudiez, trans. T. Gora and A. Jardine [New York: Columbia University Press, 1980], 64–91) carried this forward with her coining of the term "intertextuality," restricting the term to the relationship between texts. She famously distills from Bakhtin the insight that "every text is constructed like a mosaic of quotations, every text is an absorption and a transformation of another text." Julia Kristeva, *The Kristeva Reader*, ed. Toril Moi (New York: Columbia University Press, 1986), 37.

58. Benjamin D. Sommer, "Exegesis, Allusion and Intertextuality in the Hebrew Bible: A Response to Lyle Eslinger," *VT* 46, no. 4 (1996): 488.

59. Ellen van Volde. "Texts in Dialogue with Texts: Intertextuality in the Ruth and Tamar Narratives," *BibInt* 5, no. 1 (1997): 5–7.

60. Wolde, "Texts in Dialogue," 6.

61. The term was coined by Nahum Sarna, "Psalm 89: A Study in Inner Biblical Exegesis," in *Biblical and Other Studies*, ed. Alexander Altmann (Cambridge, MA: Harvard University Press, 1963), 29–46.

The most significant work since then includes: Aryeh Toeg, "Num 15.22–31 Midrash Halacha," *Tarbiẓ* 43 (1973–74): 1–20 (Hebrew); Michael Fishbane, *Biblical Interpretation in Ancient Israel* (Oxford: Clarendon, 1985); Yair Zakovitch, *An Introduction to Inner-Biblical Interpretation* (Even-Yehuda: Reches, 1992) (Hebrew); Bernard M. Levinson, *Deuteronomy and the Hermeneutics of Legal Innovation* (Oxford: Oxford University Press, 1997); Benjamin D. Sommer, *A Prophet Reads Scripture: Allusion in Isaiah 40–66* (Stanford, CA: Stanford University Press, 1998).

62. Lyle Eslinger, "Inner-Biblical Exegesis and Inner-Biblical Allusion: The Question of Category," *VT* 1 (1992): 48n2. As Eslinger points out, "many instances of literary interconnection in the Bible do not go beyond the playfulness of simply touching on a literary antecedent." Indeed, "some may even be unconscious on the part of the author yet eminently [*sic*] significant to the reading community." Sommer ("Exegesis, Allusion and Intertextuality," 486–87) takes Eslinger further to tease apart inner-biblical allusion (or influence) from (limited-sense, reception-centered) intertextuality.

resists investigations into processes historical. Beale offers an example of such resistance: "every text is a locus of intersections, overlaps, and collisions between other texts," so much so that attempting to work out the precise vector of influence between one text and another is "endless and, quite literally, pointless."[63] Instead, as van Wolde puts it, the reader is directed by the words of the texts and the motifs they mediate, relating them by *iconicity*—that is, in the sharing of an image; in other words, by evoking the analogous, or the isomorphic. Instead of pursuing a compulsory relationship between the texts, the reader postulates potential relationships.[64] The caveat here is that the reader must mediate intertextual conversations cautiously, avoiding the slippery slope of "creating meaning as the result of the free association of textual elements in the text with a limitless number of intertexts."[65] Having identified valid intertexts (we will come back to this in a bit), "productive intertextual reading must be concerned not only with the meaning of one text (T1) in its encounter with another text (T2), but also with the new text created by the interaction of both texts."[66] Alkier does not exaggerate when he promises that through "reciprocal reading, highly surprising and unpredictable effects of meaning will result" simply because such reading alters the "meaning potential of the individual writings."[67] Discovering the *effect* of such intertextual conversation is the interest of the exegete.[68]

More recently, this clean line between author- and reader-centered intertextuality, between the diachronic and the synchronic, between the historical and the literary, has been smudged, if not nearly erased. Barton argues that "the absolute polarization of these two approaches is probably exaggerated."[69] At best, they are "devices for describing different reading emphases, but ultimately, hermeneutics cannot be hermetically sealed off into one approach or the other."[70] The two are both autonomous *and*

---

63. Timothy K. Beale, "Intertextuality," in *Handbook of Postmodern Biblical Interpretation*, ed. A. Adams (St. Louis: Chalice, 2000), 128–29.

64. Wolde, "Texts in Dialogue," 6–7.

65. Richard L. Schultz, "Intertextuality, Canon, and 'Undecidability': Understanding Isaiah's 'New Heavens and New Earth' (Isaiah 65:17–25)," *BBR* 20, no. 1 (2010): 27.

66. Wolde, "Texts in Dialogue," 8.

67. Stefan Alkier, "Intertextuality and the Semiotics of Biblical Texts," in *Reading the Bible Intertextually*, ed. Richard B. Hays, Stefan Alkier, and Leroy A. Huizenga (Waco, TX: Baylor University Press, 2009), 12.

68. Van Wolde, "Texts in Dialogue with Texts," 8.

69. John Barton, "*Déjà Lu*: Intertextuality, Method or Theory?" in *Reading Job Intertextually*, ed. Katharine Dell and Will Kynes (New York: Bloomsbury, 2013), 7. He prefers to use for these two approaches the terms "temporal" and "spatial" (7).

70. Katherine Dell, introduction to *Reading Job Intertextually*, *Reading Job Intertextually* (New York: Bloomsbury, 2013), xxii.

interdependent.[71] The intersection of author- and reader-centered intertextuality is probably where imaginative exegesis lies.

In this study, our "reading emphasis" is on the reception-centered, synchronic, and literary understanding of intertextuality; it is an exercise in attentive listening because, as Fewell puts it, "texts talk to one another; they echo one another; they push one another; they war with one another. They are voices in chorus, in conflict and in competition."[72] This could be said of the interaction between the Genesis flood story and the *Epic of Gilgamesh*, as much as of an encounter between the biblical account of creation and Darwin's *Origin of Species*.[73] However, in this book we will restrict ourselves to the Hebrew canon because I am persuaded that we have not listened—in a sufficiently sustained manner—to the conversations the Song has with isomorphic canonical texts. In this regard, I agree with Fishbane that "intertextuality is the core of the canonical imagination," since "a canon . . . presupposes the possibility of correlations among its parts."[74] While the intracanonical conversation is our focal interest, we will occasionally lend an ear to the chatter between the Hebrew Bible and parallel ancient West Asian literature.

So, persuaded that "all canonical texts have an intertextual disposition *independent from their intratextually perceptible references to other texts*,"[75] we will engage four of the Song's main themes with parallel texts that explicitly deploy the YHWH-Israel marriage metaphor. In the first section, we examine the theme of love-in-separation in which the lover seeks the beloved (Song 2:8–3:5), reading it intertextually with Hosea 2, in which a husband ponders how he should return his wife's affections to himself. The second section examines the theme of beauty through the praise poem in which the female lover delights in her beloved's body (Song 5:9–6:3). This praise of beauty we will read alongside Ezekiel 16:1–22, a man's description of his beautiful foundling wife. The third section looks at the theme of gardens as a metaphor for the female lover (Song 4:8–5:1), holding it up in conversation with Isaiah 5:1–7, in which a husband speaks of his disappointment with his wife, whom he pictures as a vineyard he has tended. The fourth section studies the theme of love and its jealousy (Song 8:5–14), pairing it with Ezekiel 23:1–21, 40–44,

71. Dell, "Introduction," xxii, following Ferdinand de Saussure, *Course in General Linguistics* (Chicago: Open Court, 1983), 87.

72. Donna Nolan Fewell, "Introduction: Writing, Reading and Relating," in *Reading Between Texts: Intertextuality and the Hebrew Bible*, ed. Donna Nolan Fewell, Literary Currents in Biblical Interpretation (Louisville: Westminster John Knox, 1992), 12.

73. Barton, "*Déjà Lu*," 6.

74. Michael Fishbane, "Types of Biblical Intertextuality," in *Congress Volume: Oslo 1998*, ed. André Lemaire and Magne Sæbø, VTSup 8 (Leiden: Brill, 2000), 39.

75. Alkier, "Intertextuality," 11.

which is the monologue of a husband who expected love and received the opposite.

CONCLUSION

What we are going to do, then, is to embark on an intertextual reading of the Song of Songs. By "intertextuality" we do not mean production-centered intertextuality; that is, we will not address historical questions regarding the direction of influence or authorial intention. Rather, we will consider reception-centered intertextuality, the literary exercise in which we pay attention to what conversations may arise when texts are introduced to each other.

The validity of reading the Song of Songs intertextually with prophetic texts that explicitly use the YHWH-Israel marriage metaphor may be inferred from the Song's reception history. Given their under-standing of gender vis-à-vis power relations, it appears that the commu-nity of ancient Israel had no problem appropriating the Song along dual planes—the human-human and the divine-human. Even in the second century CE, they could sing it in taverns and on special occasions just as well as in festival liturgy.[76]

The expectation of this study is that when the Song is laid alongside its partner prophetic texts, the ensuing interaction will help us profile the canonical ideal for "male" and "female" partners in love relationships at two levels, the human-human and the divine-human. The texts them-selves, through the world they create, will round out the ideal for human male-female love. For the divine-human aspect, we will briefly sample the allegorical exegesis of medieval Jewish and early Christian commen-tators to understand how they treat each of the four themes. If divine-human love is "governed by much the same principles as male-female love on the human level," we may discover ways in which the affective dynamics of deity and devotee mirror the heterosexual ideal.

What we hope to discern, through a reading of theme-matched pairs of texts, are the prescriptions the Hebrew canon makes for the relation-ship between man and woman, and between deity and devotee.

---

76. Thus Rabbi Akiva's well-known injunction: "Whoever warbles the Song of Songs at banqueting houses, treating it like an ordinary song, has no portion in the World to come." t. Sanh. 12:10.

PART I

Love in Separation

2.

The Streets and Squares

An enduring trope of the romantic genre is the lover at the window or rose-trellised balcony of the object of his affection. The Song of Songs makes sure to feature one such vignette, but only as part of a larger—and deeply reflective—treatment of lovers in the situation of separation. In the Song, separation and seeking are twin themes that are sometimes foregrounded and sometimes recessed. Sometimes it is the man who seeks, and sometimes it is the woman. We will examine the poems in Song 2:8–3:5 and 5:2–6:3 to compare and contrast the man and woman in their roles as seeker.

Exum shows that these two seeking-and-finding poems have similar contours, with a significant level of correspondence[1] at multiple levels: the verbal level, the story level, and, certainly, at the conceptual level. Each speech features first the man and then the woman, each seeking the other so as to end the state of separation. The man's endeavor is presented as a visit to the house of the woman, a well-recognized trope. The woman's effort is more unconventional, and even sits uneasily with the social norms of ancient Israel. She combs the city streets for him, and she does it at night.

SEPARATION AND SEEKING IN SONG 2:8–3:5

Song 2:8–3:5 breaks quite naturally into two units, which we may call the daytime poem (2:8–17) and the nighttime poem (3:1–5). The latter is acknowledged as a unit spoken by the woman. There is sufficient agree-

1. J. Cheryl Exum, *Song of Songs: A Commentary* (Louisville: Westminster John Knox, 2005), 186–87.

ment that the former is similarly unified by a single voice.[2] Whose? Even though the unit contains a core stretch where the man speaks, his words are embedded into the matrix of the woman's voice. She recollects and repeats to her audience lines that the man has spoken to her in the past.

In the daytime poem, the man comes seeking. The nighttime one describes the woman's search for the man. The two poems are sequential with no clear narrative link between them, but with sufficient verbal links to invite the reader to consider them together.

THE MAN SEEKS: SONG 2:8–17

Listen! My beloved! [קוֹל דּוֹדִי]
Look! Here he comes [הִנֵּה־זֶה בָּא],
Leaping [מְדַלֵּג] across the mountains,
Bounding [מְקַפֵּץ] over the hills.
My beloved is like a gazelle or a young stag.
Look! There he stands [עוֹמֵד] behind our wall [כָּתְלֵנוּ],
gazing [מַשְׁגִּיחַ] through the windows,
peering [מֵצִיץ] through the lattice. (Song 2:8–9)

The poem opens with an abrupt and hurried two-word exclamation, קוֹל דּוֹדִי: "I hear my beloved!"[3] or, "Listen! My beloved!"[4] Either the woman has been waiting just for this,[5] or she is unexpectedly startled by his coming. In either case, the exclamation anticipates a happy end to separation. קוֹל probably describes the sound of his arrival rather than his voice.[6] If this is a secret rendezvous, as is usually the case with lovers at windows, it is unlikely that he is giving himself away by calling to her from a distance. Rather, the sounds of his approach are probably familiar to her ears. From how readily (and unerringly) she can identify his

---

2. Among those who see Song 2:8–17 as a unified poem spoken by the woman are Elie Assis, *Flashes of Fire: A Literary Analysis of the Song of Songs* (New York: T&T Clark, 2009), 76–77; Diane Bergant, *The Song of Songs*, Berit Olam (Collegeville, MN: Liturgical, 2001), 27; Robert W. Jenson, *Song of Songs*, Interpretation (Louisville: John Knox, 2005), 33–34; Exum, *Song of Songs*, 122; Roland E. Murphy, *The Song of Songs*, Hermeneia (Minneapolis: Augsburg Fortress, 1990), 140; John G. Snaith, *The Song of Songs*, NCB (Grand Rapids: Eerdmans, 1993), 34; Tremper Longman III, *Song of Songs* (Grand Rapids: Eerdmans, 2001), 117.

3. קוֹל followed by a genitive is often used as an exclamation. Paul Joüon and T. Muraoka, *A Grammar of Biblical Hebrew*, vol. 2, *Subsidia Biblica* 14/II (Rome: Pontifical Biblical Institute, 2005), § 162e.

4. See Marvin H. Pope, *Song of Songs: A New Translation with Introduction and Commentary*, Anchor Bible 7C (New Haven: Yale University Press, 1977), 389.

5. Ariel Bloch and Chana Bloch, *The Song of Songs: A New Translation with an Introduction and Commentary* (New York: Random House, 1995), 153.

6. See Bloch and Bloch, *Song of Songs*, 153; Pope, *Song of Songs*, 389.

arrival, this does not seem to be the first time he has come to this trysting place.

Clearly, both parties long to end the separation. If she hasn't been at the window already waiting for a prearranged meeting,[7] we know she has scrambled to it because hardly a heartbeat passes before her eyes catch up with her ears: הִנֵּה־זֶה בָּא. "Look! Here he comes." She can see him making his way to her. For his part, there is urgency in his steps, communicated to the reader by the string of participles—he is "coming," and that coming is by way of "leaping" and "bounding." While her senses are straining, directed toward the sounds and sights that will reunite her with the man, the man closes the space between them with energy, making haste to get to where she is. As she watches him close the distance, it is this energy fueled by his eagerness that she describes: "leaping across the mountains, bounding over the hills. My beloved is like a gazelle or a young stag."

Certainly, this is animal imagery that, in the culture from which this literature arises, evokes the sensual. Gazelles and stags are symbolic of not only agility but also virility.[8] However, here the description is sandwiched between two exclamations of seeing. "Look!" she exclaims on first catching sight of him at some distance. "Look!" she exclaims again, seeing him now as close as he can get in this situation, on the other side of her window. In both exclamations, the זֶה in הִנֵּה־זֶה, serves to emphasize the action in progress.[9] In between the exclamations, speed has operated—the swiftness (and grace) of a stag, even a vigorous "young stag," and this is the emphasis of metaphor.[10]

Now he has reached his destination, and he is "standing" on the other side of the wall of her house. The blur of stag-like motion is replaced with motionlessness, but the energy is now transferred to his eyes.[11] The flow of participles resumes. He is "gazing through the windows,[12]

7. A parallel in Egyptian love poetry is: "To the outer door / I set my face: / my brother is coming to me! / My eyes are turned to the road, / and my ears listen / for the [unknown word] of the neglectful one" (pap. Harris 500, Group B: 15, translated in Michael V. Fox, The Song of Songs and the Ancient Egyptian Love Songs [Madison: University of Wisconsin Press, 1985], 24).

8. See Pope, Song of Songs, 386; Othmar Keel, The Song of Songs: A Continental Commentary, trans. Frederick J. Gaiser (Minneapolis: Augsburg Fortress, 1994), 92–94, 96–97, 117; Robert Gordis, The Song of Songs: A Study, Modern Translation and Commentary, Text and Studies of the Jewish Theological Seminary of America 20 (New York: Jewish Theological Seminary of America, 1954), 26.

9. Exum, Song of Songs, 121; Fox, Ancient Egyptian Love Songs, 112.

10. Pope, Song of Songs, 390.

11. Bergant, Song of Songs, 29; Richard S. Hess, Song of Songs, Baker Commentary on the Old Testament (Grand Rapids: Baker, 2005), 90; Keel, Song of Songs, 98.

12. Pope suggests that חַלֹּנוֹת is a plural of indetermination. The man is not running from window to window. Song of Songs, 391.

peering through the lattice" in a continued endeavor to reach her. As far as catching sight of the beloved goes, the man is clearly disadvantaged. She can watch him at will. He must seek.

Verses 2:8 and 2:9 share a parallel structure:[13]

2:8	2:9
My beloved [דּוֹדִי] . . . look! [הִנֵּה־זֶה]	My beloved [דּוֹדִי] . . . look! [הִנֵּה־זֶה]
he is coming [בָּא]	he is standing [עוֹמֵד]
leaping [מְדַלֵּג] across the mountains,	gazing [מַשְׁגִּיחַ] through the windows,
bounding [מְקַפֵּץ] over the hills.	peering [מֵצִיץ] through the lattice.

The ear catches the even tempo through the four matching participles. All alliteratively carry the *mem* preformative;[14] the first pair is in assonance in *piel*; the second pair is in assonance in *hiphil*. Elie Assis observes that the "recurring structure" provides a rhythm to the lines and mediates a sense of "the man as acting ardently and swiftly in coming to the woman."[15] Indeed, elsewhere in the Old Testament, gazelles are associated with swiftness of foot (2 Sam 2:18; 1 Chr 12:9 [EV 12:8]; Ps 18:34 [EV 18:33]; Isa 35:6).[16] Further, Assis draws attention to the heaping up of verbs that "express [the man's] desire to hurry and to reach his beloved": when he is at a distance, he comes, leaps, bounds; when he is close, he stands, peers, gazes.[17] Bergant arranges the verbs differently but to similar effect. She notes that it takes verb pairs to describe the man's actions, as if a single verb will not sufficiently express his intensity. He leaps and bounds (2:8); he gazes and peers (2:9). Shortly, he will speak and say (2:10); and when he invites the woman, he asks her to arise and come (2:13).[18] Till this point, the reader is in no doubt that the longing is mutual, for her animated recital suggests that her desire to end the separation fully reciprocates his.

We now have a narrative connector: עָנָה דוֹדִי וְאָמַר. This may be translated with past tense, allowing it to be the woman's recollection of an event: "My beloved spoke and said to me . . ."[19] Or, in keeping with the tenor of the heavy use of participles so far, it could be translated in the

13. Assis, *Flashes of Fire*, 78. Bergant, *Song of Songs*, 28. See also Mary T. Elliott, *The Literary Unity of the Canticle* (Frankfurt: Lang, 1989), 68–69.

14. Duane Garrett, "Song of Songs," in *Song of Songs, Lamentations*, ed. Duane Garrett and Paul R. House, WBC 23B (Nashville: Thomas Nelson, 2004), 157–58.

15. Assis, *Flashes of Fire*, 79.

16. Assis, *Flashes of Fire*, 80.

17. Assis, *Flashes of Fire*, 80.

18. Bergant, *Song of Songs*, 29.

19. E.g., NIV, NET, NLT.

present tense, retaining the sense of immediacy, maintaining the fiction of an ongoing encounter: "My lover speaks; he says to me . . ."[20] Either way, this connector breaks the tension. The perfect verbs break the run of seven participles,[21] and indicate something is about to happen.[22] What happens is that description makes way for speech.

The man's speech-within-a-speech is an invitation to the woman to come away with him. It falls into two stanzas, 2:10b–13 and 2:14, the first stanza delimited by an inclusio:[23]

Arise [קוּמִי],
my darling [רַעְיָתִי], my beautiful one [יָפָתִי],
come away [וּלְכִי־לָךְ] (2:10b)

. . .

Arise [קוּמִי], come [לְכִי],
my darling [רַעְיָתִי], my beautiful one [יָפָתִי],
come away [וּלְכִי־לָךְ] (2:13b)

The man addresses his audience of one with a rhyming double reference (רַעְיָתִי יָפָתִי) bearing the possessive pronoun "my":[24] "*my* darling, *my* beautiful one." The overall effect is not just charming but implicitly a claim for union. He and she belong. The separation is unwarranted. So, she must come away with him. Richard S. Hess observes that this claim to union plays out in the -*i* endings of the imperatives and the adjectives. The imperatives relate to the woman; the adjectives, with their first-person pronoun suffixes ("my"), belong to the man. The sound unites the two lovers, underscoring the man's appeal for an end to separation.[25] When he repeats the appeal, he increments it with the extra imperative, "Come!" So, "Arise!" meshes with "Come!"[26] in a hendiadys of urging, leaving us, who are overhearing this conversation, in no doubt about the man's earnestness.

Within this frame of inclusion, the man gives a reason why his beloved should leave her house to join him. Earlier, her eyes had

---

20. E.g., NAB, NRSV. This verb pair (ענה with אמר) is a common rhetorical collocation. See for example Deut 26:5 and multiple occurrences in Job (4:1, 6:1, 8:1, etc.) (Bloch and Bloch, *Song of Songs*, 154). Pope points also to the clichéd use in the Gospels where it is said of Jesus that "he answered and said." *Song of Songs*, 393.

21. Fox, *Ancient Egyptian Love Songs*, 112.

22. Snaith, *Song of Songs*, 36.

23. For this division, see Assis, *Flashes of Fire*, 81.

24. Assis, *Flashes of Fire*, 82; Hess, *Song of Songs*, 91.

25. Hess, *Song of Songs*, 92.

26. Keel points out the frequent pairing of these verbs (e.g., 2 Sam 13:15; 1 Kgs 14:12; 2 Kgs 8:1; Mic 2:10), which literally should be "arise and go." The context in the Song prefers "arise and come." Keel, *Song of Songs*, 100.

followed him as he made his way to her window, and watched his eyes searching for her through the lattice. Her gaze had been focused on the man: הִנֵּה־זֶה ("Look! Here . . ."). Now he directs her gaze beyond him to a world ready to receive them: כִּי־הִנֵּה ("Look! Because . . . "). As Hess points out, what follows the man's "Look!" provides the reason why the woman should arise and come away with him.[27]

> See! The winter is past;
> the rains are over and gone [הַסְּתָו הָלַךְ לוֹ].
> Flowers appear on the earth;
> the season of singing/pruning [הַזָּמִיר] has come,
> the cooing of doves [תּוֹר] is heard in our land.
> The fig tree forms [חָנְטָה] its early fruit;
> the blossoming vines spread their fragrance. (2:12–13)[28]

Like a traveler, winter has journeyed over and across the land,[29] taking the rains with him. The passing of the rains is described with הָלַךְ הָלַךְ לוֹ. The double weight of two verbs, similar in shape and sound, make the point that the rain is "completely past, over and gone."[30]

With the curtain of rain lifted, we see images that aggregate into an overwhelming sensory cluster.[31] The flowers appeal to the eyes, a tumble of heady colors. The throaty warble of doves fills the ears in this season of song—the word "turtledove" itself, תּוֹר, is onomatopoeic. Ropes of flowering vines seduce the sense of smell. The figs evoke multiple senses all at once. The tree is forming (חנט) its early fruit. The verb carries the idea of ripening by changing color,[32] but could also convey the sense of sweetening.[33] If so, the image conjured up is of red- and yellow-streaked fruit,[34] with an anticipation of luscious sweetness filling the mouth.

The season itself is described with a verb that probably does double duty: זמר could mean both "to prune" and "to sing." In this Janus parallelism, it points back to the passing of winter and announces the arrival

---

27. Hess, *Song of Songs*, 93.

28. This arrangement of two couplets framing a tricolon is from Wilfred G. E. Watson, *Classical Hebrew Poetry: A Guide to Its Techniques*, 2nd ed., JSOTSup 26 (Sheffield: Sheffield Academic, 1995), 369. It shows the Janus verb זמר in the middle line of the arrangement.

29. G. Lloyd Carr, *The Song of Solomon: An Introduction and Commentary*, TOTC (Leicester: InterVarsity, 1984), 97.

30. Pope, *Song of Songs*, 394.

31. See Patrick Hunt, *Poetry in the Song of Songs: A Literary Analysis*, SBL 96 (New York: Peter Lang, 2008), 91.

32. חנט I, *HALOT*; Murphy, *Song of Songs*, 139; Snaith, *Song of Songs*, 39.

33. Thus, in reference to embalming, חנט is a process which uses aromatic spices (Gen 50:2, 3, 26). Bloch and Bloch, *Song of Songs*, 155; Exum, *Song of Songs*, 122.

34. Pope, *Song of Songs*, 397.

of the season of pruning; and it points forward to the sound of the returning migratory turtledove and declares the onset of the season of birdsong.[35] The one verb evokes both the tactile and the auditory—the feel of fresh foliage and the melodies of spring. From her window, the woman may enjoy the sights and sounds of spring. But, as Hess points out, to smell and touch and taste, she must do as the man says, "Come away!"[36]

The man's words are at once delicious and lovely, fragrant and resonant. A season becomes a tangible, irresistible world. What he describes as "our land" (2:12) is simply the immediate countryside familiar to them both,[37] but the invitation is so couched that "our land" could well be a world for two. Indeed, beneath the images the man conjures up is a groundswell of sensuality.[38] Nature is in an orgy. Doves call to each other, seeking mates; flowers are opening out with abandon, inviting pollination; the fig tree is with child already and is growing its fruit.[39] It is a world that has moved from the bleak barrenness of winter to the profligate fertility of springtime.[40] How desirable this world is against the present one in which walls and windows—and even "mountains" and "hills" (2:8), metaphorical or otherwise—stand between the two lovers.

Perhaps the woman is at a loss for response. Perhaps she is constrained by the lattice without the freedom to come and go as her heart pleases. Perhaps she is just playfully hiding behind the window.[41] So, the man seems to settle now for something less. If the separation cannot be overcome, then at least, he begs, let it be mitigated.

My dove in the clefts of the rock
in the hiding places of the mountainside
Show me your face/form[42] [הַרְאִינִי אֶת־מַרְאַיִךְ],
let me hear your voice [הַשְׁמִיעִינִי אֶת־קוֹלֵךְ];

---

35. Cyrus H. Gordon, "New Directions," *BASP* 15 (1978): 59–66; Bloch and Bloch, *Song of Songs*, 154–55; Exum, *Song of Songs*, 27; Garrett, *Song of Songs*, 159; Fox, *Ancient Egyptian Love Songs*, 113.

36. Hess, *Song of Songs*, 95.

37. Bloch and Bloch, *Song of Songs*, 155.

38. Hess, *Song of Songs*, 94; Keel, *Song of Songs*, 100, 102; Bergant, *Song of Songs*, 30.

39. Pope (*Song of Songs*, 397) draws attention to the rabbis using the fig as a symbol for the stages of a woman's physical maturity. Before puberty, she was an unripe fig; at maidenhood, she was in early ripening; a woman was a ripe fig.

40. Tom Gledhill, *The Message of the Song of Songs: The Lyrics of Love*, The Bible Speaks Today (Leicester: InterVarsity, 1994), 133.

41. Bloch and Bloch, *Song of Songs*, 155–56.

42. מַרְאֶה is better translated more fully as "form" or "appearance," rather than just "face." See Bloch and Bloch, *Song of Songs*, 156; Edward M. Curtis, *Ecclesiastes and Song of Songs*, Teach the Text Commentary Series (Grand Rapids: Baker, 2013), 127; Exum, *Song of Songs*, 122; Murphy, *Song of Songs*, 139; Pope, *Song of Songs*, 401; Longman, *Song of Songs*, 123.

for your voice is sweet [עָרֵב],
and your face/form [מַרְאֵךְ] is lovely. (2:14)

At the start of this poem, the woman likened the man to a gazelle or
stag, a picture of elegance in motion. Now, to the man, the woman is
"my dove." As with the gazelle or stag, this vocabulary is drawn from the
standard sexual imagery of ancient West Asia.[43] But, again, the emphasis corresponds to the situation. If the man was stag-like in speed, the
woman is dove-like in inaccessibility. The metaphors underscore the
contrast.[44] His action toward ending their separation is frustrated by her
continued unavailability, a motif that recurs in the Song (4:8, 12; 5:2–4;
8:1, 9).[45] She is like a dove nesting on the broken face of a cliff.[46] From
below, one may catch a glimpse of her before she retreats back on her
ledge and is lost to sight.

The man implores his dove in a prettily constructed chiasm: face/
form—voice—voice—face/form. Further, the two imperatives—"Show
me," "Let me hear"—follow hurriedly one on the heels of the other, communicating enamored insistence. The imperatives are in the causative
stem: "Cause [your face] to be seen by me . . . cause [your voice] to be
heard by me." This makes sense, because the one on the outside of the
lattice can see or hear only if it pleases the one on the inside of the lattice
to show or speak. His seeing and hearing require her action. As an incen-
tive, the man follows up his imperatives with adjectives that describe this
appearance and voice his eyes and ears long for. She is sweet to listen to
and lovely to behold.

Even if the second stanza does not contain the fulsome invitation of
the first stanza, the two are thoroughly interlaced by resonating vocabulary:[47]

2:12	2:14
	My dove [יוֹנָה] in the clefts of the rock,
	in the hiding places on the mountainside,
Flowers appear [ראה] on the earth;	show me [ראה] your appearance [מַרְאֶה],
the season of singing has come,	let me hear [שמע] your voice [קוֹל];

43. Keel, *Song of Songs*, 103–6; Pope, *Song of Songs*, 399–400.

44. Daniel J. Estes, "The Song of Songs," in *Ecclesiastes and the Song of Songs*, ed. Daniel C.
Fredericks and Daniel J. Estes, Apollos Old Testament Commentary 16 (Downers Grove, IL:
InterVarsity, 2010), 326.

45. Garrett, *Song of Songs*, 160.

46. Pope points us to Jer 48:28 and Isa 40:8 (*Song of Songs*, 400).

47. With minor adaptation from Assis, *Flashes of Fire*, 83; see also Elliott, *Literary Unity*,
72–73.

the voice [קוֹל] of the turtledove [תּוֹר]   for your voice [קוֹל] is sweet,

is heard [שׁמע] in our land.   and your face [מַרְאֶה] is lovely.

The verbs "see" (ראה) and "hear" (שׁמע) are strikingly transferred from an impersonal description of nature to coaxing love talk, and what is more, morphed and multiplied. This lexical spillover underscores the unity of sense between the two stanzas. The second stanza is as much an appeal to end separation as is the first. In fact, it is a far more stirring appeal, loaded as it is with the personal since the first- and second-person singular pronouns "me" and "your," so recurrent in the second stanza, are absent in the main body of the first stanza (2:11–13a).

However, as we have already said, the union achievable in the second stanza is inferior. Perhaps this is obliquely suggested by the fact that the first stanza evokes the senses of sight, hearing, smell, and taste. The second stanza restricts itself to just sight and hearing, as emphasized through chiasm (seeing—hearing—hearing—seeing)[48] and the repetition of the seeing-hearing vocabulary.[49] If taste is evoked at all, it is roundabout by synesthesia, that is, a choice of word that calls up both the auditory and the gustatory.[50] The woman's voice is עָרֵב, which may be translated "delicious."[51]

As regards appeal to sensory experience, the Song usually pairs off sight with sound and smell with taste. The first pair is, of course, much less intimate than the second.[52] The point is this: even though the union achievable through sight and hearing is far less satisfying, the man would have this rather than continue in separation. Thus, we may infer that the second stanza, by lessening what is achievable, communicates even more intensely than the first stanza the desire of the man for union with his beloved.

At this point, the poem has come full circle in its use of metaphors: The eager stag is balanced by the inaccessible dove. Though his was the freedom of unbounded spaces and hers the limitation of a latticed window, it is ironic that all through the poem she can freely hear him

48. See Robert Alter, afterword to *The Song of Songs: A New Translation with an Introduction and Commentary*, by Ariel Bloch and Chana Bloch (New York: Random House, 1995), 122.

49. Assis (*Flashes of Fire*, 84) points out the absence of only the sense of smell, and draws from it a different inference than mine: that the developing relationship between the lovers has yet to reach full physical intimacy.

50. Hunt, *Poetry in the Song of Songs*, 91.

51. Bloch and Bloch point out that עָרֵב is usually used in reference to taste and smell, and translate it with "delicious." *Song of Songs,* 156. Hess, *Song of Songs*, 96 points out its use in Prov 20:17.

52. Hunt, *Poetry in the Song of Songs*, 85–87; Alter, afterword, 122.

and watch him, while he is restricted from the sight and sound of her. It is not hard to decide who merits sympathy! We, listening in on this conversation, wonder if the woman is deliberately playing the coquette. The opening lines of her response, when it finally comes, might confirm our suspicion.

> Catch for us the foxes,
> the little foxes that ruin the vineyards,
> our vineyards that are in bloom. (2:15)

If we read these lines—notoriously difficult to attribute to a given speaker[53]—as from the lips of the woman, then it may be best to read them as a snatch from a popular ditty. The parallelism by internal repetition (foxes, the little foxes . . . vineyards, our vineyards) makes for rhythm, suggesting a folk song.[54] She lets him hear her voice, even trilling out the lyrics perhaps, but the words are not what he might want to hear. Cleverly, she has found a song that echoes his description of springtime. Indeed, the vineyards are in full and fragrant flower, but that only brings on the foxes. The world he invites her into is less than perfect, even dangerous! If she is a vineyard in bloom (1:6; 8:8), then is this suitor outside her window a little fox to be wary of?[55] Such suitors are well known for despoiling girl-grapevines.

In the Song, playful banter is not solely a female prerogative. In another conversation, the man is a tease (1:7–8). But, before the man can

53. The possibilities are young women addressing an indeterminate addressee (Keel, *Song of Songs*, 108) or the couple (Garrett, *Song of Songs*, 161); the couple in unison (Hess, *Song of Songs*, 97); the man speaking to the daughters of Jerusalem (LXX); the brothers speaking (Bloch and Bloch, *Song of Songs*, 157); the woman speaking (Elliott, *Literary Unity*, 73; tentatively, Fox, *Ancient Egyptian Love Songs*, 114; Murphy, *Song of Songs*, 141; Exum, *Song of Songs*, 128; Assis, *Flashes of Fire*, 85; Bergant, *Song of Songs*, 31; Snaith, *Song of Songs*, 41; Estes, "Song of Songs," 331–32). Of course, the meaning of the text and its implication for the immediate literary context varies according to the speaker.

54. Bergant, *Song of Songs*, 31; Bloch and Bloch, *Song of Songs*, 157; Murphy, *Song of Songs*, 141. On the matter of foxes and grapevines, one explanation is that foxes (or fox cubs) laid waste to young (flowering) vines by digging around their roots for grubs. Fox hunts were thus a routine springtime exercise, at which songs such as this may have been popular. Bergant, *Song of Songs*, 31; Bloch and Bloch, *Song of Songs*, 157; Keel, *Song of Songs*, 108, 110.

55. There is wide agreement that the metaphor here is of young women as vines and lustful young men as foxes. Gordis, *Song of Songs*, 82; Fox, *Ancient Egyptian Love Songs*, 114; Marcia Falk, *The Song of Songs: A New Translation and Interpretation* (New York: HarperCollins, 1973), 155; Exum, *Song of Songs*, 129; Elizabeth Huwiler, "Song of Songs," in *Proverbs, Ecclesiastes and Song of Songs*, by Roland E Murphy and Elizabeth Huwiler, NIBC (Peabody, MA: Hendrickson, 1999), 260; Murphy, *Song of Songs*, 141; Estes, "Song of Songs," 332. See Keel, *Song of Songs*, 109–10, for ancient depictions of foxy philanderers. For detailed Greek parallels, see Anselm C. Hagedorn, "Of Foxes and Vineyards: Greek Perspectives on the Song of Songs," *VT* 53, no. 3 (2003): 337–52.

construct a suitable repartee, the woman ceases to be elusive. Suddenly, she is in dead earnest:

My beloved is mine and I am his [דּוֹדִי לִי וַאֲנִי לוֹ];
He browses among the lilies [הָרֹעֶה בַּשּׁוֹשַׁנִּים]. (2:16)

Her suitor is not a fox, grown or little. Unlike other men, known for their philandering, this man is devoted in love. So clearly is this the case that the woman can stake an exclusive claim to his affections, an exclusivity that is reciprocal.[56] He is hers and she is his. In the order of the four Hebrew words (דּוֹדִי לִי וַאֲנִי לוֹ), the woman occupies the center space. She is nested within him in belonging. Yet, there is an undercurrent of initiative here, perhaps even of aggression. In the sequence of words, her possession of him precedes his possession of her. Rather than be a vineyard acted upon, as other maidens might be, *she* acts upon the object of her desire, making him her own.

Meanwhile, rather than joining the raucous band of vineyard-raiding foxes, he sets himself apart in the pursuit of the one he loves. Revisiting for the second time the man's motif of springtime, the woman describes him in what appears to be a continuation of double entendre. He is one who feeds[57] among lilies. If the foxes greedily and indiscriminately root up the grapevines, then her suitor carefully chooses where he will take his pleasure.[58] In exquisite contrast, he grazes among lilies, in other words, herself (2:1–2; 7:3 [EV 2]; cf. 6:2).[59] Hunt perceives this image to be "one of the cleverest multiple sensory clusters" in the Song, especially because of what it packs into just two words: הָרֹעֶה בַּשּׁוֹשַׁנִּים. The metaphor is immediately visual; grazing suggests both feel and taste; the lilies evoke fragrance[60]—in all, an exquisite circumlocution.

This is all very well, the reader will say, but what action does the woman take on the separation between her beloved and herself, the burden of the poem? Does she leave her place by the window and walk into that riotous springtime, into the arms of her lover? We cannot tell.

---

56. An identical modern Palestinian parallel is: "He is my beloved and I am his" (H. Stephan, *Modern Palestinian Parallels to the Song of Songs*, Studies in Palestinian Customs and Folklore 3 [Jerusalem: Palestine Oriental Society, 1923], 32).

57. This is reading the verb רעה intransitively, following Murphy, *Song of Songs*, 139.

58. Estes, "Song of Songs," 331.

59. This metaphorical reading is common: Fox, *Ancient Egyptian Love Songs*, 115; Murphy, *Song of Songs*, 142; Hess, *Song of Songs*, 99; Exum, *Song of Songs*, 130; Pope, *Song of Songs*, 405–7; Longman, *Song of Songs*, 125; Garrett, *Song of Songs*, 162. For the sexual connotations of the lily or lotus from the ancient world, see Keel, *Song of Songs*, 114–15.

60. Hunt, *Poetry in the Song of Songs*, 92.

Her closing lines lazily curl back into the opening ones, abandoning the reader in an unending loop:

Until the day breaks [עַד שֶׁיָּפוּחַ הַיּוֹם] and the shadows flee [וְנָסוּ הַצְּלָלִים],
turn, my beloved [סֹב דְּמֵה־לְךָ],
and be like a gazelle [לִצְבִי] or like a young stag [אוֹ לְעֹפֶר הָאַיָּלִים]
on the rugged hills [עַל־הָרֵי בָתֶר]. (2:17)

We hear the same cluster of nouns here as we did at the start (2:8b–9a): gazelle (צְבִי), young stag (עֹפֶר הָאַיָּלִים), mountains or hills (הרים). What should we make of this line? Its problematic vocabulary and phrasing have been well documented.

First, what time of the day is it that "the day breathes" (עַד שֶׁיָּפוּחַ הַיּוֹם)? It is either the fresh early morning or when the evening sea breeze comes in. It is the same time as when the "shadows flee." When is that? Shadows could be said to flee at the rising of the sun,[61] or, at its setting, when they lengthen and run into darkness.[62] Second, what action is meant by "turn" (סֹב)? The man is either being asked to "turn/circle away from" her and depart, or "turn to(ward)" her—diametrically opposite meanings.[63] And third, what are the "hills of Bether" (הָרֵי בָתֶר, literally "mountains of separation"[64]) to which he must turn? Here, we are spoilt for options: metaphorically, a place or places on the woman's body suggestive of cleft hills (cf. Song 4:6);[65] "spice-laden" mountains, either literal or metaphorical (cf. Song 8:14);[66] literal hills of that name;[67] a literal cleft or rugged hills.[68]

Taken together, the permutations for translation are indeed many. However, one starting point is this: if there is any logic to the poem, the woman's last words should make an intelligible response to the present problem of separation, one the man clearly wishes to remedy. So, does she say he should turn and come to her[69] for the night (or for the rest

61. Hess, *Song of Songs*, 99; Fox, *Ancient Egyptian Love Songs*, 115; Carr, *Song of Solomon*, 103; Pope, *Song of Songs*, 408; Gledhill, *Message of the Song of Songs*, 141–42; Garrett, *Song of Songs*, 162.

62. Exum, *Song of Songs*, 120, 133; Keel, *Song of Songs*, 115. Snaith, *Song of Songs*, 43.

63. A third possibility is that the man should return another day. This is more likely if the temporal indicator that begins the verse, עַד־שֶׁ, is read "*When* the day breathes . . . , (re)turn." See Pope, *Song of Songs*, 408; Exum, *Song of Songs*, 131.

64. See Murphy, *Song of Songs*, 139; Exum, *Song of Songs*, 132.

65. Michael D Goulder, *The Song of Fourteen Songs*, JSOTSup 36 (Sheffield: JSOT Press, 1986); Garrett, *Song of Songs*, 163.

66. Keel, *Song of Songs*, 115–18; Murphy, *Song of Songs*, 139; Snaith, *Song of Songs*, 44.

67. Aquila; Symmachus; Vulgate; Hess, *Song of Songs*, 101; Fox, *Ancient Egyptian Love Songs*, 116.

68. Some ancient and contemporary English versions: LXX; NIV; NLT; NET.

69. Exum, *Song of Songs*, 132–33; Keel, *Song of Songs*, 117–18; Murphy, *Song of Songs*, 139;

of the day), for it pleases her body to be the terrain of this virile stag? Or, does she say he should go away[70] circling over the rugged hills, swift and graceful as a stag, till the next morning (or next evening)? Or is the woman resuming her teasing and throwing out a(nother) double entendre that the man may act on according to his interpretation?[71] The text is ambiguous,[72] mischievously—or perhaps, sophisticatedly—so.

By returning us to where we started, the poem perpetuates the theme of separation. In this poem, there is no certainty of resolution. Indeed, as Exum perceptively observes, the tension present in 2:17 is further exacerbated in a similar situation in 8:14. In 8:14, the man (again) asks to hear the woman's voice. The woman repeats her line from 2:17 but with two significant differences. Instead of the ambiguous "turn" (סבב), the imperative used is "flee" (דמה). On the face of it, it is hard to mistake this for an invitation. However, the destination is not "the rugged hills" (הָרֵי בָתֶר) but "the mountains of spices" (הָרֵי בְשָׂמִים). Considering the man's earlier erotic use of this phrase to refer to the woman (4:6), he surely understands this as summoning. Thus, 8:14 "foreground[s] the dual impulses already at work in 2:17."[73] What are we to make of the woman of the Song? Does she desire an end to their separation or does she not?

At the start of the poem, the woman seemed eager to meet the man. However, while we anticipated a response to his charmingly composed invitation, at first there was none. Instead, she disappeared from her own narrative. We heard the man imploring her to let herself be heard and seen. We inferred that she was playfully concealing herself and indulged in her game of hide-and-seek. When she did break her silence, it was with a snatch of song. More teasing, we thought. Then, in a sudden turnaround, she made a declaration of love that surely gratified the man and made his labors worthwhile. Eventually, she makes her reply to the invitation to come away. But, we're not sure what she means by her reply.

We could read the woman's concluding words as a counter-invitation. The man asked her to come away into the world outside. She has a better

Longman, *Song of Songs*, 126; Estes, "Song of Songs," 332; Garrett, *Song of Songs*, 162–63; Francis Landy, *Paradoxes of Paradise: Identity and Difference in the Song of Songs*, 2nd ed. (Sheffield: Phoenix, 2011), 64, though he does accede the ambiguity of the text.

70. Fox, *Ancient Egyptian Love Songs*, 115–16; Assis, *Flashes of Fire*, 88; Bloch and Bloch, *Song of Songs*, 157–58; Curtis, *Ecclesiastes and Song of Songs*, 128; Hess, *Song of Songs*, 99–100; Elliott, *Literary Unity*, 76–77.

71. Exum, *Song of Songs*, 132; Gledhill, *Message of the Song of Songs*, 141.

72. Fox, *Ancient Egyptian Love Songs*, 115; Bergant, *Song of Songs*, 32–33; Huwiler, "Song of Songs," 261; Gledhill, *Message of the Song of Songs*, 142–43.

73. Exum, *Song of Songs*, 133.

idea. She welcomes him to the world within her walls (cf. 8:1–2). Rather than move from the world within to the world without, she asks *him* to change domains: to move from the public into the private, from the outside to the inside, from the side of the lattice where she is absent to the side of the lattice where she is present. If separation is to be solved, hers is the superior solution. The union achievable on the other side of the window is hardly comparable to the one available on this side of it. Any attractions of the hills of which he has experience pale against the allure of the cleft hills she can offer. The picture he painted of springtime was a heady one, unmistakably shot through with the sensual. However, her double entendre outdoes his. Brushing aside circumlocutions through images of nature in the tumult of passion, she briskly (and unabashedly!) gets to the point. She proposes what is possible between them—and helpfully mentions for how long. Clearly, she anticipates more than just graceful fleet-footedness from her virile stag. If the reader takes it that this is the sense in which the man understands her closing words, then, the reader is content to add in an ellipsis and leave it to the couple to complete the poem in private.

However, the other way to read the woman is that for all her initial enthusiasm, when she is pressed for a decision, she retreats. She hides behind lattices; she lets herself be beseeched for sight and sound of her; she tantalizes the man with a snatch of song; she declares utter devotion, but finishes off with equivocation—or worse, by expressly sending him away. Gledhill sees that "the ambiguity of the language indicates the ambiguity of human responses. She wants him. She does not want him."[74] On the one hand, she wishes him to "graze among the lilies" (2:16). This is more than the closeness of two bodies. The tactile moves on to the gustatory, and the woman may almost be said to be internalized by the man.[75] On the other hand, she is content to dispatch him to the far side of the הָרֵי בָתֶר, the "mountains of separation" (2:17). This is beyond the most far-reaching of the senses, beyond the range of sight. And in the tension between these two impulses, the woman remains elusive. When the poem ends, she continues inaccessible behind her window. Separation remains unaddressed.

While our picture of the woman remains blurred with uncertainty, we are in no doubt about the man. The separation fills him with intense longing for the woman's presence. It is a situation he is impatient—almost desperate—to reverse. Though the entire poem was spoken by the woman, it is the man who dominates by the fervor of his seeking.

---

74. Gledhill, *Message of the Song of Songs*, 142–43.
75. Hunt, *Poetry in the Song of Songs*, 85.

But if the inconclusive ending leaves the man (and the reader!) frustrated, the poem that follows more than compensates.

THE WOMAN SEEKS: SONG 3:1–5

The woman's voice continues into the next poem. The setting remains the same: the woman is in her mother's house. But instead of dallying by the window, she is deeper within the house. She is in her bedroom, lying on her bed. It is not daytime, but night. The effect of these adjustments to setting is to magnify several times over the isolation of the woman from the man. In 2:8–17, the universal motif of separated lovers received a delightful treatment. They were separated, and yet separated by a mere lattice. Across it, the couple exchanged glances and words and banter and emotions, not to mention a folk song. In 3:1–5, the theme of separation slides to the dark end of the scale.

In the earlier poem the woman had playfully disappeared from the narrative, only to reappear (2:14–15). Here, the man's absence is complete and continues painfully line after line almost to a breaking point. Hints of anxiety we may have detected before ("Show me your face . . . let me hear your voice," 2:14) have amplified into desperation. Shadows received a passing mention there (2:17). Now they have lengthened into night, and darkness dominates. A world bursting with songbirds and vines and lovers has, for the most part, shrunk to a world of one. The throb of springtime energy pulsing through all things living is replaced by the dull tread of a faceless city patrol.

So dark and verging on the bizarre is the poem, especially in contrast to the almost stereotypical depiction of romantic love that preceded, that the reader wonders if this is to be taken as a real event.[76] The consensus is that the episode is too improbable for it to have happened, and so perhaps it happens in the woman's mind. It is either a fantasy[77] or a dream—or if she is half-dozing, maybe it is a daydream.[78]

The question of setting may be the wrong one to ask.[79] The Song constantly blurs the distinctions between the real and the surreal, between the factual world and the world-of-two that the couple inhabits. Those familiar with the song-and-dance sequences of popular Indian

---

76. Fox, *Ancient Egyptian Love Songs*, 117–18; Hess, *Song of Songs*, 102.

77. Falk, *Song of Songs*, 116.

78. See the argument that "on my bed" could mean "in my dreams" in J. T. Willis, "On the Text of Micah 2:1aα–β," *Bib* 48 (1967): 538. Preferring the dream explanation are Gordis, *Song of Songs*, 55; Huwiler, "Song of Songs," 263–64; Snaith, *Song of Songs*, 45–46. Preferring daydream are Assis, *Flashes of Fire*, 96; Murphy, *Song of Songs*, 145.

79. Exum, *Song of Songs*, 136.

cinema[80] might readily appreciate this. The couple in love is suddenly transported into a parallel existence[81] where what one is thinking about the other plays out. The piece is marked by kaleidoscopic changes in setting that range from the recognizable to the abstract, by a script improbable in real life, by "extras" making unexpected entries and sudden exits. This cinematic device is a proven success at mediating mood. For an audience willing to temporarily suspend disbelief, it substantiates the intangible. It foregrounds the implicit. Weaving in and out between the real and the imaginary, between the conscious and the subliminal, between what can be said and what must remain unspoken, between what is allowed and what is not, all normal boundaries dissolve. Time and space, states of mind and planes of existence all whirl together to create a fractured-yet-coherent narrative that presents just this: what the protagonist *feels*. Here in the Song, the woman *feels* separated from the man. The poem dramatizes that mood.[82]

> All night long on my bed
> I looked for [בִּקַּשְׁתִּי] the one my heart loves [אֵת שֶׁאָהֲבָה נַפְשִׁי];
> I looked for him [בִּקַּשְׁתִּיו] but did not find him [וְלֹא מְצָאתִיו].   (3:1)

Night after night,[83] on her bed, the woman has "looked for" or "sought" the man.[84] The verb (בקשׁ) here moves beyond this basic sense and carries the undercurrent of longing or yearning.[85] Perhaps the man has the freedom to come to the woman and has not come. Or, perhaps the woman lies in bed attempting to conjure up the man but without satisfaction.[86] In bed, in a place normally associated with rest and inactivity, the woman's thoughts allow her neither.[87]

---

80. Present-day music videos often do much the same thing.

81. See Keel, *Song of Songs*, 120; Longman, *Song of Songs*, 127.

82. Longman, *Song of Songs*, 161, thinks that all the Song's poems are doing just this—"creating moods and sensations."

83. Or, taking the plural "nights" (בַּלֵּילוֹת) into consideration, this may be the frequentative sense of "night after night." See Bergant, *Song of Songs*, 34; Bloch and Bloch, *Song of Songs*, 158; Exum, *Song of Songs*, 122; Garrett, *Song of Songs*, 170; Fox, *Ancient Egyptian Love Songs*, 118.

84. If we were considering the section Song 2:8–3:5 as a single narrative unit, we might assume that the woman lies awake regretting that she has sent the man away in 2:17. We do not necessarily make this inference since we are reading the units in this section as independent poems.

85. Keel, *Song of Songs*, 122; Fox, *Ancient Egyptian Love Songs*, 118.

86. See Keel, *Song of Songs*, 122, for reference to a sketch on an Egyptian shard that shows a woman kept similarly awake.

87. Keel, *Song of Songs*, 122. Stephan, *Modern Palestinian Parallels*, 12, provides a parallel in modern Palestinian love poetry: "I was enjoying sleep in my bed / when your form came to my mind and deranged me."

She names the object of her affection in two words: שֶׁאָהֲבָה נַפְשִׁי; "the one my heart loves." The weight of נֶפֶשׁ suggests a rendering more intense: "the one whom I love with every fiber of my being." In Othmar Keel's words, "her whole desire, all her yearnings, her thoughts, her feelings, and her physical needs are directed toward him."[88] Hess (reading נֶפֶשׁ alongside Prov 16:26) concludes that the emotion expressed by the phrase is equivalent in strength to the desire to live.[89]

The intensity of the woman's feeling is communicated through three elements: the weight of the vocabulary; the compressed lines (the Hebrew uses far fewer words than the English); and the repetition of words within the compression. The twice-repeated verb "I looked for" emphasizes the seriousness of the initiative, and simultaneously, the disappointment at the outcome: "I did not find." Clearly, there is a gap between desire and reality.[90] As we shall see, this state of affairs is emphasized by repeating the vocabulary of seeking-and-(not)-finding in widening spirals as the action moves from bedchamber to city.

The seeking has failed, and the waiting has exceeded the tolerable. She takes it upon herself to resolve this debilitating impasse of uncertainty.[91] Action progresses to the second step:

I will get up now [אָקוּמָה נָא] and go about [וַאֲסוֹבְבָה] the city [בָעִיר],
through its streets [בַּשְּׁוָקִים] and squares [וּבָרְחֹבוֹת];
I will look for [אֲבַקְשָׁה] the one my heart loves [אֵת שֶׁאָהֲבָה נַפְשִׁי].
So I looked for him [בִּקַּשְׁתִּיו] but did not find him [וְלֹא מְצָאתִיו]. (2:2)

One verb opened the action of the first initiative, and it was in the perfect (בִּקַּשְׁתִּי "I sought"). Two verbs commence the second step, and they are in the cohortative: "Let me now get up. Let me go about . . ." Or, "I *will* get up now. I *will* go about . . ." The pair of verbs with the self-motivation indicates an increase in the effort to find the object of the search. What is more, the search now moves out of the bedchamber.

The field of the search is described in three words: in the city (בָעִיר), in the streets (בַּשְּׁוָקִים), and in the squares (וּבָרְחֹבוֹת). The initial *beth* links them alliteratively.[92] The mention of the city leads to streets, and

---

88. Keel, *Song of Songs*, 121.

89. Hess, *Song of Songs*, 103.

90. Assis, *Flashes of Fire*, 98. There is an interesting LXX addition to Song 3:1: ἐκάλεσα αὐτόν καὶ οὐχ ὑπήκουσέν μου; "I called him, but he did not hearken to me." Here, then, is a woman who looks for, and calls out to, her lover so as to end the state of separation. Such a seeker would be a perfect match for the man in the daytime poem who looks for his lover through the lattice, and who calls out to her to come away.

91. Gledhill, *Message of the Song of Songs*, 146.

92. Elliott, *Literary Unity*, 79.

the streets flow into squares. Even as the woman speaks, the words have led the reader out of her bedroom. "In the streets" (בַּשְׁוָקִים) shares consonants with "I sought" (בִּקַּשְׁתִּי), aurally interlocking the place with the purpose.[93]

So by the time we hear the third cohortative ("I *will* look for"), for us, the search has already begun. We are by her side as she hurries along this street, turns into that one, and darts across the square and into yet another street. She is searching as widely and thoroughly as she can.[94] She is also traversing dangerous places. City squares are where prostitutes entice potential clients.[95]

Meanwhile, we assume the search is random, for she has not told us she has any idea of where the man may be.[96] If so, the enterprise is fueled by desperation and is unlikely to succeed. It is not long before our misgivings are confirmed. The search in the city ends as did the one in her bedroom. Even the words that announce it are identical: "I sought him but did not find him" (3:2b). In both cases, the search and its result are described similarly: the energy built up by the quick double repetition of "I sought" is abruptly negated by "I did not find." The eager seeking falters to a halt at not finding. The repetition of vocabulary gives the reader the sense that the search, instead of progressing further, has simply returned to the starting point.[97]

We expect that with this second, and rash, initiative having reached a dead end, the woman will now retrace her steps and return to the safety of her house. Suddenly, the story picks up again with the same verb. Having now heard of two non-findings, we are taken by surprise that there is now a finding.

> The watchmen found me
> as they made their rounds [הַסֹּבְבִים] in the city.
> "Have you seen the one my heart loves?" (3:3)

In an unexpected turnaround, the subject of the action becomes its object. The night patrol finds *her*.[98] They share with her the intention of going around the city—they are הַסֹּבְבִים, the circumambulators.[99] For her, circumambulation—especially at this time of the night—is a choice. For them, it is part of their routine. How ironic, then, that they, who

93. See Hess, *Song of Songs*, 104.
94. Assis, *Flashes of Fire*, 98; Bergant, *Song of Songs*, 35;
95. Estes, "Song of Songs," 334. Cf. Ezek 16:24, 31; Prov 7:12.
96. Jenson, *Song of Songs*, 37.
97. Assis, *Flashes of Fire*, 98.
98. Bergant, *Song of Songs*, 35.
99. Assis, *Flashes of Fire*, 98.

were not particularly seeking, find, while she who has been desperately seeking has still not found.[100] This night, they have probably been making the rounds of the city longer than she has. They are many, while she is one. These considerations ignite her third initiative. She ropes them into her quest by asking if they have sighted the object of her search.

The woman's question to the watchmen is not introduced with the usual narrative connector "I asked them . . ." If the watchmen's appearance was abrupt, her voice breaks the silence of the night just as abruptly. This dramatization of the woman's mood is moving swiftly, impatiently skipping the usual formulations of a proper sequential narration.

Her question is a strange one and is unusually ordered. "The one my heart loves, have you seen?" The uncommon Hebrew word sequence throws up what is foremost in her mind, the man.[101] But the description would hardly help the patrol identify the missing person. However, we remind ourselves, the audience of the poem is not the watchmen but us, the readers. The poem is communicating to us the mood of its protagonist. This third repetition of the endearment works like a refrain, drawing us back yet again to the object of the search.[102] Her whole being is taken up by this other person, her mind completely pervaded by thoughts of him, her faculties channeled into finding him, her emotions focused on the pain of the separation.

Do the watchmen say anything in reply? We are not told. We would be surprised if they could offer any helpful response to so incoherent a question. While the patrol stands there, either formulating a counterquestion or momentarily bewildered into silence by the strangeness of the encounter, the woman turns away. Either she has sensed there is no help forthcoming from the watchmen, or the woman sets their reply aside as unnecessary incidental information.[103] The function the patrol performs in this bizarre narrative seems to be to throw into relief that the quest is a solitary one. It belongs to the woman alone.

However, her third attempt has followed the pattern of the first two. If even the city guards—who should know—are of no help, this search is clearly futile.[104] Will she now give up and return home? In answer to that, we note that there is no repeat of the *leitwörter* "I sought" and "I did not find" that closed the first two search attempts. That puzzles us. Is the poem (and thus, the woman) hurrying on to some denouement we have not anticipated? As it turns out, the positive use of מצא in the finding

---

100. Murphy, *Song of Songs*, 145; Exum, *Song of Songs*, 135; Murphy, *Song of Songs*, 145.

101. Exum, *Song of* Songs, 136. See Bloch and Bloch, *Song of Songs*, 158.

102. Hess, *Song of Songs*, 101.

103. Exum, *Song of Songs*, 137.

104. Hess, *Song of Songs*, 104.

of the woman by the watchmen marked an upturn in the flow of the episode.[105]

> Scarcely had I passed them [כִּמְעַט שֶׁעָבַרְתִּי מֵהֶם]
> when I found [שֶׁמָּצָאתִי] the one my heart loves. (3:4a)

The woman passes beyond the patrol. This suggests that she has moved on further in her search,[106] rather than that she is now ceding failure and returning home. Should we frown at her foolhardiness? Should we admire her grim optimism? Before we can make up our minds, she collides with the object of her search. The only notice we get for this surprise is the brief build-up of anticipation: "Scarcely had I passed them . . ."[107] The city streets are full of surprises! In retrospect, we commend her for not giving up.

The introduction of the man into the narrative is even stranger than the appearance of the patrol. Just a little further down the street, or perhaps just around the next corner, the man materializes out of the night. She seems to know him right away, even in the dark streets of the city, even at a time when she was more likely to bump into some undesirable element prowling the city.

> I seized him [אֲחַזְתִּיו] and would not let him go[108] [וְלֹא אַרְפֶּנּוּ]
> till I had brought him [עַד־שֶׁהֲבֵאתִיו] to my mother's house,
> to the room of the one who conceived me. (3:4b)

Following fast on the heels of the fourth and climactic מצא, her finding of the man, comes a verb pair made up of antonyms. She seizes (אחז) him, and will not let him go (ארף). The first verb is a positive action. The second reinforces it through a negative. The episode closes with a reentry into the house, completing the cycle of the narrative from the house, into the city, and back into the house.[109] Though the narrative circles around on itself, the mood has changed. There is a movement from "restlessness to rest, from solitude to companionship."[110] Indeed, as the narrative swiftly spirals inward through the concentric circles of

---

105. See Hess, *Song of Songs*, 101, 104.

106. Hess, *Song of Songs*, 105.

107. Snaith (*Song of Songs*, 48) draws attention to the position of this adverb "scarcely" (כִּמְעַט), located unusually at the head of the sentence to give it prominence.

108. See Murphy, *Song of Songs*, 420–21; Bloch and Bloch, *Song of Songs*, 158; Fox, *Ancient Egyptian Love Songs*, 118; Exum, *Song of Songs*, 134 for an alternative translation possibility.

109. Assis, *Flashes of Fire*, 95; Estes, "Song of Songs," 335.

110. Landy, *Paradoxes of Paradise*, 42.

city, mother's house, and bedchamber,[111] the bizarre and dangerous is replaced by the normal and safe.

The increasing tension of the first three-fourths is defused in the last quarter with the single familiar word "I-found!" (3:4a). Twice before, we heard it negated, and once we heard it associated with an unlikely object. Now it is a cry of exultant surprise. The poem has moved from yearning to an irrational fear of abandonment to panic-driven action to a rush of relief.[112] Now, a formulaic address to the daughters of Jerusalem closes the poem (see 2:7; 8:4).

Daughters of Jerusalem, I charge you
by the gazelles and by the does of the field:
Do not arouse or awaken love
until it so desires. (3:5)

The address consists of an oath formula and an adjuration. The oath seems to bear a likeness to the more solemn oath formula invoking God,[113] but it is made with reference to does and gazelles, typically sex symbols.[114] Perhaps the solemn oath is turned into a light-hearted version in keeping with the sylvan settings of the Song.[115]

But what is the meaning of the adjuration?[116] One possibility is that the woman has now changed her mind about proceeding further with the man, either for fear that the man should think her brazen,[117] or to protect herself against indulging herself prematurely.[118] Both are rather unlikely given the drift of the narrative. On the contrary, the adjuration may be a "Do Not Disturb!" sign put up as the door closes on the couple.[119] Or perhaps the woman is throwing out some good advice to her audience, advising them not to be untimely in matters sexual or attempt to force love into relationships, especially considering its severe

111. Jill M. Munro, *Spikenard and Saffron: A Study in the Poetic Language of the Song of Songs* JSOTSup 203 (Sheffield: Sheffield Academic, 1995), 134–35. Hess agrees that there is more than parallelism to "mother's house" and "chamber"; there is forward movement (*Song of Songs*, 106).

112. Gledhill, *Message of the Song of Songs*, 144, 146.

113. Cf. Gen 24:3. So Assis, *Flashes of Fire*, 73; Gordis, *Song of Songs*, 27–28; Fox, *Ancient Egyptian Love Songs*, 110; Bergant, *Song of Songs*, 26; Daniel Grossberg, "Nature, Humanity, and Love in Song of Songs," *Int* 59, no. 3 (2005): 231.

114. As in Prov 5:19. So Assis, *Flashes of Fire*, 73; Bergant, *Song of Songs*, 26.

115. Exum, *Song of Songs*, 119; Longman, *Song of Songs*, 116.

116. For a survey of eight different interpretations, see Brian P. Gault, "An Admonition against 'Rousing Love': The Meaning of the Enigmatic Refrain in Song of Songs," *BBR* 20, no. 2 (2010): 161–84.

117. Assis, *Flashes of Fire*, 74, 102.

118. Estes, "Song of Songs," 337; Gledhill, *Message of the Song of Songs*, 145.

119. Fox, *Ancient Egyptian Love Songs*, 118–19; Brian P. Gault, "A 'Do Not Disturb' Sign? Reexamining the Adjuration Refrain in Song of Songs," *JSOT* 36, no. 1 (2011): 93–104.

demands.[120] Or, with a slightly different nuance, perhaps the woman cautions the audience that it is futile to try and awaken love, because love will happen only when it happens—as it has happened with her—and so they should not attempt it.[121]

The adjuration affirms to us, at any rate, that the separation between the man and the woman is ended. The audience is handed caveats, but the couple is beyond them.

COMPARING THE SEEKING POEMS

Standing back from the section 2:8–3:5, we can appreciate the interplay between its two strikingly vivid poems. Both begin abruptly. Both start indoors, within the woman's house. In the daytime poem, the view is restricted. We are looking through the woman's eyes from the inside to the world outside or through the man's from the outside into the house. Movement in either direction is missing altogether. We had hoped that the woman would take up the invitation to go out to the man, but that did not happen. Perhaps the man came in to the woman, but we are left unsure.

In the nighttime poem, there is free movement, and with that, an opening up of view. The woman moves outdoors—not in response to the man's invitation as might have happened in the daytime poem, but driven by her inner urges. That she was unavailable to come out by day emphasizes the feverish agitation that moves her out at night. What is more, that urgency multiples further with the woman (rather than the man as was the case earlier) initiating an end to separation. Socially and culturally, the woman surprises us in the role of the seeking lover.

The woman had been coyly unresponsive to the man's invitation to "arise" (קוּם) and come away with him. In the nighttime poem, she arises (קוּם) and leaves the house of her own volition. Indeed, his imperative use of the verb is balanced by her cohortative. In the second poem, she needs no invitation. She exhorts herself. This gives her seeking a sharp edge that was missing in the man's (rather sweet) seeking of her.

The verb "turn/go around" (סבב) links the poems. She had asked the man to "turn" (2:17). Now she goes around, circumambulating the city. The man's סבב is linked to hills (whether literal or otherwise) in day-

---

120. Garrett, *Song of Songs*, 173; Hess, *Song of Songs*, 106–7; Longman, *Song of Songs*, 115–16; Murphy, *Song of Songs*, 147.

121. Exum, *Song of* Songs, 118–19, 138.

time, but her סבב takes place in the city, and at night.[122] The city, with its maze of streets and squares, hides its secrets better than the wide-open spaces. She must seek harder. Indeed, when סבב is applied to the watchmen, it takes the simple *qal* form, while with the woman, it appears with the intensive nuance of the *polel*.[123] What is more, the man knew where the woman could be found, while the woman has no clue. He had a destination. She searches with frantic uncertainty, taking her chances at random.

In the daytime poem, the seeker employs an appealing range of endearments, all in the context of seeking the beloved. The woman is his beloved, his beautiful one, his dove. In marked contrast, the woman uses just the one descriptor, "the one my heart loves." She speaks the phrase four times (in as many verses), evenly distributing it across the narrative. She seems to know of no other language for him, and uses it even when it is meaningless in its context (3:3). The phrase carries alliteration and assonance. שֶׁאָהֲבָה נַפְשִׁי is bookended by *sh*, and repeats the vowel sound -*a*. These internal echoes and the fourfold repetition of the endearment create a monotony that verges on fixation. Apparently, the phrase most deeply expresses what the woman feels for the man, and she has no use for anything that may be prettier but less loaded. Indeed, the man's endearments, drawn as they are from stock romantic vocabulary, almost seem frothily insubstantial against the visceral punch packed into "the one my נֶפֶשׁ loves."

The man uses a cluster of verbs in relation to seeking to end separation: arise, come away, come, show, let me hear. The woman has a narrower range of verbs attached to her endearment: seek, see, find. "Seek" and "find" are of unusually high frequency, both occurring four times each. For the seven times the man uses his seeking verbs, the woman's count is nine and that in a poem about two-thirds shorter. If vocabulary is any indicator, the nighttime poem is by far the more intensely concentrated on the theme of seeking.

Further, there is one seeking verb that links the poems: "to see" (ראה). In the daytime poem, this verb twice spills over into the noun "appearance" (מַרְאֶה) in the context of the man asking his inaccessible dove to show him her appearance (2:14). We are not sure if she complies. In a strange turn of events, the nighttime poem has the woman desperately asking the city guards if they have seen (ראה) her beloved. If they have sighted him, the possibility is that that could help lead to her seeing him.

122. See Keel, *Song of Songs*, 119–21, on the sociocultural probability of a woman out in the city at night.
123. Murphy, *Song of Songs*, 145.

The man had the advantage of proximity and could plead directly for a sight of her. She, on the other contrary, has no idea where he is, and must ask a third party to mediate so that she can see him. Her chances of sighting him are halved twice. What is more, the man's view was hindered by a wall, or even less, by a latticed window (2:9). What prevents her catching sight of him is more complex. The walls that make up the labyrinthine streets and enclose the squares—these repeatedly close in on her view, multiplying the obstacle to sight many times over. The odds are stacked against the woman, but remarkably, she persists. Love moves her to "abandon convenience, comfort, and even safety."[124]

Verbs also play a significant role in setting the mood of each poem. The daytime poem opens with a burst of seven participles all stacking up into a positive event, the man's arrival. None of the verbs that follow are negated. The nighttime poem, in contrast, is dominated by loss. Not only is the seeking verb בקשׁ in high frequency, but also the finding verb מצא is negated twice. Even after the man is found, the woman remains insecure as one more negated verb (רפה) might indicate: she will not let go. As if these three negations (by the particle לֹא) were not enough, even the closing adjuration twice negates the verb "to awaken" (עוּר, using the particle אִם). The overall effect is that the poem becomes saturated with deeply unhappy emotions ranging from anxiety to despair.

Not only the verbs but also the verb suffixes in the nighttime poem are telling. The first-person singular dominates. Other than in the encounter with the patrol, the woman is the subject of the verbs. But even when she is a verb's object, the guards are so impersonal and faceless that the encounter increases the attention on the woman. Meanwhile, the man is without exception acted on by the woman. The story does not concern itself with any detail about him—his whereabouts or the reason for his absence.[125] The poem keeps its focus fixed on the woman as seeker, perhaps intentionally contrasting it with the man's seeking. The woman's search has a certain masculine aggression, in line with her forceful declaration of possession in the daytime poem: "My beloved is mine" (2:16). This is a feisty, spirited woman!

When finally the woman finds the man, she seizes him. The verb (אחז) recalls the ditty in the daytime poem. Read metaphorically, each woman was to catch herself a fox. If that reading is valid, then the woman has figuratively done just that. She was the elusive one earlier. In the nighttime poem, the man disappears altogether. So, if catching foxes in springtime was an entertaining communal exercise, the contrast

---

124. Estes, "Song of Songs," 338.
125. Bergant, *Song of Songs*, 35.

is that for this woman, fox-catching has been a solitary ordeal. But there is more than just determination here. There is an undercurrent of the possessiveness that we saw before in 2:16: "My beloved is mine." Without meaning to objectify the man, we could say that her desperation arises from having lost a precious belonging.

So, now that she has him in her grasp, she does not let go till she has brought him (בוא) into her mother's house. She fears she may lose him again.[126] The daytime poem opened with this same verb, "to come" (בוא): "Look! Here he comes!" (2:8). There, it announced that the man was on his way to the woman's house; it declared the end to separation. Here, the verb ends the poem. The woman does not leave it to the man to spontaneously reunite them by coming to her. Rather, with a fourth and final initiative toward union, the woman ensures that the man comes into her house.

This is the dwelling whose wall the woman had earlier described as "our wall" (2:9). Then, the possessive pronoun "our" indicated that the house was her family's residence. Now there is a subtle change in ownership. The woman brings the man to the house of her mother,[127] and further in, to her mother's bedchamber. In the daytime poem, he had been shut out by walls and windows. Now, he has the use of a private and privileged space in the house because the woman wills it. So complete is her claim of this inner room on behalf of them both that the narrative reaches a resting point here. The door discreetly shuts, we understand, and a parting adjuration closes the episode.

The daytime poem ended with what is possibly a double entendre in that the gazelle/stag was perhaps encouraged to explore the "cleft hills" of his lover's body. The nighttime poem also ends with a mention of gazelles (and does), and this is explicitly in a context of arousing love. But, the double entendre of the nighttime poem really lies in the couple entering the "room of the one who conceived" the woman

126. Assis, *Flashes of Fire*, 99.

127. Why does the woman refer to this house as her mother's and not her father's? Proposed answers are: (1) When it comes to matters of the heart, a girl feels closer to her mother (Assis, *Flashes of Fire*, 99; C. Meyers, "To Her Mother's House: Considering a Counterpart to the Israelite *Bet 'ab*," in *The Bible and Politics of Exegesis: Essays in Honour of Norman K. Gottwald on His Sixty Fifth Birthday*, ed. D. Jobling et al. [Cleveland: Pilgrim, 1991], 46; C. Meyers, "Gender Imagery in the Song of Songs," *HAR* 10 [1986]: 218–19; D. Grossberg, "Two Kinds of Sexual Relationships in the Bible," *HS* [1994]: 21–22). (2) The poet follows a parallel with ancient West Asian mythology. In Sumerian cultic marriage poetry, the groom formally consummated the marriage in the bride's house (Pope, *Song of Songs*, 421–22). (3) The mother's place signifies security (Munro, *Spikenard and Saffron*, 70; Hess, *Song of Songs*, 105–6). (4) The "mother's house" symbolizes freedom, while the "father's house" symbolizes law and order (André LaCocque, *Romance She Wrote: A Hermeneutical Essay on Song of Songs* [Harrisburg, PA: Trinity, 1998], 96).

(3:4).[128] In the earlier poem, we are never sure if the woman's proposition is understood as one and acted on. Here, we are left in no doubt. Separation is remedied fully and without ambiguity. Earlier, the couple were restricted to seeing and hearing each other. The more intimate senses were missing—touch, smell, and taste. These were tantalizingly present in the metaphor of the man feeding among the lilies, but that metaphor was not explicitly realized. The nighttime poem remains empty of sensory contact, till the tactile takes over suddenly and violently. The woman seizes, will not let go, brings the man in. The first poem claimed metaphorically that the man internalized the woman by feeding among the lilies. Here, there is also an internalization of sorts, one in which the woman takes the man into what is clearly her private space, the room where she was conceived.

Our comparison of the poems' depictions of the man and the woman as seekers leads us to this conclusion: in contravention of romantic (and social) stereotypes, the woman outdoes the man at seeking. There is a certain muscularity to her quest, a raw edge to her emotions. If he is like a gentle breeze, she is a whirlwind.

SEPARATION AND SEEKING IN SONG 5:2–6:3

We come to the woman's other seeking-finding speech, 5:2–6:3. In this, the two episodes of seeking (one by the man and the other by the woman) are not merely lain out side by side. They segue into a narrative whole through the dialogue between the woman and the daughters of Jerusalem, giving the reader a seamless sequence of events.[129] The unity of the whole is signaled with the bookends "I . . . my beloved" (אֲנִי and דּוֹדִי; 5:2; 6:3),[130] showcasing the protagonists of the speech.

Within this larger piece is nested the woman's search (5:2–8) delimited by the bracketing word "I" (אֲנִי). This poem is a parallel version of the nighttime poem in 3:1–5. It has an identical storyline and cast: the woman, the man, the night watch, and the daughters of Jerusalem.

As we examine the poem in 5:2–6:3 to compare the two seekers, we will make reference to the parallel text in 2:8–3:5, reading the thematic and verbal resonance between the texts as an invitation to do so.

128. Bergant (Song of Songs, 36) points out that in the Song enclosed spaces are invariably associated with erotic activity. See 1:4; 1:12; 2:4; 8:1–3.

129. Gordis, Song of Songs, 87; Fox, Ancient Egyptian Love Songs, 141; Elliott, Literary Unity, 122–23; Murphy, Song of Songs, 168; Exum, Song of Songs, 186.

130. Elliott, Literary Unity, 122.

THE MAN SEEKS: 5:2–4

I slept [אֲנִי יְשֵׁנָה] but my heart [וְלִבִּי] was awake [עֵר].
Listen! My beloved is knocking [קוֹל דּוֹדִי דוֹפֵק]:
"Open to me, my sister, my darling,
my dove, my flawless one.
My head is drenched with dew,
my hair with the dampness of the night." (5:2)

In 3:1–5, the woman was lying awake on her bed, her agitation keeping her from sleep. Now she is much more at rest, dozing lightly. She couches this state in charming poetry. She (the emphatic אֲנִי) is asleep but her heart (לִבִּי is used in metonymy) is astir (עוּר)[131]—the same verb used in the adjuration to the daughters of Jerusalem not to arouse love. She is asleep and awake both at once.[132]

It is in this state that she hears the man. She signals his presence to the reader with the same words as before: "Listen! My beloved . . ." As before, it is the sound[133] of him that her attentive ears have picked up. Again, as before, the narrative opens with participles—waking, knocking.[134] As in a drama, the action is unfolding before the reader. Indeed, the immediacy is increased by the lack of narrative introduction to the man's speech. There is no introductory "My beloved spoke and said to me . . ." (2:10).[135]

When last we heard the man, it was day, and the man invited his beloved to come outdoors, to him. Now, it is night, and the man requests his beloved to let him come indoors, to her. She was to come out because

131. See Keel, *Song of Songs*, 162–63, on the heart as the organ of thought.

132. A similar sentiment in modern Palestinian love poetry is: "Though I sleep at night my eye is awake; / Can the promised one not sleep? / We spread the couch and prepared the bed, / The cock crowed, yet we have not seen our beloved." Stephan, *Modern Palestinian Parallels*, 72.

133. See comment on 3:8 for the preferential use of "sound" to "voice." As Exum points out, דּוֹדִי דוֹפֵק is even onomatopoeic. *Song of Songs*, 193.

134. There is much room in this monologue for double entendre. See Exum, *Song of Songs*, 190–92; Pope, *Song of Songs*, 514–18. Garrett even thinks this is a description of the man forcing himself on the woman (*Song of Songs*, 206–17). Carey Ellen Walsh (*Exquisite Desire: Religion, the Erotic, and the Song of Songs* [Minneapolis: Fortress Press, 2000], 105–14), reads the entire poem as the woman's "wet dream." Lyle Eslinger, "The Case of an Immodest Lady Wrestler in Deuteronomy XXV 11–12," *VT* 31 (1981): 275–76, posits "hand" as a euphemism for genitals in legal literature.

Others read the monologue more at face value, as relating a missed encounter: Elliott, *Literary Unity*, 129; Bloch and Bloch, *Song of Songs*, 181; Fox, *Ancient Egyptian Love Songs*, 144–45; Bergant, *Song of Songs*, 64.

Double entendre is only to be expected in love poetry. In this monologue, however, maximizing the double entendre does not help to establish the sequence of events. At most, it adds sexual flavor and cleverly sets the tension between fulfillment and desire deferred.

135. Bloch and Bloch, *Song of Songs*, 180.

it was enjoyable outside in springtime. Now, he wants to be let in because it is uncomfortable outside. Maybe he has travelled a distance to get to her door, as he did earlier to reach her window. In the process, his hair is wet with night dew.[136] It is doubtful that he presents this as a *reason* to be let in.[137] Rather, it is more likely to be a roundabout declaration of his eagerness to be with her. The self-description indicates the trouble he has taken to be where he now is, at her door.[138]

The man's affection for the woman tumbles out in a string of endearments. Each endearment is a single Hebrew word, and each ends with an identical final syllable: *-ti*.[139] It is a rhythmically rhyming word cluster that fills the night air with music. The first-person possessive pronoun suffix "my" (י-) unites the couple. There is no reason why a door should stand between them.[140] He speaks four endearments: she is his "own" (so JPS), his loved one, his dove, his flawless one. Unpacked, the endearments read: she is as dear to him as if she were his own flesh and blood; she rules the passions of his heart; her rounded dove-like contours enthrall him; in all, she is perfect for him. This string of four consecutive endearments is the longest in the Song. Clearly, there is nothing the man wants more at this moment other than to be with the woman. So, he asks her to "open to" him, to let him in.

We recall that in the daytime poem, her response to his invitation had probably been momentary silence, causing him to plead to hear her voice (3:14). Here, does she again hesitate to speak, or does she throw him back a teasing reply as she did earlier with her song (3:15)? We are not sure.[141] Either she addresses the man on the other side of the bolted door, or she thinks her thoughts aloud to us:

136. A modern Palestinian poetic parallel is: "Look, O my eyes, my beloved is standing outside, / And his shock of hair is waving" (Stephan, *Modern Palestinian Parallels*, 11).

137. Exum, *Song of Songs*, 188; Bergant, *Song of Songs*, 62; Assis, *Flashes of Fire*, 152; Huwiler, "Song of Songs," 274; Jenson, *Song of Songs*, 53.

138. Fox categorizes this trope as the *paraclausithyron*—the trope in which "a youth stands outside a girl's house complaining of his exclusion and his longing to be let in" (*Ancient Egyptian Love Songs*, 282). A modern Palestinian love song says what the response to the beloved's knocking should ideally be: "He knocked at the door with grace; / I opened it for him gently, / And served him a dish with '*knâfe*,' / The dessert being from his rosy cheeks" (Stephan, *Modern Palestinian Parallels*, 32).

139. Hess, *Song of Songs*, 168.

140. Bergant, *Song of Songs*, 61.

141. The possibilities are: (1) the woman is teasing (Murphy, *Song of Songs*, 170; Exum, *Song of Songs*, 194; Gordis, *Song of Songs*, 62; Bloch and Bloch, *Song of Songs*, 182; Hess, *Song of Songs*, 170–71; Pope, *Song of Songs*, 516); (2) she is half-asleep and confused (Goulder, *Song of Fourteen Songs*, 41; Elliott, *Literary Unity*, 126–27); (3) she muses within herself (Falk, *Song of Songs*, 122); (4) she is resisting his entry (Longman, *Song of Songs*, 166–67).

> I have taken off my robe;   must I put it on again?
>
> I have washed   my feet;   must I soil them again? (5:3)

If this is banter, we are not overly surprised. We have seen her at it before and, even if we had not, such teasing would hardly be unexpected between lovers. But if this is an aside to the reader, then it is reason for some disquiet. Either the woman has made up her mind not to attend to the door, and the questions are entirely rhetorical, or she is of two minds and is talking herself through to a decision. Her closing reply to the man's invitation to come away had shown something of this tension, though it could have been dismissed as a clever double entendre: "Turn, my beloved, and be like a gazelle or like a young stag on the cleft hills" (2:17). But, here is that tension again. As much as she loves him, the woman is not always pining for the man's company. That other night, it was intolerable that she should be separated from him. This night, she is not so sure she wants him with her—even though she may well have prepared for his arrival by perfuming herself and her bed with myrrh (5:5).[142]

Meanwhile, either in response to her teasing or anxious about her silence, the man redoubles his effort,[143] moving from words to action. In the earlier poem, he only addressed her through openings, but now he puts his hand through them:[144]

> My beloved thrust his hand through the latch-opening;
> my heart began to pound for him. (5:4)

Suddenly, there is a rush of the visual, the auditory, and the tactile. All at once, she can see and hear him. His fingers, trying to work the bolt open, stimulate her sense of touch. The door is still shut, but he has invaded the room! The sensory overload shoots a frisson through her body.[145] Spontaneously, she gets up. Hess has it right: "The keyhole marks the turning point from a pursuing male and a passive or resistant female, to a retreating male and a pursuing female."[146]

142. Cf. Ruth 3:3; Prov 7:17 (Bloch and Bloch, *Song of Songs*, 181–82; Exum, *Song of Songs*, 195).

143. Bergant, *Song of Songs*, 63.

144. Fox, *Ancient Egyptian Love Songs*, 144. For an explanation of the mechanics of doors and how they were secured, see Keel, *Song of Songs*, 190, 192–93; Bloch and Bloch, *Song of Songs*, 181; Pope, *Song of Songs*, 518–19.

145. Literally, "my insides murmured for him." For a similar use of חמה to communicate deep emotion, see Jer 4:19. For other instances of "insides" as the locus of intense feeling, see Isa 16:11; Lam 1:20; 2:11; Job 30:27.

146. Hess, *Song of Songs*, 172.

THE WOMAN SEEKS: 5:5–6:3

I arose to open for my beloved,
and my hands dripped with myrrh,
my fingers with flowing myrrh,
on the handles of the lock. (5:5)

For the second time, there is the emphatic use of "I" (אֲנִי), marking the milestones in the narrative: "I, I arose . . ." Attention now shifts from his hand to her hands. The gaze dwells longer here. Where his hand burst into view and then vanished from the narrative, her hands are described as if in slow motion and with increasing detail. Her fingers drip with liquid myrrh, smearing the handles of the lock. Her grip slips and she must try again and again till the door unbolts. The aggregation of sensory stimuli is directed at the reader this time—the sight of the woman's hands clumsily at work, the sound of the bolt being worked, and the feel of oiled fingers against the door's lock. In addition to these three sensory stimuli, which were also present with the male hand, is the fragrance released by the dripping oil of myrrh (see Esth 2:12). With this aggregation of the more intimate senses (namely, touch and smell), the reader is alerted that this poem has upped the ante from its parallel in 3:1–5, in which the woman also seeks the man.

The pace of seeking momentarily retards, but unfortunately at a critical moment. In all, there have been two pauses so far, once when the woman deliberated on getting out of bed, and next with the slippery bolt. Paronomasia links the two. She hesitates to soil (טנף) her freshly washed feet, while her hands drip (נטף) with liquid myrrh.[147] Both hands and feet are unwilling participants, and there will be a price to pay.

I opened for my beloved [פָּתַחְתִּי אֲנִי לְדוֹדִי],
But my beloved had left; he was gone [וְדוֹדִי חָמַק עָבָר].
My heart sank [נַפְשִׁי יָצְאָה] at his departure [בְדַבְּרוֹ].
I looked for him [בִּקַּשְׁתִּיהוּ] but did not find him [וְלֹא מְצָאתִיהוּ].
I called him [קְרָאתִיו] but he did not answer [וְלֹא עָנָנִי]. (5:6)

The act of opening the door is described with a third repetition of the emphatic "I": "I, I opened for my beloved" (5:6). However, the lapse between his request "Open . . ." (5:3) and the actual opening of the door is considerable. Assis perceptively observes that half the poem (5:2–8) has gone by before the door finally swings open.[148]

147. See Y. Zakovitch, *Das Hohelied*, HThKAT (Freiburg: Herder, 2004), 216.
148. Assis, *Flashes of Fire*, 154. Hess notes that time to recite more than forty words have passed (*Song of Songs*, 174).

Meanwhile, even as slickly perfumed fingers were struggling with the bolt, the man has made an exit from the narrative. Assis notes a play on words linking the two. The flowing (עבר) myrrh dripped from her fingers, while the man passed on (עבר).[149]

As suddenly as he appeared in the city streets (3:4), he disappears from her threshold.

Murphy notes the tight chiasm that highlights this, with the subject "my beloved" as the focus:[150]

$$\text{פָּתַחְתִּי אֲנִי לְדוֹדִי וְדוֹדִי חָמַק עָבָר}$$

Opened . . . my beloved . . . my beloved . . . turned and gone

The departure is announced with a verb pair, and we are reminded of the multiple verb pairs that described his arrival in the daytime poem. This one baldly sets out that he turned away (חָמַק) and moved on (עָבָר). The verbs possibly function as a hendiadys,[151] indicating either his rapid departure or his total disappearance (or both).[152]

Each verb in this pair echoes a previous poem. The woman has asked the man to turn (סבב) to the "hills" (2:17). If these were literal, then it appears that now the man has disappeared over them. In the other nighttime poem, the woman found the man just after she passed by (עבר) the night watch (3:4). Perhaps this is what she must do now—seek him again in the streets of the city.

The woman's body had thrilled in anticipation when the man's hand broke into her bedroom. Now, her whole being (נֶפֶשׁ) expires at his departure, so severely does she feel the loss at this missed opportunity.[153]

---

149. Assis, *Flashes of Fire*, 154.

150. Murphy, *Song of Songs*, 165.

151. Longman, *Song of Songs*, 168; Pope, *Song of Songs*, 525.

152. See Bergant, *Song of Songs*, 65.

153. In a similar collocation, the verb יצא is used with נֶפֶשׁ to recount the death of Rachel (Gen 35:18). Further, the verb דבר is rendered either as "turn/flee" from an Arabic/Akkadian cognate (Pope, *Song of Songs*, 525–26; Murphy, *Song of Songs*, 165) or as the usual "speak" (Fox, *Ancient Egyptian Love Songs*, 145; Falk, *Song of Songs*, 184–85; Bloch and Bloch, *Song of Songs*, 182). Thus: (1) "My heart sank at his departure" (NIV); (2) "My soul failed me when he spoke" (NRSV). The latter makes more sense for the story sequence.

Modern Palestinian parallels are: "Alas, I stand at the door alone, / Drying my tears with my handkerchief" (Stephan, *Modern Palestinian Parallels*, 34); "My beloved is away / And my heart has melted— / For a long while / He has sent no message. / Examine me, / O physician, / As to what I suffered / On behalf of the beloved one" (Stephan, *Modern Palestinian Parallels*, 80); "I love him, I love him, and would die with (longing for) him" (Stephan, *Modern Palestinian Parallels*, 7). In an Egyptian parallel: "O my heart, don't make me foolish! / Why do you act crazy? / Sit still, cool down, until the brother comes to you / . . . Don't let people say about me: / 'This woman has collapsed out of love.' / Stand firm whenever you think of him, / my heart,

She looks about anxiously, and she calls out hoping he is still within earshot.[154] There is neither sight nor sound of him. At another time, she had playfully hid from him while he urged her to show herself and make herself heard (2:14). This disappearance is not a game, however. On the contrary, the poem signals the mood by borrowing the motif from her previous search: "I looked for him but did not find him" (3:1, 2). Then, she had searched for the "one my heart loves" (שֶׁאָהֲבָה נַפְשִׁי; 3:1–4). Here, her "heart" (נֶפֶשׁ) sinks. Keel translates more vividly: "I was completely stunned."[155] Perhaps, this time, the sense of loss is even greater. Last time, the man had been gone for a length of time. This time, he was just on the other side of her door, with only a bolt separating them. While he had taken the extra measure of attempting to undo the bolt, she had dallied and then further been delayed by her disobliging fingers. Neither her head nor her hands had been ready, or swift, to let him in. So, to the pain of the man's absence is added a heavy burden of self-recrimination. The possibility that he is gone for good has increased, and with it, her desperation.

The narrative rushes forward, eliding a narrative connector to the next event. In stark contrast to her hesitation to get out of bed, she loses no time in getting into the city. With no narrative to smooth the transition in scene, we are launched headlong into another night encounter with the city patrol.

a   The watchmen [הַשֹּׁמְרִים] found me [מְצָאֻנִי] as they made their rounds in the city.

b   They beat me [הִכּוּנִי], they bruised me [פְצָעוּנִי];

b′   they took away my cloak [נָשְׂאוּ אֶת־רְדִידִי מֵעָלַי],

a′   those watchmen of the walls [שֹׁמְרֵי הַחֹמוֹת]! (5:7)

The meeting with the night guard is related in words identical to 3:3. For a moment, we are led to expect a resolution similar to the last one. But with the same speed that hurled us from the doorstep into the city streets, the familiar plot takes a violent turn.[156]

What happens next is narrated in a chiasm. The watchmen (a a′) close in on the woman (b b′). The word "walls" contributes further. It is as if the men form around her the "walls" they are supposed to guard. The

and scurry not away" (pap. Chester Beatty I, Group A: 34. translated in Fox, *Ancient Egyptian Love Songs*, 53–54).

154. Exum, *Song of Songs*, 196.

155. Keel, *Song of Songs*, 194.

156. For the hostility associated with the Song's public settings (as against the security of enclosed spaces), see Falk, *Song of Songs*, 139–43.

woman is lost to sight as they take her place as the grammatical subject. They have *found* her, and now they *beat* her, *bruise* her, and *strip* her. The series of four perfect verbs resonates faintly with the string of four endearments the man had used earlier, but in distressing contrast. Words of affection, delicately composed, are replaced with the brute thud of a body being struck. Then, a man she knew and loved had reached his hand toward her. Here, faceless strangers manhandle her. In her bedroom, she had unclothed herself for the night. In the streets, others strip her. She had modestly dressed herself again for a certain man; she is now undressed before many. She is beaten so as to be bruised, and her bruised body is exposed. When the episode ends, the woman's state of undress returns us to where she started. The ugly difference is that she lies unclothed, not in the privacy of her bedchamber, but out in public space, in the city streets.[157] The woman's shock at this turn of events comes through in her unusual syntax.[158] She puts the subject at the end of the sentence, coloring it with horror and accusation: "They beat me . . . *those watchmen of the walls!*"

What is the reason for this assault? Does the guard take her for a prostitute?[159] Beyond that, what is the implication of the encounter for the larger story? Is the woman punishing herself for the mismanaged relationship?[160] We shall return to these questions shortly. Meanwhile, there is one certainty, and that is the direction the poem is moving in. The poem (and thus the woman) continues the quest.

Just as the woman drew the city guards into the search the last time, she now—having experienced their ferocity—turns to another group for help, the daughters of Jerusalem. As before, she moves beyond the group. Only this time, the demand on her resources is multiplied both mentally

---

157. There is disagreement over the extent to which the woman suffers exposure. Bloch and Bloch think there may have been none since the garment (רְדִיד) was "a stylish bit of finery rather than a basic article of clothing" (*Song of Songs*, 182). At the other end of the range, Gledhill thinks she was left "half naked" (*Message of the Song of Songs*, 178; see also Fox, *Ancient Egyptian Love Songs*, 146). However, note Exum, who rightly holds that "for men to strip off a part of a woman's clothing, even if it is not an essential piece of clothing, is a contemptuous act of exposure" (*Song of Songs*, 197). From the woman's description of the event and from her tone of shock, we may assume that her dignity was not respected, and that there was a significant degree of exposure.

158. Bloch and Bloch, *Song of Songs*, 183.

159. For this explanation, see Gordis, *Song of Songs*, 89; Pope, *Song of Songs*, 527; Fox, *Ancient Egyptian Love Songs*, 142; Keel, *Song of Songs*, 195; also Fokkelien van Dijk-Hemmes, "Traces of Women's Texts in the Hebrew Bible," in *On Gendering Texts: Female and Male Voices in the Hebrew Bible*, ed. Athalya Brenner and Fokkelien van Dijk-Hemmes (Leiden: Brill, 1993), 79.

160. Assis, *Flashes of Fire*, 156–58, 160–61, gives a psychological reason. By dreaming this encounter the woman is punishing herself for her tardiness in responding to the man. Polaski, "What Will Ye See?," 78–79, similarly infers that this is self-flagellation for forbidden desires.

and physically. Her damaged body must pull itself together, as must her traumatized mind. She who had thought twice about walking across her bedroom thinks nothing of crisscrossing the city till the man is found.

She addresses the daughters of Jerusalem, the recipients of her formulaic adjurations (2:7; 3:5). So far, they have been silent onlookers. Here, they are drawn into the plot, called in to participate, to solve the impasse.

> Daughters of Jerusalem, I charge you—
> if you find [אִם־תִּמְצְאוּ] my beloved,
> what will you tell him?
> Tell him I am faint with love [שֶׁחוֹלַת אַהֲבָה אָנִי]. (5:8)

The seeking verb (מצא), which was a *leitwort* in her other seeking poem (3:1–5), makes its third appearance in this poem. She has not found him. The night guard has found the seeker instead of the sought. Both parties having failed, the woman passes on the task to the daughters of Jerusalem. She hopes they may succeed. If they find him, they are to convey a brief message of three words.[161] The message describes her current state with the verb חלה, meaning to be faint or weak, as when taken ill. However, it is not the assault that has weakened her, but love. He should be told that she is lovesick.[162] This is what she thinks will bring him back to her, the knowledge that she is pining for him. Keel remarks: "The only one able to cure this type of illness is the one who caused it."[163] With this, the first half of the poem comes to an end, as indicated by the pronoun "I" that opens and closes this section (5:2–8).[164]

Scholars point out the four emphatic occurrences of the first-person pronoun "I" (אָנִי) in the poem.[165] In each instance, "I" is linked closely with "my beloved" (דּוֹדִי)[166] and "accentuates four moments in the woman's longing for her beloved."[167]

---

161. Fox, *Ancient Egyptian Love Songs*, 146–47, argues that the particle אם carries the same sense of negation as in the other formulae of adjuration, and concludes that the woman is proscribing the daughters of Jerusalem from telling the man about her experience in the city. The Egyptian parallel he cites is one in which the girl, embarrassed at the condition of her heart, admonishes it with: "Don't make people say about me, 'This woman is lost because of love.'" ("Scholia to Canticles," *VT* 33, no. 2 [1983]: 204–5). Contra Exum, *Song of Songs*, 201.

162. Similarly, modern Palestinian love poetry: "Alas, I stand at the door alone, / Drying my tears with my handkerchief. / And should the youths ask about me— / (Tell them): I am in love and have parted from my friend." Stephan, *Modern Palestinian Parallels*, 34.

163. Keel, *Song of Songs*, 195.

164. Assis, *Flashes of Fire*, 150.

165. E.g., Carr, *Song of Solomon*, 131.

166. Elliott, *Literary Unity*, 123–24.

167. Bergant, *Song of Songs*, 60.

5:2:   I slept [אֲנִי יְשֵׁנָה] . . . my beloved [דּוֹדִי] is knocking

5:5:   I arose [קַמְתִּי אֲנִי] to open for my beloved [דּוֹדִי]

5:6:   I opened [פָּתַחְתִּי אֲנִי] for my beloved [דּוֹדִי]

5:8:   If you find my beloved [דּוֹדִי] . . . tell him I am faint [שֶׁחוֹלַת אַהֲבָה אָנִי]

But more than this, this list of four contains the three instances in the story where she was most deeply affected: when she saw his hand through the key hole, her body shuddered with ecstasy (5:4); when she realized he had gone, her whole being expired (5:6); when the search comes to a dead end, she is faint with love (5:8). How remarkable that the public beating does not figure in the list! Perhaps it is from this omission that we can infer the significance of the assault for the mood of the poem.

So, to return to the questions we left unanswered: the poem is unhelpful on the reason for the attack. We cannot be sure why she was attacked, especially when in the previous nighttime episode, she had the freedom to inquire of the guards and pass on unharmed. As for how the assault contributes to the poem, the obvious answer seems to be that it exacerbates the ordeal presented by the parallel story (3:1–5). By doing so, it intensifies one of the topoi of the romantic genre. Lovers demonstrate the worth of their affections by enduring hardship for the sake of their beloved.[168] Ancient West Asian poems are a testimony to this, as are classics from Indian cinema.[169]

The nighttime poem of 3:1–5 showed the audience the extent to which the woman was willing to inconvenience herself for the sake of her beloved. The parallel poem of 5:2–8 pushes the boundaries further. She can endure not just the vulnerability of being out at night, the uncertainty of a random search in a maze of dark streets, or the sheer exhaustion of such a search. More than that, she can even take a brutal

---

168. On a similar note, see Exum, *Song of Songs*, 199–200; Fox, *Ancient Egyptian Love Songs*, 291.

169. For example, the 1960 historical epic movie *Mughal-e-Azam*, set in the Mughal period, tells of the forbidden love between the crown prince Salim and the courtesan Anarkali. She refuses to give up her love for Prince Salim, suffers many hardships for his sake, and eventually offers to trade her life for his by suffering the punishment of being entombed alive.

A parallel Egyptian love song runs: "I [will not] abandon it / Until blows drive [me] away / to spend my days in the marshes, / [until blows banish me] / to the land of Syria with sticks and rods, / to the land of Nubia with palms, / to the highlands with switches, / to the lowlands with cudgels. / I will not listen to their advice / to abandon the one I desire" (pap. Harris 500, Group A: 4, translated in Fox, *Ancient Egyptian Love Songs*, 10). Another parallel is Palestinian: "The quarrel rose between me and him: / They dragged me to the *sarai*; / They beat me a thousand strokes; / They beat me on my ankles" (Stephan, *Modern Palestinian Parallels*, 18).

attack by a group of armed men and not let it hinder her quest for the man. Before, she had shown herself willing to defy cultural restrictions. Here, she goes further. She proves that she can cope with the consequence of her unorthodox excursions, even if it is the ultimate shame of beating and exposure at the hands of the guardians of the "walls," representatives of the normative. In 5:2–8, the woman showed herself explicitly ambivalent about her desire for the man, more than was the case in the daytime poem of 2:8–17. Subsequently, she proved her love in proportion to that ambivalence. Thus, the first venture passed without event, but the second stretched the limits of endurance. What makes the suffering worthwhile for her is the one for whom she endures it. The man remains the focus of both poems. In 3:1–5, he is the "one my heart loves" (four times) and in 5:2–8, he is "my beloved" (six times).

COMPARING THE TWO SEEKING POEMS

We mentioned at the start of this chapter that the two seeking poems have a similar shape. We may detect similarities at the lexical level, as well as at the story level. Exum demonstrates this in a table, presented below with some modification:[170]

THE MAN SEEKS THE WOMAN

2:8–17	*5:2–5*
"Listen! My beloved . . ." (2:8)	"Listen! My beloved . . ." (5:2)
The man is outside:	The man is outside:
coming, leaping, bounding, standing, gazing, peering (2:8–9)	knocking (5:2)
He calls to the woman: "Arise," "come" (2:10, 13)	He calls to the woman: "Open" (5:2)
Endearments:	Endearments:
my friend, my beautiful one, my dove (2:10, 13–14)	my sister, my friend, my dove, my perfect one (5:2)
Reason for call (2:10–13):	Reason for call (5:2):
it is springtime outside	it is wet outside
she must come out to him	she must let him come in to her

170. Exum, *Song of Songs*, 186–87.

The woman hides (2:14)	The woman delays (5:3)
The man pleads to see and hear her (2:14)	The man attempts to enter (5:4)
The man may not gain admission:	The man does not gain admission:
"turn" (2:17)	"turned away" and "gone" (5:6)
Refrain:	(*Refrain delayed*)
"My beloved is mine and I am his" (2:16)	

THE WOMAN SEEKS THE MAN

3:1–5	*5:6–6:3*
"all night long on my bed" (3:1)	"I slept . . . was awake" (5:2)
"I will arise" (3:2)	"I arose" (5:5)
"I sought him but did not find him" (3:1, 2)	"I sought him but did not find him" (5:6)
"the watchmen found me—the ones who make the rounds of the city" (3:3)	"the watchmen found me—the ones who make the rounds of the city" (5:7)
The watchmen are unresponsive	The watchmen manhandle the woman
The man is found, leading to oath placed on the daughters of Jerusalem (3:4–5)	Oath is placed on the daughters of Jerusalem, leading to finding the man (5:8–6:2)
	Refrain: "I am my beloved's and my beloved is mine" (6:3)

The male of these poems is a dream lover. He is eager and ardent and shows it. Like an Asahel in love, this gazelle comes bounding over the horizon of hills, his feet flying to reach his beloved's window (2 Sam 2:18). Or, he stands bedewed and wet at her door at night. In neither instance is he immediately gratified. He must search for her through the lattice; he must knock asking for admittance. Beyond that, he must prettily invite her to come out or plead to be invited in. His speeches to this effect are an exquisite concoction of tender imperatives and passionate endearments. But like cold water poured over his earnestness, the woman's response is ambivalent. She plays hard to get, dallying behind lattices, too petulant to leave her bed. He must further plead for her presence, or literally take the matter into his own hands and attempt to let himself in. It is possible that both his endeavors end without fulfillment. Certainly in the second, he removes himself from the scene without notice or explanation. On one hand, he is an inversion of the Old Testament motif of the woman at the window (Judg 5:28; 2 Kgs 9:30).[171] If we may extrapolate from that motif, his are the anxious eyes of Sisera's mother watching for her son to return from the battlefield. His is the keen gaze of Jezebel waiting for Jehu to bring her the final challenge, watching with senses heightened and heart pounding. But on the other hand, this male Jezebel slides easily from enthusiasm to exasperation. He can throw up his hands and leave. He can live with his quest left hanging.

What can we say about the woman? She can be a tiresome tease. Or, worse, she can turn her lover away from her window or door. She can live on the knife-edge of wanting him with her and wanting him away from her. But, whereas he has a way with sweet nothings, she can deliver a public eulogy to him in the middle of the night, as she does to the daughters of Jerusalem (5:10–16). She meets his anxious pleading with bold assertions of mutual belonging—made both on her behalf and on his. If he is passionate about her, her feelings for him are visceral. She loves him as she loves living (3:1); her insides churn at his nearness (5:4); she almost dies at his departure (5:6); she is faint with lovesickness (5:8). She presents the full range of experiences that describe and define love—its agony and its ecstasy, its frustration and its fulfillment. If his journeys to find her are starry-eyed romances, her journeys to find him are ruthlessly self-endangering—she is "the tougher, more determined, more vehement lover."[172] In seeking, she has the tenacity it takes to find. Like Ruth, she is willing to imperil her reputation if by it she can gain the man.[173] Like Lady Folly, she audaciously steps out into the night "unruly and defiant,"[174] to seek—not out of lust but out of love. With respect to seeking, the man remains within the expected. She bursts through boundaries. And that is why she finds.

171. Estes, "Song of Songs," 327.
172. See Fox, *Ancient Egyptian Love Songs*, 310.
173. Ruth 3.
174. Prov 7:11.

3.

The Wilderness

Like the two seeking poems of the Song, Hosea 2 is a monologue.[1] Unlike Song 2, it is not an interior monologue. Like Song 5, in which the woman was in conversation with a group called the "daughters of Jerusalem," Hosea 2 also seems to have an addressee, the speaker's children. The speaking parts, however, are reversed. In the Song, the woman speaks, embedding the man's speech within hers. In Hosea, the man speaks, embedding the woman's lines within his.[2] Like the Song's poems, Hosea 2 is emotive; the speaker uninhibitedly bares his soul. The emotions, however, reveal a relationship that is almost the antithesis of the idyll presented in the Song.[3] The characterization of the woman shocks: "She is from the outset a woman whose main and explicitly mentioned attribute is that she is promiscuous."[4] In fact, we enter the narrative at an explosive moment in what appears to be longstanding and severe familial dysfunction.

---

1. Other (much shorter) texts in the Old Testament that play on the theme of searching are: Jer 29:13; Hos 3:5; 5:6, 15; and to a lesser extent Isa 65:1, 12; Jer 7:27; Zech 8:21–22.

2. My treatment of the poem is through the conjugal metaphor. We will ignore references to identification of the "man" with YHWH and the "woman" with Israel (or her lovers with the Baalim). Thus, the protagonists remain in the singular, husband and wife, ignoring pronouns for Israel such as "they" (2:8) and "them" (2:18) and even, "he" (2:23).

3. For a comparative feminist reading of Hosea 2 with various parallel texts in the Song of Songs, see Fokkelien van Dijk-Hemmes, "The Imagination of Power and the Power of Imagination: An Intertextual Analysis of Two Biblical Love Songs: The Song of Songs and Hosea 2," *JSOT* 44 (1989): 75–88. Van Dijk-Hemmes argues that Hosea 2 can be read as the woman's love song for her lovers. The man's voice controls and subverts this reading.

4. Ehud Ben Zvi, "Observations on the Marital Metaphor of YHWH and Israel in its Ancient Israelite Context: General Considerations and Particular Images in Hosea 1.2," *JSOT* 28, no. 3 (2004): 379.

ESTRANGEMENT: HOSEA 2:2–5

2 Rebuke your mother, rebuke her,[5]
for she is not my wife,
and I am not her husband.
Let her remove the adulterous look from her face
and the unfaithfulness from between her breasts.
3 Otherwise I will strip her naked
and make her as bare as on the day she was born;
I will make her like a desert,
turn her into a parched land,
and slay her with thirst.
4 I will not show my love to her children,
because they are the children of adultery.
5 Their mother has been unfaithful
and has conceived them in disgrace.
She said, "I will go after my lovers,
who give me my food and my water,
my wool and my linen, my olive oil and my drink." (2:2–5)

Within a domestic setting, the speaker is drawing the children into his quarrel, urging them to contend on his behalf against his wife.[6] (He will end by casting off these children as bastard born.) The breakdown in relationship seems to have reached the point of no return. Six bald words pronounce the separation twice over:[7] הִיא לֹא אִשְׁתִּי וְאָנֹכִי לֹא

5. For the convenience of the reader following the English version, we have used the verse numbering of most English versions. The corresponding verse in the MT is obtained by adding two to the verse number in the English version.

6. A minority view is that it is the wife initiating divorce, and that the husband is asking the children to plead (rather than contend; thus RSV's rendering of the verb רִיב) with her to change her mind. See H. D. Beeby, *Grace Abounding: A Commentary on the Book of Hosea* (Grand Rapids: Eerdmans, 1989), 22–23; Bruce C. Birch, *Hosea, Joel, and Amos*, Westminster Bible Companion (Louisville: Westminster John Knox, 1997), 28.

7. Some scholars read this as a statement of divorce: Hans Walter Wolff, *Hosea*, trans. Gary Stansell, Hermeneia (Philadelphia: Fortress Press, 1974), 33; Mordechai A. Friedman, "Israel's Response in Hosea 2:17b: 'You Are My Husband,'" *JBL* 99, no. 2 (1980): 202; Charles H. Silva, "The Literary Structure of Hosea 1–3," *BSac* 164 (2007): 192; Markham J. Geller, "The Elephantine Papyri and Hosea 2,3: Evidence for the Form of the Early Jewish Divorce Writ," *JSJ* 8, no. 2 (1977): 139–48. We will read it as spoken within a domestic exchange, since the husband continues to have authority over his wife as the ensuing sections show. He thinks through (rather than enacts sequentially) the alternatives of using threats, restrictions, public shaming, and seduction to restore the relationship. So Renita J. Weems, "Gomer: Victim of Violence or Victim of Metaphor?," *Semeia* 47 (1989): 97; David J. A. Clines, "Hosea 2: Structure and Interpretation," in *On the Way to the Postmodern: Old Testament Essays, 1967–1988*, vol. 1, ed. David J. A. Clines, JSOTSup 292 (Sheffield: Sheffield Academic, 1998), 298n17; James Luther Mays, *Hosea*, OTL (London: SCM, 1969), 37–38; Francis I. Andersen and David Noel Freedman, *Hosea: A New Translation with Introduction and Commentary*, AB (New Haven: Yale University

אִישָׁה "She is not my wife, and I am not her husband" (2:2).[8] Here is the antithesis of the Song's declaration of mutual belonging: דּוֹדִי לִי וַאֲנִי לוֹ; "My beloved is mine and I am his" (Song 2:16).[9] In the place of the לִי and לוֹ that merge the speaker with her beloved is the negation לֹא, separating out the two components of the marriage relationship like oil from water—the husband from the wife. Indeed, the fact that the man speaks *about* his wife right through with not a word *to* her is a measure of the estrangement.[10]

In words reminiscent of the Song,[11] the husband elaborates the reason for the words of severance. The marriage has been in disarray for a long time now, with enough adultery on her part to have borne several children. But if the husband's long years of patience surprise us, we are taken aback at the violence he now says he will unleash on her with mounting severity.[12] Perhaps this is a poetic version of the legal injunction that an adulterous woman must be put to death (Lev 20:10; Deut 22:20–21),[13]

Press, 1980), 220–24; A. A. Macintosh, *Hosea: A Critical and Exegetical Commentary*, ICC (Edinburgh: T&T Clark, 1997), 41.

8. For a summary of research on whether this is a divorce formula parallel to that in the Elephantine Papyri, see M. Dass, "Divorce (?) Formula in Hosea 2:4a," *Indian Theological Studies*, 34 (1997): 56–88.

9. See Francis Landy, *Hosea*, 2nd ed. (Sheffield: Sheffield Phoenix, 2011), 32–33.

10. John L. Mackay, *Hosea*, Mentor Series (Fearn: Christian Focus, 2012), 74.

11. The marks of adultery are between her breasts (and on her face) (Wolff, *Hosea*, 33–34). See speculations and connections with Song 1:13 ("a sachet of myrrh resting between my breasts") in Andersen and Freedman, *Hosea*, 224–25; Landy, *Hosea*, 32.

12. Hosea 1–3 is among those prophetic texts that so offends present-day social sensibilities that it has been classed as "pornoprophetic," especially by feminist critics.

For an interpretation of the metaphor of harlotry vis-à-vis the socioeconomic and political realities of the setting of the book of Hosea, see, e.g., Alice A. Keefe, *Woman's Body and the Social Body in Hosea*, JSOTSup 338, Gender, Culture, Theory 10 (Sheffield: Sheffield Academic, 2001); Gale A. Yee, "'She Is Not My Wife and I Am Not Her Husband': A Materialist Analysis of Hosea 1–2," *BibInt* 9, no. 4 (2001): 345–83.

For an interpretation of the marriage metaphor arising from the covenant between YHWH and Israel, see, e.g., Peggy L. Day, "Yahweh's Broken Marriages as Metaphoric Vehicle in the Hebrew Bible Prophets," in *Sacred Marriages: The Divine-Human Sexual Metaphor from Sumer to Early Christianity*, ed. Martti Nissinen and Risto Uro (Winona Lake, IN: Eisenbrauns, 2008), 232–33; Elaine June Adler, "The Background of the Metaphor of Covenant as Marriage in the Hebrew Bible" (PhD diss., University of California, 1990); Sharon Moughtin-Mumby, *Sexual and Marital Metaphors in Hosea, Jeremiah, Isaiah and Ezekiel*, Oxford Theological Monographs (Oxford: Oxford University Press, 2008).

Gerlinde Baumann provides a survey of the ancient Near Eastern practices for the punishment of adulterous women as suggested by the prophetic texts employing the divine marriage metaphor, including sections on covenant treaty curses and wartime actions as possible contexts for reading these problematic texts (*Love and Violence: Marriage as Metaphor for the Relationship between YHWH and Israel in the Prophetic Books*, trans. Linda M. Maloney [Collegeville, MN: Liturgical, 2003], 69–81).

13. Scholars are divided over whether exposure was a mode of execution of adulterous wives in ancient West Asia. Some think this may have been the case (e.g., G. I. Davies, *Hosea*, New

or an action the husband could rightfully take prior to or instead of the death penalty (cf. Jer 13:22, 26–27; Ezek 16:37–39; 23:29; Nah 3:4–5), or as divorce proceedings.[14]

The man will strip her (פשט) so as to slay her (מות). The vocabulary is painful: stripped naked; bare as when born; like a desert; parched land; killed by thirst. Exposed, she gradually dehydrates and desiccates to death. The Song's woman, on the contrary, uncovered herself at will, undressing to lay down in bed, her hands dripping with the abundance of myrrh-scented oil (Song 5:3, 5). In Hosea, the naked state of the woman recalls her birth (ילד) but moves her toward death.

In the Song, the woman recalls her conception (הרה) as she moves toward the act that can impregnate her with new life. Indeed, the locale in the Song is the "house of my mother . . . the room of the one who conceived me" (בֵּית אִמִּי . . . חֶדֶר הוֹרָתִי, Song 3:4). The only other text where אֵם and the *qal* feminine participle of הרה occur juxtaposed is in Hosea 2:5.[15] Whereas in the Song the association of words promised the consummation of exclusive love, in Hosea it indicts a "mother" who has "conceived" in multiple, disgraceful mésalliances.

Just as there is a third party in Song 5, the "daughters of Jerusalem," so Hosea 2 has a third party. The wife's "lovers" are an unseen presence in the monologue (2:5, 7, 10, 12, 13). The difference is that while the daughters of Jerusalem are eager to assist in the reunion of the separated couple, the "lovers" in Hosea are the very reason for the separation of the husband and wife.

That the third party—"lovers"—has caused separation becomes apparent as now, for the first time, we hear the wife speak. Her words are conveyed through the male voice. What we hear appears to be the conclusion of a deliberation on her next steps.[16] She concludes, quite

Century Bible Commentary [Grand Rapids: Eerdmans, 1992], 71); others think this is language that fits the metaphor of Israel as land from which God withdraws his gift of rain, resulting in drought (e.g., Ben Zvi, "Observations," 368).

For stripping as an alternative to the death penalty, see Wolff, *Hosea*, 34. Henry McKeating, "Sanctions against Adultery in Ancient Israelite Society: With Some Reflections on Methodology in the Study of OT Ethics," *JSOT* 11 (1979): 57–72, concludes that in Hosea and parallel prophetic texts (e.g., Ezek 16:37–39; 23:29), "the case for the use of this penalty is strengthened by the fact that it was almost ubiquitous in the ancient near east" (61).

14. For stripping as an act prior to enforcing the death penalty, see P. Kruger, "Israel, the Harlot," JSNL 11 (1987): 111–12. Anthony Phillips, "Another Look at Adultery," *JSOT* 20 (1981): 16, thinks stripping of the wife may have preceded the pronouncement of the divorce formula, "not simply to indicate that her husband was no longer under any obligation to clothe his wife, but to proclaim publicly the shameful reason for the divorce."

15. Duane Garrett, "Song of Songs," in *Song of Songs, Lamentations*, ed. Duane Garrett and Paul R. House, WBC 23B (Nashville: Thomas Nelson, 2004), 174: The *qal* fs ptc. of הרה only occurs in these two texts. Also, see van Dijk-Hemmes, "Imagination of Power," 80.

16. Andersen and Freedman, *Hosea*, 229–30.

emphatically, that she should seek out her lovers: אֵלְכָה, which could be rendered either "let me go" or "I want to go after my lovers."[17] She follows up her decision with good reason. Her lovers keep her supplied with all her basic necessities. The list of commodities—the first of three in this poem—is composed in three pairs:

לַחְמִי וּמֵימַי	my bread and my water
צַמְרִי וּפִשְׁתִּי	my wool and my linen
שַׁמְנִי וְשִׁקּוּיָי	my oil and my drink

The list sounds like a measured chant,[18] as the woman ticks off the advantages of her pursuit. *Shin* and *mem* tumble from word into word, creating an aurally attractive daisy-chain of six nouns. If וּפִשְׁתִּי were to be re-vocalized to וּפִשְׁתַּי,[19] we would have the first items of each pair ending in -*i* and the second ending -*ay*, adding rhyme to already mellifluous lines. There are textures here to feel: warm wool, light linen; there is a bouquet of fragrance: olive oil and drink; there is the taste of food: bread and wine and the clear wash of water. But, for all its sensory appeal, the list is thoroughly mundane, covering no more than the bare necessities of life.[20] We cannot help contrasting it with the verbal string the man puts together when he first speaks in the poem of Song 5: "my own, my darling, my dove, my flawless one": אֲחֹתִי רַעְיָתִי יוֹנָתִי תַמָּתִי. That too captivated the ear. More significantly, its components similarly ended with the -*i* of the possessive pronoun "my."[21] But, while the man focuses on his beloved, enumerating all that he finds desirable in her, Hosea's woman keeps her mind on the materials her lovers can provide her. That basic difference immediately discredits the vigor of her pursuit, for while the Song's lover springs across hills in leaps and bounds to get to his sole beloved (Song 2:8), this woman will go (הלך) after her many men (2:5), chasing (רדף) them so as to catch up (נשׂג) with them (2:7).

With this we come to the first of the three *therefores* that naturally divide the poem (לָכֵן; 2:6; 2:9; 2:14). Each "therefore" will open a strategy for dealing with the current situation of emotional separation (2:6–8;

---

17. David Allan Hubbard, *Hosea: An Introduction and Commentary*, TOTC (Leicester: Inter-Varsity, 1989), 76.

18. Andersen and Freedman, *Hosea*, 232: the lines are "rhythmic to the point of being poetic."

19. K. A. Tangberg, "A Note on *Pisti* in Hosea II 7, 11," *VT* 27, no. 2 (1977): 222–24.

20. Andersen and Freedman, *Hosea*, 232. Wolff (*Hosea*, 35) thinks the last pair are a luxury—oil for anointing the skin and drink for pleasure.

21. See Andersen and Freedman, *Hosea*, 231–32, for an alternative dative reading or for a double meaning encompassing both dative and possessive.

2:9–13; 2:14–23). Does this mean that the husband tries a plan, finds that it fails to achieve the desired result, and then devises and attempts the next one?[22] Since the outcome of each strategy is not communicated, this monologue is more likely to be a projection of possibilities. The aggrieved party works through three strategies, constructed as alternatives.

2:2   She is not my wife, and I am not her husband

2:5   She said, I will go after my lovers

   Who give me my food and my water, my wool and my linen, my olive oil and my drink

2:6   Therefore [לָכֵן] [*because she said she would go after her lovers (2:5)*]

   I will block her path . . . wall her in

2:8   She has not acknowledged that I [אָנֹכִי], I gave . . .

2:9   Therefore [לָכֵן] [*because she thinks her lovers provide her goods (2:5)*]

   I will take away my grain . . . wine . . . wool . . . linen

2:13 Me [אֹתִי] she forgot

2:14 Therefore [לָכֵן] [*in order to help her go, not after her lovers (5:5), but to her husband*]

2:14 I will allure her . . . lead her . . . speak tenderly to her . . . betroth her

2:23 "You are my people"; "You are my God"

Clines posits that the poem presents "the judgments of imprisonment (vv. 8–10) and deprivation (vv. 11–15) as a sequence of possibilities that Yahweh passes in review, only to decide *against* them and *for* the third possibility: restoration (vv. 16–17)."[23] The starting point for each alterna-

22. Many scholars take the poem's sections as a linear plot (see Weems, "Gomer," 97–98). In this case, the man's purpose is to restore the woman through what Wyrtzen creatively calls "restorative confrontation." David B. Wyrtzen, "The Theological Centre of the Book of Hosea," *BSac* 141, no. 564 (1984): 315–29. Along the same lines, see Wolff, *Hosea*, 32.

23. Clines, "Hosea 2," 298. Along similar lines, Frederick W. Keene, "Anger and Pain in Hosea," *Continuum* 3 (1994): 204–17; Andersen and Freedman, *Hosea*, 236. Clines's reading is an alternative to engage against the (often feminist) position that Hosea 2 is a sample of domestic violence against the wife.

For helpful approaches to the problem of domestic violence in Hosea 2, samples are: John L. Thompson, "Hosea and Gomer," in *Reading the Bible with the Dead* (Grand Rapids: Eerdmans, 2007), 93–111, who argues that the reader should separate the text's intention from its unintended effects; Drorah Setel, "Prophets and Pornography: Female Sexual Imagery in Hosea," in *Feminist Interpretation of the Bible*, ed. Letty M. Russell (Oxford: Blackwell, 1985), 86–95, who offers that the "pornographic" content remains a challenge to present day readers, but also recalibrates for ancient Israel its relationship to YHWH; R. Abma, *Bonds of Love: Methodic Studies of Prophetic Texts with Marriage Imagery (Isaiah 50:1–3 and 54:1–10, Hosea 1–3, Jeremiah 2–3)*

tive is the woman's speech in 2:5.[24] Like a moth drawn to fire, the man's thoughts return in circles to her words of infidelity. It is only with the third cycle that there is resolution to the problem of estrangement that opens the poem (2:2).

THE FIRST "THEREFORE": HOSEA 2:6–8

[6] Therefore I will block [לָכֵן הִנְנִי־שָׂךְ] her path with thornbushes;
I will wall her in [וְגָדַרְתִּי אֶת־גְּדֵרָהּ] so that she cannot find her way [וּנְתִיבוֹתֶיהָ לֹא תִמְצָא].
[7] She will chase after [וְרִדְּפָה] her lovers [אֶת־מְאַהֲבֶיהָ] but not catch them [וְלֹא־תַשִּׂיג אֹתָם];
she will look for them [וּבִקְשָׁתַם] but not find them [וְלֹא תִמְצָא].
Then she will say,
"I will go back to my husband as at first [אִישִׁי הָרִאשׁוֹן],
for then I was better off [כִּי טוֹב לִי] than now."
[8] She has not acknowledged that I was the one
who gave her the grain, the new wine and oil,
who lavished on her the silver and gold—
which they used for Baal. (2:6–8)

The first thought cycle opens with an "urgent announcement of ominous intention."[25] It starts with the construction הִנְנִי ("Look! I . . .") and follows up with the participle שָׂךְ ("blocking"). This sequence indicates imminent action.[26] Since the wife brazenly (and ardently!)[27] seeks out lovers, the immediate solution is to use containment. Her quest must be thwarted with physical obstacles till she gives up and returns to her husband.[28] In the man's imagination, he sees her running after (2:7) her former patrons. A rank of thornbushes rises, cutting her off. She turns to take a detour, only to find her way barricaded by a wall. The cognate accusative construction (וְגָדַרְתִּי אֶת־גְּדֵרָהּ) is an emphatic literary device:[29] "I will build a wall to wall her way." The result is predictable:

(Assen: Van Gorcum, 1999), who argues for a difference between understanding Hosea 1–3 and adopting its values.

24. So also Clines, *Hosea*, 299. However, my table for the flow of the poem varies in several places from his.

25. Andersen and Freedman, *Hosea*, 236.

26. Andersen and Freedman, *Hosea*, 236. So: "Therefore, I will soon fence her in with thorns" (NET).

27. The verb רדף (2:7) is used in the intensive piel.

28. An often-used image for cutting off thoroughfare: cf. Lam 3:7, 9; Job 3:23; 19:8; Prov 15:19.

29. See Bruce K. Waltke and M. O'Connor, *An Introduction to Biblical Hebrew Syntax* (Winona Lake, IN: Eisenbrauns, 1990), § 10.2.1f. The third-person feminine singular suffix functions as a dative of disadvantage: "as a wall against her."

not only can she not find (מצא) her lovers, she cannot even find (מצא) her way to them.

The scene is as surreal as its counterpart in the Song, where the woman seeks her beloved at night. The verbal resonance is strong. Hosea's woman will "look for [her lovers] but not find them." The Song's woman "looked for [her beloved] but did not find him" (3:2; 5:6). Both seek (בקש) the one(s) they love (אהב) and do not find (מצא). However, there is a fundamental difference. In Hosea, the seeker who matters is the husband. This is his quest to find and restore his wanton wife. The wife's seeking is a spurious one, a parody. Unlike the Song's woman, who searches for her own beloved, this one seeks a clutch of men, none of whom are her husband. Though she uses the word "lover" to relate herself to them, it is not love but lust for goods that propels her. Unlike the Song's woman who perseveres, carrying on beyond the watchmen, Hosea's woman gives up. The inconveniences of bramble and brick skid her quest to a halt. In the Song, the woman endures being bruised and stripped. This one stops before the thorns can scratch and rip. Her start was feisty,[30] as energetic as in the Song, but we see how little it takes to deflate her enthusiasm. This Hosea narrative recalls the Song, but only in caricature.

After a cold calculation, she redirects her efforts toward what is the more expedient option. She will return (שוב) to her husband. In a context like this one, the verb "to return" is usually layered with the associated sense of "to repent."[31] But we see no remorse.[32] In contrast to her lovers, the husband is described without emotion. He is, clinically, אִישִׁי הָרִאשׁוֹן, "my first husband" or "my husband as at first." The return is mercenary, for it serves her interests: "for then I was better off than now." At least, she is consistent in following what she thinks works best for her.[33] If hers is a quest at all, its path orbits tightly around her good (טוב). Husband and lovers, finding them or not finding them—these are incidental.

If this is the case, it is not the wife but the husband who is the counterpart of the Song's seeking woman. His is the anguished mind that runs through a maze of possible solutions, the equivalent of dark streets and city squares. He perseveres at seeking until he finds.

At this point in the poem, the man pauses at this thought: his wife cannot rightly acknowledge her provider. So, he counters her list of pro-

---

30. Andersen and Freedman, *Hosea*, 238: "There is sustained emphasis on the initiative of the woman."

31. Diane Jacobson, "Hosea 2: A Case Study on Biblical Authority," *CTM* 23, no. 3 (1996): 167.

32. See Clines, "Hosea 1," 298–99.

33. See Landy, *Hosea*, 31.

visions with his. He posits that not only has he *given* her grain, wine, and oil, but beyond these basic necessities,[34] he has *lavished* silver and gold on her, which, ironically, she has used on her lovers. He is emphatic in his claim: "I, I gave . . ." (אָנֹכִי נָתַתִּי). With this counter-list, the flow of thought has looped back to the woman's words in 2:5: "I will go after my lovers, who give me . . ." The man devised containment to prevent the woman from going. That plan dissolves and a new strategy takes shape, this one arising from her belief that her lovers give her goods.

THE SECOND "THEREFORE": HOSEA 2:9–13

When the woman listed her goods, she consistently appended the possessive pronoun "my" to each item. She claimed them as hers. However, this claim was as a beneficiary. The husband now presses his greater claim to the same goods, and his claim is as benefactor, as the patron who made these available to the wife in the first place. Beyond mis-acknowledging these provisions (2:5),[35] the wife misused the wealth for adultery (2:8). So, in a turnaround of devastating proportions, the husband recovers what he, in honorable discharge of his obligations (cf. Exod 21:10–11), had provided.[36] "Gone was the time when [he] was willing to donate the means for his own cuckolding."[37] Item after item disappear from the woman's possession. This time, the "my" affixed to each item is the husband's, forcefully and conclusively overriding the woman's "my."

[9] Therefore [לָכֵן] I will take away [אָשׁוּב וְלָקַחְתִּי] my grain when it ripens,
and my new wine when it is ready.
I will take back [וְהִצַּלְתִּי] my wool and my linen,
intended to cover her naked body.
[10] So now I will expose [אֲגַלֶּה] her lewdness
before the eyes of her lovers;
no one will take her out [לֹא־יַצִּילֶנָּה] of my hands.
[11] I will stop [וְהִשְׁבַּתִּי] all her celebrations:
her yearly festivals, her New Moons,
her Sabbath days—all her appointed festivals.

34. Wolff, *Hosea*, 35, suggests that the infrequent שִׁקּוּיִים possibly refers to beverages like wine and beer, and were a luxury.

35. Here, as regularly in the Old Testament, poetic justice is in operation: inability to recognize the giver results in the loss of what is given. Beeby, *Grace Abounding*, 26.

36. Cf. similar legal provision for a wronged husband in ancient West Asia: James B Pritchard, *Ancient Near Eastern Texts: An Anthology of Texts and Pictures* (Princeton: Princeton University Press, 2011), 160, 534. See Andersen and Freedman, *Hosea*, 245.

37. Beeby, *Grace Abounding*, 26.

¹² I will ruin [וַהֲשִׁמֹּתִי] her vines and her fig trees [תְּאֵנָתָהּ],
Which she said were her pay [אֶתְנָה] from her lovers;
I will make them a thicket,
and wild animals will devour them [וַאֲכָלָתַם].
¹³ I will punish her [וּפָקַדְתִּי עָלֶיהָ] for the days
she burned incense to the Baals;
she decked herself with rings and jewelry,
and went after her lovers,
but me she forgot [וְאֹתִי שָׁכְחָה], declares the Lord. (2:9–13)

There is a torrent of verbs here, an outpouring of emotion as the man sets out what he will do. The first two function together as a hendiadys, with שׁוּב in an auxiliary function to לקח: "I will take back."³⁸ Each verb is paronomastic. The woman pursued her lovers because they gave (נתן) her gifts (2:5). Tiring of her pursuit, she decided to return (שׁוּב) to her first husband (2:9). Now, her שׁוּב is countered with his: "The wife will not *return*, so the husband will *change* [or *turn*] his attitude."³⁹ Similarly, the lovers' giving (נתן) is countered with the husband's taking back (לקח). What is more, he takes back with a vengeance. He had given to (נתן) and lavished upon (רבה). In swift reversal, a new pair of verbs is implemented. He takes (לקח) and violently snatches away from (נצל).

As we watch, the woman is depleted. The grain and the wine go slowly, each taken away according to the agricultural calendar. Then, without warning, the hand falls on her person. She is stripped (גלה) of wool and linen.⁴⁰ The verbs turn increasingly ferocious, going from "I will take back" (לכח) to "I will snatch" (נצל) to "I will strip bare" (גלה). His last act lays open "the literal site of the woman's . . . transgression," her genitalia.⁴¹ Then we have the verb "snatch" (נצל) again, but used in further escalation of violence: he dares her lovers to snatch the exposed body of his wife from his hands. "The husband, in exhibiting his wife, simultaneously discards her, and asserts his prerogative over her."⁴² Meanwhile, it is a means of shaming a woman, one that Indians are familiar with. It plays out in mythology: in the Sanskrit epic called the *Mahabharata*, a crux in the family feud is the public disrobing of a princess by the chief warrior prince of the opposite camp.⁴³ It happens in

38. Andersen and Freedman, *Hosea*, 244.
39. Andersen and Freedman, *Hosea*, 245.
40. The Targum and Peshitta add here a further reference to the owner, which the NEB follows: "I will take away the wool and the flax which I gave her to cover her naked body." For a debate on whether there is indeed a naked woman in Hos 2:9–10, see Matthew W. Mitchell, "Finding the Naked Woman in Hosea ii 11," *VT* 57 (2007): 114–23.
41. Yee, "She Is Not My Wife," 378.
42. Landy, *Hosea*, 28.
43. See discussion at Satya Chaitanya, "Was Draupadi Disrobed in the Dice Hall of Hasti-

real life: newspapers routinely report incidents from rural India in which women are paraded naked so as to teach their family or their community "a lesson."[44]

With this, we understand the purpose of the man's actions. He has contrived a scheme that (to use a violent metaphor) kills two birds with one stone. As Weems puts it: "Stripping her naked before her lovers will not only expose her body and the foolishness of her ways, it will also prove, contrary to her claims, how feeble and impotent are her lovers to protect and provide for her."[45] Her lovers either do not dare to come to her aid or do not care to.[46]

Before we return to follow the thread of verbs, we pay attention to a second pile-up of nouns in this unit: celebrations, yearly festivals, new moons, Sabbath days, all appointed festivals. All these are affixed with "her." Within the relationship between Israel and YHWH (her national deity), all these are really his. He instituted them for her to celebrate him. She however, has directed them to the service of other parties. So, he relinquishes his association with these festivities. For the second time there is a change in ownership. On the one hand, he takes away her possessions because they are not hers but his. On the other hand, he gives away to her all the appointed festival days because they are no longer his, but hers. What could be more indicative of separation than this bifurcation of ownership!

Coming back to follow the husband's intended actions: three more verbs follow, all signaling an end to existence—cease (שׁבת), ruin (שׁמם), devour (אכל). He will ruin "her vines and her fig trees," hers only in error; she thinks these are "her pay from her lovers." Again, poetic justice is accentuated by paronomasia: she loses her fig trees (תְּאֵנָתָהּ) because she wrongfully attributed them to the pay (אֶתְנָה) from her lovers.[47] By using the word "pay" (אֶתְנָה) she implicates herself over again, since this term is used for a prostitute's fee.[48] The forest will take over these tracts of fertile land, and wild beasts will "devour them."[49] Landy points out that this threat is the antithesis of the earlier threat of exposure by which he

napura?," Boloji, March 6, 2015, https://tinyurl.com/y74ye8pc. The Indian epic (ed. Krishna-Dwaipayana Vyasa; trans. Kisari Mohan Ganguli; 1883–96) is available in the public domain at the Internet Sacred Text Archive, https://tinyurl.com/ya4hdr3t.

44. E.g., "Indian Woman Paraded Naked on Donkey," BBC News, November 10, 2014, https://tinyurl.com/y83clazv.

45. Weems, "Gomer," 97.

46. Andersen and Freedman, *Hosea*, 249.

47. Hubbard, *Hosea*, 79; Wolff, *Hosea*, 38.

48. Landy, *Hosea*, 27; Wolff, 38; Yee, "She Is Not My Wife," 378. Cf. Deut 23:19; Ezek 16:31, 34, 41; Hos 9:1.

49. Andersen and Freedman (*Hosea*, 252–56) argue at length that since beasts are unlikely to fall upon grapes and figs, "them" here refers to the woman's children.

would turn her into a parched desert land. Whereas that threat was passive, "with the woman abandoned," the latter is active with the aggression of wild animals.[50] By this point, the actor is not human but beast. Ferocity makes way for the feral.[51] In this, the man has the law on his side—an adulterous woman attracts the death penalty (Deut 22:22).

The final verb in the series of eight captures the motivation for these intended actions. The husband means to punish his wife (פקד על). For what? The five verbs of which she is the subject set out the crime. She misattributed her possessions to her lovers, saying (אמר) they were her "pay" for services rendered. So she burns incense to gratify them (קטר); she makes herself attractive for them (עדה);[52] and she goes (הלך) after them to pleasure them—driven by the misguided notion that the more she offers them, the better her gains will be. In all this, she has let herself forget the true identity of her benefactor: "but me she forgot" (וְאֹתִי שָׁכְחָה). The frontloading of the object forgotten emphasizes the thrust of the husband's case. Further, the "me" now stands immediately after "her lovers" clearly showing the contrasting treatment each party receives at her hands: "went after . . . lovers . . . me . . . forgot."[53]

The punishment fits the crime. Andersen and Freedman explain: "Just as in the past the errant wife had sought out her lovers and eagerly disrobed in their presence for the purposes of sexual gratification, so now she will be forcibly exposed in the same situation, and publicly humiliated."[54] What is more, "what she did secretly and for pleasure will now be done to her openly and for her disgrace."[55]

Of the three "therefore" units, this one is the most emotive. The intended actions start with the vindictive, increase in violence to constitute an atrocity against human dignity, and climax at the murderous. Distributed evenly across the outpouring of rage are three references to the wife's lovers (2:10, 12, 13). In each case they are invoked with an intention to expose them as impotent. They cannot rescue the woman as she is being publicly humiliated; they cannot defend her property for her—supposedly, their gifts; they cannot intervene to prevent her utter ruin. The man's outrageous acts, though performed on the woman, are

50. Landy, *Hosea*, 29.

51. Landy, *Hosea*, 28.

52. See Andersen and Freedman, *Hosea*, 260–61, for the erotic associations of one of the items of adornment, the הֶלְיָה.

53. Andersen and Freedman, *Hosea*, 262.

54. Andersen and Freedman, *Hosea*, 249. Weems ("Gomer," 98) sees the law of *talion* functioning more specifically. The woman dresses like a prostitute (2:2–3, 13) and refuses to remove this show of infidelity. The public stripping fits the crime of indecent apparel.

55. Andersen and Freedman, *Hosea*, 249.

all in relation to them. In uncovering her nakedness, it is their impotence he exposes.

By this is betrayed the underlying emotions of jealousy at losing, and intolerance at the loss of, the object of his affections. She is not merely a possession he must destroy so that she becomes unavailable for the enjoyment of another. He desires her love. Under the gamut of emotions—"pain, anguish, uncertainty, anger"—is the "determination to win back his wife."[56] It is this volatile mix of anguish and fury that drive him to the extreme of taking a family matter out into the streets. Stripping a wife in full public view is the ultimate disgrace for the wife, *and* also for the husband. In any Eastern community—and this is true of present-day India—nothing brings greater shame to a man than an adulterous wife.[57]

The powerful emotions of the seeker in Hosea 2 find a parallel in those of the seeker of Song 5. When she opens the door only to find the man has left already, hopelessness overwhelms her. She nearly dies (נַפְשִׁי יָצְאָה; Song 5:6). She looks, she calls out, and before we know it she is in the city, searching wildly. The encounter with the city guards comes as a shock, complicating her despair with humiliation at the hands of strangers. But even this disgrace is tolerable in the search for her beloved. She is "faint with love." In a way, this is the case with the seeker in Hosea 2. If he had put his scheme into action, it would have been suicidal for his own standing. But he contemplates wreaking havoc on his own reputation if it will regain for him the affection for which he is competing, if it will return his wife to him. Both seekers are what we would describe colloquially as "out of their minds." They can think of no other. So, each conjures up the loved one. For the woman in the Song, the man she describes is beautiful, and all that beauty is hers: "This is *my* beloved" (Song 5:16). The mind of the man in Hosea also is full of memories. He recalls her done up in "rings and jewelry." However, that beauty was for the visual pleasure of other lovers, not him.

In Hosea 2, eventually desolation overtakes rage. She "went after her lovers," he reminisces (וַתֵּלֶךְ אַחֲרֵי מְאַהֲבֶיהָ), his thoughts looping back to exactly where they left off in 2:5: She said, "I will go after my lovers" (אֵלְכָה אַחֲרֵי מְאַהֲבַי). Two cycles of thought yielded two proposals, containment and retaliation. But like a dog chasing its tail, both have expended their energies in futile circularity. The speaker, tirelessly the seeker, essays a third alternative.

---

56. Weems, "Gomer," 97.

57. See Ben Zvi, "Observations," 381; Andersen and Freedman, *Hosea*, 229.

THE THIRD "THEREFORE": HOSEA 2:14–23

For the third time, the starting point is 2:5, but this last alternative thoroughly undoes the logic of *lex talionis* followed until now. Dearman insightfully points out that, according to the legal code, once a marriage had been violated, there was no way the offender could initiate restoration. Restoration was only possible if the offended party took extraordinary steps.[58] This is what the husband in Hosea proposes.

The woman's feet are restless ones. The husband will take advantage of those moving feet and lead them to himself. Weems is right that the "same amount of pathos that went into threatening [the woman] is now spent in seducing her" since the man's "only desire is to win his wife back."[59] The enthusiasm is as marked as in the first "therefore" section. Thus, again, the speaker begins with a "Look!" (הִנֵּה) and follows it up with a pronoun and participle, "I am alluring her" (אָנֹכִי מְפַתֶּיהָ). The sense is that he will do what he plans to do without wasting any further time thinking through any more alternatives. The sudden turnaround is all the more heightened when read against the previous sentence: "me she forgot [but] . . . I will allure her."[60]

[14] Therefore [לָכֵן] I am now going to allure her [הִנֵּה אָנֹכִי מְפַתֶּיהָ];
I will lead her into the wilderness [וְהֹלַכְתִּיהָ הַמִּדְבָּר] and speak tenderly to her [וְדִבַּרְתִּי עַל־לִבָּהּ].
[15] There I will give her back her vineyards,
and will make the Valley of Achor a door of hope.
There she will respond [וְעָנְתָה] as in the days of her youth,
as in the day she came up out of Egypt.
[16] In that day, declares the Lord,
you will call me 'my husband;' [אִישִׁי]
you will no longer call me 'my master.' [בַּעְלִי]
[17] I will remove the names of the Baals from her lips;
No longer will their names be invoked.
[18] In that day I will make a covenant for them
with the beasts of the field, the birds in the sky
and the creatures that move along the ground.
Bow and sword and battle
I will abolish from the land,
so that all may lie down in safety.

---

58. J. Andrew Dearman, *The Book of Hosea*, NICOT (Grand Rapids: Eerdmans, 2010), 115.
59. Weems, "Gomer," 96.
60. Andersen and Freedman, *Hosea*, 271. Though the vocabulary is that of seduction, it need not mean self-interest. Dearman (*Hosea*, 121) rightly suggests this is a "whole-hearted appeal" "to the rational faculties and the will (= heart) of a person" "based on personal commitment" as in Gen 50:21, Ruth 2:13, Isa 40:2.

¹⁹ I will betroth you forever;
I will betroth you in righteousness and justice,
in love and compassion.
²⁰ I will betroth you in faithfulness,
and you will acknowledge the Lord.
²¹ In that day I will respond [אֶעֱנֶה], declares the Lord—
I will respond [אֶעֱנֶה] to the skies,
and they will respond [יַעֲנוּ] to the earth;
²² and the earth will respond [תַּעֲנֶה] to the grain,
the new wine and the olive oil,
and they will respond [יַעֲנוּ] to Jezreel.
²³ I will plant her for myself in the land;
I will show my love to the one I called 'Not my loved one.'
I will say to those called 'Not my people,' 'You are my people;' [עַמִּי אַתָּה]
and they will say, 'You are my God' [אֱלֹהָי] (2:14–23)

Clines describes this section as a "delightful reversal of the expected."[61]
The mood of coercion that marked the first proposal and the language of
revenge that permeated the second disappear altogether. In their place is
a love song.[62] Even if the word "love" is never in the speaker's mouth,[63]
the section is as vulnerable and confident, as anxious and hopeful, as tender and forceful as only a love poem can be.

By its nature, this section cancels or reverses sentiments expressed
hitherto. The desert (מִדְבָּר; 2:3, 14) will not describe the shameful circumstances of her death but instead serve as the location for a return to
dignity; a "murderous fantasy"[64] is replaced by romance. Instead of seiz-
ing the woman's grain (דָּגָן; 2:9, 22) and new wine (תִּירוֹשׁ; 2:9, 22),
the husband will supply them.[65] Instead of setting wild beasts against her,

61. Clines, "Hosea 2," 297.
62. Using the (perhaps limited) parameters of form criticism, Smith identifies the genre of
this poem as an oracle of salvation, which, read in the context of Israel's salvation history, it is.
He categorizes Hosea 14:5–7 as a "love song." See Charles H. Silva, "Literary Features in the
Book of Hosea," *BSac* 164 (2007): 44, 47.
63. For expressions of divine love in Hosea, see Ralph L. Smith, "Major Motifs of Hosea,"
SwJT 18, no. 1 (1975): 25–28, esp. 26; Carsten Vang, "God's Love According to Hosea and
Deuteronomy: A Prophetic Re-working of a Deuteronomic Concept?," *TynBul* 62, no. 2
(2011): 181–85.
64. Francis Landy, "In the Wilderness of Speech: Problems of Metaphor in Hosea," *BibInt* 3,
no. 1 (1995): 51.
65. Tabulating the lists helps us to see the offense, the deserved penalty, and the husband's
actual action:
2:5: what the woman thinks her lovers provided: bread; water; wool; flax; oil
2:8: what the man provided: grain; wine; oil; silver; gold
2:9: what the man could seize: grain; wine; wool; silver
2:22: instead, what the man will continue to provide: grain; wine; oil
Adapted from Dearman, *Hosea*, 113.

he wishes her to live in harmony with nature (חַיַּת הַשָּׂדֶה; 2:12, 18). Instead of pronouncing the dissolution of the family, he speaks reconciliation. He will restore to himself the children he cast off (2:4, 22–23). Most remarkable is his hope that the wife he disowned will call him husband again (2:2, 16).[66] And, in the process of gaining her back, here is an itemizing of the bride price the man will pay. It far supersedes the lists of material possessions that populates Hosea 2: righteousness, justice, love, compassion, and faithfulness (2:19–20).

Clines beautifully builds a case for the idea of belonging as the "crucial datum of the poem" and elaborates the concept through a series of motifs. We will build on two of these as they apply to this particular section of the poem.[67]

The first motif of belonging is that of speech and response. Till the third "therefore" section, the woman speaks thrice, each time in reference to her lovers. She takes pleasure in the pay she thinks she receives from her lovers (2:12); she decides to go after her lovers (2:5); and she changes her mind and redirects herself to her former husband (2:7). Meanwhile, the husband never speaks directly to the wife. Indeed, any words he has for her he couriers through the children (2:2). Clines rightly observes that "this is on his part an alienating device, or at least a signal of his own sense of alienation [from his wife]."[68] However, this speech pattern is reversed in this section. The husband's plan of action is to bring his wayward wife to a place where he can speak tenderly to her, "to her heart."[69] "Whatever the content of this speech," says Landy, "it appeals to the organ responsible for affective life."[70] He will woo her until she responds as she once did.

Now the husband speaks directly to the woman, urging her to call him "my husband" rather than the usual "my master." "The desire to be called an אִישׁ not a בעל," observes Landy, is to initiate a paradigm of mutuality, and is a subversion of patriarchy.[71]

In direct speech again, he commits himself to be betrothed to her. Hosea 2:21–22 (EV 19–20):

---

66. For other elements of reversal, some involving Hosea 1, see Andersen and Freedman, *Hosea*, 264.

67. Clines, "Hosea 2," 300–311.

68. Clines, "Hosea 2," 302.

69. It is regularly noted that the phrase וְדִבַּרְתִּי עַל־לִבָּהּ occurs in Gen 34:3 (Shechem and Dinah), Ruth 2:13 (Boaz and Ruth), and Judg 19:3 (the Levite and his concubine).

70. Landy, "In the Wilderness," 50.

71. Landy, "In the Wilderness," 54. See along the same lines, Douglas Stuart, *Hosea-Jonah*, WBC 31 (Waco, TX: Word, 987), 57; Wolff, *Hosea*, 49; Mays, *Hosea*, 48; Beeby, *Grace Abounding*, 29; Dearman, *Hosea*, 124; Hubbard, *Hosea*, 87. Contra Yee, "She Is Not My Wife," 380; Macintosh, *Hosea*, 78.

וְאֵרַשְׂתִּיךְ לִי לְעוֹלָם
וְאֵרַשְׂתִּיךְ לִי בְּצֶדֶק וּבְמִשְׁפָּט וּבְחֶסֶד וּבְרַחֲמִים
וְאֵרַשְׂתִּיךְ לִי בֶּאֱמוּנָה
וְיָדַעַתְּ אֶת־יְהוָה

The solemn words of betrothal repeat thrice over, like a liturgical chant. One is reminded of the thrice-said *talaaq*[72] with which a Muslim divorces his wife. Here, the triple אֵרַשְׂתִּיךְ לִי ("I will betroth you to me")[73] annuls the painful words of separation spoken in 2:2. The repeating לִי ("to me") embraces the woman back into the relationship.[74] In an audacious overturning of the usual state of conjugal affairs, we are given to understand that the divorce was for a moment, but that this betrothal is "forever."

The result of this initiative is spectacular. The wife who could not acknowledge her husband (2:8) is now able to. Across the canon, when the verb "to know" (ידע) is used in the context of sexual activity, the woman is invariably the object. Here in the wilderness, when the husband seduces and re-betroths himself and his wife, there is a sexually charged reversal of the usual male subject: *she* will "know" (ידע)[75] *him* (2:20).[76] His "speaking tenderly" to her powerfully reverses the flow of her affections.

With communication reestablished, the Hosea poem begins to look more like the Song's seeking poems. In the Song, words flowed between the man and the woman, word responding to word sometimes playfully (Song 2:15) and sometimes in dead earnest (Song 2:16); relational words that entwined one lover with the other in endearments (Song 3:1–4; 5:2); words that, if left unspoken, were pleaded for (Song 2:14); words that, when absent, were called out for (Song 5:6); and beyond words, ears that listened for the sound of the beloved (Song 2:8; 5:2). In Hosea, the poem ends climactically with the very first words directly exchanged between man and wife.[77] He speaks two (עַמִּי־אַתָּה; "You are my people") and she, just one (אֱלֹהָי; "my God"). But they suffice. Their latent

---

72. In Arabic, "divorce."

73. Landy (*Hosea*, 43) points out that Hos 2:19–20 (MT 21–22) is recited every morning by Jews while putting on phylacteries.

74. A betrothal is not the same as courtship, and is more binding than an engagement, since it involved the payment of the bride-price to the father (cf. David's betrothal to Saul's daughter Michal at the price of a hundred Philistine foreskins; 2 Sam 3:14) (Derek Kidner, *Love to the Loveless: The Story and Message of Hosea*, Bible Speaks Today [Leicester: InterVarsity, 1981], 34). A betrothal seems to have been as binding as marriage in the eyes of the law. Cf. Exod 22:16–17; Deut 20:7; 22:23–29) (Stuart, *Hosea-Jonah*, 59).

75. Of course, the plain sense here, as in 2:8, is that of acknowledging.

76. See Brenner, "Pornoprophetics Revisited: Some Additional Reflections," 82.

77. Clines, "Hosea 2," 302.

force nullifies the anti-belonging ("not my wife" and "not my husband") that opened the poem.

A second motif of belonging Clines sets out is that of the spatial: the movements of the woman. Earlier in the poem, she goes away from her husband (2:5) and then returns (2:7). Her going is determined, but her return is indifferent, undertaken when she has run out of options. In this section, the man and woman keep step. He leads her (the *hiphil* of הלך) into the wilderness.[78] From this ground they walk together through a "door of hope," into the land[79] where at last her feet can cease their wandering. Clines describes the woman's journey thus:

> The reversal of movement *away from* Yahweh initiated by Israel's passion for the Baalim has come to a full stop. Israel no longer suffers the self-cancelling and ineffectual motion of going and coming, and now comes to rest in a place where she will put down roots—so the imagery implies—and where her planted-ness will announce her belonging-ness: "I will sow her—for myself (לי)."[80]

"I will sow her to me," though clumsy in the English,[81] segues with the formula of betrothal: וְאֵרַשְׂתִּיךְ לִי is followed through with וּזְרַעְתִּיהָ לִי. The engagement leads to marriage, the latter expressed in the language of consummation.[82]

The man in Hosea 2 makes an extraordinary move in going after a wife who herself is pursuing sundry clients. Socially, a prostitute is "tolerated, while an adulterous, promiscuous wife would never be."[83] The cost of even standing by such a one would be enormous. How much greater, then, the derision the man invites upon himself by following where she goes, so that he can lead her away from her lovers.

The Song uses movement well to express the motif of belonging. Indeed, the lines are dizzy with the protagonists' comings and goings—always with the man and woman moving toward each other. The man cannot wait to get to his beloved's window or to her side of the door. But, the journeys that haunt us are those of the woman. Compared to Hosea's man, the Song's woman makes just as unusual a foray

---

78. Clines, "Hosea 2," 305.

79. Clines, "Hosea 2," 305.

80. Clines, "Hosea 2," 306.

81. זרע is a word play on Jezreel (יִזְרְעֶאל; Hosea 1:4) and reverses the negative associations with that name. See Wolff, *Hosea*, 54, for an attempt at untying the grammatical knots; also Dearman, *Hosea*, 95, 100–101.

82. Andersen and Freedman, *Hosea*, 288.

83. See Yee, "She Is Not My Wife," 371.

to retrieve the one she loves. Like the man in Hosea, she too will not rest till she leads her beloved back home.

The seeking in both books finishes off with potential happily-ever-after endings. As a love poem would, both end with the couple returned to their world-of-two. The Song signs off with its typical circumlocutions for the pleasures of reunion: the couple enters the bedchamber (Song 3:4); the man comes to his garden to gather lilies (Song 6:2). Hosea is less coy. All of nature is thrown into "an orgy of responsiveness,"[84] with the verb "respond" (ענה) echoing antiphonally through the created orders. The skies respond to the earth, we presume with rain, because the earth responds back to yield grain, new wine, and olive oil. We cannot help recalling the Song's springtime images of nature in a frenzy of procreation (Song 2:11–13). Commingled with the fertility of earth is the fertility of the reunited couple. As Yee puts it, the woman, who had hitherto given herself to be "ploughed" and "seeded" by other lovers, now returns to a state of exclusive belonging. The husband impregnates her,[85] and she produces legitimate offspring the man can love and rightfully call his own.[86]

CONCLUSION TO HOSEA 2

The poem of Hosea 2 establishes the husband as the untiring seeker. As the husband of an errant wife, he had two options: divorce or her death by stoning. He chose neither. Even his words of separation (2:2) contained embedded a seed of hope in the word "lest"/"otherwise" (פֶּן; 2:5)—let her make amends, lest I take action, he warns.[87] The situation is still open-ended. His affection for her will not let him let her go. But the woman remains intractable.

Clines sets out the options before the man. Should he act to block her access to her lovers, this will return her to him but only as a knee-jerk reaction to unfavorable circumstances. She does not "know" him. The reunion does not lead to restoration. Should he act in judgment, she still remains in the state of having "forgot[ten]" him. The greater risk is that she may not survive the punishment, dissolving the very possibility of restoration. Thus, "the first two options lead nowhere, or at least, lead only to a fixation of the unacceptable state of affairs that has called forth the initial 'protest' (ריב) of the poem."[88] The man, therefore, dis-

---

84. Clines, *Hosea*, 302.
85. Hos 2:22: Jezreel means "God plants."
86. Yee, "She Is Not My Wife," 372, 381.
87. The particle governs five clauses of punishment (Andersen and Freedman, *Hosea*, 225).
88. Clines, "Hosea 2," 313.

misses these alternatives and takes the third way. This makes a remarkably logical route to reconciliation. From divorce, the poem moves back to the starting point of the relationship between the man and woman—to courtship (2:14), which moves to betrothal with a bride price (2:19–20), and consummation (2:23).[89] By moving back in time it moves forward to a desirable end.

LOVE-IN-SEPARATION: MAN AND WOMAN

The poems of Hosea 2 and the Song converse with each other simply by their location in the same canon. To the reader, they present two versions of exclusive love between a man and a woman. One wrestles with love that has gone terribly wrong. The other celebrates love that is nearly perfect. What inferences may we draw from the interplay between these texts as it concerns the idea of the seeking lover?

In Hosea 2, at first the woman appears to be the seeker. On closer inspection, we see that her seeking is a counterfeit of the real thing. Her first quest is illegitimate; her second is poorly motivated. If there is to be a resolution of the separation, the man must assume the role of seeker. While we may consider the entire poem as an exercise in seeking, the final section delineates the strategy he eventually uses for reunion. He models to the woman what ideal seeking may look like. It is not pursuit of material goods, for genuine seeking sets aside self-interest. It is not casual redirection from lovers to husband, but seeking that is deeply intentional.

In his seeking, the man appears motivated by the pain of separation. "There is no quest without pain . . . no lover who is not also a martyr."[90] The tormented mind comes through in the tortuous convolutions of the long poem. Even when pushed to the extreme that a spouse can tolerate, the man cannot give his wife up.[91] And, even if his present domestic condition is extraordinarily distressing, he sees divorce not as a solution to the pain, but as even more painful.

Which of the seekers in the Song is most like this man? It would be

---

89. See Mordechai A. Friedman, "Israel's Response in Hosea 2:17b: 'You Are My Husband,'" *JBL* 99, no. 2 (1980): 199–204, who argues that the "marriage" is indicated as early as 2:17. He reads the woman calling the man her אִישׁ as her part in the marriage vow formula such as it existed in the ancient world. Thus, this text cancels, or reverses, the divorce pronouncement of 2:2. See also Matthew W. Mitchell, "Hosea 1–2 and the Search for Unity," *JSOT* 29, no. 1 (2004): 125–26, for an observation on the "complete jumbling of the logical order of events" in this poem: courtship, the reinstatement of the title "husband," and after that, betrothal.

90. Evelyn Underhill, *Mysticism* (New York: Dutton, 1961), 222, citing the Blessed Henry Suso.

91. Hos 11:8–9 sets this out in a passionate outpouring of inner turmoil.

the Song's female protagonist, rather than the male. Her seeking is motivated by a mood matching that of the man in Hosea 2. She cannot bear
that her beloved should be where she is not. Separation throws her into
an agitation which quickly exceeds the limits of tolerance. She *must* find
the man. Given this, we might say that if we were to match lovers across
the canon, the Song's woman makes the perfect equivalent to the husband in Hosea; she best replaces her inadequate Hosean counterpart.

However, that is not all. The Song's second poem (5:2–6:3) shows yet
another motivation. The woman discovers that her delay in opening the
door was critical. She has missed the opportunity to be with her beloved.
Without explicitly stating it, the poem communicates a sense of deep
remorse. It tells us she almost died; it describes a search even more fren-
zied than the one previous. If this is the case, then, the Song's woman
doubly compensates for the one in Hosea: she is *like* the husband, and
she is *not like* the wife. Unlike the wife who flaunts her adultery in the
face of her husband (Hos 2:2), who seeks out lovers like an animal in
heat (Hos 2:5, 7) but forgets her husband (Hos 2:13), who misattributes
the goodness of her husband toward her and misuses his gifts in the service of her lovers (Hos 2:8), whose mouth is filled with the names of her
lovers (Hos 2:17), and whose body is bedecked for their viewing pleasure
(Hos 2:13)—unlike this woman, abnormally hard of heart, the woman in
the Song is distraught that she may have offended her beloved by a few
minutes of hesitation. Unlike the woman of Hosea 2, she is regretful and
hurries to remedy her fault.

Laying the poems of Hosea and the Song side by side, we arrive at the
human ideal of love-in-separation.

LOVE-IN-SEPARATION: DEITY AND DEVOTEE

Allegorical readings of the Song's "seeking lover" texts come readily to
Judaism. Whether it is the male or the female lover, the passages are
unanimously read into one of the periods of Israel's national history
when the people were in some manner of *golah* ("dispersion")—the
sojourn in Egypt or the Babylonian exile. The readings may vary in the
details of the application made, but largely flow together, and often take
their lead from the *Targum*.

Thus, the male lover eagerly bounding toward his beloved's window
is "as if God hurriedly leaped and skipped to redeem the Jews before the
pre-determined End." Though the period set for the affliction was 400
years (Gen 15:13), of which only 210 had passed, God disregarded the
calculations by leaping over them to pronounce liberation from slavery

190 years in advance.[92] The wall that stops him from reaching his people is their grievous sin. Nevertheless he stands behind it, "compassionately watching over" them by peering through the cracks in that wall of sin, "made by the virtue of our righteous [ones]."[93] "Arise, My love . . . and come away," he calls, asking Israel to "bestir" itself, because he is going to lead them out of the "winter" of their affliction.[94] "As rain is the harshest part of the winter, so the harshest part of the 210 years of Egyptian bondage was the 86 years from the birth of Miriam," but, "they, too, are now 'over and gone.'"[95]

In the exodus event, beloved Israel is the "dove" trapped at the Red Sea, threatened by the hawk Pharaoh from without and by a fiery serpent from within.[96] In such perilous circumstances, Israel still joins in the song of Moses, and that voice is sweet because it expresses her confidence in God.[97] According to Rashi, however, the poem closes with the departure of the *Shechinah* (Song 2:17), which is angered by Israel's sin in the events following the crossing of the Red Sea. What the next poem (Song 3:1–5) describes is how Israel "longingly sought after" a God they had estranged.[98]

The "night" in which a "tormented, insomniac Israel" lies "twisting and turning sleeplessly" ruing its separation from God could refer to either the wilderness wandering or the Babylonian exile,[99] both consequences of their sin. But rather than continue in bed, Israel is "determined to arise and seek Him out by every possible avenue."[100] In the exile, Israel might have said: "I will . . . roam about the countries among who we are dispersed. . . . The heathen nations in whose midst I find myself in servitude found me and I asked them: 'Have you seen a God like ours?'"[101]

In another reading, the "guards" are either Moses and Aaron, or Ezra and Nehemiah,[102] of whom Israel agitatedly asks for the whereabouts of

92. Rashi cited in Meir Zlotowitz, compiler, *Shir haShirim/Song of Songs: An Allegorical Translation based upon Rashi with a Commentary Anthologized from Talmudic, Midrashic and Rabbinic Sources* (New York: Mesorah, 1979), 105.

93. *Tz'ror HaMor*, cited in Zlotowitz, *Shir haShirim*, 106.

94. Rashi, cited in Zlotowitz, *Shir haShirim*, 107–8.

95. Midrash, cited in Zlotowitz, *Shir haShirim*, 108.

96. *Aramaic Targum to Song of Songs* (trans. Jay Treat; Hebrew text compiled from *Mikraot Gedolot* and Raphael Hai Melamed, *The Targum to Canticles according to Six Yemen MSS* [1921], https://tinyurl.com/yb37vrk4, 2.14.

97. *Midrash* cited in Zlotowitz, *Shir haShirim*, 112.

98. Rashi cited in Zlotowitz, *Shir haShirim*, 115.

99. Rashi and Alshich, cited in Zlotowitz, *Shir haShirim*, 116.

100. Alshich, cited in Zlotowitz, *Shir haShirim*, 117.

101. *Midrash Lekach Tov*, cited in Zlotowitz, *Shir haShirim*, 119.

102. Zlotowitz, *Shir haShirim*, 117–18.

God, but, even these authorities have no answer. Eventually, when the period of separation ended and God returned, Israel clung to him, enjoying her relationship with him in the chamber of her "mother's house," whether that was the tabernacle at Shiloh or the Second Temple.[103]

As for the second seeking poem in Song 5, Ibn Ezra's reading, which partly follows the *Targum* and the *Midrash*, is a representative sample of Jewish allegorical interpretation. Again, the parallels are historical. Israel slumbers in the Babylonian captivity, though her heart is awake in its desire "to reunite with the *Shechinah* as before." God responds. He declares that his hair, anthropomorphically speaking, is drenched with the tears of their supplicatory prayers. So, God knocks; that is, he moves Cyrus to decree that Israel may return to her homeland. However, Israel is reluctant to return to the land and rebuild the Temple. Only 42,000 heed the call, while millions prefer to stay behind in the relative comfort of Babylon. Eventually, Israel rises to open the door for her Beloved; that is, the Temple is rebuilt. But to her dismay, her Beloved is already gone—the *Shechinah* does not enter the Second Temple as it had done with Solomon's Temple. Israel seeks him in desperation, with no success. Not only is the *Shechinah* absent, but shortly thereafter, prophecy ceases. In her state of distress, watchmen fall upon her—the kings of Greece, who strike and wound her "by their evil decrees." Nevertheless, Israel remains faithful in her seeking, and as the nations of the world of that time could testify, she demonstrated herself to be "sick for His love."[104]

The theme of love-in-separation also easily resonates with Christian exegetes. Unlike Jewish readings, which incorporate the Song into their national experience, Christian interpretations apply it at the levels of both the church and the individual Christian. Our sample will include a taste of both.

God, the seeking lover, is often portrayed more specifically as Christ. Gregory the Great is delighted by the allegorical possibility here. "If I can put it this way," he says, "by coming for our redemption, the Lord leaped! My friends, do you want to become acquainted with these leaps of his? From heaven he came to the womb, from the womb to the manger, from the manger to the cross, from the cross to the sepulcher, and from the sepulcher he returned to heaven."[105]

Parallel to Jewish readings, Christ stands separated by the wall of human sin (cf. Isa 59:2) and by his advent disassembles it (cf. Eph 2:14;

103. Zlotowitz, *Shir haShirim*, 118–19.

104. Ibn Ezra, cited in Zlotowitz, *Shir haShirim*, 151–52n.

105. Gregory the Great, *Forty Gospel Homilies* 29, cited in J. Robert Wright, ed., *Proverbs, Ecclesiastes, Song of Solomon*, ACCS, Old Testament 9 (Downers Grove, IL: InterVarsity, 2005), 318.

Col 1:20).[106] Before he came seeking lost humanity, it was winter. After his coming, there are flowers, the time for harvest arrives, and the fig tree that was previously barren begins to bear fruit.[107]

The church passionately reciprocates Christ as the seeking lover. When she "was still lying prostrate . . . among the nations" and "could not find the true God there," she roused herself to a strenuous search that took her into the streets of the city. "When she speaks of this city, she is referring to the design of the divine Law . . . which contains a public square and avenues, streets and homes, walls vast and high made strong by their impregnable solidity." So her search through the city is a search through the whole Law. This search is rudely interrupted by the guardians of the Law, the scribes and Pharisees. But, passing them by, she finds Christ. Clinging to him, the church journeys toward her mother's house which is the heavenly Jerusalem.[108]

Along similar lines, Gregory the Great applies this seeking to the individual:

> We seek the one we love upon our beds when we sigh with longing for our Redeemer during our short period of rest during the present life. We seek him during the night, because even though our hearts are already watchful for him, our eyes are still darkened. But it remains for the person who does not find the one he loves to rise and go about the city, that is, he must travel about the holy church of the elect with an inquiring heart. He must seek her through its streets and squares, making his way, that is, through narrow and broad places, on the watch to make inquiries if any traces of her can be found in them, because there are some, even of those leading worldly lives, who have something worth imitating of virtue in their actions. The watchmen who guard the city find us as we search, because the holy fathers who guard the church's orthodoxy come to meet our good efforts, to teach us, by their words of their writings. Scarcely have we passed them by when we find him whom we love. Although in his humility our Redeemer was a human being, in his divinity he was above human beings. Therefore once the watchmen have been passed by, the beloved is found.[109]

If the first seeking poem (Song 3) is often read as telling the story of how the church first finds Christ, the second poem (Song 5) is often read as narrating her proclivity to fail, followed by her eagerness to make

---

106. Apponius, *In Canticum Canticorum Exposito* 4.16–17, cited in Norris, *Song of Songs*, 119–20.

107. Ambrose of Milan, *De Isaac* 4.32–37, cited in Norris, *Song of Songs*, 121.

108. Gregory of Elvira, *In Canticum Canticorum* 5.5–14, cited in Norris, *Song of Songs*, 137–39.

109. Gregory the Great, *Forty Gospel Homilies* 25, cited in Wright, *Proverbs, Ecclesiastes, Song of Solomon*, 326.

amends. Here is the church that lies abed, "untroubled, occupied with the pleasures of the flesh . . . walled about by the devices of the Enemy." Christ "knocks at the gate of her mind, so that, roused from her deadly sleep, she may see that she is surrounded with dangers and may pray her Helper to come in to her."[110] That he comes by night reprises the "nocturnal rising of the Jews against him (cf. John 13:30; 18:3)." The bedewed head signifies his death, "which touched the hairs of his head, and not himself." His plea to her is: "Since . . . I underwent death for your sake, and suffered these things on your account, open to me and let me in."[111] She, meanwhile, shamelessly lies "stripped of the garment that the grace of Christ bestowed on her" and with her feet bare when they should have been shod "by the hope of attaining blessedness" through "the gospel of peace" (Eph 6:15). "She does not blush to rise up from the bed of evil custom, and by repentance to open the door of her mind to the Christ who knocks."[112]

Eventually, "the church of the penitent" rises to open the door, by which time Christ has gone. She desperately seeks the Beloved she "[has] lost by [her] own fault." Who should find her but the guards, that is, "the leaders of the church"? They find her as she goes "seeking and calling, full of sins and abominations." They "struck [her] with fear of judgment and of sins; they wounded [her] with remorse and penitence; they . . . took away [her] mantle, that is to say, the multitude of sins in which [she] was wrapped, by means of the penitence they enjoined." Or, alternatively, they stripped away her veil of ignorance by explaining her condition to her. "Therefore, to the guards of the city . . . who found me in such a state and treated me as they did," she makes this confession: "Because of my love of him I am sick and tired of things earthly and desire only things heavenly."[113]

CONCLUSION

In this section, we began with the pair of seeking poems in Song 2:8–3:5, each featuring one of the lovers engaging the condition of love-in-separation. Comparing the two, the woman emerged with the stronger profiling. She sought the termination of their separation with an intensity that overwhelmed the reader, recklessly essaying the peril of dark,

110. Apponius, *In Canticum Canticorum Expositio* 5.25–26, cited in Norris, *Song of Songs*, 198.

111. Theodoret of Cyrus, *Interpretatio in Canticum Canticorum*, cited in Norris, *Song of Songs*, 197.

112. Apponius, *In Canticum Canticorum Expositio* 5.25–26, cited in Norris, *Song of Songs*, 198.

113. Honorius of Autun, *Expositio in Cantica Canticorum*, cited in Norris, *Song of Songs*, 207–8.

strange places. Next, we studied the poem of 5:2–6:3, which also provides the opportunity to compare the protagonists as seekers. Here, the man faded even more into the penumbra, while the woman plunged further into the darkness, realizing upon herself the pain and the price of seeking.

We moved to the intertext, Hosea 2, to encounter there a betrayed husband seeking an end to long years of separation. While his wife seeks after her lovers, he moves through cycles of roiling emotions to arrive at a strategy—countercultural and counterintuitive—that can re-betroth them.

It appears, then, that Hosea's man and the Song's woman reciprocate each other. They love with identical passion, feel separation with equal agony, and seek their beloved with matching vehemence. Intertextuality erases the boundaries of canonical placement, and demonstrates—as a prescription to human love relationships—that this man and this woman are made for each other.

Meanwhile, Jewish and Christian applications of the Song's seeking poems present both deity and devotee as exemplars of seeking. Deity hastens to his beloved with leaps and bounds. Bringing springtime to her desolate wintry world, he urges her into freedom. The devotee's response may initially be apathetic, mirroring the behavior of Israel and the church in other canonical treatments of the marital metaphor. However, she repents with commendable alacrity and goes on to make tearful compensation for her indolence. Such a devotee, one whose feet restlessly seek the company of her God, is best reciprocated by the God depicted in Hosea.

If not for the Song of Songs, the Hebrew Bible would lack a woman whose tenacious pursuit of her separated beloved matches that of the husband in Hosea. If not for the Song, the Old Testament's divine-human marital metaphor would locate the devotee in the company of sundry lovers, leaving deity inhabiting a state of love-in-separation.

PART II

In Praise of the Beloved

4.

The Golden One

When the enthralled gaze moves admiringly over the beloved's body, one possible outcome is the praise poem. In the Song, the four poems in admiration of the beloved's body are often assigned to the category of the *wasf*,[1] which in Arabic means "description." The *wasf* refers to a type of poem traditionally used in Arab marriage celebrations in which the physical charms of the couple—more usually, the bride—are described. When the Song's poems are equated with the *wasf*, the nuptial life setting is usually not a consideration, so perhaps its praise poems should be more correctly categorized as examples of the "human-body-descriptive song."[2]

In the ancient world, the Song's praise poems largely find their parallels in Ramesside Egyptian love poetry and in Sumerian liturgy celebrating the sacred marriage of deities.[3] In Jewish literature, there is

1. Discussions of the *wasf*, including comprehensive bibliography, can be found in Michael V. Fox, *The Song of Songs and the Ancient Egyptian Love Songs* (Madison: University of Wisconsin Press, 1985), 232, 269–78; Othmar Keel, *The Song of Songs: A Continental Commentary*, trans. Frederick J. Gaiser (Minneapolis: Augsburg, 1994), 22–24; Marvin H. Pope, *Song of Songs: A New Translation with Introduction and Commentary*, Anchor Bible 7C (New Haven: Yale University Press, 1977), 54–58, 67; Wilfred G. E. Watson, *Classical Hebrew Poetry: A Guide to Its Techniques*, 2nd ed., JSOTSup 26 (Sheffield: Sheffield Academic, 1995), 353–56; Richard D. Soulen, "The *Wasfs* of Song of Songs and Hermeneutic," *JBL* 86 (1967): 183–90; Marcia Falk, *The Song of Songs: A New Translation and Interpretation* (New York: HarperCollins, 1973), 127–35.

2. David Bernat, "Biblical *Wasfs* beyond Song of Songs," *JSOT* 28, no. 3 (2004): 334.

3. See Robert Gordis, *Song of Songs: A Study, Modern Translation and Commentary*, Text and Studies of the Jewish Theological Seminary of America 20 (New York: Jewish Theological Seminary of America, 1954), 30–34; Keel, *Song of Songs*, 20–24; Tremper Longman III, *Song of Songs* (Grand Rapids: Eerdmans, 2001), 49–53, Roland Murphy, *The Song of Songs*, Hermeneia

the praise of Sarah's beauty in *Genesis Apocryphon* 20.2–8.[4] Similar also
are the descriptions of the splendors of the high priest Simon in Sirach
50:5–10, and of the patriarch Jacob in *Joseph and Aseneth* 22:7, though
these are not in the category of love poetry.

Three of the Song's *wasf*s are in praise of the woman (4:1–7; 6:4–9;
7:2–10 [EV 7:1–9]). The less usual one is the woman's description of the
man (5:10–16).[5] A similar rare case may be found in Ugaritic mythological love songs, where a description of the male body follows the same
order as here in the Song, starting from the head, moving down the
body, and returning to the mouth.[6]

A formal feature of the *wasf* is that it follows the schema of "list
poetry." That is, the poem is essentially a listing of itemized body parts,
each of which is accompanied by "elaboration, description or other
supplementary language,"[7] usually through the devices of simile and
metaphor. The man's *wasf*s of the woman are constructed through the
gaze; the woman's praise of the man is constructed from memory. He
details his beloved's assets as his eyes drink them in, while the woman
conjures him up in absentia. The narrative plot in which her poem is set
requires this.

THE CONTEXT OF THE PRAISE POEM

The woman's *wasf* is prompted by a question. She has been in a futile
search for her beloved, and coming to the end of her resources, she more
or less recruits the daughters of Jerusalem. The daughters of Jerusalem
are willing to participate in the search, but want to be given sufficient
grounds for undertaking it.

> How is your beloved better than others [מַה־דּוֹדֵךְ מִדּוֹד],
> most beautiful of women?
> How is your beloved better than others,
> that you so charge us? (5:9)

(Minneapolis: Augsburg Fortress, 1990), 41–56; Pope, *Song of Songs*, 69–85. Fox, *Ancient Egyptian Love Songs*, is devoted entirely to Song of Songs in comparative perspective.

4. The Genesis Apocryphon *wasf* was first noted by M. H. Goshen-Gottstein, "Philologisch
e Miszellen zu den Qumrantexten," *RevQ* 2 (1959–60): 43–51. See also Pope, *Song of Songs*,
55–56, and Joseph A. Fitzmyer, *The Genesis Apocryphon of Qumran Cave I* (Rome: Pontifical
Institute Press, 1971), 119–20.

5. Songs in praise of the male body are rare in both the biblical canon and AWA literature.
Murphy, *Song of Songs*, 169n9, gives two examples: the brief description of Judah's princes (Lam
4:7) and the longer one of Simon the priest (Sir 50:5–10).

6. P. C. Craigie, "The Poetry of Ugarit and Israel," *TynBul* 22 (1971): 11.

7. Bernat, "Biblical *Wasf*s," 330.

The question may be understood as: What does your beloved look like?[8] More likely, the question asks if there is anything that puts this man above the ordinary.[9] If the woman can persuade the daughters of Jerusalem that the object of the search is worth their while, they may join in. Asked in this way, the question may have a teasing, mildly skeptical tone,[10] or perhaps one of challenge, or even sarcasm.[11] The woman makes a feisty response with her *wasf*.

The *wasf* lies nested within layers of the term of endearment, "my beloved" (דּוֹדִי). This narrative frame is created by the ongoing dialogue between the woman and the daughters of Jerusalem:

5:8	woman	דּוֹדִי	if you find *my beloved*
5:9	daughters of Jerusalem	דּוֹדֵךְ	how is *your beloved* better
		דּוֹדֵךְ	how is *your beloved* better
5:10	woman	דּוֹדִי	*my beloved* is radiant and ruddy
5:10–16		**PRAISE POEM**	
5:16	woman	דּוֹדִי	this is *my beloved*
6:1	daughters of Jerusalem	דּוֹדֵךְ	where has *your beloved* gone
		דּוֹדֵךְ	which way did *your beloved* turn
6:2	woman	דּוֹדִי	*my beloved* has gone down to his garden

The setting discharges two functions. First, by literally making the man the centerpiece of the dialogue, the concentric structure presents him like a pearl in an oyster, exquisitely set off. It leaves us in no doubt at all that the focus of the poem is the man. Second, the surrounding dialogue provides the motivation for the *wasf*. Unlike the other praise poems in

8. Mary T. Elliott, *The Literary Unity of the Canticle* (Frankfurt: Lang, 1989), 135.

9. Ariel Bloch and Chana Bloch, *The Song of Songs: A New Translation with an Introduction and Commentary* (New York: Random House, 1995), 184, explain at length their reading of the מִן as differentiating rather than comparing following postbiblical phraseology as in the question at the Passover Haggadah, "How is this night different from all other nights?" See Gianni Barbiero, *Song of Songs: A Close Reading*, trans. Michael Tait, VTSS (Leiden: Brill, 2011), 283–84.

10. Jill M. Munro, *Spikenard and Saffron: A Study in the Poetic Language of the Song of Songs*, JSOTSup 203 (Sheffield: Sheffield Academic, 1995), 46; Fox, *Ancient Egyptian Love Songs*, 143.

11. G. Lloyd Carr, *Song of Solomon: An Introduction and Commentary*, TOTC (Leicester: InterVarsity, 1984), 138–39; Robert W. Jenson, *Song of Songs*, Interpretation (Louisville: John Knox, 2005), 56; Elie Assis, *Flashes of Fire: A Literary Analysis of the Song of Songs* (New York: T&T Clark, 2009), 166; Keel, *Song of Songs*, 198; Cheryl J. Exum, *Song of Songs: A Commentary* (Louisville: Westminster John Knox, 2005), 202; Tom Gledhill, *The Message of the Song of Songs: The Lyrics of Love*, Bible Speaks Today (Leicester: InterVarsity, 1994), 182.

which the man is stirred by aesthetics, the woman speaks from a deep sense of loss. She is "faint" with love (5:8), specifically, love-in-separation. She fears she has brought upon herself an irrecoverable loss of her beloved (5:6). When she describes him, she speaks in painful realization of what the lost one means to her. While the man's poems are driven by admiration, the woman's *wasf* is fueled by an emotion more intense. She speaks of his immeasurable value to her, a value so great that she is willing to risk the dangers of the dark city streets to find him—a value so great that, desperate at the loss, she absurdly attempts to recruit into the search a group of strangers who have never seen him before.

If we appreciate this to be the literary matrix in which the *wasf* lies embedded, we are better able to challenge the assessment of those who think it rather lifeless, cold, and distant. It appears that those who see the *wasf* as an expression of the value of the woman's beloved are reading it more in line with the literary context of the *wasf*.[12]

THE PRAISE POEM

The *wasf* itself opens and closes with an overall claim of the beloved's uniqueness. To begin with, he is "outstanding among ten thousand" (5:10); to finish off, "he is altogether lovely" (5:16). Between these hyperbolic descriptions, the woman's eye rests tenderly on her beloved's various bodily assets, her admiring glance moving from the head downward.

> My beloved is radiant and ruddy (צַח וְאָדוֹם)
> Outstanding among ten thousand (דָּגוּל מֵרְבָבָה). (5:10)

She begins with what would usually be a first impression. He is צַח וְאָדוֹם. How are we to read this phrase? A helpful parallel is the description of Jerusalem's princes in Lamentations 4:7, which contain both the words צַח and אָדוֹם: "brighter than snow (זַכּוּ . . . מִשֶּׁלֶג) and whiter than milk (צַחוּ מֵחָלָב), their bodies more ruddy than corals (אָדְמוּ עֶצֶם מִפְּנִינִים)."

Just as useful a reference for צַח is Isaiah 18:4, where the word is an eye-blinding blend of heat (חֹם) and light (אוֹר). צַח is variously rendered as: "shimmering heat in the sunshine" (NIV); "glowing heat of sunshine" (NAB); "dazzling heat in the sunshine" (NASB). Those who live in hot climates get the idea immediately. The man is radiant (Ps

---

12. Exum, *Song of Songs*, 202.

104:15).[13] This could be the sparkle of *joie de vivre*, the energy of being alive.

Added to this glow—so much more evident in a youthful face—the beloved is ruddy (אָדוֹם), or, as Bloch and Bloch put it more literally, "earth-colored"[14]—as in the case of the princes of Jerusalem whose "bodies [were] more ruddy than coral" (Lam 4:7). Of course, the description of David comes to mind—ruddy, youthful, and handsome (1 Sam 16:12; 17:42). Among brown-skinned peoples with their range of skin color, "red" sometimes describes the most desirable tone when speaking of either male or female beauty.[15] Keel points out that in Egyptian art, the male body is traditionally painted dark red-brown.[16] Murphy agrees that the *wasf* "begins with what seems to be a general statement about his color."[17] If this is the aesthetic being praised in the Song, then the feature being described is not only his robust physical state (as in the idiom applicable to Caucasians, "in the pink of health"), but also the culturally desirable color of his skin. White-skinned races might see here an admirably tanned look.

So here is the first impression the daughters of Jerusalem receive of the man they are to help find, and it is only reasonable that the woman starts with the man's face, the prime signifier of one's identity. But the terms of description easily move out to apply to his whole person. His ruddy countenance promises robustness, and the vitality of his face bespeaks an attractive temperament. Here is a man who would stand out in a multitude—"outstanding among ten thousand" (דָּגוּל מֵרְבָבָה; 5:10). Here, Gordis explains the Akkadian cognate of the verb דגל ("outstanding") as carrying the sense of "to look upon, gaze, behold." A special nuance in Akkadian usage is "look with astonishment" or "look with admiration."[18]

---

13. In South India, there is a word used of a lively face, *kala* (vivacity), common to Kannada, Telugu, and Tamil. Irrespective of the beauty of the facial features or the age of person whose it is, a face is said either to possess or to be devoid of *kala*.

Palestinian love poetry has this parallel to the Song: "Visit me, O you with the radiant face / And heal my heart from its miseries." H. Stephan, *Modern Palestinian Parallels to the Song of Songs*, Studies in Palestinian Customs and Folklore 3 (Jerusalem: Palestine Oriental Society, 1923), 52.

14. Bloch and Bloch, *Song of Songs*, 184.

15. This is the case in South Indian languages, perhaps because "white" as a skin tone is not obtainable in the genetic pool. Even when a South Indian speaks of "white" skin, the vocabulary used describes a pale shade of brown. Thus, *erra* in Telugu, *kempu* in Kannada, *seguppe* in Tamil, and *sevappe* in Malayalam all mean "red" of skin, a color that is culturally desirable; whereas in North India, more influenced by the Aryan ideal of aesthetics and the gene pool, "white" (*gora*) is possible and is the epitome of desirable skin color.

16. Keel, *Song of Songs*, 198.

17. Murphy, *Song of Songs*, 171.

18. Robert Gordis, "The Root דגל in the Song of Songs," *JBL* 88, no. 2 (1969): 203–4.

From these senses, the passive participle דָּגוּל may be read according to Pope's preference: the beloved is "conspicuous" among ten thousand.[19] Of course, "ten thousand" is a hyperbolic figure signifying the superlative "countless."[20] Thus, the woman returns an answer to the question the daughters of Jerusalem ask. How is her beloved better than any other beloved? He stands out, he catches the eye, even in a sea of people.

She now goes on to describe in detail the attributes that make this the case.

His head is purest gold [רֹאשׁוֹ כֶּתֶם פָּז];
His hair is wavy [קְוֻצּוֹתָיו תַּלְתַּלִּים] and black as a raven [שְׁחֹרוֹת כָּעוֹרֵב]. (5:11)

Now begins the *wasf* proper, the line-up of physical attractions. The beloved's "head is purest gold." The pairing of two words both meaning "gold" (כֶּתֶם and פָּז) makes for a phrase translatable as "pure gold."[21] How is this "golden head" best understood? Decidedly, the reference is not to a head of blonde hair. Soon we will hear that his hair is as black as a raven. Later, the woman will use "gold" to describe the man's head, arms, and feet. To West and South Asian communities, both ancient and modern, the value of gold is proverbial.[22] There is no metal prized beyond it, as was the case in ancient Israel.[23] One Egyptian love poem invokes the beloved as "O Golden One."[24] In South Asia, the most common endearment for children or for the female loved one is the word for gold,[25] which is also widely used as a proper name for both males and females. A bride's dowry is never complete without a requisite amount of gold jewelry, valued above hard cash as a reserve for difficult times. As for purity, anything less than the optimal 22 carats is considered inferior—an opinion with its equivalent in biblical Israel and shared in this poem.[26] If this is the sense in which the *wasf* describes the man's head and

19. Pope, *Song of Songs*, 532.

20. Pope, *Song of Songs*, 532–33. See, e.g., Deut 33:2, 17; 1 Sam 18:7; Ps 91:7; Mic 6:7.

21. Bloch and Bloch, *Song of Songs*, 185. Pope, *Song of Songs*, 534–35, points to 2 Chr 9:17 interpreting such a pairing in 1 Kgs 10:18. Cf. Dan 10:5.

22. Cf. Ps 19:11 [EV 10]; 72:15; etc.

23. Richard S. Hess, *Song of Songs*, Baker Commentary on the Old Testament (Grand Rapids: Baker, 2005), 184. Thus, gold occupies a prime place in the furnishings of the tabernacle (Exodus 35–39) and the temple (1 Kings 6–7).

24. John Bradley White, *A Study of the Language of Love in the Song of Songs and Ancient Egyptian Poetry*, SBLDS 38 (Missoula, MT: Scholars, 1978), 180.

25. Thus, *sona/sonu* (Hindi), *thangam* and *ponne* (Tamil and Malayalam), *chinna* (Kannada) and *bangaaru* (Telugu). My departed mother named me Havilah for its association with gold (Gen 2:11), and used for me the endearment *bangaaru*.

26. Cf. Ps 72:15, 119:127, etc.

other body parts as being gold, it is a forceful statement of his worth.[27] As for the criticism that the woman's metallic imagery leaves the reader cold, it can be said that the Easterner well appreciates in the metaphor the warm glow of gold enfleshed.[28]

The man's hair is תַּלְתַּלִּים. This may be a compliment to its thickness.[29] Or it may be in admiration of its waves.[30] Either way, it satisfies the classical standards for Asian beauty by the depth of its blackness.[31] An Egyptian love poem has this parallel: "Fairest of women . . . Blacker is her hair than the blackness of night, / than the grapes of the *idb*-vines."[32] His has the midnight sheen of a raven's wing,[33] setting off to even greater advantage his glowing face. Metaphorically, the black hair and the golden head make a striking interplay of light and darkness. Even more pointed is the contrast between birds of opposite colors, the raven and the dove, for his eyes will soon be likened to the latter.

His eyes are like doves [עֵינָיו כְּיוֹנִים] by the water streams [עַל־אֲפִיקֵי מָיִם], Washed in milk [רֹחֲצוֹת בֶּחָלָב], fitly set [יֹשְׁבוֹת עַל־מִלֵּאת]. (5:12)

The description of the eyes is not only the longest but also the most fanciful. As windows to the soul, they deserve the space. Image layers over image until it is hard to say what exactly one is supposed to envision. The beloved's "eyes are like doves by the water streams, washed in milk," and יֹשְׁבוֹת עַל־מִלֵּאת. Any attempt to match the signified to the signifier leaves the cluster of images in shambles. What is being washed in milk, one begins asking: Eyes? Doves? Even jewels (NLT)? What does יֹשְׁבוֹת עַל־מִלֵּאת mean? Does it continue with the picture of doves, and

27. So Assis, *Flashes of Fire*, 168; Diane Bergant, *Song of Songs*, Berit Olam (Collegeville, MN: Liturgical, 2001), 69; Exum, *Song of Songs*, 204.

28. The correlation between the glow of precious materials and good health may be seen in this Babylonian poem for the recovery of a sick person (Gordis, *Song of Songs*, 33):
Like lapis lazuli I want to cleanse his body,
Like marble his features should shine,
Like pure silver, like red gold,
I want to make clean what is dull.

29. The idea is based on Arabic cognates to this hapax, where it refers to the fronds of a palm. So Pope, *Song of Songs*, 536; Murphy, *Song of Songs*, 166; Keel, *Song of Songs*, 199.

30. Based on Mishnaic Hebrew, where it means "hill upon hill." Bloch and Bloch, *Song of Songs*, 185; Snaith, *The Song of Songs*, NCB (Grand Rapids: Eerdmans, 1993), 80; Fox, *Ancient Egyptian Love Songs*, 147. Stephan, *Modern Palestinian Parallels*, 11, cites a modern Palestinian poem which describes the man's hair similarly: "His shock of hair is waving."

31. See Pope, *Song of Songs*, 536.

32. White, *Study of the Language*, 189.

33. Keel's suggestion of a demonic element (*Song of Songs*, 199) is perhaps Eurocentric in its inability to appreciate cultures in which shining black hair is considered desirable.

if so, should מִלֵּאת be translated as "full" and the reader to imagine doves sitting by (or over)[34] something brimming over, such as a pond?[35] Or should מִלֵּאת be translated in terms of craftsmanship, and if so, is this a picture of something superbly mounted, such as jewels (Exod 28:17)?[36]

Without straining the details, the picture that comes through is of eyes whose irises are set in a field of unblemished white, as white as doves—which themselves are so spotless that poetic license imagines them washed in milk. What is more, these are sparkling eyes, the sparkle suggested by the images of water streams and jewels. (Since the Hebrew for "springs/fountains" and "eyes" is the same [עֵינַיִם], the association is immediate.) Here are eyes lustrous with the twinkle of sunbeams gliding off water or light refracting through gemstones. And just as precious stones should be well set, these eyes are delicately framed by eyelashes, surely as jet black as his hair. These are eyes that sit well in a head of gold.

In every way, these are an exquisite pair of eyes, and a match for hers. He had also described hers as doves (יוֹנִים, 4:1) and as pools (עֵינַיִם, 7:4), ascribing to them spotless whiteness and gleam. Indeed, he begged that she should turn her eyes away for "they overwhelm" him (6:5). He even complained that she had "stolen his heart with one glance of your eyes (עֵינַיִךְ), with one jewel[37] (עֲנָק) of your necklace" (4:9). If jewels are intended in her *wasf* of the man, she deftly merges the images, making his eyes brilliant gems set in his golden head.

The next to be described is his face:

His cheeks	are like a bed of spices	towers of sweet-scented herbs.
לְחָיָו	כַּעֲרוּגַת הַבֹּשֶׂם	מִגְדְּלוֹת מֶרְקָחִים

His lips	are lilies	dripping with myrrh.
שִׂפְתוֹתָיו	שׁוֹשַׁנִּים	נֹטְפוֹת מוֹר עֹבֵר (5:13)

The man's face reminds his beloved of sweet-smelling, growing herbs—so much so that the reader wonders if the description is of a beard rather than of clean-shaven cheeks.[38] Beds and mounds (literally,

---

34. Keel has the doves sitting at the rim of a basin brimming with water, and in that sense "over" it. *Song of Songs*, 196, 199–20.

35. For example, ESV and JPS following the LXX: καθήμεναι ἐπὶ πληρώματα ὑδάτων.

36. As most English versions, e.g., KJV, NRSV, NIV, NASB, NAB, NET, NLT. Pope (*Song of Songs*, 239) thinks that the ancient practice of making a statue's eyes using jewel inlays supports this reading.

37. Or "bead" or "strand."

38. Duane Garrett, "Song of Songs," in *Song of Songs, Lamentations*, ed. Duane Garrett and

"towers") are shapes easily associated with the cheeks. Bloch and Bloch explain the hyperbole well: the woman thinks her beloved's cheeks are "beds of . . . no, towers of" fragrant spices.[39]

But continuing the garden simile to lily-like lips rather stretches the imagination. Rather than associate the lips with the curves of the petals, Exum offers a subtler connection. The woman had spoken of her beloved feeding among the lilies (2:16; 6:3), while both of them had referred to her as a lily (2:1–2; cf. 7:2). She reverses the image of the lily to this specific part of his body, his lips. Since toward the end of the poem she will comment on the sweetness of his mouth, this turns the image of feeding right around to make *her* the one who feeds on his lily-like parts[40]—a charming reciprocation of metaphors.

We notice that the poem has switched sensory stimuli. The head, hair, and eyes were largely visualized. The images for cheeks and lips are densely olfactory. The woman uses the sense of smell when describing cheeks, as if she has mentally closed the distance and rests her face against his, breathing in his fragrance. Dripping (נטף) lips evoke the tactile and perhaps even the gustatory, strengthened by the association between lilies and the idea of grazing among them. Scents and tastes, unlike the other senses, require taking into one's body something of the other's body and thus recall the sexual act.[41] In this, the woman's image is more intimate than that of the man's who says her lips are "like a scarlet ribbon" (4:3). The thoroughly visual image suggests distance between the viewer and the viewed. However, he does parallel her language in a line outside the *wasfs*, even deploying the same verb: "Your lips drip [נטף] sweetness as the honeycomb" (4:11).

Other than appeal to the senses, spices and myrrh reiterate the idea of value. Like gold, they are exotic, luxurious goods imported from distant lands and available for the use of the privileged. Bloch and Bloch remind that Hezekiah's spices were locked away in the royal treasuries or storehouses along with silver and gold and precious stones (2 Chr 32:27),[42] and Keel notes that myrrh "always connotes great value."[43] As the poem moves downward from the head and face, it pursues this idea of worth even more vigorously. The arms, torso, and legs—strictly,

Paul R. House, WBC 23B (Nashville: Thomas Nelson, 2004), 221; Pope, *Song of Songs*, 240; Longman, *Song of Songs*, 172; Snaith, *Song of Songs*, 81. Contra: Keel, *Song of Songs*, 201.

39. Bloch and Bloch, *Song of Songs*, 186.

40. Exum, *Song of Songs*, 206.

41. See Matthew Boersma, "Scent in Song: Exploring Scented Symbols in the Song of Songs," *Conversations with the Biblical World* 31 (2011): 80–94.

42. Bloch and Bloch, *Song of Songs*, 186.

43. Keel, *Song of Songs*, 202.

hands, belly, and thighs[44]—are described in rhythm, with triple correspondence between the descriptions:[45]

His arms	are rods of	gold	set	with topaz.
בַּתַּרְשִׁישׁ	מְמֻלָּאִים	זָהָב	גְּלִילֵי	יָדָיו

His body	is slabs of	ivory	decorated	with lapis lazuli.
סַפִּירִים	מְעֻלֶּפֶת	שֵׁן	עֶשֶׁת	מֵעָיו

His legs	are pillars of	marble	set	on bases of pure gold.	(5:14–15a)
עַל־אַדְנֵי־פָז	מְיֻסָּדִים	שֵׁשׁ	עַמּוּדֵי	שׁוֹקָיו	

In contrast with spice beds and lilies, which are yielding and even delicate, the materials in this section are hard: gold, gemstones, ivory, and marble or alabaster. While softness is desirable in the face, the ideal male body must be firm, solid to the touch. Alter agrees that one reason the "semantic field of artifact dominates" over the nature imagery is because "the celebration of the male body concentrates on the beautiful hardness of arms, thighs and loins."[46]

The body parts are described in terms of architecture. A Sumerian parallel has a woman saying something similar:

O my pure pillar, my pure pillar
Sweet are your charms!
Pillar of alabaster set in lapis lazuli
Sweet are your charms![47]

A modern Arabic love poem comes close with: "His arms (are) staffs of pure silver, / his fingers golden pencils."[48]

Architecture is a device the man uses in his praise poems when he

44. Exum, reading יָדַיִם as "hands," understands the glass-lustered topaz inlay as fingernails (*Song of Songs*, 207). We read יָדַיִם in their more general sense of arms rather than as hands. See Bloch and Bloch, *Song of Songs*, 186; Pope (*Song of Songs*, 542) quotes the Ugaritic describing King Keret's washing: "He washed his hands to the elbow / his fingers up to the shoulder."

Reading "arms" is in keeping with reading of מֵעֶה as "body" rather than "abdomen" or "loins," and שֹׁקַיִם as "legs" rather than "thighs" (cf. Ps 147:10; Prov 7:8; 26:7; Isa 47:2). Thus, the body is described in broad sweeps: arms, torso and abdomen, and legs.

45. The body part / a noun in the construct state / the precious substance / a participle / a second precious substance (Elliott, *Literary Unity*, 140).

46. Robert Alter, *The Art of Biblical Poetry* (New York: Basic Books, 2011), 246; Exum, *Song of Songs*, 21.

47. Exum, *Song of Songs*, 208.

48. Keel, *Song of Songs*, 24–25.

likens her neck or nose to a tower (2:4; 7:4). Her literary skills are more sophisticated. She uses rods, slabs, and pillars to construct a structure—not of a building but of a demi-god. He is merely reminded of architecture at the sight of her body parts: "Your neck is like an ivory tower" (7:4). She takes the idea to extravagant lengths: his arms are gold, his body ivory, and his legs marble. With the arms, the reader imagines the warm golden tan. For the torso, the word (עֶשֶׁת) in Mishnaic Hebrew refers to a "specific work of artistry" in which the material is brought to a smooth finish.[49] Here is a creamy white body "carefully polished" and "dully gleaming."[50] As for the legs, if שֵׁשׁ is to be identified as alabaster (rather than as marble), then it is the sculptor's material of choice to reproduce flesh tones.[51]

The body as precious material skillfully worked upon is a familiar metaphor in Sumerian royal love songs:

> O my lapis lazuli beard!
>   O my roped locks!
> My one with beard mottled
>   like a slab of lapis lazuli,
>   my one with locks arranged ropewise!
> You are my turban pin,
>   my gold I wear,
> my trinket fashioned
>   by a cunning craftsman,
> my trinket worked on
>   by a cunning craftsman![52]

Modern Palestinian love poetry has something similar: "He has a mouth (like) a gold ring, set with pearls."[53] In all these poems, the idea of the aesthetic is inextricable from the idea of priceless value. The gold is precious, as is the ivory. We are reminded that while the Temple was overlaid with gold, palaces used the exotic import commodity ivory.[54] An index of luxurious living, ivory enters prophetic warnings against decadence (1 Kgs 22:39; Ezek 7:6, 15; Amos 3:15; 6:4).

Further, both poems move beyond precious metals to gemstones. If

49. Fox, *Ancient Egyptian Love Songs*, 148–49.

50. Keel, *Song of Songs*, 204–5.

51. Hunt, *Poetry in the Song of Songs*, 274.

52. Exum, *Song of Songs*, 56.

53. Stephan, *Modern Palestinian Parallels*, 13. Similarly, a woman describes herself: "My breast is a marble slab . . . My thighs are marble pillars . . . My mouth is like King Solomon's signet" (Stephan, *Modern Palestinian Parallels*, 39–40).

54. 1 Kgs 10:18–22; 22:39; Amos 3:15; 6:4.

the best the man can do is to speak of jewelry that adorns the woman's ivory neck (4:4, 9), the woman simply encases the man's body parts with gems. The gold is *studded* (מְמֻלָּאִים) with topaz, the body is *decorated* (מְעֻלֶּפֶת) with lapis, and the legs are *anchored* (מְיֻסָּדִים) in gold. Each verb is lavish, indicating no shortage: the gold is simply encrusted[55] with topaz, as the ivory is smothered[56] with lapis, and the marble is solidly secured into gold.[57] Extravagance seems to be the point of the verbs.[58] Besides, the verbs are in passive participle form, melodic with the alliterating *m* and assonant with the *u*. The aural aesthetic flows over the visual beauty of the final noun in each sequence: the brilliance of topaz (or beryl or chrysolite) on gold arms creating highlights, the lovely blue of lapis (or sapphires) on ivory suggesting veining, the contrast of gold with the marble (or alabaster) of the legs.

The closest the man came to this lavish show of wealth and craftsmanship was his description of the woman's legs: "Your rounded thighs are like jewels, the work of an artist's hands" (7:1). His phrase "the work of" (מַעֲשֵׂה) is reciprocated and then completely overwhelmed by her verb triplet—studded, overlaid, anchored. The suggestion is sometimes made that the man is adorned with jewelry, especially that his hands are decorated with jeweled rings or his arms with armlets.[59] However, here the triple parallelism suggests that this may not be the case. In fact, it may even defeat the purpose the woman has in mind. It appears she is describing a man who is breathtaking in his natural beauty.

This is the section that elicits the criticism that the man has been converted into a piece of statuary. Assis, for example, complains that the woman's *waṣf* of the man is "frozen" and "static," and that its images are largely drawn from the inanimate—from metals and gemstones.[60] Jenson thinks this statue-like body is "impersonally describable."[61] Whedbee presents the description as bordering on the ludicrous: "the image of the man who appears bigger-than-life, standing somewhat awkwardly as a gargantuan, immobile, distant figure."[62] Clines thinks "there is some-

---

55. From the verb מלא which means "to be full."

56. Bloch and Bloch point to the use of the verb עלף in Gen 38:14 where it describes the action to "wrap up in" (*Song of Songs*, 187).

57. The image of marble legs secured in bases of gold is parallel to Sir 26:18, which describes the legs and feet of a woman: "Like golden pillars on silver bases, / so are shapely legs and steadfast feet." Silver does not seem to be valuable enough to make it into this *waṣf*.

58. Keel, *Song of Songs*, 205.

59. For example, Bergant, *Song of Songs*, 72; Keel, *Song of Songs*, 204. Contra Murphy, *Song of Songs*, 172.

60. Assis, *Flashes of Fire*, 170–71.

61. Jenson, *Song of Songs*, 56–57.

62. J. William Whedbee, "Paradox and Parody in the Song of Solomon: Towards a Comic

thing odd about it, and its significance remains a little elusive."[63] Three considerations counter this reading.

First, if the male beloved seems to us to appear "remote, sculptured and statuesque,"[64] it may be because the *wasf*'s language follows a trope from this part of the ancient world. The Sumerian poem "The Message of Ludingira to his Mother" is helpful here. The man describes his mother to a messenger so that he may recognize her and give her his message:

> My mother is brilliant in the heavens, a doe in the mountains,
> A morning star abroad at noon,
> Precious carnelian, a topaz from Marhashi,
> A prize for the king's daughter, full of charm,
> A nir-stone seal, an ornament like the sun,
> A bracelet of tin, a ring of antasura,
> A shining piece of gold and silver,
> . . .
> An alabaster statuette set on a lapis pedestal,
> A living rod of ivory, whose limbs are filled with charm.[65]

Geographically closer to Israel is a snippet from an Ugaritic text in which a maiden's beauty is extolled similarly: "The pupils (of whose eyes) are of pure lapis lazuli, / whose eyes are like alabaster bowls, / who is girded with ruby."[66] Similarly, Sirach 26:18 says of the virtuous woman: "Pillars of gold on a base of silver, so are beautiful legs on well-formed feet." The operative principle in this trope, as Fox explains it, seems to be "metaphoric distance" between the image and the referent. The incongruity ignites "psychological arousal" that releases "aesthetic pleasure." "Without significant metaphorical distance," the description would be reduced to the "banal."[67]

Second is the attention to the theme of priceless worth that runs through the *wasf*. A golden head has as its focal feature a pair of jewel-like eyes. The cheeks and lips smell of spices and myrrh. The arms, body, and legs are worth a king's ransom. With the same word for gold being

Reading of the Most Sublime Song," in *A Feminist Companion to the Song of Songs*, ed. Athalya Brenner, FCB (Sheffield: Sheffield Academic, 1993), 274.

63. David J. A. Clines, "Why Is There a Song of Songs and What Does It Do to You If You Read It?," in *Interested Parties: The Ideology of Writers and Readers of the Hebrew Bible*, ed. David J. A. Clines, JSOTSup 205 (Sheffield: Sheffield Academic, 1995), 120.

64. Kathryn Harding, "'I Sought Him but I Did Not Find Him': The Elusive Lover in the Song of Songs," *BibInt* 16 (2008): 56.

65. Jerrold S. Cooper, "New Cuneiform Parallels to the Song of Songs," *JBL* 90 (1971): 160.

66. Longman, *Song of Songs*, 53.

67. Michael V. Fox, "Love, Passion and Perception in Israelite and Egyptian Love Poetry," *JBL* 102, no. 2 (1983): 226, citing C. Martindale, *Romantic Progression* (New York: Hemisphere, 1975), 23–30, 119–29.

used for both his head and his feet, the man is made up of the most valuable materials obtainable, from head to toe. What is more, as we shall see in the next verse, his appearance in its entirety suggests a tree whose expensive wood adorns palaces—the cedar. Commenting on the parallels between this *wasf* and poems on cultic statuary, Keel rightly remarks, "The main interest in 5:15–16 is not the purity, the divinity, or the artistry of these materials but their value."[68] Black remarks, "He is an amalgamation of exotic goods brought from the world over, ivory, sapphires, jasper, alabaster, gold."[69] Fox points out the parallel to ancient Egyptian love poetry where one also sees stock tropes emphasizing the preciousness of the beloved using the language of things of value, for example, "Her hair [is] true lapis lazuli, / her arms surpass gold."[70] Fox agrees that these are general asseverations of preciousness.[71]

Third, there is in this section a subtle sensuality, restrained in its expression, which those who reduce it to a mass of metal seem to miss.[72] Soulen, for example, is persuaded that there is "a difference in erotic imagination between poet and poetess."[73] Others emphasize the influence of Egyptian pictorial art[74] or statuary craft[75] on the *wasf*. Gerleman concedes that "the expressive power of these images is associated to a very high degree with their derivation from an erotic content that is bound up with feeling," so much so that the images are to be "acknowledged as sensuous even when there is a minimum of reality expressed by them."[76]

Whether this imagery is indeed a "minimum of reality" is arguable. Black, for example, explains that though the body of the man is largely "static and hard," his face and head compensate: his hair suggests waving palm fronds; his cheeks are verdant spice beds; his lips are myrrh-dripping lilies; and his eyes are doves.[77]

Exum sees the hardness of the materials chosen to describe the torso

68. Keel, *Song of Songs*, 204.
69. Fiona C. Black, "Beauty or the Beast? The Grotesque Body in the Song of Songs," *BibInt* 8, no. 3 (2000): 316.
70. Pap. Chester Beatty, Group A: 31, translated in Fox, *Ancient Egyptian Love Songs*, 52.
71. Fox, "Love, Passion and Perception," 223.
72. Some hold that compared to the man's praise poems, the woman's lacks or underplays sensuality and desire: Assis, *Flashes of Fire*, 171; Athalya Brenner, "Come Back, Come Back the Shulammite," in *On Humour and the Comic in the Hebrew Bible*, ed. Y. T. Radday and Athalya Brenner (Sheffield: Almond, 1990), 251–76. Contra, e.g., Exum, *Song of Songs*, 21–22.
73. Soulen, "*Wasfs*," 184n6.
74. E.g., Watson, *Classical Hebrew Poetry*, 353–56.
75. E.g., Cooper, "New Cuneiform Parallels," 160; G. Gerleman, *Ruth, Das Hohelied*, BKAT 18 (Neukirchen-Vluyn: Neukirchener), 68–72.
76. Gerleman, *Ruth, Das Hohelied*, 177.
77. Black, "Beauty or the Beast?," 316.

and thighs as erotic, an appreciation of the feel of the man during inter-course.[78] In the same direction is the much-pondered question this sec-tion raises of whether the man is being described naked or clothed. The tantalizing answer is that the description hovers delicately between the two states. Does מֵעָיו, literally "his inward parts," make reference to something more private than the abdomen? If so, is Murphy right in rendering מֵעָיו עֶשֶׁת שֵׁן מְעֻלֶּפֶת סַפִּירִים as "his loins, a shaft of ivory, ensconced in lapis lazuli"?[79] And considering ivory is readily associated with the tusk, could this be taken as a veiled allusion to the male organ[80] "on the grounds that somewhere in the Song there must be mention of an item so necessary for the couple's lovemaking"?[81] As much as any of the Song's *wasf*s for the female beloved, this one could "force a readerly encounter with the body, itemized for erotic consumption."[82]

At any rate, it can be vigorously refuted that this section is coldly life-less. If anything, the images are carefully designed to reflect a real, living human. Garrett may have a point when he notices that gold describes the head, arms, and feet, while ivory and marble describe the torso and legs, suggesting that the more exposed parts of the body are tanned golden—his arms even have topaz highlights!—while the parts usually covered by clothing are paler.[83] So careful is the detailing that the ivory of the torso throbs with veins of lapis. Each substance declares the rela-tional value of this man to the woman. This is the sentiment that contin-ues into the final lines:

His appearance | is like Lebanon,

מַרְאֵהוּ | כַּלְּבָנוֹן

choice | as cedars.

בָּחוּר | כָּאֲרָזִים (5:15)

His mouth [חִכּוֹ] is sweetness itself [מַמְתַקִּים];

He is altogether lovely [וְכֻלּוֹ מַחֲמַדִּים].

This is my beloved [זֶה דוֹדִי], this is my friend [וְזֶה רֵעִי], daughters of Jerusalem.

78. Exum, *Song of Songs*, 207.

79. Murphy, *Song of Songs*, 75n305.

80. Keel, *Song of Songs*, 204–5; Garrett, "Song of Songs," 223–24; Longman, *Song of Songs*, 173; Michael D. Goulder, *The Song of Fourteen Songs*, JSOTSup 36 (Sheffield: JSOT Press, 1986), 6.

81. Jenson, *Song of Songs*, 56.

82. Black, "Beauty or the Beast?" 307.

83. Garrett, "Song of Songs," 223.

One look at him inspires the thought of Lebanon, a word that at once invokes not just the towering mountains but its stately cedars, incomparable for their majestic girth and height.[84] The picture may at first suggest a sense of distance, as if the man is being viewed at long range. But any separation between viewer and viewed is simultaneously compensated by the olfactory stimulus at the mention of Lebanon's choice cedars, for the cedar is an aromatic wood. Suddenly one can smell the man's natural fragrance—he is up close and personal.

Why does the *wasf*, having travelled from head to foot, finish with the mouth? Perhaps here is a mouth so sweet in its kisses that the woman's thoughts return to it one last time before she signs off the poem. Having described him in such detail, it is "as though she cannot resist kissing him,"[85] because his mouth is the "most sensuous part" of his body.[86] On the other hand, the mouth could carry associations with not only the gustatory but also the aural.[87] Since, strictly, it is his "palate" or organ of speech mentioned here (cf. Job 31:30; Prov 8:7), the text could also be completing the picture of the man by matching his entrancing appearance to a personality just as captivating. Jenson follows the Targum's "the words of his palate" to press "a wholly different kind of desirability" since returning to a mouth that kisses would "wreck the physical inventory's otherwise painstaking order." Here is one whose "words delight his enraptured hearer." Matching his perfect body, he is the perfect companion.[88] If the man's description of the woman's mouth is read similarly with both senses in mind (4:11), here is yet another reciprocation between the two.

In summary, we stand back and spot an *inclusio* between the opening and closing section (other than 5:10b with 5:16b, mentioned earlier).

---

84. In Sumerian poetry, the king was described as "a good shade [for the land] like a cedar" (Samuel Noah Kramer, *The Sacred Marriage Rite: Aspects of Faith, Myth and Ritual in Ancient Sumer* [Bloomington: Indiana University Press, 1969], 43). In modern Palestinian love songs, a "man of fine stature is likened to a palm tree" (Stephan, *Modern Palestinian Parallels*, 23). Also, other trees can be pressed into service: "O you, whose height is that of the teak and the tile tree" (Stephan, *Modern Palestinian Parallels*, 77).

85. Elizabeth Huwiler, "Song of Songs," in Roland E. Murphy and Elizabeth Huwiler, *Proverbs, Ecclesiastes and Song of Songs*, NIBC (Peabody, MA: Hendrickson, 1999), 276.

86. Hess, *Song of Songs*, 170.

87. Bergant, *Song of Songs*, 72–73; Bloch and Bloch, *Song of Songs*, 188; Daniel J. Estes, "The Song of Songs," in *Ecclesiastes and the Song of Songs*, ed. Daniel C. Fredericks and Daniel J. Estes, AOTC 16 (Downers Grove, IL: InterVarsity, 2010), 376; Exum, *Song of Songs*, 209; Fox, *Ancient Egyptian Love Songs*, 149; Elliott, *Literary Unity*, 141.

88. Jenson, *Song of Songs*, 57.

5:10a	A	My beloved is radiant and ruddy
5:10b	B	Conspicuous among ten thousand
5:15b	B'	His appearance is like Lebanon
5:16b	A'	He is altogether lovely

That he is radiantly ruddy matches his being "altogether lovely." His "appearance" (רֹאֶה) loops back to his conspicuity among myriads (דָּגוּל).[89] The first impression the woman gave the daughters of Jerusalem was that of a dazzling youth at the prime of his life. The closing affirmation, coming at the end of a listing of his attractions, is that he is "altogether lovely" with not a blemish to mar his perfection. This is an exact match to what he thinks of her: "You are altogether beautiful, my darling; there is no flaw in you" (כֻּלָּךְ יָפָה רַעְיָתִי וּמוּם אֵין בָּךְ, 4:7). Pope renders the woman's summarizing compliment as "He is utterly desirable (כֻּלּוֹ מַחֲמַדִּים)."[90] If this is the emphasis, then the memory of the mouth could infuse this statement with sensuality: "His mouth is sweetness itself; he is utterly desirable" (5:16).

The woman presents this paragon of manly beauty, so utterly desirable, to her audience with the words "This is my friend/darling (רֵעִי)." The woman uses the same word—darling—that the man uses for her at other points in the Song, so much so that it can be said to be his favorite endearment for her.[91] By using the masculine counterpart, the poem emphasizes once more the reciprocity between these two. They even talk about each other with matching vocabulary.

While we have shown how this *wasf* well matches, and sometimes even outdoes, the man's poems in praise of the woman, there is an obvious difference to consider. All three of the man's poems are direct addresses to the woman. Each begins with an exclamation: "How beautiful you are, my darling!" (4:1); "You are as beautiful as Tirzah, my darling" (6:4); "How beautiful your sandaled feet, O prince's daughter!" (7:1). The man speaks impulsively, his words articulating what his eyes see as his gaze moves either upward or downward over her body.

The woman's poem of praise, however, is addressed to a third party. It is a construction of him from memory, and for that reason is even more remarkable for its passion—every bit as spontaneous and real as if he stood before her eyes in flesh and blood. She can remember details—the

---

89. Similarly, Exum, *Song of Songs*, 209, also recalls that the beloved was as singular as an apple tree among the forest trees (2:3).

90. Pope, *Song of Songs*, 549.

91. Hess, *Song of Songs*, 188.

waves in his hair, the sparkle in his eyes, the fragrance of his cheeks, the flecks of blue on his belly. Considering that she describes him to an interested audience, she manages the images with skill. Uncontrolled, the poem could strip the dignity of the described, laying him bare to the voyeuristic gaze of a clutch of curious women. Overly controlled, the poem could harden into a functional description, bland and bereft of feeling.

The trick by which the woman makes the man simultaneously available for public consumption and yet restricted within the circle of exclusive love is that she carefully frames the poem with the phrase "my beloved." All that is said in the interim is contained and referenced by her possession of him. All this beauty is hers alone.

THE EFFECT OF THE PRAISE POEM

If the man is perfect, the *wasf* that describes him is almost perfect in itself. Far from being a bloodless construction of metal and stone, the poem is a delightful concoction. There are enough textures to stimulate the sense of touch: from feather-soft doves to rough, springy herbs to highly finished, unyielding marble or ivory. There is a balance between the delicateness of lilies and the strength of cedars. For contrast we have the milk-white dove against the pitch-black raven, and the clear, creamy tones of ivory against the mottled blue of lapis lazuli. There is contrast too between the hard, straight lines evoked by rods, pillars, and slabs, held against the curves of wavy hair and pool-like eyes. Some images are of the fixed and static. Such are the legs that end solidly in their bases. Some images evoke movement. Such are the herbs, the lilies, and the cedars moving with the wind; the flowing water streams; the milk splashing and scattering as doves bathe in it; the myrrh dripping. Every sensory stimulus is present. The man shimmers in his aura of radiance. If you touched him it would be muscle as hard and smooth as polished ivory. Step up close and you can drink in his fragrance. Come even closer, and his mouth is delectable. Or if it is conversation that is meant, the ear thrills to the sound of his words. "The peculiar heaping of sensual splendors . . . does not present the verisimilar, but by means of the entire group, the poet suggests the superlative."[92]

The ears of the daughters of Jerusalem are certainly tickled by the description, for it moves them to offer their services in the search for the missing beloved. And why not, one would ask! The woman has made

92. Daniel Grossberg, *Centripetal and Centrifugal Structures in Biblical Poetry* (Atlanta: Scholars, 1989), 65.

a vigorous and matching rejoinder to the question that prompted their *wasf*:

How is your *beloved*	this is my *beloved*
more than any other *beloved*	and this is my *darling*
most beautiful of women?	daughters of Jerusalem[93]

The poem accomplishes what it set out to do. It exalts the woman's beloved in the eyes of a third party simply by showing him off. More than that, it does what Soulen suggests: "the imagery of the *wasf* [is] a means of arousing emotions consonant with those experienced by the . . . maiden as she speaks of her beloved" in order that the audience can "share [her] joy, awe and delight."[94] Within the text, this audience is the daughters of Jerusalem; outside of it, it is readers down the ages.

One significant literary device that helps to create the larger-than-life beauty of the beloved is the trope of "royal fiction," a distinctive theme in Egyptian love poetry.[95] In the Song, too, the lovers play "king and queen." She is, in his eyes, a "prince's daughter" (7:1), or even better than one. Not even a harem full of "sixty queens . . . eighty concubines, and virgins beyond number" can compare with her. So "perfect" and "unique" is she that even these royal women praise her (6:8–9).

The woman expends even more persistence in investing her beloved with a royal persona. Her opening words make him out to be a king bringing her "into his chambers" (1:4) where they repose at a royal banquet, he "resting between [her] breasts" (1:12–13; cf. 2:4). The longer conceit is her description of the man's approach in 3:6–11. His arrival is heralded with a "column of smoke," perhaps a reference to the clouds of myrrh and incense preceding him. He is Solomon himself, travelling in grand state. An elite convoy of sixty of Israel's noblest warriors accompanies him. His palanquin is custom designed, made of fragrant, expensive cedar with a gold platform and silver carrying-poles. He himself is in magnificent royal array, crowned. It is a sight for the city to come out to see.

---

93. Assis, *Flashes of Fire*, 165.

94. Soulen, "*Wasfs*," 189–90.

95. See White, *Study of the Language*, 110–11. An example is the woman's self-description as she nears the trysting place, in which she uses the royal title: "My face faces the cottage; / my arms are filled with persea (branches); / my hair is heavy with resin. / I am like the Lady of the Two Lands. / I am with you" (pap. Harris 500, Group A: 8 translated in White, *Study of the Language*, 151). Stephan, *Modern Palestinian Parallels*, 8, observes that in some parts of modern-day northern Mesopotamia, the bridegroom is *sultan* for the period of the wedding feast, and acts as such.

This Solomonic metaphor appears to make up the bones of the praise poem. Gold was literally a part of the golden age of Solomon. His ships brought back fabulous quantities of this prized metal once every three years (1 Kgs 9:28; 10:11, 22). Gold lavishly adorned the Temple and its furnishings (1 Kgs 7; cf. 1 Chr 29:4), decorated the royal palace, and even made its household articles. Precious stones and exotic woods also made their way to Jerusalem from Ophir, brought in great cargo loads (1 Kgs 10:11). Ivory was another import that added to the legend. While later Israelite royalty could employ ivory only in decorative inlays (1 Kgs 22:39), Solomon sat on a throne made of solid ivory of which it could be said that "nothing like it had ever been made for any other kingdom" (1 Kgs 10:18–20). As for cedar from neighboring Phoenicia, Solomon's palaces, both those for administrative and for personal uses, were from no other wood. One of them took its very name from the cedar of which it was built: the Palace of the Forest of Lebanon (1 Kgs 7:1–11). Indeed, in his day, "cedar" became "as plentiful as sycamore-fig trees in the foothills" (1 Kgs 10:27). When royalty such as the queen of Sheba came on a state visit, Solomon was brought not only more gold and precious stones but also spices in a "very great caravan" (1 Kgs 10:2).

Gold and precious stones, ivory and spices, and choice cedar—these are the materials that construct the one who stands out among a myriad, much like Solomon did among his royal contemporaries. Worthy of note is that in the five instances where gold is mentioned in the Song, four times it is associated with the man (3:10; 5:11, 14, 15), and only once with the woman, and even here, as a gift from him to her: "We will make you earrings of gold" (1:11). If there is no mention of silver in the praise poem, perhaps its absence is also in reflection of the legend, for "silver was considered of little value in Solomon's days," and even "as common in Jerusalem as stones" (1 Kgs 10:21, 27). "Whenever the poet alludes to queens and concubines, horses and chariots, the cedars of Lebanon, gold, ivory, and spices, the reader is imaginatively invited into King Solomon's court . . . the Song lingers appreciatively over that world of opulence."[96]

Solomon may not be the only royal evoked by this praise poem. The man's complexion is ruddy, a distinctive of the youthful David (אַדְמוֹנִי; 1 Sam 16:12). What is more, like David, this one too stands out among tens of thousands (רְבָבָה; 1 Sam 18:7). There are faint echoes of other royals, each at one time the darling of the masses, whose stature and appearance put them above all others. He is like Saul who stood head and shoulders over the rest, and of whom it could be said, "There is no one like him among all the people" (1 Sam 10:23–24). And he is

---

96. Bloch and Bloch, "Introduction," *Song of Songs*, 10–11.

like Absalom of the enviable hair and the handsome looks of whom it was said, "From the top of his head to the sole of his foot there was no blemish in him" (2 Sam 14:25). There is also significantly high sharing of vocabulary with a post-exilic description of the glory days of Judah. This is literally the golden age, described in terms common to the *wasf*—gold (זָהָב) and fine gold (כֶּתֶם and פָּז) (Lam 4:1–2); its royalty boasted of "princes [who] were brighter than snow and whiter than milk, their bodies more ruddy than rubies, their appearance like lapis lazuli (Lam 4:7)."[97]

What the royal fiction achieves for the *wasf* is a transfiguration by love. And, by this vaulting over from the real into the surreal, the poem as a whole effectively communicates the relational value the woman places on her beloved.

THE FUNCTION OF THE PRAISE POEM

What is the function of the poem within the immediate narrative context? Presented with a picture of this exquisite creature, the daughters of Jerusalem set out a second question, constructed in the same repetitive, undulating rhythm as their first:[98]

Where has he gone [אָנָה הָלַךְ]   your beloved? [דּוֹדֵךְ] . . .

Where has he turned aside [אָנָה פָּנָה]   your beloved? [דּוֹדֵךְ] (6:1)

Perhaps there is irony in asking why one so beloved should be missing,[99] or even outright mockery:[100] does such a one even exist? On the contrary, it is possible that the women are completely bowled over and wish to join the search. As Gledhill puts it, they are "convinced that this paragon of masculine beauty, this almost god-like figure, is worth finding, and they want to catch a glimpse of him."[101] Can the woman point them in the direction she thinks he may have gone? Her answer surprises us:

97. Barbiero, *Song of Songs*, 285–86.

98. Exum, *Song of Songs*, 202; Bergant, *Song of Songs*, 73.

99. Bergant, *Song of Songs*, 73–74; Barbiero, *Song of Songs,* 307; Andre LaCocque, *Romance She Wrote: A Hermeneutical Essay on Song of Songs* (Harrisburg: Trinity, 1998), 127.

100. Assis, *Flashes of Fire*, 178–79; LaCocque, *Romance She Wrote*, 127.

101. Gledhill, *Message of the Song of Songs*, 185. So also Fox, *Ancient Egyptian Love Songs*, 149; Murphy, *Song of Songs*, 173; Longman, *Song of Songs*, 175.

My beloved has gone down to his garden,
to the beds of spices,
to browse in the gardens[102] and to gather lilies. (6:2)

In the Song, the garden is the locale of intimacy (4:12, 15, 16; 5:1), just as much as spice beds are a reference to sexual pleasure (4:16; 5:1; 8:14). The woman, by her circumlocutory answer, tells the daughters of Jerusalem that she is calling off the search because she has found her beloved. Perhaps the man was playing hide-and-seek, as the two are wont to do, and reappears at this point.[103] Less likely is the proposal that the man was never absent, and the woman realizes this only at this point.[104] Just as improbable is that the woman detects mockery in the questions being asked, and defends the relationship with a reference to past intimacies and with a final assertion.[105]

A more satisfying possibility is that of "finding-by-praise."[106] Fox explains it like this: "It is as if the woman's praise brings about his presence: he is absent, she describes him, and he is immediately at her side."[107] Part of the Song's poetics is the constant "temporal slippage," as Exum calls it, a blurring of the boundaries between anticipation and experience.[108] Perhaps the woman's answer belongs within the range of this literary device, in which losing and finding coalesce. And in this the chorus helps her, first by asking a question that requires her to describe the man, and then by asking a second question that gives her the opportunity to discover she has found him. Now she celebrates her finding with a declaration of mutual belonging that is familiar to us:

---

102. Francis Landy notes the tension between the singular and the plural "garden/gardens" (גַּן/גַּנִּים) (*Paradoxes of Paradise: Identity and Difference in the Song of Songs*, 2nd ed. [Sheffield: Phoenix, 2011], 192–93). It is largely taken as a plural of generalization (Joüon and Muraoka, *A Grammar of Biblical Hebrew*, § 136j). Barbiero proposes a "plural of love" (*Song of Songs*, 311–12). Iain Provan, *Ecclesiastes, Song of Songs*, NIVAC (Grand Rapids: Zondervan, 2001), 337, suggests it is the various parts of the woman.

103. Longman, *Song of Songs*, 175.

104. Murphy, *Song of Songs*, 173; Elliott, *Literary Unity*, 144–46; Hess, *Song of Songs*, 190; Longman, *Song of Songs*, 175. Keel calls it a "delightful confusion"; *Song of Songs*, 209. D. Philip Roberts, *Let Me See Your Form: Seeking Poetic Structure in the Song of Songs* (Lanham, MD: University Press of America, 2007), 223–25; Barbiero, *Song of Songs*, 314; Provan, *Ecclesiastes, Song of Songs*, 337.

105. Assis, *Flashes of Fire*, 177–84.

106. Exum, *Song of Songs*, 188, 210. She attributes it to Albert Cook, *The Root of the Thing: A Study of Job and the Song of Songs* (Bloomington: Indiana University Press, 1968), 134. Similarly, Clines, "Why Is There a Song," 104; Harding, "I Sought Him," 58.

107. Fox, *Ancient Egyptian Love Songs*, 143.

108. Exum, *Song of Songs*, 11.

I am my beloved's and my beloved is mine,
he browses among the lilies. (6:3)

The first line is reversed from when we heard it last in 2:16: "My beloved is mine and I am his." Perhaps the reversal is chiastic, with the chiasm framing the two episodes of the woman's seeking (2:16; 6:3).[109] At any rate, the woman's paean of praise conjures him up, and she is blissfully reunited with her lost one. Exum puts it well: "As if in response to articulated desire, the lover materializes, brought into being—by poetic imagination."[110] Finding is the narrative function the *wasf* fulfills.

CONCLUSION

In a world in which men own the gaze and woman are the gazed at, this *wasf* is not simply unusual but astonishing.[111] Not only does the woman do the looking, but her eyes become the windows at which a group of other women settle down, first out of curiosity and then increasingly out of incredulity at what they see. Indeed, we are just as incredulous at the image the woman conjures up.

The fantastic nature of the image relates to the literary context of the poem. The setting is one of desperation in loss. As we mapped out, the *wasf* is the centerpiece of a conversation on that loss. This being the case, it is only reasonable to expect that the poem's thrust will be the value of the object lost, and thus the enormity of the loss.

Where the poem exceeds the expected is that while performing a function demanded by the narrative, it masterfully conveys the relational. There is in each item described a giveaway of the woman's experience of this item, be it fragrant cheeks or hard thighs or delicious mouth. Whether the woman intends it or not, there are memories of sensuous encounters, glimpses of past pleasures. It is an unselfconscious sensuality, one that instead of making an exhibition of itself, seals the woman's claim to the object lost. When the praise poem ends, the woman has shown off her prized possession and, to everyone's surprise, found him. It is as if her recollection of the past (and precious!) delights of ownership recovers him in the present.

109. Exum, *Song of Songs*, 188.
110. Exum, *Song of Songs*, 7.
111. Athalya Brenner, *The Intercourse of Knowledge: On Gendering Desire and 'Sexuality' in the Hebrew Bible* (Leiden: Brill, 1997), 39–43, 168–70.

5.

The Foundling

A commonplace in love songs is the male admiring his beloved. The Song stocks up nicely in this department, ensuring it has three *wasf*s in praise of the woman's assets. Where in the canon may we find a similar composition? Ezekiel 16:3–22 is a possible candidate.

In Song 5, the woman loses and finds her beloved. In Ezekiel 16, a man tells the story of a woman he found and then lost. In the Song, the woman describes her beloved to the reader piece by piece. Ezekiel 16 is not a *wasf*. It does not make up a descriptive list. However, its narrative has a readily identified body bias. Common to the two texts is the beauty of the loved one reconstructed through the memory of the one who loves.

We must start the Ezekiel story, however, at its shocking beginning in 16:3–5.

BIRTH: EZEKIEL 16:3–5

Your ancestry and birth were in the land of the Canaanites; your father was an Amorite and your mother a Hittite.

מְכֹרֹתַיִךְ וּמֹלְדֹתַיִךְ מֵאֶרֶץ הַכְּנַעֲנִי אָבִיךְ הָאֱמֹרִי וְאִמֵּךְ חִתִּית

On the day you were born your cord was not cut, nor were you washed with water to make you clean, nor were you rubbed with salt or wrapped in cloths.

וּמוֹלְדוֹתַיִךְ בְּיוֹם הוּלֶּדֶת אֹתָךְ לֹא־כָרַּת שָׁרֵּךְ וּבְמַיִם לֹא־רֻחַצְתְּ לְמִשְׁעִי וְהָמְלֵחַ לֹא הֻמְלַחַתְּ וְהָחְתֵּל לֹא חֻתָּלְתְּ

No one looked at you with pity or had compassion enough to do any of these things for you.

לֹא־חָסָה עָלַיִךְ עַיִן לַעֲשׂוֹת לָךְ אַחַת מֵאֵלֶּה לְחֻמְלָה עָלָיִךְ

Rather, you were thrown out into the open field, for on the day you were born you were despised.

(16:3–5) וַתֻּשְׁלְכִי אֶל־פְּנֵי הַשָּׂדֶה בְּגֹעַל נַפְשֵׁךְ בְּיוֹם הֻלֶּדֶת אֹתָךְ

The person in the story is introduced first by ancestry and then by the events of the day of her birth. Neither are promising. She is a product of the land of the Canaanites, with Amorite and Hittite bloodlines.[1] Read from an Israelite point of view, this ancestry is enough to damn her. Nothing good can come of such ethnic stock. But well before she can grow up to demonstrate her bad blood and deserve contempt, she receives it at the very moment of her birth. If pedigree is against her, those who receive her into the world are even more so.

A series of four negatives (לֹא) lists what was not done for this child at birth. Her umbilical cord is not properly cut; she is not washed, not rubbed with salt, not swaddled. None of these are indicative of extraordinary care. Rather, they are the most basic actions performed for any newborn. The first two are universally practiced. Massaging with saline is common in Arab households, perhaps to clean, dry, and toughen the baby's skin, or as an apotropaic action, or as an antibacterial agent to maintain hygiene. The swaddling may have been to promote the development of straight limbs.[2]

Why were these caring acts not performed? A fifth and final negative (לֹא) sums up the situation. In the family and community into which she

1. Indeed, Jerusalem's Canaanite origins predate its Israelite history by at least half a millennium. Strictly speaking, it was a Jebusite city rather than Amorite or Hittite. However, these two were among the most significant ethnic groups in pre-conquest Canaan. In adopting their practices, Israel had made herself their progeny. Daniel I. Block, *The Book of Ezekiel: Chapters 1–24*, NICOT (Grand Rapids: Eerdmans, 1997), 474–75; Walther Eichrodt, *Ezekiel*, trans. Cosslett Quin, OTL (London: SCM, 1970), 204; Moshe Greenberg, *Ezekiel 1–20: A New Translation with Introduction and Commentary*, AB 22 (Garden City, NY: Doubleday, 1983), 274; John W. Wevers, ed., *Ezekiel*, NCB (London: Thomas Nelson, 1969), 120; Walther Zimmerli, *Ezekiel 1: A Commentary on the Book of the Prophet Ezekiel Chapters 1–24*, trans. Ronald E. Clements, Hermeneia (Philadelphia: Fortress Press, 1979), 337–38.

2. Block, *Ezekiel 1–24*, 475. For the four actions, see J. Morgenstern, *Rites of Birth, Marriage, Death, and Kindred Occasions among the Semites* (Cincinnati: Hebrew Union College Press, 1966), 8–9; R. Patai, *Family, Love and the Bible* (Garden City, NY: Doubleday, 1960), 168–70. See Greenberg, who explains that Talmudic rabbis permitted these procedures on newborn infants even in violation of the Sabbath (*Ezekiel 1–20*, 274). C. F. Keil, *Ezekiel, Daniel*, trans. James Martin and M. G. Easton, Commentary on the Old Testament 9 (Peabody, MA: Hendrickson, 1996), 113–14; Zimmerli, *Ezekiel 1–24*, 338–39; William H. Brownlee, *Ezekiel 1–19*, WBC 28 (Waco, TX: Word, 1986), 223.

is born, not an eye looks on her with pity or compassion. Not one pair of eyes—not even her mother's—cares. Rather, she is detested at birth. For no reason other than the fact of her existence, the baby is found loathsome. So repugnant is she that she is literally ejected from womb to wasteland, snarled in umbilical cord and placenta, covered in her birth fluid and her mother's blood. This is the only action performed upon her, to be flung out (שלך) instantly into the field,[3] where she would not have lasted more than a few hours. Rather than inhabit the security of a home, she lies exposed in the open. Rather than be lovingly owned, she is the property of no one. The account begins by associating her ominously with a land (אֶרֶץ) known for its atrocities; but even this does not prepare the reader for her gruesome location on a field (שָׂדֶה) mere moments after birth.

There could be no greater contrast between the opening lines of this story and those of the *wasf* in Song 5. The man is the object of adoration just as much as this newborn is the object of contempt. He is a specimen of manhood at its most desirable—glowing with beauty, ruddy (אָדוֹם) of complexion. Her condition is utterly wretched—any "redness" is only gobs of blood congealing on her filthy, unwashed little body. Whereas he is the paradigm of well-being, there is every indication that she will die. He is conspicuous (דָּגוּל) even in a multitude. No eye (עַיִן) so much as glances at her. Indeed, he is beloved while she is found repulsive. Rather than receive endearments, she receives every sign of intentional neglect. He is the proud possession of one who calls him hers (*my beloved*). Out in the field, she belongs to none.

FINDING: EZEKIEL 16:6–8

Then I passed by and saw you kicking about in your blood, and as you lay there in your blood I said to you, "Live!" (and as you lay there in your blood I said to you, "Live!")[4]

וָאֶעֱבֹר עָלַיִךְ וָאֶרְאֵךְ מִתְבּוֹסֶסֶת בְּדָמָיִךְ וָאֹמַר לָךְ בְּדָמַיִךְ חֲיִי

---

3. Cogan argues the hiphil form (השׁליך) can be a legal-technical term for the common ancient practice of exposing children; other examples are Ishmael (Gen 21:15); Joseph (Gen 37:22, 24); Pharaoh's command concerning Hebrew male infants (Exod 1:22); and Jeremiah (Jer 38:3) (Mordechai Cogan, "A Technical Term for Exposure," *JNES* 27 [1968]: 133–35).

4. On the possible dittography here, see Zimmerli, *Ezekiel 1–24*, 323–34. The translation depends on where the division is made for וָאֹמַר לָךְ בְּדָמַיִךְ חֲיִי giving either: "I said to thee, 'In thy blood, live;" or "I said to thee in thy blood, 'Live.'" E.g., Keil prefers the latter: "Although lying in thy blood, in which thou wouldst inevitably bleed to death, thou shalt live." *Ezekiel*, 115. Wevers prefers the former, suggesting that the phrase to "live in blood" means to live in health, and sees here a clever wordplay. *Ezekiel*, 121n6.

I made you grow like a plant of the field.

רְבָבָה כְּצֶמַח הַשָּׂדֶה נְתַתִּיךְ

You grew and developed and entered puberty.

וַתִּרְבִּי וַתִּגְדְּלִי וַתָּבֹאִי בַּעֲדִי עֲדָיִים

Your breasts had formed and your hair had grown, yet you were stark naked.

(16:6–7)   שָׁדַיִם נָכֹנוּ וּשְׂעָרֵךְ צִמֵּחַ וְאַתְּ עֵרֹם וְעֶרְיָה

At this point the narrator enters the story. He is the chance passerby. The baby's wails surely caught his attention before the sight of her did, but it is the latter that arrests him mid-stride. There lies an infant, flailing in her blood. So gory must be the sight that the text morbidly repeats the observation that the baby lies "in [her] blood." The man wills the infant to live.

From this point on, the man assumes responsibility for the infant.[5] Explaining instances of infant exposure and adoption in ancient West Asia, Malul gives the example of a legal case. It proceeds in two stages. The mother first relinquishes her right to her son by exposing him in a no-man's land. Such an infant would technically be one "who has neither father nor mother."[6] From here, the adopter may pick him up to be his own, free of any legal encumbrances. What is more, the infant becomes incontestably the adopter's if the infant has been exposed without any postnatal care, since the latter would suggest that the biological parents wished to keep him. Washing, cleansing, and clothing would legitimate the baby. Thus: "If a man has taken in adoption an infant still (bathed in) his amniotic fluid and raised him up, that adopted child shall not be (re)claimed!"[7]

There appear to be echoes of this legal procedure in the story of Ezekiel 16. The man wills her to live, and she responds vigorously to his interest in her. Instead of succumbing to that wasteland, she takes root and flourishes like "plant of the field." Her growth is described with the word רְבָבָה, which usually means "myriad" or "multitude." Here it

---

5. Julie Galambush, for example, argues that there is no adoption indicated here since there is no mention of the infant being reared or cared for in any way (*Jerusalem in the Book of Ezekiel: City as Yahweh's Wife*, SBLDS 130 [Atlanta: Scholars, 1992], 94n16).

6. Meir Malul, "Adoption of Foundlings in the Bible and Mesopotamian Documents: A Study of Legal Metaphors in Ezekiel 16:1–7," *JSOT* 46 (1990): 100–106. See a dissenting review of Malul in S. Tamar Kamionkowski, "'In Your Blood, Live' (Ezekiel 16:6): A Reconsideration of Meir Malul's Adoption Formula," in *Bringing the Hidden to Light: Studies in Honor of Stephen A. Geller*, ed. Kathryn F. Kravitz and Diane M. Sharon (Winona Lake, IN: Eisenbrauns, 2007), 103–13.

7. Malul, "Adoption of Foundlings," 106–10.

uniquely functions to mean "great" and suggests "development" (rather than multiplication):[8] "I caused you to flourish."[9]

Before long, she is showing all the signs of pubescence. The circumlocutory phrase describing this attainment of womanhood is literally "you came into (or, became) the ornament of ornaments."[10] Though figurative, the phrase "most beautiful of jewels" evokes in its context a body flowering into maidenhood, stirring the beholder to admiration. The offensive sight of an infant weltering in discharge is displaced by the eye-pleasing aesthetic of female nubility. Yet she remains "stark naked." The correspondence between phrases indicates the danger of this:

you grew	your breasts had formed
וַתִּרְבִּי	שָׁדַיִם נָכֹנוּ
and developed	and your hair had grown
וַתִּגְדְּלִי	וּשְׂעָרֵךְ צִמֵּחַ
and entered puberty	yet you were stark naked.

וְאַתְּ עֵרֹם וְעֶרְיָה   וַתָּבֹאִי בַּעֲדִי עֲדָיִים

As a girl who has reached puberty and is utterly uncovered, she stands in even greater danger now than she did at birth. She can suffer the proverbial "fate worse than death." A man must take her under his protection so that she is protected from unwelcome attention. This is a reminder that she is still outside society, very much a wild plant.

> (Later) I passed by, and when I looked at you and saw that you were old enough for love, I spread the corner of my garment over you and covered your naked body.
>
> וָאֶעֱבֹר עָלַיִךְ וָאֶרְאֵךְ וְהִנֵּה עִתֵּךְ עֵת דֹּדִים וָאֶפְרֹשׂ כְּנָפִי עָלַיִךְ וָאֲכַסֶּה עֶרְוָתֵךְ
>
> I gave you my solemn oath and entered into a covenant with you . . . and you became mine.
>
> (16:8) וָאֶשָּׁבַע לָךְ וָאָבוֹא בִבְרִית אֹתָךְ . . . וַתִּהְיִי לִי

When next the man passes her way, his gaze is arrested yet again. With his interjection, "look!" (הִנֵּה), we see what his eyes see. The foundling is sexually ripe—the vocabulary used is specifically sexual in reference

---

8. Block, *Ezekiel 1–24*, 481: Greenberg, *Ezekiel 1–20*, 276.

9. Paul M. Joyce, *Ezekiel: A Commentary*, LHBOTS 482 (London: T&T Clark, 2007), 131.

10. See Zimmerli, *Ezekiel 1–24*, 324.

(דּוֹדִים; e.g., Song 4:10; 7:13). She is in even greater need of protection than before.

For the second time the man speaks to the foundling, and as before, he does so to address her critical need. This time he speaks an oath of marriage.[11] Once again, the power of his words moves the addressee from one realm into the next. Before, she had moved from death to life. Now she is relocated from outside society into its mainstream. The rite of passage is marriage.[12] A man covers her with the corner of his garment and speaks the formal words of matrimony. Her condition of being an outcast (literally!) is reversed. One who belonged to none is now someone's: "you became mine."

THE RISE: EZEKIEL 16:9–14

For the birth procedures denied her, she is compensated by nuptial procedures. She had not been washed with water (וּבְמַיִם); now he washes her with water (בַּמַּיִם). She had not been cleansed of blood (בְּדָמָיִךְ); she is now washed clean of blood (דָּמַיִךְ). She had not been rubbed with salt; her body is now perfumed with ointments.[13] She had not been swaddled; she is now covered with clothes.[14]

The detail about blood is subtly ambiguous. Linked back to the fact of the girl's puberty, it would seem to be menstrual blood. But if associated with her being taken in marriage, it would seem to be hymeneal. If the second, it is evidence that the girl is a virgin. Her chastity at this point will be in stark contrast to her eventual promiscuity. Either way, what surprises is the picture of the groom doing what the girl herself, or slaves, should be doing. In this cultural context, the bathing—not to mention washing intimate parts of the body—is women's business. It is impossible to think of anything more extraordinary for a traditional Eastern man to put his hands to. But that is exactly the emphasis of the triple tasks:

---

11. This is the usual reading of וָאֶפְרֹשׂ כְּנָפִי עָלַיִךְ: P. A. Kruger, "The Hem of the Garment in Marriage: The Meaning of the Symbolic Gesture in Ruth 3:9 and Ezek. 16:8," *JSNL* 12 (1984): 86; R. Patai, *Sex and Family in the Bible and the Middle East* (Garden City, NY: Doubleday, 1959), 197–98.

12. An alternate, and perhaps much less tenable, position is that at this point the man formally adopts the foundling. See Mary E. Shields, "Self-response to 'Multiple Exposures,'" in *A Feminist Companion to Prophets and Daniel*, ed. Athalya Brenner, FCB, Series 2 (Sheffield: Sheffield Academic, 2001), 160–63.

13. Greenberg proposes that the woman is compensated by being treated with ointment since the newborn was traditionally rubbed with salt and oil. *Ezekiel 1–20*, 278.

14. Linda Day, "Rhetoric and Domestic Violence in Ezekiel 16," *BibInt* 8, no. 3 (2000): 208–9.

I bathed you	with water
וָאֶרְחָצֵךְ	בַּמַּיִם

I washed . . . from you	the blood
וָאֶשְׁטֹף . . . מֵעָלָיִךְ	דָּמַיִךְ

I anointed . . . you	with ointments
וָאֲסֻכֵךְ	בַּשָּׁמֶן (16:9)

Having completed for her the basic toilette of washing and perfuming, he dresses her up. Whereas the purpose of swaddling the baby had been to ensure basic bodily aesthetics (of straight limbs), the husband elevates the woman to all the beauty that could be achieved through clothing. The materials are extravagant. Embroidered dresses belonged to princesses (Judg 5:30; Ps 45:15). Such material and the luxury-quality leather[15] with which her shoes are made were used for the tabernacle (Exod 26:14, 36).[16] Again, the husband is the source. He does not simply supply but puts each item on with his own hands, including the sandals. He becomes her handmaid.[17]

I clothed you	with embroidered cloth
וָאַלְבִּישֵׁךְ	רִקְמָה

I shod you	with fine leather
וָאֶנְעֲלֵךְ	תָּחַשׁ

I wrapped you	in fine linen
וָאֶחְבְּשֵׁךְ	בַּשֵּׁשׁ

15. Possibly the skin of a seal-like animal. E.g., John B. Taylor, *Ezekiel: An Introduction and Commentary* (Leicester: InterVarsity, 1969), 136.

16. For echoes of the tabernacle and Israel's wilderness journey, see Greenberg, *Ezekiel 1–20*, 302; Block, *Ezekiel 1–24*, 485; Christopher J. H. Wright, *The Message of Ezekiel: A New Heart and a New Spirit*, Bible Speaks Today (Leicester: InterVarsity, 2001), 135; Zimmerli, *Ezekiel 1–24*, 340–41.

17. "The same motif of the groom adorning the bride and her gaining a new, higher status is also found in a much later Neo-Assyrian text of the marriage of Nabu and Tasmetu" (Pirjo Lapinkivi, "The Adorning of the Bride: Providing Her with Wisdom," in *Sex and Gender in the Ancient Near East: Proceedings of the 47th Rencontre Assyriologique Internationale, Helsinki, July 2–6, 2001*, part 1, ed. S. Parpola and R. M. Whiting [Helsinki: Neo-Assyrian Text Corpus Project, 2002], 327–28).

I covered you   with silk[18]

וָאֲכַסֵּךְ   מֶשִׁי   (16:10)

The task of dressing done, one last service remains: adorning with jewelry. For a woman in ancient West Asia (or in contemporary South Asia), this is an elaborate procedure, for jewelry involves a whole array of items.

I adorned you   with jewelry

וָאֶעְדֵּךְ   עֶדִי

I put   bracelets   on your arms

וָאֶתְּנָה   צְמִידִים   עַל־יָדַיִךְ

and a necklace   around your neck

וְרָבִיד   עַל־גְּרוֹנֵךְ

and I put   a ring   on your nose

וָאֶתֵּן   נֶזֶם   עַל־אַפֵּךְ

earrings   on your ears

וַעֲגִילִים   עַל־אָזְנָיִךְ

and a beautiful crown   on your head

וַעֲטֶרֶת תִּפְאֶרֶת   בְּרֹאשֵׁךְ   (16:11–12)

After the general statement that he adorned her with jewelry, he lists the specifics, matching each item to the body part bedecked. The man begins with her forearms and proceeds upward. The arms (or wrists, more realistically) receive bracelets; the neck is decorated with a necklace; a nose ring embellishes the face; a pair of earrings frame it; and finally, the head is crowned with a tiara. While this could be just the ceremonial coronet used over the bridal week (cf. Ps 45; Song 3:11), the other possibility is that it actually elevates the foundling into the ranks of royalty (16:13).[19] The crown is described in construct with the noun תִּפְאֶרֶת, which here could be rendered "beautiful" (Exod 28:2) or "splen-

---

18. See Greenberg, *Ezekiel 1–20*, 278–79; Zimmerli, *Ezekiel 1–24*, 324.
19. Block, *Ezekiel 1–24*, 485; Greenberg, *Ezekiel 1–20*, 279; Keil, *Ezekiel*, 116.

did" (Isa 60:7). The girl with not a stitch on her back now lacks nothing, not even a magnificent crown.

We notice that at each of the stages of toilette, there is a list. The most basic stage of preparation lists three tasks: bathing, washing of intimate parts, and anointing. The stage of putting on apparel lists four verbs of service: clothing, sandaling, wrapping, and covering. The final stage of adornment lists five items of jewelry: bracelets, necklace, nose ring, earrings, and tiara. The stages not only grow more elaborate, but the requirements for each grow increasingly expensive. Even within each series, the list begins with something basic and finishes off with a luxury. Bathing, clothing, and adornment would be the usual routine for a woman. But to be pampered with unguents, smothered in silk, and crowned with a resplendent diadem—these are the stuff of a girl's dream, a girl who dreams of being a princess.

The narrator-husband steps back and surveys his wife and her situation.

So you were adorned	with gold and silver		
וַתַּעְדִּי	זָהָב וָכֶסֶף		
your clothes were	of fine linen	and silk (?)	and embroidered cloth
וּמַלְבּוּשֵׁךְ	שֵׁשׁ	וָמֶשִׁי	וְרִקְמָה
finest flour	and honey	and olive oil	you ate
סֹלֶת	וּדְבַשׁ	וָשֶׁמֶן	אָכָלְתְּ
You became very	beautiful	and advanced to be royalty	
בִּמְאֹד מְאֹד	וַתִּיפִי	וַתִּצְלְחִי לִמְלוּכָה (16:13)	

Framed by two shorter outer lines are two lists of three items each. One is a list already familiar. It details the materials that clothe the woman. She swishes about in fine linen, silk, and embroidered fabric. The second list is new to the reader. It tells us what is served at her table. For one who grew up wild, these are delicacies beyond her imagination. Her food is made with the finest flour, honey, and oil. The two lists run together into one long sequence, with the one who enjoys this lifestyle enclosing it: "Your clothes were . . . (the list of six items) . . . you ate."

The outer lines match each other: first, the woman is adorned; ultimately, she grows into great beauty. Her adornment is with gold and silver; befitting these metals associated with royalty, she rises to be a queen.[20] Her food too is associated with royalty—fine flour is part of the rations of Solomon's household (1 Kgs 5:2 [EV 4:22]). But the zenith is still to come.

And your fame spread among the nations on account of your beauty

וַיֵּצֵא לָךְ שֵׁם בַּגּוֹיִם בְּיָפְיֵךְ

for it was perfect because of my splendor which I had bestowed upon you

(16:14) כִּי כָּלִיל הוּא בַּהֲדָרִי אֲשֶׁר־שַׂמְתִּי עָלַיִךְ

The section hits the climax with its last line, a line incandescent with its heaping-up of shining words: fame (שֵׁם), beauty (יְפִי), perfection (כָּלִיל), splendor (הָדָר). The husband continues his survey of his foundling wife, observing the range of the ripples she creates with her loveliness. The nations hear of her perfect beauty.

As much as the previous verses in this section (16:9–12) were dominated by the first person ("I"), these latter verses (16:13–14) mark a shift. The "I" makes way for "you." It is only at the very end of the sentence that the first person returns. And it makes a claim that the narrative can well attest: it was "my splendor" that perfected "your beauty." Her splendor is a reflection of his.[21] The woman's one single asset is the promise of natural beauty (16:13). If not for the man's wealth lavished on her by way of fine food and expensive apparel, this promise of beauty might never have been fulfilled. We appreciate why the woman's meteoric rise to beauty (16:9–12) is narrated with the man as subject. Without his agency, none of this would have come to be.

---

20. Within the canon, the plot parallels that of Moses (Exod 2:1–10), a foundling who rose to royalty. His story, in turn, bears remarkable similarity to the Legend of Sargon:

Sargon, the mighty king, king of Agade, am I.
My mother was a changeling, my father I knew not. . . .
My changeling mother conceived me, in secret she bore me.
She set me a basket of rushes; with bitumen she sealed my lid.
She cast me into the river which rose not [over] me.
The river bore me up and carried me to Akki, the drawer of water.
Akki, the drawer of water, lifted me out as his dipped his e[w]er.
Akki, the drawer of water, [took me] as his son [and] reared me.
Akki, the drawer of water, appointed me as his gardener.
While I was a gardener, Ishtar granted me [her] love,
And for four and [. . .] years I exercised kingship.
(Pritchard, *Ancient Near Eastern Texts*, 82)

21. Block, *Ezekiel 1–24*, 485.

THE FALL: EZEKIEL 16:15–19

The story swings on a hinge at this point, and that hinge is the triple use of the word so key to the narrative, "beauty":

you became exceedingly beautiful [יפה]
your beauty [יָפְיֵ] . . . was perfect because of [me]
you trusted in your beauty [יָפְיֵ] (16:13–15)

Placing this word into its narrative context, Block draws up a concentric structure that demonstrates the woman's beauty to be the fulcrum of the story (16:1–22):

A   "squirming in your blood" (מִתְבּוֹסֶסֶת בְּדָמָיִךְ)   (v. 6)

B   "you were naked and bare" (עֵרֹם וְעֶרְיָה)   (v. 7)

C   "The declaration of the Lord Yahweh"   (v. 8)

D   Yahweh's personal endowments   (vv. 9–13)

E   The fame (שֵׁם) of Jerusalem   (v.14aα)

F   "on account of your beauty"   (v.14aβ)

F′   "on account of your beauty"   (v. 15aα)

E′   The fame (שֵׁם) of Jerusalem   (v. 15aβ)

D′   Yahweh's personal endowments   (vv. 16–19a)

C′   "The declaration of the Lord Yahweh"   (v. 19b)

B′   "you were naked and bare" (עֵרֹם וְעֶרְיָה)   (v. 22bα)

A′   "squirming in your blood" (מִתְבּוֹסֶסֶת בְּדָמָיִךְ)   (v. 22bβ)[22]

Once the first half builds up the story to the completion of her beauty, post-pivot, we are told the consequence of this beauty. It makes her queenly and brings her fame (16:13–14). But it also causes her to misuse her fame to play the wanton:

But you trusted in your beauty and used your fame to become a prostitute.
וַתִּבְטְחִי בְיָפְיֵךְ וַתִּזְנִי עַל־שְׁמֵךְ

---

22. Block, *Ezekiel 1–24*, 472.

You lavished your (sexual) favors on anyone who passed by, and it (your beauty) became his.[23]

(16:15) וַתִּשְׁפְּכִי אֶת־תַּזְנוּתַיִךְ עַל־כָּל־עוֹבֵר לוֹ יֶהִי

So then, this is the unexpected and dramatic turn the story takes. "Beauty has brought its own peril."[24] The beauty that was exclusively the man's (16:8) now becomes public property. The chronological sequence is laid out through a concentric structure: royalty (מְלוּכָה)—fame (שֵׁם)—fame (שֵׁם)—prostitution (זנה). The second half of the story pointedly uses the verb "to take" four times, over the course of which the woman's status spirals downward from queen to common whore. Here are the first three occurrences of the verb:

> You took [וַתִּקְחִי] some of your garments [מִבְּגָדַיִךְ] to make gaudy high places, when you carried on your prostitution. You went to him, and he possessed your beauty.

> You also took [וַתִּקְחִי] the fine jewelry [כְּלֵי תִפְאַרְתֵּךְ] made of my gold [מִזְּהָבִי] and my silver [וּמִכַּסְפִּי] which I gave you [אֲשֶׁר נָתַתִּי לָךְ], and you made for yourself male idols and engaged in prostitution with them.

> And you took [וַתִּקְחִי] your embroidered clothes [בִּגְדֵי רִקְמָתֵךְ] to put on them, and you offered my oil [שַׁמְנִי] and my incense [קְטָרְתִּי] before them. Also my food [וְלַחְמִי] I provided for you [אֲשֶׁר־נָתַתִּי לָךְ]—the flour, olive oil, and honey [סֹלֶת וָשֶׁמֶן וּדְבַשׁ] I gave you to eat [הֶאֱכַלְתִּיךְ]—you offered as fragrant incense before them. (16:16–19)

The woman begins by first taking what she needs to set up the dens. The clothes come in handy as decoration, reminding the reader of the cautionary tale in Proverbs, in which the adulteress lures the foolish with similar enticements:[25] "I have covered my bed with colored linens from Egypt. I have perfumed my bed with myrrh, aloes and cinnamon" (Prov 7:16).

Next she takes what is necessary for attracting clients. The jewelry is useful because it provides the necessary precious metals to melt down and convert into objects necessary for her trade. The third time she takes, the already bizarre situation exceeds reasonable limits. She takes so that she can make gifts to her customers. The expected direction of pay for sexual favors is turned on its head. Rather than be the recipient of payment and gifts, this woman offers incentives to her clients to use her

---

23. See Zimmerli, *Ezekiel 1–24*, 325–26, for textual issues in Ezek 16:15.
24. Peter C. Craigie, *Ezekiel* (Philadelphia: Westminster, 1983), 111.
25. Greenberg, *Ezekiel 1–20*, 280.

services (16:32–34). She takes and places at their use her embroidered garments; the food of flour, oil, and honey; and an item not mentioned earlier, incense. (The woman will take a fourth item, which we will come to shortly.)

In this series of taking, the narrator deploys the first- and second-person pronouns to striking effect. In 16:9–12, the personal pronoun "I" dominated over the "you," the former as the donor and the latter as the passive recipient. In 16:13–14, the gaze was directed upon "you" with only a single (but sharp!) reminder at the close that the "you" was indebted to the "I." Now in 16:15–21, the two protagonists share equal space. "You" performs the actions, but those actions are performed with articles that "I" sourced.

Crediting the husband with all these goods is done in three ways. First, items taken away from the household may carry the pronoun suffix "my": my gold, my silver, my oil, my incense, my food. Second is a repeated reminder of who the real owner is: "which I gave you" (אֲשֶׁר נָתַתִּי לָךְ, 16:17, 19), varied once as "which I gave you to eat" (הֶאֱכַלְתִּיךְ, 16:19). Third, except for the incense, all the articles listed are familiar to us. We know them as bounty the husband expended on his bride, a foundling rescued from the wayside. That background makes this present abuse incomprehensible.

By the use of the pronouns, the narrative simultaneously establishes the husband as the rightful owner of these household goods and incriminates the wife as committing gross disservice. She brazenly pillages his house.

Another point worth noting is the number of different verbs of which the woman is the actor. Up to this point in the narrative, she has been acted upon. The family she was born into "threw" her out of the birthing chamber (16:5). The man who eventually married her directed upon her all those actions by which she survived a perilous infancy to grow into puberty, enter a family again, and realize the full potential of her natural asset of beauty. Now, the husband recedes into the background, and she acts. The sudden and "extreme change of syntax is an indicator that the *fact* of her action is just as significant as the *content* of her actions."[26]

16:15: she trusts [בטח] in her beauty; whores [זנה]; pours out [שפך] sexual favors

16:16: she takes [לקח]; makes [עשׂה] dens of vice; whores [זנה]

26. S. Tamar Kamionkowski, "Gender Reversal in Ezekiel 16," in *A Feminist Companion to Prophets and Daniel*, ed. Athalya Brenner, FCB, Series 2 (Sheffield: Sheffield Academic, 2001), 174.

16:17:   she takes [לקח]; makes [עשׂה] lovers; whores [זנה]

16:18:   she takes [לקח]; covers [כסה] lovers with clothes; gives [נתן] incentives

16:19:   she gives [נתן] incentives

The speed with which action follows action is astonishing. Just as astonishing is how irrational these actions are. As much as the husband gave without restraint, the wife now takes and gives away without restraint.[27] Material wealth flows from the woman to a third party—no more than "strangers" (16:32)—and we are not sure she receives anything in return other than gratification of her lust. While the clients are made richer with silver and gold, while they are beautified with expensive fabric, while they are fed fine food, and while they luxuriate in clouds of fragrance, the woman is systematically and increasingly deprived of these same goods. Their enrichment is directly in proportion to her impoverishment. What is more, her impoverishment has a bearing on her beauty, the theme of this narrative. Just as her beauty had been built up by being invested with clothes, jewelry, and a fine diet, it is deconstructed by their removal, item by item. When she is done, we wonder if she has not returned herself, by her own deliberate acts, to the nakedness of her premarital state. Stripped bare of all that made her the famous beauty she was, she inhabits public space again (16:24–25, 31), available to the gaze of any passerby (כָּל־עוֹבֵר; 16:15, 25) as once she was (עבר; 16:6, 8).

As in the Song, physical beauty and sensuality are inseparable. The praise poem was delicate in its expression of sensuality, letting double entendre do the work. Thus, we are never sure what the woman means us to see when she describes מֵעָיו, made of "polished ivory" and covered with blue lapis (Song 5:14). Is this veined skin? If so, is this a reference to his private parts? We cannot be sure what she means by חִכּוֹ being "sweetness itself" (Song 5:16). Since the word is literally "palate" rather than "mouth," one is left wondering if she means his amiable conversation or more private intimacies.

The narrative in Ezekiel sweeps such niceties aside. The woman "pours out" (שׁפך) her whoring. Here is a verb that better fits the man's part in an encounter such as this (Ezek 23:8). Her sexual aggression seems best described in male terms.[28] What is more, this pouring out of whoring is freely available to any passerby who cares to stop to appro-

---

27. Block, *Ezekiel 1–24*, 488; Ronald M. Hals, *Ezekiel*, FOTL 19 (Grand Rapids: Eerdmans, 1989), 106.

28. See S. Tamar Kamionkowski, *Gender Reversal and Cosmic Chaos: A Study on the Book of Ezekiel*, JSOTSup 368 (Sheffield: Sheffield Academic, 2003), esp. 92–127. She sets out Ezekiel 16 as a subversion of the gender order where female Israel begins to behave as man.

priate her physical assets (16:15, 25). And after she has enticed and used these men, this lustful woman still has energy left over. This she expends on "male idols," phallic objects (16:17).[29]

As much as the Song's praise poem left us wondering if the man being described was clothed or nude, Ezekiel 16 leaves nothing to the imagination. Song 5 gave the impression that the woman was carefully manipulating her metaphors to keep control of her exclusive rights to her beloved, allowing her audience to see only what she was happy to release to public view. At the other end of the spectrum, the problem with the woman in Ezekiel 16 is her dissatisfaction with a single man, a husband (16:32). She prefers many to one, and seeks men out in the city squares and street corners.[30] She craves variety, so she goes from Egyptians to Assyrians to Babylonians, each round only increasing her appetite (16:24–26, 28–29). Thus, while the speaker of Song 5 delighted in "my beloved" (Song 5:10, 16), the woman in Ezekiel 16 lives in a perpetual orgy. In the Song, only the woman knows what fragrance the nearness of her beloved's cheeks affords (Song 5:13). In Ezekiel, the woman's incense is readily available to random noses. In the Song, only the woman knows the taste of the man's "sweet" mouth with its myrrh-dripping lips (Song 5:13). In Ezekiel, the woman sets out her honey before anyone who cares to sample it. If the Song's man was a choice, exceptional cedar (Song 5:15), the Ezekiel woman is "a plant of the field" (16:7) in the commonest and coarsest sense.

To sum up the contrast, while the Song displays a guarded reticence when speaking of the sensuality of beauty, Ezekiel exhibits it with nauseating license—the publicly opened legs (16:25), the female fluid produced by arousal (16:36), and the baring of the genitalia (16:36). The erotic makes way for the pornographic. And so the husband can say that what was once beauty becomes an obscenity (וַתְּתַעֲבִי אֶת־יָפְיֵךְ; 16:25).

THE CYCLE COMPLETED: EZEKIEL 16:20–22

We come to the fourth and last of the woman's "taking" actions, and this proves not simply irrational, as the first three were, but grossly and gratuitously cruel.

---

29. See Block, *Ezekiel 1–24*, 488–89; Eichrodt, *Ezekiel*, 207.

30. Block notes that the word used for this woman's promiscuous behavior is not "adultery" (נאף) but "prostitution" (זנה). The latter term is a better fit because it describes her "habitual, iterative activity," her "motive of personal gain" (16:33–34), and her "multiple partners" (16:17, 25–29) (Block, *Ezekiel 1–24*, 465). Greenberg remarks, "By extending the metaphor in time, Ezekiel provides the adulterous wife of Hosea and Jeremiah with a biography" (*Ezekiel 1–20*, 299).

And you took your sons and daughters whom you bore to me and sacrificed [זבח] them as food to the idols. Was your prostitution [זנה] not enough? You slaughtered [שחט] my children and sacrificed them [וַתִּתְּנִים בְּהַעֲבִיר אוֹתָם] to the idols. In all your detestable practices [וְאֵת כָּל־תּוֹתַבֹתַיִךְ] and your prostitution [זנה] you did not remember [לֹא זָכַרְתְּ] the days of your youth [וְמֵי נְעוּרָיִךְ], when you were stark naked [בִּהְיוֹתֵךְ עֵרֹם וְעֶרְיָה], kicking about in your blood [מִתְבּוֹסֶסֶת בְּדָמֵךְ הָיִית]. (16:20–22)

She who was abandoned to the perils of the open field by her own mother now subjects her children to what goes well beyond the heartless. She systematically and cold-bloodedly engages in activity that violates the norms of motherhood. Three verbs describe the horror. She slaughters (זבח), she butchers (שחט), she engulfs in flame as in a holocaust.[31] By this last, especially, she betrays her Canaanite ancestry.[32]

With this the husband circles back to the start of the narrative to locate the problem. The problem, as he states it, is that the woman "did not remember" her beginnings—she had a "severe case of amnesia."[33] If she could have revisited her memory, she would particularly have remembered that her husband did not wish the death of children. She owed her very existence to the fact that this man had desired her to live.[34]

In Hebrew, the act of remembering (זכר) is not merely a cognitive exercise. One remembers so as to act upon that which is called to mind. The woman is expected to order her actions in line with her history. The man brings up three images: the days of her youth, nakedness, and weltering in blood. The images blur together two different points on the timeline, with nakedness flowing both ways as a connective. She is called on to recall her bare pubescent body. She is to recall also the exposed infant body that wriggled in its blood. Blood then becomes another connective between two phases of nakedness—menstrual blood and birth blood. There are several effects of these twin images. First is the nature of nakedness and female-related blood. Canonically, post-fall nakedness is something to be ashamed of (Gen 3:7). As for female discharges, canon law considers both childbirth and menstruation unclean (Lev 12:1–8; 15:19–33). The images point back at a disadvantaged past.

Second, as concerns the aesthetic, neither image is an attractive sight.

---

31. The last is an economical conflation of two idioms for sacrifice: "to devote one's offspring to Molech" and "to pass one's son or daughter through the fire to Molech." In both cases, the result is a fiery end. See Block, *Ezekiel 1–24*, 490; Brownlee, *Ezekiel 1–19*, 231.

32. Block, *Ezekiel 1–24*, 491. Cf. the practices in 2 Kgs 16:3; 17:17; 21:6; 23:10, which are referred to and strictly forbidden in Lev 18:21; 20:2–15; Deut 12:31; 18:10.

33. Block, *Ezekiel 1–24*, 491; Craigie, *Ezekiel*, 112.

34. Margaret S. Odell, *Ezekiel*, Smyth and Helwys Bible Commentary Series (Macon, GA: Smyth & Helwys, 2005), 191.

A newborn slimy with amniotic fluid, covered with gobs of placental blood, and tangled in an uncut umbilical cord hardly pleases the eye. Just as disagreeable is the image of a naked young girl, thighs streaked with menstrual blood.

Third, both conditions stir pathos. There is nothing more poignant than the sight of an infant abandoned to certain death who yet thrashes about because her natural instinct is to survive. Just as distressing is the idea of a girl on the cusp between childhood and maidenhood who is confused by the changes in her body, anxious about the bleeding, and vulnerable to human male predators. Both the baby and the girl are defenseless and dependent.

Unclean, unlovely, and utterly vulnerable as she once was, the grown woman has no past to be proud of. Yet, once her beauty elevates her into the echelons of fame, she promptly forgets that her past must direct her present, that loyalty to the one who rescued her must dictate her life and her love. The woman in Song 5 remembers well. She can recreate in her mind's eye the twinkle in her beloved's eyes, the luxuriant wave of his hair, the highlights on his golden skin. In her memory she can smell him and taste him; she can hear him speak; she can feel the hardness of his muscled body. The memories order her present state of complete dedication: "I am my beloved's" (Song 6:3).

Beyond this, memory serves the woman in Song 5 well. Because she can remember, she finds her lost beloved by conjuring him up. Her words coalesce into flesh and blood. Her metaphors knit together into sinews and skin. Barely has she finished speaking when she finds him by her side (Song 6:2). What is lost is found. In Ezekiel, the woman forgets. Thereby, what is found is lost. The man loses his foundling wife. The woman, having found a life eminently worth living, loses it all to disgrace. By her forgetting, she both causes and experiences loss.

What precipitates the woman's amnesia? It is her beauty. In Song 5, the beloved's beauty serves the lover. The woman can proudly show off her man as one heart-stopping concentration of masculine desirables. In Ezekiel 16, beauty serves the one who possesses it. She trusts in it enough to haughtily dismiss (implied in 16:15; cf. 16:50) everything that affords her security, both husband and home. Because of her beauty, she can take to the streets and take lovers.

In a narrative in which beauty moves the lover to remember and recall past delights, the end is rhapsodic. The woman pronounces her beloved "utterly desirable" (Song 5:16). In a narrative in which beauty becomes the reason for forgetting past relationships, the end appalls. The outraged husband declares his wife's actions "detestable" (16:22).

BEAUTY: MAN AND WOMAN

Song 5 and Ezekiel 16 overlap in their approach to the idea of beauty. Indeed, the beauty of the beloved is central to both narratives. Though the Song does not use the word "beautiful" (יפה), the poem itself is cast as a *wasf*, dedicated to the praise of the beloved's face and form. In Ezekiel 16, the story revolves around the fact of the foundling's beauty. It is described in no uncertain terms. The woman is "exceedingly" (בִּמְאֹד מְאֹד) beautiful (יפה), so much so that this beauty may be said to have reached perfection (כָּלִיל).

And since it is physical beauty that both texts make so much of, both narratives place the beloved's body center-stage. This is clearly the case in Song 5, in which the woman's memory travels lingeringly from one part to another of the beloved's body. Ezekiel 16 is subtler, but just as focused on the body. The infant girl has nothing done for her body—neither cutting of the cord, nor washing, nor rubbing, nor swaddling. Next, we are informed that she has grown into the age for love (דֹּדִים, as in the Song)—the male gaze notices her new-formed breasts and (pubic) hair. At marriage, it is her "naked body" (16:8) that continues to receive attention. (Indeed, nakedness is the theme of this piece.[35]) Her body is washed and then covered, first by the covenantal cloak and then with clothing. The story continues to be told in terms of what happens to the woman's body—its increasing desirability and its use by men. When the section ends, it is with a flashback to what this body looked like when first the man laid eyes on it.[36]

Having affirmed that both texts are built around the idea of the aesthetically pleasing body, we examine three points of comparison between Song 5 and Ezekiel 16.

CREATING THE BEAUTIFUL BELOVED

Common to the two texts is the role the speakers play with regard to the beauty of the respective beloved. In Song 5, neither the daughters of Jerusalem nor the reader has any idea what the man looks like until the woman describes him. Setting aside the question of the reliability of her testimony, the fact remains that his beauty resides entirely in her

35. M. G. Swanpoel, "Ezekiel 16: Abandoned Child, Bride Adorned or Unfaithful Wife?," in *Among the Prophets: Language, Image and Structure in the Prophetic Writings*, ed. Philip R. Davies and David J. A. Clines, JSOTSup 144 (Sheffield: Sheffield Academic, 1993), 89–90.

36. Mary E. Shields, "Multiple Exposures: Body Rhetoric and Gender Characterization in Ezekiel 16," *JFSR* 14, no. 1 (1998): 5–18.

words. She makes him beautiful, so much so that the immediate audience is enchanted by the vision. A similar agency is operative in Ezekiel 16. The first mention of the foundling's beauty comes at the end of a long list of what the man does for her (16:13), suggesting that were it not for his exertions, her beauty may never have materialized. In line with this idea is the chiastic arrangement of the central section of the story:

A   "your fame" (16:14)

   B   "on account of your beauty" (16:14)

      X   *the splendor I had given you* (16:14)

   B'   "on account of your beauty" (16:15)

A'   "your fame" (16:15)

The husband's part in the foundling's internationally renowned beauty is central. Thus in both stories, the beauty of the loved one may be credited to the one who loves.

ESTABLISHING THE BELOVED AS BEAUTIFUL

A second point common to the two texts is the manner in which a concept as subjective as beauty is objectively established. One way to establish beauty is by public affirmation. In the Song, the point of the *wasf* would have been lost if the daughters of Jerusalem had responded with disbelief. Rather, their eagerness to join in the search (Song 6:1) is an indication that they consider the man worth the effort of seeking. He is too handsome to ignore. Further, within the praise poem itself, the man is held up as one who would attract the attention of an onlooker even if he was immersed in a sea of people. Ezekiel 16 outdoes this image. The woman's extraordinary beauty draws the eyes of a sea of people; however, these are not merely individuals but whole nations. In counterpart to the Song's daughters of Jerusalem are the daughters of Philistia (16:27), the daughters of Sodom and Samaria (16:53), and the daughters of Edom (16:57). Conversely, the woman's beauty counts for nothing when these groups are unimpressed: "you are now scorned by the daughters of Edom and all her neighbors and the daughters of the Philistines—all those around you who despise you" (16:57).

This idea of objectively establishing a human as beautiful by public affirmation may be explored further. The Ezekiel text, especially, raises the interesting possibility that human beauty is in some way bound up with honor. We start with the idea we have already considered, the idea well entrenched in the Israelite community that nakedness is shameful. Thus, the young girl is in a state of shame. Though she may have attained the phase that is described as the "ornament of ornaments," by remaining unclothed she lacks something fundamental to her wholeness. Her condition is described with emphasis by using a pair of words, עֵרֹם וְעֶרְיָה, "naked and bare," or if rendered as a hendiadys, "stark naked." The change in her social status begins at exactly the point when the man, idiomatically, spread his garment over her and "covered [her] naked body." Literal covering-up follows. Using a series of three verbs, we are told that the groom "clothed" (לבשׁ), "dressed" (חבשׁ), and "covered" (כסה) his bride with embroidered fabric, fine linen, and silk. It is through being dressed—more than that, extravagantly arrayed—that she attains the pinnacle of beauty.

Her descent from this height is described by a reversion to nakedness. She gradually strips herself of garments (16:16, 18). Eventually, the man pronounces the worst that can happen with this threat: "I will . . . strip you [וְגִלֵּיתִי עֶרְוָתֵךְ] in front of them, and they will see you completely naked [וְרָאוּ אֶת־כָּל־עֶרְוָתֵךְ]" (16:37; cf. 16:39). In this unclothed state, it does not seem to matter at all how well-formed her body is. Rather by her voluntary public exposure (spreading her legs), she has rendered that beauty (יפה) obscene (16:25) (תעב)—indeed, others cringe at it (16:27). This public stripping, too, will hardly be an occasion for any to admire the beauty of her body. Rather, she will be shamed by this disgrace (16:52) (כְּלִמָּה). The fact of her nakedness dramatically changes her status from one of wholeness to one of disgrace, from כָּלִיל to כְּלִמָּה.

In Song 5, does beauty collapse into the repulsive under the public gaze? As we have observed, the woman so carefully controls what her audience sees that the man can never be said to be naked. He is clothed in metaphors,[37] metaphors that invest him with an aura. Bare flesh is dressed with a radiant glow. His body flashes color, encrusted as it is with topaz and lapis. The viewer's gaze cannot penetrate the shimmer of a golden head and feet, the gleam of polished ivory, the sheen of marble. His splendor hides him. In biblical literature, it appears that one cannot tease apart the nude from the naked, assigning one to the realm of the erotic and the other to the pornographic. Any public exposure attracts shame, whatever may be the motivation of the one who does the exposing. If this is the case, the Ezekiel woman finishes off the way she began—publicly naked, and for that reason, unbeautiful. The man in

37. Cheryl J. Exum, *Song of Songs: A Commentary* (Louisville: Westminster John Knox, 2005), 6.

Song 5, figuratively shielded by the luminescence of his beauty, earns the respect of his audience. He is thereby established objectively as beautiful.

Another way beauty is established is by relating it to royalty—indeed, "the fitness of beauty for royalty is a commonplace."[38] Reading Song 5 and Ezekiel 16 canonically, the reader cannot miss the references to the regal. With Song 5, we have observed the associations with Israel's early royal figures, all legends in their own right—Saul, David, Absalom, and most of all, Solomon. If any lover could be constructed out of gold and gemstones, cedar and spices, it has to be Solomon.

Ezekiel 16 deploys the same hyperbole. The woman is plainly declared as royal. In addition, there is a piling-up of associations. If her elaborate toilette is preparation for marriage, the reader recalls Esther, another attractive commoner who rose into royalty. Esther, who "had a lovely figure and was beautiful" (Esth 2:7), entered the Persian harem as a prospective queen. To make her ready to meet the king, she was given "beauty treatments and special food," and a retinue of seven maids (Esth 2:9). The treatments lasted a whole year, the first half of which was dedicated to oil of myrrh and the second half to perfumes and cosmetics. We may safely assume clothes and jewelry formed a part of this preparation, because later, when Esther seeks audience with the king, she is careful to "put on her royal robes" (Esth 5:1).

As for royal robes, the foundling receives clothes so special that one is reminded of the princess Tamar's special robe, rendered sometimes as "ornamented robe" (כְּתֹנֶת הַפַּסִּים; 2 Sam 13:19). The groom's gifts recall the dowry Rebekah received when her wedding to a clan chieftain's son was arranged: "gold and silver jewelry and articles of clothing" (Gen 24:53). These are in addition to the "gold nose ring" and "two gold bracelets" (Gen 24:22). And when it comes to beauty, the reader remembers all the famous "mothers of Israel" who were possessed of stunning looks: Sarah (Gen 12:14), Rebekah (Gen 26:7), and Rachel (Gen 29:17). Adding up the weight of these associations, it seems that the narrator could not have bestowed on the woman a more honorable profile.

Both texts, then, establish the beloved as objectively beautiful by appealing to public affirmation in terms of honor and by subtly associating them with royalty.

---

38. Greenberg, *Ezekiel 1–20*, 279.

LOSING THE BEAUTIFUL BELOVED

Song 5 and Ezekiel 16 are generated under similar emotional circum-stances. In both cases, the protagonist is experiencing the loss of the loved one. The loss is the reason for the text. In Song 5, the woman is fraught with remorse that she turned her beloved away, even if unwit-tingly. Having sought without success, the last resort is to describe him to a group that may help find him. In Ezekiel 16, the husband is at a cri-sis point. Having lost his wife to other men, he recalls their meeting and marriage before he can set out his next step.

By setting each recollection into its background of internal turmoil, we are able to appreciate that the burden of each text is heavily relational. The speaker reflects on the personal value of the object lost. What is being recounted is not merely a description of the beautiful one. Under-lying the description is the love felt for the lost one. In the Song, the woman's emotions come through more clearly because of the narrative context. Her request of the daughters of Jerusalem is charged with emo-tion: "If you find my beloved . . . tell him I am faint with love" (Song 5:8). Each line of description gives away the speaker's affection, and the poem itself is nested within endearments.

With Ezekiel 16, the man's feelings for the wife remain unspoken. Thus, reading the man like Halperin does is possible: "Hosea and Jere-miah, even at their most severe, manage some measure of tenderness for their errant ladies. . . . In Ezekiel, the prevailing emotion is pornographic fury."[39] The audience must deduce from the telling of the story whether this is the case.

To begin with, the point the man makes in listing all that was not done for the newborn is that not a single "eye" (עַיִן) looked upon her with pity or compassion (16:5). In contrast, he "saw" (רָאָה) her. We may assume that at the sight, he was moved by these emotions. He, a stranger and a passerby, takes it upon himself to compensate her for her parents' neglect. That compensation, then, must include the basic ingredient for the care of a child, affection. We must deduce his affection from the out-come that the infant not only survives but thrives into girlhood. Indeed, for Origen, pity or compassion is the affective aspect of love.[40] And here,

39. David J. Halperin, *Seeking Ezekiel: Text and Psychology* (University Park: Pennsylvania State University Press, 1993), 142.

40. Origen, *The Song of Songs Commentaries and Homilies*, trans. R. P. Lawson, ACW 26 (Westminster, MD: Newman, 1947), cited in Robert W. Jenson, *Ezekiel*, (London: SCM, 2009), 128.

it is striking that he loved her when she was not only unloved but also unlovely.[41]

Further, his care for her accommodates her needs. When her survival demands that a man take her in marriage, he takes the responsibility upon himself. The deep sense of obligation is conveyed through the narration: "I gave you my solemn oath and entered into a covenant with you" (16:8). In a culture in which marriage liaisons take into account such things as family and pedigree, the man's choice of a foundling of Hittite and Amorite origins is remarkable. One recalls Ruth the Moabite's astonishment at the Israelite Boaz taking notice of her: "Why have I found such favor in your eyes that you notice me—a foreigner?" (Ruth 2:10). Just as incredible is what the man does for this castaway born of traditionally despised ethnicities: when the girl does not have the privilege of maids (Gen 29:24, 29) or a community to help prepare her for marriage, the man fills that gap voluntarily, doing her services that Eastern men would consider undignified.

In his capacity as husband, the man launches his bride into a fairytale existence. Her clothes are exotic; she is bedecked in all manner of jewelry; and her table groans with the finest of food. Even if it was compassion that set in motion this chain of events, his care of the foundling at every stage so outdoes all cultural obligations and expectations that the reader recognizes here a deep and genuine affection. Wright correctly understands that his actions arise "from totally self-motivated and unconditional love," especially since they were "not compelled by or dependent on anything that the wallowing infant might be or do or deserve."[42]

When this affection is betrayed, the response is outrage. His thoughts return to that open field in which a castaway wallowed in blood. Is he aggrieved to find that her nature lacked even the gratitude that could have kept her faithful? There seems to be more than this. His anguish is that having done the utmost he could, he has failed to win her affection—she prefers other men (16:32). The disappointment is perhaps all the greater because she was found so unexpectedly and now lost even more unexpectedly; because the long years of careful nurturing have turned viciously against him; and because where he had anticipated she was ready for love, she turned out to have a proclivity for promiscuity. The "semipornographic style" he uses to describe her offenses could well be "a deliberate rhetorical device" to communicate the strength of his

41. Craigie, *Ezekiel*, 109.

42. Wright, *Message of Ezekiel*, 133. The aspect of unconditional love is well demonstrated by reading this Ezekiel text alongside the Song of Moses in Deuteronomy 32. The plot lines are uncannily similar, and there is an overlap of significant vocabulary. See Jason Gile, "Ezekiel 16 and the Song of Moses: A Prophetic Transformation?" *JBL* 130, no. 1 (2011): 87–108.

emotions.[43] Commenting on the tenor of Ezekiel 16 and 23, Halperin sees "the ill-disciplined outpourings of a human being in nearly unbearable psychic pain."[44] It is reasonable to assume, as we did with Song 5, that the pain is an index of the speaker's love for the beloved.

With this, we have shown Song 5 and Ezekiel 16 to overlap in their treatment of the theme of the beautiful beloved. In both, (1) the protagonist is the creator of beauty; (2) the protagonist publicly establishes the lover as beautiful; (3) the protagonist's love is evidenced by pain at the loss of the object of love.

BEAUTY: DEITY AND DEVOTEE

How does the theme of beauty apply to the relationship between deity and devotee? Beyond associating the male beloved with the most famous of Israelite kings and princelings, the praise poem of Song 5 moves into the realm of the gods. The poem abounds in "fantastic hyperboles and superlatives that imply that the woman's beloved evokes notions of divinity."[45] In this, it is thought that perhaps the poem bears resemblance to Egyptian literature describing the statues of gods. These were wrought with extravagantly expensive materials. Eventually, these descriptions began to be used as if describing the actual bodies of deities.[46] For instance, the Egyptian "Myth of the Cow of Heaven," similar to a later hymn to Amon-Re, describes the sun god's body thus: "His bones were of silver, his limbs were of gold, his hair was genuine lapis lazuli."[47] The sun god's earthly representative, the Pharaoh, came to be described in similar language. Rameses III is praised in statuary terms: "Your hair (is) lapis lazuli, your eyebrows are *qa'*-stone, your eyes are green malachite, your mouth (is) red jasper."[48] Gold and lapis had passed into poetry as the stuff of the bodies of deities.[49]

In ancient West Asian poetry, mortal heroes were immortalized in statues, and these statues described in poems. In the Gilgamesh epic, the hero has a statue made of his departed friend Enkidu, recruiting a "cop-

43. Block, *Ezekiel 1–24*, 467.

44. Halperin, *Seeking Ezekiel*, 157.

45. Othmar Keel, *The Song of Songs: A Continental Commentary*, trans. Frederick J. Gaiser (Minneapolis: Augsburg, 1994), 201.

46. Keel, *Song of Songs*, 202; Marvin H. Pope, *Song of Songs: A New Translation with Introduction and Commentary*, Anchor Bible 7C (New Haven: Yale University Press, 1977), 535.

47. Keel, *Song of Songs*, 202.

48. Keel, *Song of Songs*, 202–3.

49. Pope, *Song of Songs*, 543; Keel, *Song of Songs*, 203–4.

persmith, goldsmith, engraver." The resulting statue is then eulogized: "of lapis is thy breast, of gold thy body."[50]

In Egypt, it may be that the poems that first described divinity and then royalty were eventually democratized and became popularly usable.[51] In these popular poems, one gets a mix of metaphors in that body parts are sometimes identified with the gods and sometimes with precious materials, all in the same poem: "Your beauty is that of a calm pool. . . . Your head, O my lord, is adorned with the tress of a woman of Asia; your face is brighter than the Mansion of the Moon; your upper part is lapis lazuli; your hair is blacker than all the doors of the Netherworld on the day of darkness. . . . Your lungs are Nephthys; your face is Hapi and his flood. . . . Your gullet is Anubis; your body is extended with gold; your breasts are eggs of carnelian which Horus has inlaid with lapis-lazuli; your arms glitter with faience."[52]

Closer to the world of the Song, and with remarkable parallels to the praise poem of Song 5, is the hyperbolic description of a dignitary that borders on the superhuman. The high priest Simon is described thus in Sirach 50:5–10:[53]

> How glorious he was when the people gathered round him as he came out
>   of the inner sanctuary!
> Like the morning star among the clouds, like the moon when it is full;
> Like the sun shining upon the temple of the Most High, and like the rain-
>   bow gleaming in glorious clouds;
> like roses in the days of first fruits, like lilies by a spring of water,
> like a green shoot on Lebanon on a summer day; like fire and incense in the
>   censer,
> like a vessel of hammered gold adorned with all kinds of precious stones;
> like an olive tree putting forth its fruit, and like a cypress towering in the
>   clouds.

Is the woman using "divine fiction"[54] as Sirach does, because the man "has taken on larger-than-life proportions to her"?[55] Perhaps, yes. The

---

50. Keel, *Song of Songs*, 203.

51. Keel, *Song of Songs*, 22, 24; contra Michael V. Fox, *The Song of Songs and the Ancient Egyptian Love Songs* (Madison: University of Wisconsin Press, 1985), 271, who sees no connection between the erotic Description Songs and cultic Description Hymns, other than that both list body parts.

52. Keel, *Song of Songs*, 23.

53. Pointed out in Murphy, *Song of Songs*, 169–70; Pope, *Song of Songs*, 532.

54. See Keel, *Song of Songs*, 29. H.-P. Muller calls it "theomorphic language" ("Das Hohelied," in *Das Hohelied, Klagelieder, Das Buch Ester*, ed. H.-P. Muller, O. Kaiser, and J. A. Loader, ATD 16/2 [Göttingen: Vandenhoeck & Ruprecht, 1992], 59–60).

55. Tremper Longman III, *Song of Songs* (Grand Rapids: Eerdmans, 2001), 173.

beloved remains concretely human, invested only with a numinous aura deriving from this hyperbole. However, in its cultural context the literary device takes on a different color. As Keel explains, "divine fiction" in love poetry would not have been a problem for polytheistic cultures where the dividing line between the divine and the mortal is not sharply drawn. (In an Egyptian love poem, the beloved is "My god, my lotus."[56]) *Mutatis mutandis*, a similar blurring happens when Song 5 is laid into the canon of which it is part. But before we come to that, let us review the allegorical reading of Song 5 in the Jewish and Christian traditions—a reading in which the male *wasf* of Song 5 has been applied to divinity.

In Judaism, both the Midrash and the Targum to the Song tread cautiously around applying the *wasf* to the divine lover since God cannot be said to have a body, and even if he had one, the second commandment proscribes description of it. One piece of Jewish literature that throws caution to the winds is the text *Shi'ur Qomah* ("measure of stature/height"), influenced by Song 5 to one extent or another.[57] Here, the ecstatic mystic sees God enthroned and describes his gigantic anthropomorphized body. A celebration of divine beauty rather than superhuman dimensions is found in *Hekhalot Rabbati*.[58] Mainstream literature—Targum, Talmud, and Midrash—meanwhile, mostly projects the description poem of Song 5 onto the Torah, which in turn represents God. Where it does appropriate Song 5 for divinity, it does so circumspectly.

The daughters of Jerusalem set the poem rolling with their question, "How is your beloved better than others?" (Song 5:9). This enquiry is placed on the lips of the heathens who cannot understand why the Jews will not intermingle with them: "In what way is your God so superior to other gods that you are ready to be burned and tortured for Him?"[59] The Jews respond: "I will describe my Beloved to you—but in the most

---

56. Keel, *Song of Songs*, 29. Fox cites the example in Egyptian love poetry in which the lovers are "transformed" into gods: the "brother" is Re or Nefertem, and the "sister" Hathor or Sothis (*Ancient Egyptian Love Songs*, 234).

57. E.g., Saul Lieberman, "Mishnat Shir ha-Shirim," in *Jewish Gnosticism, Merkabah Mysticism, and Talmudic Tradition*, ed. Gershom Scholem, 2nd ed. (New York: Jewish Theological Seminary, 1965), 118–26; Martin S. Cohen, *The Shi'ur Qomah: Liturgy and Theurgy in Pre-Kabbalistic Jewish Mysticism* (Lanham, NY: University Press of America, 1983), 19; David J. Halperin, *The Faces of the Chariot: Early Jewish Responses to Ezekiel's Vision* (Tübingen: Mohr Siebeck, 1988), 26–27.

58. Text found in S. A. Wertheimer, ed., *Batte Misrashot*, vol. 1, 2nd ed. (Jerusalem: Ktav Vasefer, 1968), 63–136; P. Schafer, *Synopse zur Hekhalot Literatur* (Tübingen: Mohr, 1981), 81–306.

59. *Mechilta*; Rashi, both cited in Meir Zlotowitz, compiler, *Shir haShirim/Song of Songs: An Allegorical Translation based upon Rashi with a Commentary Anthologized from Talmudic, Midrashic and Rabbinic Sources* (New York: Mesorah, 1979), 154.

anthropomorphic of analogies—as a maiden describes her bridegroom. Then even you will agree that there is no other like Him."[60]

This bridegroom is described as "white" and "ruddy" for the "seemingly contradictory attributes" of purity and punishment, "both of which are embodied within Him simultaneously."[61] His "banner" (דֶּגֶל) "waves over myriads of angels who minister before Him."[62] Or, "just as a banner ... is raised above the head of a marching army, so does He tower above all the others in strength, eternity, might, and sovereignty."[63] His eyes are dove-like, for just as doves keep their gaze on their cotes, so God directs his eyes "toward synagogues and study-houses from which emanates Torah which is compared to water."[64] The fragrant cheeks allegorically refer to the "utterances at Sinai during which God displayed a friendly, smiling demeanor."[65] Or, if cheeks are regarded as synonymous to the organs of speech, then: "With every single word that went forth from the mouth of the Holy One, Blessed Be He, the whole world was filled with spices [i.e., fragrance],"[66] "for His Words spiritually purified and prepared the souls of the people—just as fragrant spices revive and rejuvenate the flesh."[67]

"Where has your beloved gone?" is a taunt by the nations in the period following the Babylonian destruction of Solomon's Temple, when "Judah lay desolate."[68] But, just as the Song's beloved goes down to his gardens, God vindicated Judah by "descending" from his heavenly realm to graze his sheep even in the "gardens" of their dispersion—"i.e., He caused his Shechinah to descend to the synagogues and study-houses of those 'sheep' who remained in the lands of Captivity."[69] Indeed, Israel can confidently counter the nations that mock her with her claim to an exclusive relationship with God consonant with the Song's declaration "I am my beloved's and my beloved is mine": "Once I have attached myself to Him, can I separate myself from Him? Once He has attached Himself to me, can He separate from me? For just as I have never forsaken Him for another god, so He has never entirely forsaken me."[70]

60. Alshich, cited in Zlotowitz, *Shir haShirim*, 155.

61. *N'tziv*, cited in Zlotowitz, *Shir haShirim*, 155.

62. Ibn Ezra; *Metzudas David*, both cited in Zlotowitz, *Shir haShirim*, 155.

63. Ibn Aknim, cited in Zlotowitz, *Shir haShirim*, 155.

64. Rashi, cited in Zlotowitz, *Shir haShirim*, 157.

65. Rashi, cited in Zlotowitz, *Shir haShirim*, 157.

66. B. Shabbat 88b, cited in Zlotowitz, *Shir haShirim*, 158.

67. Alshich, cited in Zlotowitz, *Shir haShirim*, 158.

68. B. Yoma 54a; b. Shabbat 145b; commentary to Lam 1:1, all cited in Zlotowitz, *Shir haShirim*, 160.

69. Rashi, cited in Zlotowitz, *Shir haShirim*, 161.

70. *Metzudas David*, cited in Zlotowitz, *Shir haShirim*, 162.

The Jewish declaration of mutual and exclusive belonging is appropriated with no less enthusiasm in the Christian tradition of the allegorical reading of the Song. Of interest to us, however, is the slant Gregory of Nyssa gives it: when the church asserts that she is her beloved's and her beloved is hers, she is claiming "that she is conformed to Christ—that she has recovered her very own beauty, the primordial blessedness of the human race, that is, to be arrayed in a beauty that conforms to the image and likeness of the first, the sole, and the true Beauty." This, he goes on to explain, is similar to a mirror, which "displays . . . the exact imprint of the face it reflects." In this case, the "face" is that of Christ, a face of "inviolate Beauty." So the church can claim union with her Beloved on these grounds: "Since I focus upon the face of my Kinsman with my entire being, the entire beauty of his form is seen in me."[71]

How may the "beauty of his form" be inferred from the Song's male *wasf*? The beloved "is shining white because he is the radiance of eternal light and 'light from light'" and "because he is free of all sin."[72] If he is ruddy, it is in reference to "his passion, in which . . . he was bathed in his blood."[73] Or, the two colors point to his dual nature: "as God he is shining white" while his ruddiness "indicates what is earthly."[74] He wears his earthly body as a garment: "Who is this that comes from Edom, in crimsoned garment from Bozah—he that is glorious in apparel, in might with strength" (Isa 63:1). This ruddy body is one that we may marvel at for being "splendid in beauty by comparison with the sons of men" (Ps 44:3).[75] Thus, "he is white fittingly, for he is the brightness of the Father; and ruddy, for he was born of a Virgin. The color of each nature shines and glows in him."[76] As for his head, it is no wonder that it is finest gold, because the head of Christ is God (1 Cor 11:3).[77]

The choicest myrrh that drips from the beloved's lips is "the words of his teaching." His finely wrought arms mean "that his doings are polished and finished like the work of a turner." And these arms and hands

---

71. Gregory of Nyssa, *Homiliae XV in Canticum Canticorum* 13, cited in Richard A. Norris Jr., trans. and ed., *The Song of Songs: Interpreted by Early Christian and Medieval Commentators* (Grand Rapids: Eerdmans, 2003), 230.

72. Richard of St.-Victor, *In Cantica Canticorum Explicatio*, cited in Norris, *Song of Songs*, 211; John of Ford, *CXX Sermones*, cited in Norris, *Song of Songs*, 213–15.

73. Richard of St.-Victor, *In Cantica Canticorum Explicatio*, cited in Norris, *Song of Songs*, 211.

74. Theodoret of Cyrus, *Interpretatio in Canticum Canticorum*, cited in Norris, *Song of Songs*, 212.

75. Theodoret of Cyrus, *Interpretatio in Canticum Canticorum*, cited in Norris, *Song of Songs*, 212.

76. Ambrose, *Concerning Virgins* 1.9–4.6, cited in J. Robert Wright, ed., *Proverbs, Ecclesiastes, Song of Solomon*, ACCS, Old Testament 9 (Downers Grove, IL: InterVarsity, 2005), 348.

77. Richard of St.-Victor, *In Cantica Canticorum Explicatio*, cited in Norris, *Song of Songs*, 211–12; John of Ford, *CXX Sermones*, cited in Norris, *Song of Songs*, 215–18.

"are golden because the glory of his divinity brought to perfection the virtues he cultivated in his humanity." The topaz (or purple-flowered "hyacinth") embellishing his hands symbolize the "passion of Christ . . . because on the cross they were pierced by nails and besprinkled with a color like purple thanks to the crimson of his blood." His ivory belly declares that "the frailty of his humanity is bright with the gleam of chastity." And it is set with sky blue sapphire, "signifying the sublimity of things celestial." Ivory and topaz together speak of his two natures: his "human frailty, known in hunger, temptation, weariness, and death"; his "divine majesty, known in miracles, resurrection, and ascension." His legs are described as pillars because, pillar-like, "the ways followed by his incarnation are straight and enduring." These rest on golden pedestals, namely, the prophets (cf. Eph 2:20), "because he has been manifest in the flesh even as foretold by them." If he is like Lebanon, it is because "his beauty is the splendor of all the saints, even as Lebanon is the splendor of all mountains." Indeed, like its cedars which "stand higher than all trees, so Christ surpasses all the saints." As "Lebanon stands out by reason of its height and its bulk . . . Christ shines out among all who have been born on earth." And "just as the cedar surpasses all the splendor of forests in beauty, strength, height, and fragrance, so the Beloved is exceptional in form as compared with the children of men." His mouth's sweetness is clearly "the savor and delight of his words when relished internally . . . most sweet." In all, he is "wholly desirable . . . not only in his divinity but also in his humanity—from the very beginning of his conception until the triumph of his passion, resurrection, and ascension—he is in all respects desirable."[78]

Where is this dazzling one to be found? As with Jewish readings, Christian allegorists make much of his descent into his gardens. His going down signifies "his coming down from unutterable majesty to the lowliness of our nature." The gardens, of course, are human beings, since "we are his field" (1 Cor 3:9).[79] Also, as with Jewish readings, the declaration of reciprocal belonging is key. Christ and his church "are actually two in one flesh." Thus the church's claim: "My lover belongs to me, and I to him."[80] Meanwhile, Christ is the bridegroom whose exclusive affec-

78. Honorius of Autun, *Expositio in Cantica Canticorum*, cited in Norris, *Song of Songs*, 222–23.

79. Gregory of Nyssa, *Homiliae XV in Canticum Canticorum* 15, cited in Norris, *Song of Songs*, 229.

80. Leander of Seville, *Homily on the Triumph of the Church*, cited in Wright, *Proverbs, Ecclesiastes, Song of Solomon*, 350.

tion the church "need not doubt, for he himself says, 'You are my only lover.'"[81]

The concept of Christ's beauty, as we see from these allegorical readings of the *wasf*, is almost equally applied symbolically and literally. The latter interests us particularly, since the *wasf* is a body song. Thus, Gregory of Nyssa's comment works well to summarize how the Song's *wasf* applies most directly to Jesus: "All these elements constituting the bridegroom's beauty are made known for our benefit . . . whoever looks at the visible world and understands the wisdom that has been made manifest by the beauty of creatures"—the Song's male beloved is one such creature—"can make an analogy from the visible to the invisible beauty, the fountain of beauty whose emanation established all living beings in existence."[82]

It appears, then, that where Judaism treads with caution, the Christian allegorical tradition exuberantly transposes the *wasf* on to deity—a hermeneutical move lubricated by the fact of the incarnation of Christ. We now examine whether the canon of Scripture accommodates this move.

At both the level of physical detail and the level of concept, there is, in other parts of the canon, a correlation between the Song's *wasf* and descriptions of unearthly beings. These may be dream-beings, angelic creatures, or visions of God himself.

To begin with, scholars regularly draw comparisons between the *wasf* and the statue in Nebuchadnezzar's dream (Dan 2:30–35).[83] As with the beloved, the first impression of this image is splendorous brightness (זִיוֵהּ יַתִּיר). Both have a head of pure gold (דְהַב טָב). Beyond these superficial details, however, there is little else in overlap. Unlike the man who is golden from head to toe, Nebuchadnezzar's statue must confess to its proverbial feet of clay.

The angelic being in Daniel 10:5 is eye-blinding. He evokes images not only of fiery flame but also of specific precious stones and metal. This being is available for closer viewing than the one in Ezekiel's vision, so Daniel is able to say that he is dressed in linen and has about his waist a

---

81. Leander of Seville, *Homily on the Triumph of the Church*, cited in Wright, *Proverbs, Ecclesiastes, Song of Solomon*, 351.

82. Gregory of Nyssa, *Homilies on the Song of Songs* 13, cited in Wright, *Proverbs, Ecclesiastes, Song of Solomon*, 347.

83. E.g., Assis, *Flashes of Fire*, 171; Diane Bergant, *Song of Songs*, Berit Olam (Collegeville, MN: Liturgical, 2001), 68–69; Ariel Bloch and Chana Bloch, *The Song of Songs: A New Translation with an Introduction and Commentary* (New York: Random House, 1995), 185; Keel, *Song of Songs*, 204; Jenson, *Song of Songs*, 56; John G. Snaith, *The Song of Songs*, NCB (Grand Rapids: Eerdmans, 1993), 80.

belt of gold. Again, we have the same pair of words for gold[84] as in Song 5 (כֶּתֶם אוּפָז)—his girdle is fine gold; "His body was like topaz [תַּרְשִׁישׁ], his face like lightning [בָּרָק], his eyes like torches of fire [אֵשׁ], his arms and legs/feet like the gleam of burnished bronze [נְחֹשֶׁת קָלָל]." It appears that his linen garment still gives away enough of what his unclothed body might have looked like.

However, Ezekiel's theophanic encounter with "a figure like that of a man" (Ezek 1:26–28) is the text that may make the connection between the Song's male protagonist and God himself. The "man" is positioned on a throne of lapis (סַפִּיר), and the first impression is that from the waist up, he seems to be composed of "glowing metal/amber [הַשְׁמַל], as if full of fire [אֵשׁ]," and that from the waist down, "he looked like fire [אֵשׁ]" itself. As if this similitude of conflagration was insufficient brightness, Ezekiel goes on to say that "brilliant light [נֹגַהּ] surrounded him." "Like the appearance of a rainbow in the clouds on a rainy day, so was the radiance [נֹגַהּ] around him."

Splendor is what runs common to these texts, whether they describe angels or God. Indeed, lapis is familiar from a theophany much earlier in the canon. While in Ezekiel it makes up the divine throne, in Exodus it forms the pavement under the feet of God: "a pavement made of lapis lazuli, as bright blue as the sky [לִבְנַת הַסַּפִּיר וּכְעֶצֶם הַשָּׁמַיִם לָטֹהַר]" (Exod 24:10). How remarkable that the woman should describe her beloved the way she does. In radiance, ruddiness, and lapis-like appearance, we may liken the man to Jerusalem's idealized princes (Lam 4:7). But the beloved moves well beyond them, toward those representations of the unearthly and immortal that the language of Daniel and Ezekiel strain toward. Even the reference to the cedars is not without these intimations of the divine, for cedars are "the trees of God" (Ps 80:10 [EV 11]), "the trees of YHWH . . . that he planted" (Ps 104:16).[85]

In the New Testament, the prophetic visions of Daniel and Ezekiel find their resting point in the incarnate Christ. Here is a human who is transfigured such that "his face shone like the sun, and his clothes became as white as the light" (Matt 17:2). Indeed, "his clothes became dazzling white, whiter than anyone in the world could bleach them" (Mark 9:3). The post-resurrection Christ of John's vision (Rev 1:12–16) is a daring reprise of Daniel's vision of YHWH, the Ancient of Days (Dan 7:9–10): Here is a mortal—a "son of man"—whose hair is "white like wool, as white as snow," and whose "eyes were like blazing fire." In resonance with the golden-footed beloved of the *wasf*, "his feet were like bronze

---

84. See Pope, *Song of Songs*, 534–35, for his dissection of the term.
85. Keel, *Song of Songs*, 206; Pope, *Song of Songs*, 546.

glowing in a furnace." Where the beloved was sweet of mouth, this heavenly vision has a voice "like the sound of rushing waters." Both are gloriously effulgent: "His face was like the sun shining in all its brilliance."

We see, then, that the Song's exaltation of its human lover into the realms of the unearthly takes on new depth when the reader firmly inserts the poem into the canon of sacred literature of which it is part and listens for resonances.

CONCLUSION

Having treated Song 5 and Ezekiel 16 as canonical counterparts to each other in their focus on the body beautiful, we showed how these texts work together to present a prescription for ideal human love.

When speaking of beautiful bodies, the woman of Song 5 and the man of Ezekiel 16 could make a perfect prescription for human love relationships. This is not necessarily because each is beautiful—indeed, we have no idea what Ezekiel's man looks like—but because of the overlaps in their conception of the one they love.

First, we notice that if not for the speaker, the beautiful beloved would not exist. They speak, and beauty assembles itself before our eyes. She can put it together body part by incredible body part. He can invoke it with a sequence of astonishing scenes. And all this wizardry bubbles up from a shared trait: the capacity to construct the other as beautiful, as a means of expressing the value of the other.

Second, in the process of creating beauty, both follow similar routes—suggesting equivalence in their perception of the loved one. Each sees the beloved as so praiseworthy that only royalty can sufficiently exalt him/her. Each sees the beloved as incalculably precious. The husband of Ezekiel 16 sees his foundling bride as worthy of gold and silver. The woman in Song 5 thinks of her loved one as composed of gold. Eventually, not only is beauty created but established—through the lover's agency, the loved one is publicly affirmed as beautiful.

Predictably then—and third—both respond in like measure to the loss of the beautiful beloved, with anguish.

If "beauty lies in the eyes of the beholder," then Song 5 and Ezekiel 16 present a pair of humans who could love each other into beauty beyond imagination.

Meanwhile on the plane of deity and devotee, Ezekiel 16 presents the divine husband who devotedly constructs and delights in the loveliness of his bride. The Song of Songs itself has three poems (4:1–7; 6:4–9;

7:2–10 [EV 7:1–9]) in praise of the bride, which if read allegorically, declare the divine lover's admiration of his beloved. The New Testament picks up this theme in Revelation (21:2, 9–27). As in Ezekiel 16, the bride's beauty is attributed to God's agency. When John's angelic tour guide offers to show him "the bride, the wife of the Lamb," John sees "Jerusalem" shining "with the glory of God."

Does the canon *also* present the devotee-bride reciprocally rejoicing in the beauty of her heavenly bridegroom? That is what the Song of Songs does when read as allegory. Here is the bride who proudly shows off the body beautiful of her man—a "man" invested with the incandescence of God.

PART III

Gardens

6.

The Orchard of Pomegranates

Large parts of the Song are either set in a leafy paradise or speak of one. The verdant outdoors competes with walled spaces. The lovers set up meetings in the countryside as much as they speak of withdrawing into private chambers. While on one hand the woman urges her beloved to take her into his bedroom (1:4), or hurries him into her mother's house (3:4), or longs to do so (8:2), on the other hand, she negotiates a siesta-time rendezvous on the hillsides where he tends his sheep (1:7), imagines their forest haunts to be their bedchamber (1:16–17), or suggests the outdoors as a getaway (7:11–13). Meanwhile, the man sometimes knocks on her door at night, desiring to come in (5:2), but at other times invites her to come out into the springtime countryside (2:10–13). The lovers speak of being in each other's company on the forest floor (1:16–17), under apple trees (8:5), in flowering vineyards, and under pomegranate trees with the grass beneath them fragrant with mandrakes (7:12).

Besides the literal, the Song is flush with vegetal imagery, used especially in each lover describing the other. The woman thinks of the man as "a cluster of henna blossoms" (1:14), as an apple tree in the forest (2:3), or as a cedar of Lebanon (5:15). He speaks of her as a "lily among thorns" (2:2), with temples as ruddy as pomegranates (4:3; 6:7), with a body as heady as a garden of spices (4:13–15), with a belly that reminds him of a "mound of wheat encircled by lilies" (7:2), and breasts that are as delectable as clusters of dates or grapes (7:7–8).

Other than describing each other with recourse to the botanical, their intimacies are delicately evoked by the same metaphor. Sometimes, the man is a gazelle and she the lily-strewn meadow in which he feeds (2:16; 6:3). Sometimes, she is the vineyard he tends, whose fruit he enjoys

(8:12). Sometimes, she is a garden or orchard he is invited to enter and raid (4:12–5:1; 6:2), or a spice-laden mountain he can gambol on (8:14). Further, both speak of the woman's sexual ripening in garden terms. He "went down to the grove of nut trees to look at the new growth in the valley, to see if the vines had budded or if the pomegranates were in bloom" (6:11). He thereupon is seized by "desire." She, in very similar double entendre, invites him to "go early to the vineyards to see if the vines have budded, if their blossoms have opened, and if the pomegranates are in bloom" (7:12). She thereupon promises him her "love."

The "Songs of Lebanon" is the title sometimes given to a series of three enchanting poems in the Song in which the third poem treats the woman as a metaphorical garden. Except for one interjection by the woman, the poems belong to the male voice. The three songs are located sequentially in 4:8, 4:9–11, and 4:12–5:1. We have chosen this section for our study of the theme of gardens so that we can place the Song in conversation with a parallel text in the Hebrew canon.

We find that the idea of the woman as a garden resonates with that in the love song of Isaiah 5:1–7, in which another "woman" is a vineyard. In each case, there is a man who desires to enjoy the fruit. In the Song, the metaphor is sustained over the section 4:12–5:1 with a logical progression. It begins with anticipation—"You are a garden . . . my sister" (4:12)—and finishes off with satisfaction—"I have come into my garden, my sister" (5:1). This makes it a textual parallel to the parable of Isaiah 5, in which also a certain man anticipates satisfaction from his vineyard.

However, the Song's poem is the last of a series of three Songs of Lebanon, and so has to be taken in this literary context. The series is unified by an inclusio.[1] It begins "Come with me" (4:8) and finishes with "I have come" (5:1). The series, as the title suggests, is also unified with the mention of Lebanon.[2] The first poem begins with it: "Come with me from Lebanon" (4:8). The second poem ends with it: "The fragrance of your garments is like the fragrance of Lebanon" (4:11). The third poem mentions it midway: "You are . . . a well of flowing water streaming down from Lebanon" (4:15). Thus, we study the triptych of love poems as a single literary piece, each poem setting up, and tumbling into, the next.

---

1. E.g., Elie Assis, *Flashes of Fire: A Literary Analysis of the Song of Songs* (New York: T&T Clark, 2009), 130; Mary T. Elliott, *The Literary Unity of the Canticle* (Frankfurt: Lang, 1989), 99.
2. E.g., Assis, *Flashes of Fire*, 130.

THE FIRST SONG OF LEBANON: SONG 4:8

The man invites—no, pleads!—with his loved one to come with him. He makes similar pleas for her company in other parts of the Song. In 2:10–13, she was on the other side of a latticed window. His invitation was bracketed with the imperatives, "arise [קוּמִי לָךְ] . . . come away" (לְכִי־לָךְ). In 5:2, he stands on her doorstep, urging her to let him in, again with an imperative, "open to me" (פִּתְחִי־לִי). Here, in 4:8, his invitation is just as urgent:

With me	from Lebanon	bride	
אִתִּי	מִלְּבָנוֹן	כַּלָּה	
With me	from Lebanon	come	
אִתִּי	מִלְּבָנוֹן	תָּבוֹאִי	
Descend	from the top of	Amana	
תָּשׁוּרִי	מֵרֹאשׁ	אֲמָנָה	
	from the top of	Senir	and Hermon
	מֵרֹאשׁ	שְׂנִיר	וְחֶרְמוֹן
	from the dens of	lions	
	מִמְּעֹנוֹת	אֲרָיוֹת	
	and from the mountains of	leopards	
	מֵהַרְרֵי	נְמֵרִים	

When the lines are arranged, the pattern that emerges is striking for its repeated use of "from" (מִן).[3] Three pairs of "from" line up. The first pair is identical, and notes the general region of the woman's location. She is to come away *from* Lebanon. The second pair describes specifically where in the Lebanon area she is. She is to come away *from* the head of Amana, *from* the head of Senir and Hermon. The third pair takes note of her environs. She is to come away *from* the dens of lions, *from* the haunts of leopards.

A woman coyly hiding behind a window lattice or latched in by a

---

3. See Elliott, *Literary Unity*, 102–3 for the structural function of מִן with respect to the imperatives of movement.

bedroom door was one thing. For her to stand on a mountain top, and with suggestions of being flanked by big cats, is another thing altogether. In the other two scenes, the movement is merely across a barrier. All it takes to end the separation is that either she must come out, or he must be let in. In many ways, this scenario is different.

First, the image transcends any semblance of what usually may be expected in the trope of love in separation. The man is at his creative best. He places his beloved on the highest mountain range an Israelite can think of. She is not just a dove on a cliff side, but a woman on a mountain peak—she is that much more inaccessible.[4]

Second, the image is seductive. Comparing her to a dove associated her with the goddess of love. Here, she is the goddess herself.[5] Keel explains that "goddesses enthroned on mountains are not found with great frequency in ancient Near Eastern art, but they are hardly out of the ordinary." Ishtar is depicted on a cylinder seal "as a wild mountain dweller, energetically climbing a mountain." Meanwhile, the Lebanon range, being the highest known in the region (cf. Deut 3:25), was considered the abode of gods (Ezekiel 31) with its cedars planted by the Lord himself (Ps 104:16). This idea is represented in the Gilgamesh epic, which exalts Lebanon as "the cedar mountain, abode of the gods, Throne-seat of [Ishtar]."[6]

This idea could well inform the Song's placing of the beloved woman on the icy heights of Lebanon. Senir, Amana, and Hermon probably represent the northern, middle, and southern parts of the anti-Lebanon range. Hermon, which is snow-topped for the greater part of the year, is significant for its sanctuaries with temples and altars dating into the Roman period.[7] Like the gods, then, the Song's woman inhabits the high mountains, beyond human habitation. The image is strengthened by the mention of the lion and the leopard, whose haunts these mountain

---

4. Diane Bergant, *Song of Songs*, Berit Olam (Collegeville, MN: Liturgical, 2001), 51; Richard S. Hess, *Song of Songs*, Baker Commentary on the Old Testament (Grand Rapids: Baker, 2005), 139; Roland Murphy, *The Song of Songs*, Hermeneia (Minneapolis: Augsburg Fortress, 1990), 160; Michael V. Fox, *The Song of Songs and the Ancient Egyptian Love Songs* (Madison: University of Wisconsin Press, 1985), 134.

5. Thus Duane Garrett, "Song of Songs," in *Song of Songs, Lamentations*, ed. Duane Garrett and Paul R. House, WBC 23B (Nashville: Thomas Nelson, 2004), 192–93; Tom Gledhill, *The Message of the Song of Songs: The Lyrics of Love*, Bible Speaks Today (Leicester: InterVarsity, 1994), 160–61.

6. Othmar Keel, *The Song of Songs: A Continental Commentary*, trans. Frederick J. Gaiser (Minneapolis: Augsburg, 1994), 155–56.

7. Keel, *Song of Songs*, 158; Marvin H. Pope, *Song of Songs: A New Translation with Introduction and Commentary*, Anchor Bible 7C (New Haven: Yale University Press, 1977), 475–77, thinks there are echoes here of an episode in Canaanite mythology in which the shepherd Dumuzi/Adonis flees with his beloved to the Lebanon mountains.

ranges supposedly are. Keel observes that these animals have an association with female deities that goes back to the seventh/sixth millennium BCE, with particular reference to the warlike Ishtar. "Her dominion over predatory animals illustrates her wild, unbroken, unapproachable and virgin power."[8] Icons depict her, armed with quiver and sword, with her foot on a lion that she holds by a leash (Akkadian, ca. 2200 BCE), or standing on what could be either a lioness or leopard (Neo-Assyrian, seventh century BCE). Going by the persistence of this image across space and time, from Egypt to the Greco-Roman period to the present day, it appears to have a timeless erotic appeal that transcends cultures.[9]

Like the warlike love goddess, the Song's beloved is attended by wild cats, the lion and the leopard. She is love incarnate; not just unimaginably beautiful and utterly desirable, but with an edge of the dangerous and the untamed. Some scholars see the picture of the beloved among wild cats as an indication of her being in danger, one from which she must come away so as to be safe with her man.[10] This is debatable. On the contrary, it appears that she herself is presented as the mortal hazard. She is not only beyond the pale of humanity but beyond what is safe for human consumption. Such a divine being is best located on the mountaintops, as thoroughly inaccessible as such a one should be.[11] If the man is attempting to allure his loved one with this seductive imagery, he has it right. Images of doves on unreachable rocky crags pale in comparison with this metaphor. We shall see that he does well with this start.

A third significant difference from previous love-in-separation scenes is that by placing the beloved on a (mountain of a) pedestal, the point is implicitly made that it is up to her to make the next move. There are no imperatives here as when she was behind windows and doors. A human could not presume to command a goddess! The invitations are thus more entreaties. The divine must condescend to descend to her besotted human lover who pleads for her presence. Thus, we have the sixfold "from." She must deign to come away from where she belongs,

---

8. Keel, *Song of Songs*, 158.

9. See Keel, *Song of Songs*, 157–59; Pope, *Song of Songs*, 476–77. The image is not uncommon in present day advertisements, comic books, and video games.

10. E.g., Assis, *Flashes of Fire*, 132; Daniel J. Estes, "The Song of Songs," in *Ecclesiastes and the Song of Songs*, ed. Daniel C. Fredericks and Daniel J. Estes, AOTC 16 (Downers Grove, IL: InterVarsity, 2010), 356–57; Tremper Longman III, *Song of Songs* (Grand Rapids: Eerdmans, 2001), 149; Marcia Falk, *The Song of Songs: A New Translation and Interpretation* (New York: HarperCollins, 1973), 182.

11. So Cheryl J. Exum, *Song of Songs: A Commentary* (Louisville: Westminster John Knox, 2005), 169. Ariel Bloch and Chana Bloch, *The Song of Songs: A New Translation with an Introduction and Commentary* (New York: Random House, 1995), 174, agree that the mountains are "symbols of inaccessibility and danger, and at the same time, of majestic, primeval beauty."

these awesome mountain heights clothed with snow and cloud, where the fiercest of cats stand guard at her side. His previous pleas seemed to elicit her teasing. She either tantalized him with a song (2:15) or vexed him with questions (5:3). We shall see that by positing himself as a mortal supplicant who trespasses his bounds by even raising his eyes to her, he eventually gains from her a counter-invitation every bit as passionately breathless as his.

A fourth difference is the motive in his invitation. At other times, he called her out to enjoy the countryside in springtime; or, he pleaded to be let into her chamber because he was standing in the night mist, a little bedraggled and sorry for himself. This time, the invitation is focused entirely on her. Each pair of phrases develops the theme of her as a goddess—the northern regions, the heights, the cats. The compliment he pays her is irresistible!

A final point of difference from previous invitations is the allure in the picture of him as a humble devotee who has dared to raise his eyes to her. The distance between them is insurmountable, and in picturing this separation as vertical, he places her unreachably above himself. Yet, he dares to invite her. He does not use an imperative, but rather the imperfect (תָּבוֹאִי), which fits the context well as wishful thinking: "Oh, that you would come down . . ."[12]

What is more, he uniquely addresses her as bride (כַּלָּה). Though this does not necessarily demand a marital context, it could be used in hope.[13] It is significant that this endearment is unique to the Songs of Lebanon, and occurs six times in them (4:8, 9, 10, 11, 12; 5:1). It is an audacious endearment for a mere mortal to confer on a goddess, and certainly one calculated to win her favor.

But, of course, the man has only begun. There is more seduction to come.

12. Bloch and Bloch, *Song of Songs*, 174.

13. E.g., Bergant, *Song of Songs*, 50; Bloch and Bloch, *Song of Songs*, 175; Exum, *Song of Songs*, 169–70; Garrett, *Song of Songs*, 193; Murphy, *Song of Songs*, 160; Fox, *Ancient Egyptian Love Songs*, 135; Falk, *Song of Songs*, 182. Contra Gledhill, *Message of the Song of Songs*, 163; Estes, *Song of Songs*, 353; Hess, *Song of Songs*, 139, 142; Longman, *Song of Songs*, 150; Michael D. Goulder, *The Song of Fourteen Songs*, JSOTSup 36 (Sheffield: JSOT Press, 1986), 37; Keel, *Song of Songs*, 155; Iain Provan, *Ecclesiastes, Song of Songs*, NIVAC (Grand Rapids: Zondervan, 2001), 318. Gianni Barbiero, *Song of Songs: A Close Reading*, trans. Michael Tait, VTSS (Leiden: Brill, 2011), 202, explains it as an alternative to "daughter-in-law."

THE SECOND SONG OF LEBANON: SONG 4:9–11

We must assume that the love goddess consents to the ardent plea, and descends from her mountain abode.[14] Indeed, she is now on level with him as his words would indicate. Like the previous poem, this one also begins with a double repetition of phrases:

You drive me crazy	my sister[15]		bride	you drive me crazy
לִבַּבְתִּנִי	אֲחֹתִי		כַלָּה	לִבַּבְתִּינִי

With one (glance)	of your eyes
בְּאַחַת	מֵעֵינַיִךְ

With one jewel	of your necklace
בְּאַחַד עֲנָק	מִצַּוְּרֹנָיִךְ (4:9)

The goddess stands before the mortal, and at her nearness his heart is wildly affected.[16] English translations try various renderings. She has "ravished" his heart (KJV), "captured" (NLT) or "stolen" (NIV) or "captivated" (ESV) it, or made it "beat faster" (NASB).[17] But this is not just because of her proximity. She is looking at him. One glance is sufficient to electrify the lover. Why, the glint of one jewel in her necklace does the job quite effortlessly![18]

The repeated "one" (אהד/אהת) emphasizes how little it takes to set his heart a-thud. An example from ancient Egypt brings together the effect

---

14. The implied movement of the woman—by stages—in the Songs of Lebanon is regularly observed: e.g., Estes, "Song of Songs," 356.

15. On the sibling endearment as an expression of physical bondedness, see Jill M. Munro, *Spikenard and Saffron: A Study in the Poetic Language of the Song of Songs*, JSOTSup 203 (Sheffield: Sheffield Academic, 1995), 74–79. See Pope, *Song of Songs*, 480–81, on examples in other parallel texts. Fox, *Ancient Egyptian Love Songs*, 136; Exum, *Song of Songs*, 171–72; Garrett, "Song of Songs," 194; Hess, *Song of Songs*, 142; Robert W. Jenson, *Song of Songs*, Interpretation (Louisville: John Knox, 2005), 50; Barbiero, *Song of Songs*, 203–4. H. Stephan, *Modern Palestinian Parallels to the Song of Songs*, Studies in Palestinian Customs and Folklore 3 (Jerusalem: Palestine Oriental Society, 1923), 12, gives an example of similar language in modern Palestinian love poetry: "We have brought your cousin, we have brought your kinswoman."

16. Note the alliterative wordplay between לבב and לְבָנוֹן. E.g., Assis, *Flashes of Fire*, 134.

17. See Bergant, *Song of Songs*, 51–52.

18. The phrase מֵעֵינַיִךְ may be understood to be Janus parallelism. עֵינַיִם could mean either "eyes" (which steal the man's heart; previous stich) or "jewels" (which make up her necklace; following stich) (M. Malul, "Janus Parallelism in Biblical Hebrew: Two More Cases," *BZ* 41 [1997]: 246–49). Also Fox, *Ancient Egyptian Love Songs*, 136.

of both gaze and jewelry: "with your eyes you have captured me / with your necklace you have bound me."[19] Linking the beloved's eye and its effect on the lover's heart is a modern Palestinian poem: "Her wink terrifies the heart of the lion, / O, how much sense has she stolen!"[20]

There is the recurring "from" (מִן), this time with the sense of "of." In the earlier poem it negotiated the distance between the woman on a mountain peak and her lover at the foothills. Here, the "from" implies that the great distance has miraculously closed. She is close enough for him to look into her eyes. He can admire her jewelry at close quarters. In other words, the impossible has happened, and she stands within his reach. She is terrible, bejeweled as any self-respecting goddess should be, and with flashing eyes that melt the insides—but the happy fact is that she is at arm's length. And so, taking his life in his hands, we should presume, he dares to speak to her, and tells her he is thoroughly undone.

We suppose that she finds this confession endearing, for she moves closer. Not only can he see her, but his nose catches a whiff of her perfume. The poem's opening endearment-studded schema has been successful, so in 4:10 he presses the formula into service a third and last time (cf. 4:8, 9):

How beautiful	is your lovemaking	my sister	bride
מַה־יָּפוּ	דֹּדַיִךְ	אֲחֹתִי	כַלָּה
How [much more] pleasing	is your lovemaking	than wine	
מַה־טֹּבוּ	דֹּדַיִךְ	מִיַּיִן	
	and the fragrance of your ointments	than any spice	
	וְרֵיחַ שְׁמָנַיִךְ	מִכָּל־בְּשָׂמִים	

How can he speak of lovemaking[21] when she is barely descended from the heights? We may assume he speaks in anticipation, another device

---

19. Pap. Chester Beatty I, Group C: 43, translated in Barbiero, *Song of Songs*, 206. Fox, *Ancient Egyptian Love Songs*, 73, renders the second line differently: "With her thighs she binds."

20. Gustaf H. Dalman, *Palästinischer Diwan: Als Beitrag zur Volkskunde Palästinas* (Leipzig: Hinrichs, 1901), 134. Similar lines from Palestinian poems are: "your eyes are black and they sparkle, and have slain (me) indeed" (Stephan, *Modern Palestinian Parallels*, 14); and: "the lilt of your eyes—oh, my eyes!— / Have driven me to love you frantically" (Stephan, *Modern Palestinian Parallels*, 47).

21. Another possibility is to read דדיך with the LXX: "breasts" (דַּדַּיִךְ) rather than "lovemaking" (דֹּדַיִךְ).

in his artful enticement of her. He articulates his expectation of further favors and in the meantime, breathes in her heavenly fragrance, better than that of spice (בֹּשֶׂם).[22] This is the recurring spice (4:14, 16; 5:1, 13; 6:2; 8:14) identified as balsam. Balsam's fragrance is described as "fine and pleasing, spicy, similar to lemon or rosemary, comparable to the fresh resin of the silver fir."[23] Josephus associates it with the spices (בְּשָׂמִים) the queen of Sheba gifted to Solomon (1 Kgs 10:2, 10),[24] carefully cultivated in the imperial gardens in En-gedi, perhaps in Josiah's time (seventh century BCE) or in the Persian period (sixth century BCE).[25] The beloved's fragrance rivals even that of balsam, so intoxicating is the aroma of her unguents.

Given the distance still existing between them, her aroma is the most he can appropriate. But his charming words pay off, because from the next words he speaks, we must imagine that she has closed what remains of the distance between their bodies—she is kissing him with no uncertain fervor. Thus, when he next has the opportunity to speak further, he is able to speak of the taste of her lips and tongue, and say what her clothes smell like. Clearly, the woman has capitulated into his eager arms.

(The sweetness of) honeycomb	your lips drip	bride
נֹפֶת	תִּטֹּפְנָה שִׂפְתוֹתַיִךְ	כַּלָּה
Honey and milk	are under your tongue	
דְּבַשׁ וְחָלָב	תַּחַת לְשׁוֹנֵךְ	
The fragrance	of your garments	
וְרֵיחַ	שַׂלְמֹתַיִךְ	
is like the fragrance	of Lebanon	
כְּרֵיחַ	לְבָנוֹן (4:11)	

---

22. "The sense of the colon is not that her perfumes are better than any others, but that to her lover even her everyday anointing oils smell better than the most exotic perfumes" (G. Lloyd Carr, *Song of Solomon: An Introduction and Commentary*, TOTC [Leicester: InterVarsity, 1984], 122).

23. Immanuel Löw, *Die Flora der Juden*, vol. 1, *Kryptogamae, Acanthacae, Graminaceae* (Leipzig: Wien, 1928), 300, cited in Keel, *Song of Songs*, 165.

24. Josephus, *The New Complete Works of Josephus*, trans. William Whiston, rev. and exp. ed. (Grand Rapids: Kregel, 1999), *Ant.* 8.6.174.

25. Keel, *Song of Songs*, 165.

The man continues to press the technique of repetition, but now we see repetition with increment. He describes her kisses first with the metaphor of the honeycomb,[26] and then advances it using the images of honey and milk. He first speaks about her lips and then moves on to his experience of her tongue. Some suggest that he may be making reference to the fluid sweetness of her speech. While this is plausible, it seems rather unlikely in the circumstances.[27] We have noted how her implied movements, step by step, eliminated the distance between herself and this ardent devotee.[28] The sensory sequence thus begins with the visual and moves up the scale of intimacy. First, she is visualized from afar—a distant figure on the heights of Lebanon—and then seen up close—he can see details on her jewelry. The next step induces the olfactory sense: he smells her perfume. Surely, this should be followed by the gustatory rather than the auditory. Thus, his adroit wooing is rewarded with a taste of her. And that taste he can only describe with hyperbole. "Milk and honey" is what the promised land of Canaan flows with (e.g., Exod 3:8). Indeed, milk or cream and honey are what mark paradise, whether experienced here on earth or in the world to come (Deut 32:13–14; cf. Job 20:17).[29]

Intimations of the divine are similarly evoked by the *leitwort* "Lebanon" that closes the poem. Her clothes smell like Lebanon.[30] They give off the proverbial luxurious scent of the resin-rich conifer forests (Hos 14:6) that made Lebanon a celestial garden. The lover doesn't let the metaphor drop just yet. She is close enough for him to luxuriate in the smell of not just her perfume but her clothes (4:11), but one is not to forget that she is the goddess descended from her dwelling on high.

---

26. Keel, *Song of Songs*, 165, notes the heaping up of "p" and "t" sounds in the first colon of the verse that convey the dripping of honey from its comb.

27. The seductress in Prov 5:3 is similarly described: her lips "drip honey" and her mouth is "smoother than oil." Similarly, some modern Palestinian songs: "Her saliva is like crystal sugar (or sugar candy), / O, How sweet is the sucking of her lips / sweeter than sugar or honey" (Stephan, *Modern Palestinian Parallels*, 16); "Her mouth is sweet to me / it contains a honeycomb." Gustaf H. Dalman, *Palästinischer Diwan: Als Beitrag zur Volkskunde Palästinas* (Leipzig: Hinrichs, 1901), 134. In a similar context of sexuality, see Pope, *Song of Songs*, 505–6, for honey as an element in fertility worship.

28. Similarly, Assis, *Flashes of Fire*, 136.

29. See Barbiero, *Song of Songs*, 212.

30. Cf. Psalm 45, a wedding song in which the bridegroom's "robes are fragrant with myrrh and aloes and cassia" (45:8). A modern Palestinian parallel is: "O you with the gauze mantle, let it not become dusty, / For your fragrance is musk and ambergris" (Stephan, *Modern Palestinian Parallels*, 15).

THE THIRD SONG OF LEBANON: SONG 4:12–5:1

The final act of intimacy remains to be entered into. Intent on dissolving any remaining reticence, the man deftly continues his verbal foreplay into the third and last of the series of poems. He introduces a metaphor within a metaphor. She is goddess, and what is more, her body is like an exquisite garden.[31] He sustains this sub-metaphor across four verses, shaping it as the climax of his courting of her favors. Bracketing the poem is the reference to her as a "garden" (גַּן)/"fountain of gardens" (גַּנִּים).

4:12: (You are)		4:15: (You are)	
a garden	locked up	a fountain	of gardens
גַּן	נָעוּל	מַעְיָן	גַּנִּים
a spring	enclosed	a well	of living/flowing water
גַּל	נָעוּל	בְּאֵר	מַיִם חַיִּים
a fountain	sealed	streams	from Lebanon
מַעְיָן	חָתוּם	נֹזְלִים	מִן לְבָנוֹן

Both the opening and closing brackets use a triplet of nouns (4:12 and 15), each followed by a descriptor. In the opening bracket, the three nouns are garden, spring,[32] and fountain. Each of these is pictured as in some way restricted.[33] The garden is locked up, the spring is enclosed, the fountain is sealed.[34] In other words, the man is addressing the condition of his loved one. Even though she is located in his embrace, rather

31. For an intertextual reading between the garden of Eden and the garden metaphor in the Song, see Francis Landy, "The Song of Songs and the Garden of Eden," *JBL* 98, no. 4 (1979): 521–28.

32. By emending גַּל to גַּן, the second image could be read as reiterating the first: "a garden enclosed" (so Fox, *Ancient Egyptian Love Songs*, 137). Without emendation, the word is used as in Josh 15:19 and Judg 1:15 to refer to a "spring" or "cistern." See Pope, *Song of Songs*, 488–89.

33. The restriction does not necessarily express the man's claim of sole ownership or that he alone has admission; Bergant, *Song of Songs*, 54; Gledhill, *Message of the Song of Songs*, 168 (but see also 165). Contra, Murphy, *Song of Songs*, 161; Estes, *Song of Songs*, 359; Exum, *Song of Songs*, 175–76. Christopher Meredith presents an interesting reading of the Song's gendering of spaces by invariably featuring the woman "internal and bounded, placed within the poem's numerous cavities" and beyond that, "*as* a cavity for male inhabitation" ("The Lattice and the Looking Glass: Gendered Space in Song of Songs 2:8–14," *JAAR* 80, no. 2 [2012]: 365–86, esp. 373–74).

34. See Keel, *Song of Songs*, 173–74, for an explanation with diagram for how water sources were sealed in Egypt.

than on Lebanon, she remains inaccessible.[35] Is this to be read as a petulant remark, spoken with an undertone of complaint? This is unlikely. In
Eastern communities, virginity and chastity are womanly virtues prized
above all else. Just as he admired the beloved's fragrance and taste in the
previous poem, he now eulogizes her exclusivity. In fact, the compliment on her fragrance which ends the second poem (4:11b) is what the
poet picks up and expands in the third poem, which is dedicated to the
idea of the woman as a garden of sweet-smelling spices. It is not just her
cosmetics or her garments that delight the nose—she herself is the source
of fragrance.

The sequence of nouns spills over seamlessly from the opening bracket
(4:12) to the closing bracket (4:15): garden—spring—fountain; fountain—well—streams. In the second triplet, the sense of restriction that
marked the first triplet seems to disappear. The fountain is now not a
sealed one, but one that is a "fountain of gardens," suggesting its availability to these gardens. It waters them. The well is not just a basin of
static water. It is bubbling up from the spring at its bottom. It is a well
of moving (literally, "living") water. The last item (נֹזְלִים) may be read
either as a participial verb or as a substantive. That is, it could continue the image of the well: "a well of flowing water, *streaming* from
Lebanon."[36] Or, it could be an image independent of the well: "a well of
flowing water, *streams* from Lebanon." Since the opening bracket has a
series of three images, it would be aesthetic to have a numerical match in
the closing bracket, where the noun "fountain" is paired with the noun
"streams."[37] If so, here is a picture of free-flowing mountain rills, tumbling over boulders and down into the valley.

The images of fountain, well, and stream suggest an increasing liberty
in movement.[38] With the "fountain of gardens," we picture the neatly
laid out canals and pools that it supplies. With the well, we can see
the water astir as the spring gushes within it. With the streams, we are
released from the enclosed spaces that gardens and wells are. We are
looking at a mountainside, down which the rivulets plummet, free to
choose their path. With this subtle difference marking the opening and
closing frames of the poem, we wonder if the poet is embedding into his
lines a delicate entreaty. Is the woman to understand the movement from
the inaccessible to the available as a request that she open herself to this

---

35. Hess, *Song of Songs*, 147; Longman, *Song of Songs*, 155; Barbiero, *Song of Songs*, 219–20.

36. See Bloch and Bloch, *Song of Songs*, 177–78, which requires reading the verse against the accents.

37. Cf. Prov 5:15, 18, for a woman as a well or fountain.

38. Bergant, *Song of Songs*, 56.

suitor?[39] He well appreciates that she can withhold her favors. Indeed, walled-off gardens, fenced-off springs, and sealed fountains are all the more desirable because they are unavailable. The passerby is intrigued. He wonders what lies on the other side of the wall; he wonders what the spring's water tastes like; he wonders what the fountain would feel like. So, while the man admires the loved one's aloof exclusivity, he wishes he could experience her. He anticipates the pleasure of being watered by this garden fountain, of drinking deep from the bubbling well, of splashing in the refreshing water of Lebanon's snow-fed streams. And there is the *leitwort* "Lebanon" for the last time. He ends his courtship with it. She is still the love goddess, and he a supplicant hoping to receive the ultimate of her favors. The man's speech ends as it began. She remains in some way above him. She must descend to him "from Lebanon" (4:8). She must stream down to him "from Lebanon" (4:15). How could the woman resist a suitor so worshipful!

We must return to consider the substance of the garden metaphor. While the garden as a setting for love trysts is ubiquitous in romantic genres ancient and modern, the woman herself as a garden is no less common. An Egyptian song has the woman imagining herself a garden of "fragrant plants":

> I am your favorite sister
> I am yours like the field
>   planted with flowers
>   and with all sorts of fragrant plants.
> Pleasant is the canal within it,
>   which your hand scooped out,
>   while we cooled ourselves in the north wind.[40]

We understand, of course, the "hand" and the "canal" are not referring to the man's labors at gardening. Similarly, the Sumerian text known as "The Message of Ludingira to His Mother" has a description of the beloved thus:

> My mother is . . .
> A garden of delight, full of joy,
> A watered pine, adorned with pine cones,
> A spring flower, a first-fruit,

---

39. See Garrett, *Song of Songs*, 196.
40. Pap. Harris 500, Group C: 18, translated in Fox, *Ancient Egyptian Love Songs*, 26.

An irrigation ditch carrying luxuriant waters to the garden plots,
A sweet date from Dilmun, a date chosen for the best.[41]

Again, we understand that "mother" isn't what the term usually means.[42]

Song 4:13–14 employs this poetic device of the beloved-as-garden
to depict the attractions of the beloved, who is just as "fragrant" as her
Egyptian counterpart, and perhaps even more intoxicating:[43]

> Your plants [שְׁלָחַיִךְ] are an orchard [פַּרְדֵּס] of pomegranates [רִמּוֹנִים]
>   with choice fruits [עִם פְּרִי מְגָדִים]
> Henna [כְּפָרִים] with nard [עִם־נְרָדִים], nard [נֵרְדְּ] and saffron [וְכַרְכֹּם],
>   calamus [קָנֶה] and cinnamon [וְקִנָּמוֹן]
> With every kind of incense tree [עִם כָּל־עֲצֵי לְבוֹנָה]
> Myrrh [מֹר] and aloes [וַאֲהָלוֹת] with all the finest spices [עִם כָּל־רָאשֵׁי
> בְשָׂמִים] (4:13–14)

Here is a garden designed to beggar the imagination. Consider first
its individual parts.[44] The pomegranate is a beautifully shaped fruit, its
ruddy skin protecting a treasure of juicy seeds colored pale pink or ruby
red. Henna leaves produce a lovely reddish-brown dye. From nard is
obtained thick, intensely aromatic oil. The saffron flower is a type of cro-
cus whose female parts make the most expensive of spices. Calamus may
be the sweet cane, known for its scented leaves and rhizome. Cinnamon
is aromatic tree bark, and myrrh, a fragrant gum. Aloe is known for the
aroma of its wood. The "incense tree" would be a generic term, referring
to any sweet-smelling tree.

Of these items, henna and saffron are valued for color. Henna is a popular hair colorant in present-day South Asia, as it seems to have been in
ancient West Asia. Besides tinting hair, it is traditionally used to decorate
women's hands and feet with intricate designs called *mehndi,* an essential
part of a Hindu or Muslim bride's toilette. Saffron is so expensive as to

41. Jerrold S. Cooper, "New Cuneiform Parallels to the Song of Songs," *JBL* 90 (1971):
161–62.

42. Pope, *Song of Songs,* 496–97; Cooper, "New Cuneiform Parallels," 161. A sample of the
frequent use of this metaphor in modern Palestinian poems is: "The garden of your beauty in its
bloom is fairer and more resplendent than a flower garden" (Stephan, *Modern Palestinian Parallels,* 16).

43. We note, however, that compared to the Egyptian poem, the Song's garden metaphor
has no concrete elements. Its abstractions keep it from slipping into the explicit (Assis, *Flashes of
Fire,* 138; Longman, *Song of Songs,* 156). It has no finite verbs, but rather a string of participles,
keeping the imagery static (Bergant, *Song of Songs,* 54). Some, however—typically, Pope, *Song
of Songs,* 489–91—readily see allusions to various female body parts.

44. See Longman, *Song of Songs,* 156–57; Pope, *Song of Songs,* 492–95; Keel, *Song of Songs,*
178–80; Barbiero, *Song of Songs,* 223–26.

be a luxury even in lands to which it is native. While it delicately flavors food, its warm orange color is what makes it distinctive.

If the appeal of henna and saffron is largely visual, then the pomegranate serves for taste. With its tangy-sweet seeds, it is the only edible item listed. Meanwhile, the largest grouping is that of fragrant items. Here, cinnamon serves both the nose and the taste buds, adding its sharp woody flavor to foods or working as a perfume. Nard and calamus, myrrh and aloe are best known for their use in perfumery, finding their way into oils or ointments. The garden's contents stimulate the senses. When the metaphor is peeled back, it is the body of the bride that the poet describes, a body that can knock a man senseless.

What is more, the garden declares the woman's value. Nearly all the spices are exotic. Many are articles of international trade from earliest times, being imported from regions as far-flung as India, China, southern Arabia, and eastern Africa.[45] In Jeremiah 6:20, fragrant calamus is imported from a far country, as is incense from Sheba. They are part of expensive offerings that the worshipper hopes will please God. Indeed, Isaiah 60:6 places Sheba's incense in a caravan that carries gold. In Isaiah 43:23–24, God mentions the same pair—calamus and incense—as exorbitant offerings that he never demanded of his people. The value of these goods becomes clear in Ezekiel 27, which draws up a list of Tyre's impressive imports and exports, that city renowned as the "gateway to the sea, merchant of peoples on many coasts" (Ezek 27:3). Among the trade items is calamus, sitting side by side with "the finest of all kinds of spices [בְּרֹאשׁ כָּל־בֹּשֶׂם], and precious stones, and gold" (Ezek 27:19, 22). The phrase is the same as that which closes the Song's catalogue of the garden. Listing nine items, the man finishes off with what Pope describes as a "poetic et cetera": "all the finest spices" (כָּל־רָאשֵׁי בְשָׂמִים). The emphasis is dual. These are the best spices to be had, "grade A materials." And these cover "all" the ones there are. In a context of ruler-worship in Daniel 3, the narrator extensively lists every state official or musical instrument he can think of and then implies more with the phrase "all the other" or "all kinds of"—the phrases standing for a wide-ranging et cetera (Dan 3:3, 7, 10).[46] That is what the poet does here in the Song. The image evoked by the Song's impossible garden is that of a bride whose charms are all-inclusive, exotic, and exceptionally rare, and therefore, priceless.

That this is a picture of priceless worth finds support in other parts of the canon. The oil used in the tabernacle contains calamus, myrrh,

45. Bloch and Bloch, *Song of Songs*, 177; Pope, *Song of Songs*, 493–94.

46. Pope, *Song of Songs*, 494.

and cinnamon, besides cassia. It is described as "a fragrant blend, the work of a perfumer" (Exod 30:23–25). Its use is strictly restricted to the anointing of the sacred paraphernalia and the priests. Another mention of the Song's spices is in Psalm 45, where aloes and myrrh, along with cassia, perfume the royal nuptial robes (Ps 45:9 [EV 8]). In later times, the wealthy Nicodemus brings a mixture of myrrh and aloes to prepare the body of Jesus for burial, "in accordance with Jewish burial customs" (John 19:39). The nard poured on Jesus's feet provokes the indignation it does because it is a waste of "an expensive perfume," "worth a year's wages" (John 12:3, 5; cf. Mark 14:3–5). Uses more in line with the Song are in the toilette of women, especially those whose business it is to be attractive. The women of the Persian harem use oil of myrrh as part of their year-long preparation to go to the king (Esth 2:13 [EV 12]). The seductress in Proverbs prepares her love bed with myrrh, aloes, and cinnamon (Prov 7:17).[47] But the Song exceeds all these examples. As Keel observes, the range of spices in this extravagant garden easily outdoes all the ingredients of the tabernacle's sacred oil, the king's wedding garments, and the bed of the proverbial whore![48]

The impression the text delivers, then, is that of mind-blowing profusion, of a garden that could not possibly exist—for indeed, this is a garden whose various spice beds are located on different continents. Here are herbs like nard, shrubs such as henna bushes, and trees such as the pomegranate forming levels and layers of verdure. Here are the edible and the inedible. Here is a range of fragrances gathered from different parts of plants: cinnamon from bark, saffron from flower, henna from leaves, calamus from root, and myrrh from oozing resin. The word underlying this wild luxuriance is "all" or "every" (כֹּל). There is *every* possible variety, and there are *all* the finest. The garden lacks for neither quantity nor quality. In fact, its pomegranate trees are heavy with the choicest (מְגָדִים) fruit of its kind. The word is an archaic word, perhaps intentionally chosen to associate this garden with the land the Lord blesses[49] "with the precious (מֶגֶד) dew from heaven above . . . with the best (מֶגֶד) the sun brings forth and the finest (מֶגֶד) the moon can yield; with the choicest (רֹאשׁ) gifts of the ancient mountains and the fruitfulness (מֶגֶד) of the everlasting hills; with the best (מֶגֶד) gifts of the earth and its fullness" (Deut 33:13–16). With these assets, the bride can hardly be human, one thinks! She is not just the finest specimen of the human female on the face of the earth. If this is what she is, she must be divine! Indeed, the

---

47. Keel, *Song of Songs*, 152–53, notes that myrrh and frankincense were erotic symbols.
48. Keel, *Song of Songs*, 180.
49. Keel, *Song of Songs*, 176; Pope, *Song of Songs*, 492.

word *lebona* ("incense"; לְבוֹנָה) echoes the *leitwort* "Lebanon" (לְבָנוֹן), calling up an association with the divine, for Lebanon was poetically "the garden of God" (Ezek 31:8). In terms of the plot, *lebona* is a reminder of the make-believe world of goddess and suitor of which this garden is a part.

Returning to the developing storyline, this is the third time the man has mentioned the woman in relation to fragrance. He has smelled her cosmetic ointments and her clothes, but has as yet no experience of her aromatic body. The man can only indicate that he longs to inhabit this pleasure garden, heady with the scent of spices and gurgling with the sound of running water. But it is up to the woman to decide what happens next.

THE WOMAN'S RESPONSE: SONG 4:16

The woman of the Song has in other places made invitations to the man.[50] The book begins with one: "Take me away with you—let us hurry! Let the king bring me into his chambers" (1:4). In another instance, she offers: "Come, my beloved, let us go into the countryside . . . there I will give you my love" (7:11). And then there is the twice-repeated invitation couched in code, one of which ends the book: "Turn, my beloved, and be like a gazelle or like a young stag on the rugged hills" (2:17; cf. 8:14).

Even for a book thick with invitations of this nature, the response of the woman toward the end of the Songs of Lebanon stands out. She seems to enter into the spirit of the make-believe that she is a goddess with a garden-like body, being wooed by a besotted suitor. She summons the winds:

Awake, north wind [עוּרִי צָפוֹן], and come, south wind [וּבוֹאִי תֵימָן]!
Blow on my garden [הָפִיחִי גַנִּי]. Let its spices/fragrance flow [out] [יִזְּלוּ בְשָׂמָיו]. (4:16a)

Any movement in the poem thus far has been subtly implicit. From this point on, the poem is seized with motion, intimated through a series of imperatives.[51] Winds are called upon to blow into the garden and stream

---

50. 4:16a is read by some as spoken by the man: e.g., Murphy, *Song of Songs*, 157, 161; Bergant, *Song of Songs*, 57. More usually, the lines are attributed to the woman: e.g., Exum, *Song of Songs*, 180–81; Assis, *Flashes of Fire*, 139.

51. The three imperatives (awake; come; blow) are followed by three jussives (let its fragrance waft; let my beloved come; let him eat) (Bergant, *Song of Songs*, 56–57).

its fragrance out. In the reverse direction, the man, who is thus far "out-side" the garden, is invited and enters into it.

The movement begins with a stirring invocation made in an epigram-matic style suited to the woman's role as goddess, but it could take the suitor by surprise. What is he to make of it? Considering her penchant for teasing (2:15; 5:3), does she seize this opportunity to be mischie-vous? The exaggeratedly dramatic tone could suggest this might be the case. Further, in employing his metaphor of her as a garden, she reuses some of his last words. He had spoken of her as abounding with the finest spices (בְשָׂמִים). He had finished off with referring to her as streams (נֹזְלִים). Now she asks that these spices (בְשָׂמִים) be streamed out (נֹזַל).[52] It would appear that this goddess has taken note of the remark that she is a walled-in spice garden. She wishes to alter the situation, and let her attractions be known far and wide. The winds are her appointed mes-sengers. They may spread abroad her fragrance, tantalizingly wafting it to the noses of the peoples. It is only proper that a goddess should be desired by the entire world.[53]

What is the man to understand by this? Has she now slipped into the role of the seducer, with her sights set on conquering the world? Her next words come as happy relief:

> Let my beloved come into his garden [יָבֹא דוֹדִי לְגַנּוֹ]
> and eat its/his choice fruits [וְיֹאכַל פְּרִי מְגָדָיו]. (4:16b)

The action is similar to that in lyrics from Akkadian love poetry in which

> The king goes down to the garden,
> The chief gardener to the pleasure garden.[54]

In the Song, the woman makes explicit that she is *his* garden. As such, she is eminently accessible to him—in fact, only to him. He may enter at will, and eat its/his "choice fruit," a verbatim repetition of his description of her assets. The pronoun suffix allows two possible readings depend-ing on which is used as the antecedent subject: "its" (that is, the garden's) fruit, or "his" (that is, the beloved's) fruit. The ambiguity delights the ear of her lover. Of course, he would prefer to understand that the garden is

---

52. See Bloch and Bloch, *Song of Songs*, 177–78.

53. See Keel, *Song of Songs*, 153 for the Egyptian love goddess Hathor depicted as the "Lady of Myrrh."

54. S. M. Paul, "A Lover's Garden of Verse: Literal and Metaphorical Imagery in Ancient Near Eastern Love Poetry," in *Tehillah le-Moshe: Biblical and Judaic Studies in Honour of Moshe Greenberg*, ed. M. Cogan, B. A. Eichler, and J. H. Tigay (Winona Lake, IN: Eisenbrauns, 1997), 105.

his, as is the luscious fruit thereof. In reworking his words, she uses the "from" that marked the first of the three Songs of Lebanon. She has come down "from" (מִן) the upper realms so that he can be the one who will enjoy "from" or "of" (מִן) her pleasures.

An Egyptian love song describes similar exclusive access:

> The goose soars and alights,
>   While the ordinary birds circle.
> He has disturbed the garden.

The fortunate "goose" is the lover, the "birds" are the other suitors, and the "garden" that receives the alighting goose is, of course, the girl herself.[55]

It privileges this admirer that he should be chosen to enjoy her delights—he is called her beloved and invited into (what is given over to him to be) "his garden."[56] What greater gift could a mortal hope for from the hands of a love goddess! Swirling with erotic undercurrents, here is the story of a mortal who dares, and a goddess who joyfully surrenders.

THE MAN CONCLUDES: SONG 5:1

The man says his concluding piece. Situated at the dead center of the Song of Songs,[57] it is appropriately the most explicit—yet allusively poetic—reference to the sexual act.

I have come	into my garden	my sister, bride
בָּאתִי	לְגַנִּי	אֲחֹתִי כַלָּה
I have gathered	my myrrh	with my spice
אָרִיתִי	מוֹרִי	עִם־בְּשָׂמִי
I have eaten	my honeycomb	with my honey
אָכַלְתִּי	יַעְרִי	עִם־דִּבְשִׁי

---

55. Pap. Harris 500, Group B: 11, translated in Fox, *Ancient Egyptian Love Songs*, 20. See Paul, "Lover's Garden of Verse," 105; Landy, "Song of Songs," 520.

56. Bloch and Bloch, *Song of Songs*, 178, note the parallel with the Shulammite's vineyard (1:6) becoming the vineyard that the man calls his own (8:12). See also Exum, *Song of Songs*, 180; Hess, *Song of Songs*, 153; Barbiero, *Song of Songs*, 234.

57. See Munro, *Spikenard and Saffron*, 74.

I have drunk	my wine	with my milk
שָׁתִיתִי	יֵינִי	עִם־חֲלָבִי (5:1a)

The response matches the woman's invitation word for word. The phrase "let him come" (יָבֹא) is answered with "I have come" (בָּאתִי); the phrase "into his garden" (לְגַנּוֹ) is reciprocated with "into my garden" (לְגַנִּי). She offered him the garden's fruit. He happily partakes of the feast. He gathers, he eats, he drinks. The goods consumed are laid out in pairs, as if to communicate the abundance available:[58] myrrh *with* spice, honeycomb *with* honey, wine *with* milk. Most significant is that each item is affixed with the possessive pronoun "my." All these become his because he can appropriate the woman as "my sister" and her body is "my garden." In all, eight of nine nouns are suffixed with "my," and the ninth noun, "bride," is clearly the man's possession.[59] The poems thus far were occupied with all those things that were hers. "Your" was the dominating pronoun. Suddenly, and overwhelmingly, all that was hers has now become his. "Your" has changed to "my," indicating that the goddess has surrendered all.

The Songs of Lebanon finish off with:

Eat, friends [אִכְלוּ רֵעִים], and drink [שְׁתוּ]; drink your fill of love [וְשִׁכְרוּ דּוֹדִים]. (5:1b)[60]

There is no consensus on the identity of the speaker(s).[61] Whoever the

---

58. Longman, *Song of Songs*, 159. Bloch and Bloch explain the poetic device of using "with" (עִם) as: "Not only *a*, but *b*, too"; or "*a* and, on top of it, *b*!" So also in the list of spices in 4:13–14 (*Song of Songs*, 179).

59. Bergant, *Song of Songs*, 58; Hess, *Song of Songs*, 154. Estes, "Song of Songs," 362, comments on the change from 4:12 where the woman is "*a* garden" and "*a* spring."

60. Or, "be drunk on lovemaking." E.g., Robert Gordis, *Song of Songs: A Study, Modern Translation and Commentary*, Text and Studies of the Jewish Theological Seminary of America 20 (New York: Jewish Theological Seminary of America, 1954), 61; Fox, *Ancient Egyptian Love Songs*, 139; Murphy, *Song of Songs*, 157. The LXX, Peshitta, and Vulgate prefer the more modest, but less likely, rendering for דּוֹדִים: "drink deeply, O lovers!" For parallels in Greek literature and art on the association of love and alcohol, see Anselm C. Hagedorn, "Of Foxes and Vineyards: Greek Perspectives on the Song of Songs," *VT* 53, no. 3 (2003): 348–49.

61. It could be (1) the man (and the woman) addressing unidentified others to do as he has done: e.g., Keel, *Song of Songs*, 184; Assis, *Flashes of Fire*, 143; Bloch and Bloch, *Song of Songs*, 179–80; Hess, *Song of Songs*, 156; (2) the daughters of Jerusalem: David Allan Hubbard, *Hosea: An Introduction and Commentary*, TOTC (Leicester: InterVarsity, 1989), 311; Exum, *Song of Songs*, 182–83; Longman, *Song of Songs*, 159; John G. Snaith, *The Song of Songs*, NCB (Grand Rapids: Eerdmans, 1993), 71; Fox, *Ancient Egyptian Love Songs*, 133; (3) the wedding guests: Carr, *Song of Solomon*, 129; Goulder, *Song of Fourteen Songs*, 39; (4) God: Estes, "Song of Songs," 362; (5) the author: Gledhill, *Message of the Song of Songs*, 167; Barbiero, *Song of Songs*, 240–42; Gordis, *Song of Songs*, 33–34.

addressees may be, the metaphor of consumption discreetly continues its delightful trajectory beyond this closing line.

THE POMEGRANATES OF "PARADISE"

We have read the Songs of Lebanon as an amorous masque that casts its protagonists as goddess and wooer. If the reality is that the man is a shepherd and the woman is a keeper of vineyards (1:6–8), then this would not be the only occasion on which the Song's lovers have played at make-believe.[62] Their favorite fantasy is that he is the legendary Solomon and she the woman royalty is smitten with (1:1–4). So they recline at the royal table partaking of a banquet (1:12–14; 2:4). He processes in state to their wedding, wearing a regal crown (3:6–11). The Songs of Lebanon could embed an alternative fiction, though far more implicit. There are three pointers to this play-acting.

The first is the motif of Lebanon, operating as a *leitwort* dominating the first poem (4:8), and closing the second and third poems (4:11, 15). Mountain heights are the dwelling places of the gods.[63]

The second pointer is the mention of lions and leopards. In other parts of the Song, the fauna mentioned are invariably read in association with ancient West Asian myth concerning deities presiding over matters amorous. Thus, the women picturing her beloved as a gazelle or stag (2:9, 17; 8:14) evokes images of not just his fleet feet but his virility, for these creatures were depicted in the company of a love goddess.[64] Similarly, he thinks of her as a dove (2:14). Though this is in the context of her inaccessibility, the associations are made between the dove and the various versions of the love goddesses of ancient West Asia.[65] The lions and leopards of the Lebanon Songs could well play the same role. Less amiable than gazelles and doves, they add the dangerous edge required when one speaks of a goddess in her natural setting on the remote crags of Amana, Senir, and Hermon. Here, we recall that though humans are sometimes depicted negatively in the Song, nature is always on the side of the lovers. Even if there are "little foxes" with ruinous intent, these are only figurative for young Casanovas (2:15). So, it seems that the big cats on the mountains are not posing a danger to the woman, but rather, they

---

62. Daphna V. Arbel presents the shifting scenes of the Song of Songs as strategies the author adopts to treat various facets of the theme of love ("My Vineyard, My Very Own, Is for Myself," in *The Song of Songs*, ed. Athalya Brenner and Carole R Fontaine, FCB Series 2 (Sheffield: Sheffield Academic, 2000), 90–101.

63. Landy (*Paradoxes of Paradise*, 104) sees the Lebanon motif differently.

64. Keel, *Song of Songs*, 92–94.

65. Keel, *Song of Songs*, 103–6.

are her mascots. Here in the Songs of Lebanon is the counterpart of the whimsical fiction of Solomon and his Shulammite. Instead of royalty and commoner, the lovers' inventiveness spins most gratifyingly into over-load, casting the protagonists as goddess and mortal. On such a stage, her yielding to his wooing is not simply charming. Located in the only sec-tion of the Song where the dialogue moves inexorably and explicitly to consummation, the fantasy makes a perfect fit. If there is a poem in the Song that demands a love goddess, it is the Songs of Lebanon.

This flight of fancy mediates the metaphor of the woman as a garden. To pun on the Septuagint's transliteration of the Masoretic text's *pardes* ("park" or "garden"; פַּרְדֵּס), the goddess is a παράδεισος—a "paradise" of succulent fruit and sweet-scented spices. The metaphor serves the love poem in two ways.

First, it works wonderfully to describe all that is most sought after in a bride, especially in an Eastern bride. A bride must be a virgin, and she must be attractive of face and form. A garden, unlike a field, is usually an enclosed cultivated space. As such, it well conveys the idea of space that cannot be readily entered. As for the other desirable, beauty, the metaphor helps to list the bride's assets by circumlocution. While on one hand ensuring that there is no slide into vulgarity, on the other hand, the point can be made that the bride lacks nothing desirable. The groom is to be envied for his good fortune. As any garden must have an owner, the bride is the man's to possess and enjoy.

A second way the garden metaphor works for a love poem is to accommodate a standard periphrasis for the pleasures of the flesh—feeding. The Old Testament reflects the ancient world's regular use of the imagery of eating for the man's (par)taking of the woman.[66] Clev-erly, the Song of Lebanon allows its spice garden to double as an orchard. It bears the finest fruit. So, while the man slips languidly into his scented paradise, he imagines his mouth filling with the tangy-sweet juice of pomegranate seeds. And again, the reader understands it is not pome-granates but his bride's body that his mouth is gorging on (cf. 8:3). The garden effectively conveys the taste and touch of the erotic without offending cultural sensibilities.[67]

66. The metaphor of eating and drinking to describe the sexual act is common in both the biblical canon (Gen 39:6, 9; Prov 3:20; 5:15, 19; 6:30; 7:18; 9:17; 30:20) and in ancient West Asian poetry. See Paul, "Lover's Garden of Verse," 99–110; and also, Falk, *Song of Songs,* 157–59; Pope, *Song of Songs,* 507–8; Barbiero, *Song of Songs,* 238–39. For parallels in Greek literature and art, see Hagedorn, "Of Foxes and Vineyards," 347–48. A sample from modern Palestinian love poems uses a plant also present in the Songs of Lebanon: "I entered your garden and plucked your pomegranates" (Stephan, *Modern Palestinian Parallels,* 17).

67. Carr, *Song of Solomon,* 126, posits that all the items mentioned in the garden list have erotic connotations in extant ancient West Asian poetry.

In addition to these functions, the garden metaphor continues the implicit depiction of the woman as divine.[68] Sumerian songs singing of sacred marriage described the bride as a "well-stocked garden."[69] One of these depicts Inanna, the goddess of love and fertility. (The Dumuzi-Adonis cult with its ritual sacred garden was popular enough in ancient Israel for Isaiah to disparage it repeatedly; Isa 1:29; 65:3; 66:17.)[70] Inanna sings as follows:

> My brother has brought me into the garden.
> Dumuzi has brought me into the garden . . .
> By an apple tree I kneeled as is proper.
> Before my brother coming in song,
> Before the Lord Dumuzi who came toward me . . .
> I poured out plants from my womb,
> I placed plants before him, I poured out plants before him.[71]

Significantly, Inanna is not only in a garden but is herself capable of generating one. The pomegranate in the Songs of Lebanon, Keel explains, was thought of not only as an aphrodisiac but also as a symbol of life, especially in regions of Assyrian influence. Ivory inlays from Assur show a pair of pomegranate trees flanking the "mountain of paradise" from which stream four rivers. In a similar vein, an Egyptian poem features the pomegranate's boast:[72]

> All [the trees]—except for me—
>   Have passed away from the meadow.
>   I abide twelve months in the gar[den].
> I have endured; [I]'ve cast off a blossom,
>   (but) next year's is (already) within me.

---

68. An interesting interpretation of the garden metaphor is in the later apocryphal work known as the *Testament of Solomon*. Using overlapping herb lists, Rainbow shows how the garden is read as a "magician's garden, complete with all the plants needed for casting spells—a veritable witch's brew" (Jesse Rainbow, "The Song of Songs and the *Testament of Solomon*: Solomon's Love Poetry and Christian Magic," *HTR* 100, no. 3 [2007]: 249–74, esp. 262–64).

69. Samuel Noah Kramer, *The Sacred Marriage Rite: Aspects of Faith, Myth and Ritual in Ancient Sumer* (Bloomington: Indiana University Press, 1969), 96.

70. Keel, *Song of Songs*, 172.

71. Kramer, *Sacred Marriage*, 101.

72. Keel, *Song of Songs*, 145–46. (Fox, *Ancient Egyptian Love Songs*, 44–45, 47, reads this tree as a "persea" tree.) See Edmee Kingsmill, *The Song of Songs and the Eros of God: A Study in Biblical Intertextuality* (Oxford: Oxford University Press, 2009), 160, who reads in a similar vein the pomegranate symbolism in the robes of the High Priest in Exodus 28.

Keel understands this as a reference to the life-giving property of the pomegranate. So, a later line in the same poem where the tree says "my fruit resembles her breasts" is understood not just as an equation of appearance but as an affirmation of both fruit and breasts as life sustaining. That the Song should feature a pomegranate bearing the "choicest fruit" in the garden that is the woman elusively invokes life-generating divinity.[73]

When this garden metaphor, so fraught with the erotic and with its own overtones of the celestial, is subsumed into a fantasy that the bride is the love goddess herself and the man is a love-struck mortal she surrenders to, the result comes close to a male lover's vision of "paradise."[74] If this is the picture the love songs of Lebanon set out to portray, they certainly succeed.

CONCLUSION

The metaphor of the woman as a garden functions similarly in the Songs of Lebanon as in the other parts of the Song. Occupying the central place in the book, it shows both mutual dependency and reciprocity between the lovers. The woman is abundantly and utterly delectable, and in that state, requires one who will experience her yield. The man, meanwhile, dreams of just this. He actively and artfully courts an invitation to the feast. Each round of wooing gains the expected response. Though implicit in the poems, the reader can well imagine that the woman has "descended" to the man; she has moved close enough that their eyes can meet; now he catches a whiff of her perfume; next she is kissing him, and vigorously at that; and when she finally speaks, it is with an enthusiasm that well matches his as she welcomes him to plunder her. She is an equal partner in the consummation, deriving just as much pleasure in receiving her beloved into the garden as he does by coming in.

This mutual satisfaction marks the garden imagery in the Song. In fact, the woman invariably ties her three famous declarations of exclusive, mutual belonging to this metaphor. In two instances, she claims she is her beloved's and he hers because she is the grass among whose lilies he chooses to nibble (2:16; 6:3). In the other instance, the assertion that

73. It is of interest here that the Temple ornamentation made pomegranates a motif. Jenson, *Song of Songs*, 51, observes that "the most striking feature to greet an arrival was a latticework of two hundred bronze pomegranates."

74. Trible and Landy both make a detailed thematic connection between the garden metaphor and the garden of Eden, showing how the loss of paradise is reversed in the Song (Phyllis Trible, *God and the Rhetoric of Sexuality* [Philadelphia: Fortress Press, 1978], 144–65; Landy, "Song of Songs," 513–28).

she belongs to her beloved and he to her is followed by her inviting him to the blossoming vineyards—herself—where she will give him her love (7:10).

Undeniably, the metaphor outdoes itself in the Songs of Lebanon. Not only is it extravagantly treated, but by its integration into the make-believe story of an immortal who capitulates to a mere human, it emphasizes that the woman's willingness matches the man's desire.

7.

The Vineyard

In our day, the idea of using the image of a garden or vineyard (or even a field) for one's wife would—at the very least!—raise a disapproving eyebrow. But, as we have seen in the Song, the ancients found the image a convenient one.[1] A man could use it to pay his beloved a compliment, and a woman might use it to describe herself.

Thus, in addition to the examples in the previous chapter, we have the advice given to a nobleman by the Egyptian vizier Ptah-hotep (ca. 2450 BCE): "If thou art a man of standing, thou shouldst found thy household and love thy wife at home as is fitting. Fill her belly; clothe her back. Ointment is the prescription for her body. Make her heart glad as long as thou livest. She is a profitable field for her lord."[2]

Similarly in the Tell el-Amarna tablets, the prince of Byblos, Rib-addi, quotes four times from what Albright describes as "an obviously familiar aphorism": "My field is likened to a woman without a husband, because it is not ploughed."[3] A parallel from Ugarit is the moon god Yarikhu speaking of his bride Nikkalu: "I will make her field into a vineyard, / the field of her love into a flower-garden!"[4]

---

1. For bibliography and examples of the garden and vineyard metaphor in love poetry in the ancient world, see S. M. Paul, "A Lover's Garden of Verse: Literal and Metaphorical Imagery in Ancient Near Eastern Love Poetry," in *Tehillah le-Moshe: Biblical and Judaic Studies in Honour of Moshe Greenberg*, ed. M. Cogan, B. A. Eichler, and J. H. Tigay (Winona Lake, IN: Eisenbrauns, 1997), 99–110.

2. J. T. Willis, "The Genre of Isa 5:1–7," *JBL* 96 (1977): 345.

3. W. F. Albright, "Some Canaanite-Phoenician Sources of Hebrew Wisdom," in *Wisdom in Israel and in the Ancient Near East*, ed. M. Noth and D. Winton Thomas (Leiden: Brill, 1960), 7.

4. *KTU* 1.24:22–23, cited in Marjo C. A. Korpel, "The Literary Genre of the Song of the Vineyard (Isa. 5:1–7)," in *The Structural Analysis of Biblical and Canaanite Poetry*, ed. Willem van der Meer and Johannes C. de Moor, JSOTSup 74 (Sheffield: Sheffield Academic, 1988), 125n36.

An example from a Sumerian sacred marriage song has Inanna being praised, perhaps by Dumuzi:

> Lordly Queen, your breast is your field,
> Inanna, your breast is your field,
> Your broad field that pours out plants,
> Your broad field that pours out grain . . .[5]

The image seems to work for modern Arab love songs as well, where a nighttime rendezvous with the beloved is likened to entering the gardens of paradise.[6] In another such poem, the lover extols his beloved with more of what Paul generically calls "arbor ardor":[7]

> The garden of your beauty in its bloom
> Is fairer and more resplendent than a flower garden.
> Your breast, O you, is like a pomegranate fruit . . .
> Your cheek shines as it were a Damascene apple.
> How sweet to pluck it in the morning,
> And to open the garden.[8]

Given this spread across ancient West Asian literature and within the biblical canon, it is reasonable to assume that Isaiah's audience would have understood that in a song a man composes about his vineyard, he is speaking of his wife.[9] Indeed, a vineyard describes a wife better than

---

5. Samuel Noah Kramer, *The Sacred Marriage Rite: Aspects of Faith, Myth and Ritual in Ancient Sumer* (Bloomington: Indiana University Press, 1969), 81 (see also similar poems, 100–101).

6. Othmar Keel, *The Song of Songs: A Continental Commentary*, trans. Frederick J. Gaiser (Minneapolis: Augsburg, 1994), 174.

7. Paul, "Lover's Garden of Verse," 101. For Greek parallels, see Anselm C. Hagedorn, "Of Foxes and Vineyards: Greek Perspectives on the Song of Songs," *VT* 53, no. 3 (2003): 342–48, esp. 347.

8. H. Stephan, *Modern Palestinian Parallels to the Song of Songs*, Studies in Palestinian Customs and Folklore 3 (Jerusalem: Palestine Oriental Society, 1923), 16.

9. For distribution across the canon, Hans Wildberger, *Isaiah 1–12: A Commentary*, trans. Thomas H. Trapp, Continental Commentaries (Minneapolis: Augsburg Fortress, 1991), 182, notes the parallel with Song 8:12, which speaks of Solomon's harem as his vineyard (cf. 1:14; 2:15). John F. A. Sawyer, *Isaiah*, vol. 1 (Philadelphia: Westminster, 1984), 47–48, similarly lists Song 4:12 (the beloved is a garden), 4:4 and 7:4 (her neck is a like a watchtower), 7:8 (her breasts are like clusters of grapes), and 7:9 (her kisses are sweeter than wine). Beyond the Song, he lists Ps 80:8–18; Isa 27:2–5; Jer 2:21; 12:10–11; Matt 21:33–41. Other shorter texts using the vineyard metaphor for Israel are Hos 9:10, 16; 10:1; Isa 3:14; 27:2–6.

Arguing that the vineyard metaphor was recognizable by the audience of Isaiah 5 are, for example, Gary Roye Williams, "Frustrated Expectations in Isaiah V 1–7: A Literary Interpretation," *VT* 35, no. 4 (1985): 460; Willis, "Genre of Isa 5:1–7," 346; Korpel, "Literary Genre," 125–28. Contra, H. G. M. Williamson, *Isaiah 1–5*, ICC (Edinburgh: T&T Clark, 2006), 329; he argues that Isaiah was the first to use the metaphor of the vineyard as female lover for the relationship between Israel and YHWH, 343.

a garden or a field would for two reasons. First, unlike grain fields that can be left fallow and later seeded, a vineyard must be "terraced, pruned, trained and protected, much like a sustained erotic relationship." Second, unlike the yield of fields and gardens, a vineyard's produce is intoxicating.[10]

Other than in the Song, sustained use of the metaphor is found in two texts, Psalm 80:8–19 and Isaiah 5:1–7. Both reflect a relationship between YHWH and Israel. In the psalm, the nature of the relationship is that of a patron and protégé. The Isaian text introduces itself as a "song" (שִׁירָה), and (as we shall argue) presents YHWH as the owner and keeper of a vineyard. Isaiah 5 has the stronger storyline and character profiling and appears to be a good candidate for reading alongside the Songs of Lebanon (Song 4:8–5:1). But before we can move into an intertextual reading, we must consider the Song of the Vineyard from the point of view of its genre, so as to further clarify our nomination of it as an intertext.

READING ISAIAH 5

The general understanding is that the Song of the Vineyard is a mix of more than one genre.[11] Establishing the genre types will help in understanding better how the text works, and to see how it could relate to the Songs of Lebanon in Song 4.

The opening line introduces the poem as a song a man composed about his vineyard. Given that eventually it will be revealed that the vineyard is a metaphor for a group of people (Israel and Judah), the song is generally understood as one that expresses disappointment in friendship or love. By appealing to the use of the vineyard metaphor in the marital relationship, one could take the people-group to be imaged collectively as a wife. The song would then be about a marriage relationship.

But here, we must consider that the Song of the Vineyard has the formal features of a lawsuit or disputation. These are: (1) the establishing of a binding relationship between plaintiff and defendant; (2) evidence produced by the plaintiff that he has faithfully fulfilled his obligations; (3) a complaint by the plaintiff that the defendant has defaulted on

10. David M. Carr, *The Erotic Word: Sexuality, Spirituality and the Bible* (Oxford: Oxford University Press, 2003), 59.

11. See the survey in Willis, "Genre of Isa 5:1–7," 337–62. He lists twelve different interpretations involving almost as many genres. For a bibliography of work since Willis, see Williamson, *Isaiah 1–5*, 327n38, and see his lengthy discussion on form and genre, 327–31.

obligations; (4) an appeal to the legal community to render a decision on the case.[12]

In this case, the husbandman would be the plaintiff; the vineyard would be the defendant; and the prophet would be the advocate who speaks on behalf of the plaintiff, presenting his case to the adjudicators. The plaintiff's concerns for "justice" and "righteousness" are legal concerns. But, of course, it would be unusual for a husbandman to take his vineyard to court. The poem maintains the suspense to the end, and then bursts out with its equivalents: the vineyard is Israel/Judah and the keeper is YHWH.

The part of Isaiah 5:1–7 that does not fit into the covenant lawsuit mold is that it is called a "song."[13] This problem is partially accommodated if we subsume the disputation into the larger genre of either parable or allegory.[14] A parable, unlike an allegory, makes a single point, and need not have exact equivalents. It could be argued that the main point here is that Israel has fallen far short of YHWH's expectation.[15] An allegory, on the other hand, expects multiple points of correspondence between itself and reality. Thus, if the allegory concerns the story of Israel, then: the vine is Israel, whom YHWH planted (Ps 80:9 [EV 80:8]); the protecting fences are the angels that guard YHWH's people (Ps 91:11); the tower is the Temple and the winepress, the altar; the bad grapes are Israel's sinfulness, the chief being idolatry.[16]

An alternative allegory takes the garden metaphor of the Song of Songs as its compass. Here, the Song of the Vineyard becomes an "erotic

12. Willis, "Genre of Isa 5:1–7," 350.

13. See Yee's article, which makes a comparison between the "song" of Deuteronomy 32 and the Song of the Vineyard, treating the lawsuit elements in both (Gale A. Yee, "The Form-Critical Study of Isaiah 5:1–7 as a Song and a Juridical Parable," *CBQ* 43 [1981]: 30–40). Walter Brueggemann, *Isaiah 1–39*, Westminster Bible Companion (Louisville: Westminster John Knox, 1998), 47, posits that the failure of the expected response causes a change in genre from love song to disputation. Brevard S. Childs, *Isaiah: A Commentary*, OTL (Louisville: Westminster John Knox, 2001), 45–46, holds that the initial promise of a love song "is a distraction" since the theme is not developed further. He does propose, however, that read in the light of the Old Testament canon, the poem "reverberates with the entire Mosaic witness to Israel as God's special possession (passages beginning at Exod 19:3; Deut 7:6; etc.)."

14. John N. Oswalt, *The Book of Isaiah: Chapters 1–39*, NICOT (Grand Rapids: Eerdmans, 1986), 151–52; Sawyer, *Isaiah*, 47. Edward J. Kissane, *The Book of Isaiah 1–39*, vol. 1, rev. ed. (Dublin: Browne & Nolan, 1960), 83, thinks it is "a parable, one of the most perfect of its kind in the Bible." Ronald E. Clements, *Isaiah 1–39*, NCB (Grand Rapids: Eerdmans, 1980), 56–57: "essentially . . . a parable, with a number of allegorical features." Peter D. Miscall, *Isaiah* (Sheffield: Sheffield Academic, 1993), 31, sees it as "both song and parable." Willis, "Genre of Isa 5:1–7," 358–62, makes an extended case for parable.

15. Contra Marvin A. Sweeney, *Isaiah 1–39*, FOTL 16 (Grand Rapids: Eerdmans, 1996), 126, who rejects the parable genre for allegory.

16. Willis, "Genre of Isa 5:1–7," 354–55.

allegory" in which: the husband has married a well-endowed wife who he expects will be productive in bearing him children; the husband fulfills his marriage obligations, sparing no effort to care for his wife (Exod 21:10); the wife, in return, turns unfaithful and bears children by adultery; and the incensed husband pronounces infertility on her using the image of land from which rain is withheld (2 Sam 1:21).[17]

Considering the legal elements embedded into the parabolic and allegorical matrix, the sub-category of juridical parable arises.[18] The distinctive of the juridical parable is its cunning. The story it tells functions as a decoy. It lulls listeners into thinking the story is about someone other than themselves, and so, lures them into passing judgment on themselves. The Song of the Vineyard shares this feature with Nathan's parable to David about the ewe lamb (2 Sam 12:1–7);[19] the story about the widow with two sons that the woman of Tekoa tells David (2 Sam 14:1–24); and the story an unnamed prophet tells Ahab about an escaped prisoner (1 Kgs 20:35–42). A juridical parable would carry—often as a sting in the tail—the identification of the parties and elements involved in the case. The Song of the Vineyard identifies the husbandman as YHWH, the vineyard as Israel, good grapes as justice and righteousness, and bad grapes as bloodshed and the cries of the oppressed.

Korpel examines the structure of the poem at length, concluding that it is an allegory, albeit interrupted by red herrings:

5:1aα–β:	Love Song?
5:1b–2:	No! Vintage song?
5:3–4:	No! Lawsuit?
5:5–6:	No! Still a vinegrower's complaint?
5:7:	No! Announcement of God's judgment on Israel[20]

It would seem that the poet artfully layers the genres for his intended rhetorical effect, building up to his dramatic climax.

17. Willis, "Genre of Isa 5:1–7," 355.

18. See, e.g., John D. W. Watts, *Isaiah 1–33*, WBC 24 (Waco, TX: Word, 1985), 84, for proponents; G. T. Sheppard, "More on Isaiah 5:1–7 as a Juridical Parable," *CBQ* 44 (1982): 45–47; Yee, "Form-Critical Study," 30–40.

19. Uriel Simon, "The Poor Man's Ewe Lamb: An Example of a Juridical Parable," *Bib* 48 (1967): 207–42. Hans Wildberger, *Isaiah 1–12: A Commentary*, trans. Thomas H. Trapp, CC (Minneapolis: Augsburg Fortress, 1991), 186; Clements, *Isaiah 1–39*, 57; Miscall, *Isaiah*, 31; Oswalt, *Isaiah 1–39*, 151; Sawyer, *Isaiah*, 47–48; Watts, *Isaiah 1–33*, 87; Edward J. Young, *The Book of Isaiah 1–18*, vol. 1 (Grand Rapids: Eerdmans, 1965), 198–99.

20. Korpel, "Literary Genre," 119–155, esp. 150.

Significant to our study is that while within the canon the image of a garden or vineyard or field is widely used for a wife, the Song of the Vineyard has a peculiarity in its introductory line which may support such an association. The prophet (as we shall see below) peculiarly refers to YHWH as his "beloved." If this is how the prophet sees himself in relation to YHWH, and if this is the relationship he prescribes that Israel should—but does not—have with YHWH, then there is reason here to postulate that the Song of the Vineyard implicitly draws upon the genre of love song.[21]

If this is the case, the Song of the Vineyard in Isaiah 5 is appropriate as an intertext for the Songs of Lebanon in Song 4.

THE SONG OF THE VINEYARD

The introduction to the Song of the Vineyard takes some sorting out.

I will sing for the one I love my beloved's song about his vineyard

אָשִׁירָה נָּא לִידִידִי שִׁירַת דּוֹדִי לְכַרְמוֹ (Isa 5:1a)

Who the various parties here are is not easy to agree on.[22] Who is the speaker? Who is the "loved one," referred to as יָדִיד and דּוֹד? What or who is this loved one's vineyard?

The possibility that דּוֹד could be rendered "uncle" is quickly dismissed, even though that is the meaning in more than a dozen texts

21. Otto Kaiser, *Isaiah 1–12*, trans. R. A. Wilson (London: SCM, 1972), 59–63, sets the song into a feast. The prophet assumes first the role of the friend of the bridegroom introducing a love song. The voice changes to that of a small farmer, but the audience understands that it is an allegory for a faithless bride and sympathizes with the fate of the groom. Then, unexpectedly, YHWH speaks his parallel allegation, bringing the point home to the (now sullen) hearers. Similarly, John L. Mackay, *Isaiah 1–39*, vol. 1 (Darlington, UK: Evangelical, 2008), 133; J. A. Motyer, *The Prophecy of Isaiah* (Leicester: InterVarsity, 1993), 68; David Stacey, *Isaiah 1–39*, Epworth Commentaries (London: Epworth, 1993), 31–32; and Sweeney, *Isaiah 1–39*, 129, all propose that the life setting could be the festivities following a grape harvest. In either case, the clever shift of speakers as the song progresses would have had its intended dramatic effect.

22. See discussion in John Buchanan Gray, *Isaiah 1–39*, vol. 1, ICC (Edinburgh: T&T Clark, 1912), 84–85, 87. He first dismisses the possibilities that יָדִיד in 1a could be YHWH (Isaiah, particularly, would not use, "even in parable, so familiar a term": contra, e.g., Oswalt, *Isaiah 1–39*, 152–53); could be the bride Israel ("very improbable" if in the דּוֹד and יָדִיד following are YHWH); or could be "uncle" ("obvious unsuitability"). Then, following the LXX's pronoun suffix in 1a ("my vineyard") and through emendation, Gray arrives at a first-person recital: "Let me sing of the thing that I love / The song of my love for my vineyard." "The prophet in reciting it seems at first to be referring to a vineyard of his own, and only towards the close does he allow it to be seen that he is speaking in Yahweh's name." He concedes that textual difficulties remain unreconciled. See a full treatment of the text in J. A. Emerton, "The Translation of Isaiah 5,1," in *The Scriptures and the Scrolls: Fest A. S. van der Woude*, ed. F. Garcia Martinez et al., SVT 49 (Leiden: Brill, 1992), 18–30.

across the Old Testament canon from Leviticus 10:4 to Esther 2:15. Significantly, scholars point to the Song's use of the word to mean "beloved." Even though the Song is unique in this usage, it influences the reading of the word in Isaiah 5:1. Again, this must be because the Song of the Vineyard is taken as a love song (of sorts)—thus the assumption is that the persons introduced in 5:1 are in some way in close relationship.

Working backward within the verse, the "beloved" (דּוֹד) must be the husband, because the song is composed about his vineyard, or wife. The speaker, then, must be either the wife herself, or a friend of the husband. The idea that the wife speaks the song is readily dismissed. First, it would be ironic that she addresses her husband as "beloved" when the song will show her to have regarded him as anything but that. Second, why would a wife sing a song that so deeply implicates her in wrongdoing? Third, we would struggle to find a reason why halfway through her song the husband breaks into it and begins to speak in his own voice.

The speaker, then, may be a friend of the husband.[23] A likely candidate within the cultural context is the "friend of the bridegroom" (cf. John 3:29). This is a technical term for the one who arranges the wedding and would be, in rabbinic terminology, the שׁוֹשְׁבִין or "best man at a wedding."[24] If a groom had grounds for grievance against his bride, the "friend of the bridegroom" carried the social authority needed to speak on his behalf and break the wedding contract[25] by tearing up the official wedding certificate—especially in the case that the bride's reputation became suspect—with the formal pronouncement: "It is better that she is judged as a single person than as a married person."[26] Thus, it seems plausible that the main speaker here is the groom's "best man," and represents the troubled bridegroom.

Outside this literary device of the protagonists as actors in a marriage drama, the consensus is that the speaker is the prophet, communicating YHWH's "song" to the people. Why he introduces YHWH as his "beloved" (twice in the line; יָדִיד and דּוֹד) continues to puzzle. Not only is that more suitable for a bride to use of her loved one, but also, it is unique in prophetic reference to God.[27] Is the prophet trying to say, as

23. E.g., Kaiser, *Isaiah 1–12*, 60; Sawyer, *Isaiah*, 47; Watts, *Isaiah 1–33*, 83–84.

24. Wildberger, *Isaiah 1–12*, 178.

25. Willis, "Genre of Isa 5:1–7," 349. The present-day equivalent to the "friend of the bridegroom" is clearly not the "best man." A more likely candidate is the middleman or negotiator in arranged marriages in South Asia. Should anything go wrong before or immediately after the wedding, the negotiator would be the one to represent the offended party to the offending party.

26. Wildberger, *Isaiah 1–12*, 178.

27. One way out is to read "friend" instead of "beloved" since a prophet could well be considered a friend of God. See, e.g., Mackay, *Isaiah 1–39*, 135, 137; Miscall, *Isaiah*, 31;

we surmised above, that even if Israel does not behave toward her God as if he were her beloved, he—the prophet—can declare that he loves YHWH? That is, is the use of the term "my beloved" meant as a rebuke to uncaring Israel? Perhaps it is.

At any rate, the "I" is the prophet singing for his beloved, who in the course of the song will be revealed to be YHWH. The song the prophet sings is his beloved's song, that is, one sung on his behalf. And the subject of the song is the beloved's vineyard.

The song commences and proceeds in a narrative style, telling about a man and his vineyard:

My loved one had a vineyard on a fertile hillside.

כֶּרֶם הָיָה לִידִידִי בְּקֶרֶן־שָׁמֶן

He dug it up and cleared it of stones and planted it with the choicest vines.

וַיְעַזְּקֵהוּ וַיְסַקְּלֵהוּ וַיִּטָּעֵהוּ שֹׂרֵק

He built a watchtower in it and cut out a winepress as well.

וַיִּבֶן מִגְדָּל בְּתוֹכוֹ וְגַם־יֶקֶב חָצֵב בּוֹ

Then he looked for a crop of good grapes, but it yielded only bad fruit.

וַיְקַו לַעֲשׂוֹת עֲנָבִים וַיַּעַשׂ בְּאֻשִׁים (Isa 5:1b–2)

The vineyard, or at least the plot for the proposed vineyard, is on a "horn" (קֶרֶן). This is understood by most as a topographical spur, the side of a hill. A vineyard on a hillside would have the advantage of well-drained soil and would have been sufficiently exposed to the sun—both ideal for vines.[28] What is more, the soil is indicated to be naturally fertile, "fat" (שָׁמֶן).[29] Perhaps it lay on the windward side of the hill and caught the rains (cf. 5:6). It is the word with which the elderly Isaac blesses the son he thinks is Esau: "Ah, the smell of my son is like the smell of a field (שָׂדֶה) that the Lord has blessed. May God give you (of) heaven's dew and (of) earth's fatness (מִשְׁמַנֵּי־הָאָרֶץ)—an abundance of grain and new wine" (Gen 27:28). A land's "fat" is demonstrated by its happy agricultural yield. At the outset, we see no reason for the proposed vineyard to fail. On the contrary, all the natural conditions point to successful viticulture.

The husbandman sets about the venture with enthusiasm. The land

Williams, "Frustrated Expectations," 459–60. See the lengthy discussion in Williamson, *Isaiah 1–5*, 331–35, who prefers to render the opening words as: "I will sing for my dear friend a song about my intimate friend concerning his vineyard."

28. Wildberger, *Isaiah 1–12*, 180; Mackay, *Isaiah 1–39*, 134.

29. Motyer, *Isaiah*, 68. If reading for double entendre in a love poem, we would arrive at a "vineyard" on an "oily horn." Williamson, *Isaiah 1–5*, 336, shudders at so indelicate a reading.

is previously uncultivated, we presume, since he begins by breaking the ground (עזק) and de-stoning it. In rabbinic usage, the first verb is used of the activity of digging deep enough to prepare the ground for planting.[30] The de-stoning would have been no easy task. Young recounts the Arab proverb that tells of how, when God created the world, an angel in charge of distributing stones across the earth flew down carrying a bag of stones under each arm. However, as he flew over Palestine, one of the bags broke, and that is how Palestine ended up with half of all the stones in the world![31]

When the ground is prepared, presumably after days of painstaking labor, he plants the vines. He is careful to choose choice stock (שֹׂרֵק), a variety of red grape. A parallel text is Jeremiah 2:21, in which the vine planted is "a choice vine (שֹׂרֵק) of sound and reliable stock."[32] We will learn later that the man put in a hedge or a wall (5:5). A hedge would have been a thorny fence, a rough enclosure.[33] A wall would have been of stone. Those stones removed from the soil would have come in handy in the building of such a wall.[34] The hedge and wall ensured protection from passing cattle or wild animals, or at the fruiting stage, from passersby. In the parallel text in Psalm 80, a broken-down wall allows "all who pass by [to] pick its grapes" (Ps 80:12). Going by the narrative so far, the stage is set for a harvest that the farmer will have every reason to take satisfaction in.

Indeed, so certain is the man about a long-term successful outcome that he goes on to invest in permanent structures. He builds a tower in its midst and "even" (גַּם) hews a winepress out of the hillside rock. Both structures are beyond what one would expect in a vineyard only just created out of virgin land, and as yet unproven in yield. A small shaded area (Isa 24:20) or a hut (Isa 1:8; 4:6) would be the usual.[35] But, the owner invests in a more permanent stone structure, providing much more comfortable accommodation for the keeper of the vineyard.[36] As for the winepress, Verbin points out that the word "even" suggests that it was not expected for a private vineyard. Common sense would suggest

---

30. Wildberger, *Isaiah 1–12*, 181.

31. Young, *Isaiah 1–18*, 196.

32. Wildberger, *Isaiah 1–12*, 181. He mentions the Valley of Sorek (נַחַל שֹׂרֵק; Judg 16:4), which was as famous as Masrekah (מַשְׂרֵקָה) in Edom (Gen 36:36; 1 Chr 1:47) for the high quality of grapes.

33. Perhaps of prickly pear: e.g., Gray, *Isaiah 1–39*, 86.

34. Wildberger, *Isaiah 1–12*, 181.

35. John S. Kloppenborg Verbin, "Egyptian Viticultural Practices and the Citation of Isa 5:1–7 in Mark 12:1–9," *NT* 44, no. 2 (2002): 141.

36. Wildberger, *Isaiah 1–12*, 181.

that using a nearby communal one would be more economical.[37] The winepress would require excavation of the limestone bedrock to create the vats and the construction of a pressing mechanism.[38] This is not just a risky investment of capital but also hard labor. But, with both tower and winepress, this husbandman is thinking ahead in anticipation of long years of productivity that he calculates will well offset the expense of this infrastructure.[39]

The verbs surround the nouns: built—tower—winepress—hewed. The owner's labors enclose the vineyard's structures, as if to emphasize the pains he undertakes. His efforts also include the daily and seasonal maintenance required. He provides for the most basic need of any vineyard—water (5:6). He hoes the ground as needed to keep out the thorns, and he prunes the vines in season (5:6). The activities are essential to protect the vines and maximize the yield.

Verbin makes interesting observations from the LXX version of the Song of the Vineyard. In the LXX, as in the MT, the land is already in the owner's possession, and it is situated on a fertile spur. However, the version retells the initial preparations, perhaps contextualizing it to Egyptian agricultural—and specifically, viticultural—practices. Instead of breaking the ground and removing stones from the soil, he puts up a "palisade" (φραγμός) around the plot and stakes the land with trellises. A palisade could be a wooden fence, but considering the relatively low availability of wood in Egypt, this was more likely to be a low stone wall. Indeed, later, this palisade will be "razed" (καθαιρέω). A stone wall takes on greater significance in an intensively cultivated region (as Egypt would have been), serving as a boundary marker in surveys and land registers, where it indicated the taxation scheme that this piece of agricultural land came under. And, of course, the wall discouraged animals from coming in to graze, or humans from beating a short cut through it. When the vines began to yield, the wall and the guard in the watchtower would ensure protection against animals such as foxes or wild boar (cf. Ps 80:13–14; Song 2:15), and against theft.[40] As for the trellising, the probability is that the Egyptian farmer is simply converting a plot of field crops to a vineyard for reasons of economic demand or water supply.[41] The point we note here is that the plot preparation the LXX presents is similar to that in the MT. Here is a husbandman who carefully plans for his plot, and is thorough in effecting the plans.

37. Verbin, "Egyptian Viticultural Practices," 141.
38. For details, see Wildberger, Isaiah 1–12, 181.
39. Wildberger, Isaiah 1–12, 181.
40. Verbin, "Egyptian Viticultural Practices," 145–46.
41. Verbin, "Egyptian Viticultural Practices," 144.

Given this, how great is the disappointment after months of labor and expectation! He waits (קוה) for the first harvest.[42] The verb indicates eager anticipation, or even waiting edged with apprehension. The outcome is told tersely. Instead of yielding good grapes, it yields stinkers (בְּאֻשִׁים).[43] It is not possible that good-quality stock will yield wild grapes. Thus, what is meant must be diseased grapes. What has been planted has become corrupted.[44] The word בְּאֻשִׁים is used of food that goes bad with maggots (Exod 16:20); of the smell given off by piles of dead frogs or mounds of human corpses (Exod 8:14; Isa 34:3); of wounds that fester (Ps 38:6); of ointment smelling foul because of decomposing flies (Qoh 10:1); and of loathsome persons (e.g., Gen 34:30; Exod 5:21; 1 Sam 27:12; 2 Sam 16:21). When applied to grapes, we must assume that instead of the delicious fragrance of ripened grapes, the husbandman's nose receives the sharp smell of sour fruit or perhaps of fruit spoiled by disease.[45] In the parallel text in Jeremiah 2:21, wordplay turns a choice vine (שֹׂרֵק) into a "putrid" vine (גֶּפֶן סוֹרִיָּה, with emendation).[46] It is downright obnoxious, especially if by now the audience has grasped that this is a metaphor. The expected yield of children from a fertile wife is cruelly subverted by the shock of illegitimate offspring.[47]

In the LXX, the problem is different. The man hopes for grapes, but what he gets is "thorns" (ἀκάνθας). While the MT describes the corrupt yield of the vines, the LXX stands back and describes the state of the vineyard. The fault is more that of the soil, which, instead of nourishing

---

42. Vines usually take up to three years to begin yielding. In addition is the Torah regulation forbidding the eating of fruit of the first three years of yield (Lev 19:23). At any rate, the vintner had to wait for years rather than months.

43. Gray, *Isaiah 1–39*, 86. Motyer, *Isaiah*, 68, renders it "stink-fruit." Wildberger, *Isaiah 1–12*, 182, translates: "stinking spoiled berries." Following the Latin (*labruscas*, "fruit of wild vines") and Coptic ("unripe fruit") renderings: "grapes with a tart, sour taste." G. R. Driver suggests "spoiled by anthracnosa" ("Difficult Words in the Hebrew Prophets," in *Studies in Old Testament Prophecy Presented to Professor Theodore H. Robinson*, ed. H. H. Rowley [Edinburgh: T&T Clark, 1950], 53n6). So Williamson, *Isaiah 1–5*, 320.

44. Verbin, "Egyptian Viticultural Practices," 142.

45. The thoroughly inedible nature of these grapes may contribute to the motif of eating in Isaiah that Andrew T. Abernethy develops (*Eating in Isaiah: Approaching the Role of Food and Drink in Isaiah's Structure and Message*, Biblical Interpretation 131 [Leiden: Brill, 2014]). He explores the "imperial-retributive" schema of eating, in which YHWH either provides or withholds. The Song of the Vineyard would then be an interesting reversal. Israel metaphorically produces a preposterous harvest, one which YHWH cannot "eat." In return, YHWH pronounces poor yield on Israel's fields, leaving her nothing to eat: "A ten-acre vineyard will produce only a bath of vine; a homer of seed will yield only an ephah of grain" (Isa 5:10).

46. Based on the redivision of the Masoretic Text's סוּרֵי הַגֶּפֶן to read סוֹרִיָּה גֶפֶן as suggested in the critical apparatus. This gives the *hapax legomenon* סוֹרִיָּה, which is rendered "putrid." *HALOT*, סוֹרִי. See Wildberger, *Isaiah 1–12*, 181.

47. E.g., Williams, "Frustrated Expectations," 460–61; Willis, "Genre of Isaiah 5:1–7," 348.

the grape vines, expends its resources on pushing up thorn bushes.[48] (We must assume that the man's hoeing, implied in 5:6, does not meet with success.) Either way, the venture is a terrible failure.

The Song's garden and Isaiah's vineyard share similarities. First is their fertility. The Song described its woman with the proverbial language for fertile land—she had "honey and milk" under her tongue (Song 4:11). The vineyard, similarly, enjoys the "fat" of the land. Second, both are secure pieces of property. The Song's woman is "a garden locked up" (Song 4:12), and the vineyard is walled. Third, both are extravagantly self-sufficient. The Song's garden incorporates a "well of flowing water" (Song 4:15) ensuring that the dry season will never threaten its luxuriance. The vineyard has its winepress, making it independent of the community. Fourth, the garden and vineyard are populated with good stock. The garden boasts of the "finest" (רֹאשׁ) spice beds. The vineyard is planted with good-quality red grapes. But here is the crucial difference—all the more astounding for the many similarities between the two. The garden produces "choice" (מֶגֶד) pomegranates, while the vineyard puts forth stinking grapes.[49] The vineyard's behavior defies all logic!

The frustrated husbandman breaks into the narration, and for the first time, speaks. Now, "the mask begins to slip"[50] as the speaker shifts gears with "And now (וְעַתָּה) . . ."[51]

Now you dwellers in Jerusalem and people of Judah,
judge between me and my vineyard.

וְעַתָּה יוֹשֵׁב יְרוּשָׁלַם וְאִישׁ יְהוּדָה
שִׁפְטוּ־נָא בֵּינִי וּבֵן כַּרְמִי

			for my vineyard	than (what) I have done	for it?
What	more was there to do				
מַה־	לַעֲשׂוֹת עוֹד		לְכַרְמִי	וְלֹא עָשִׂיתִי	בּוֹ
Why	when I expected it to "do"		good grapes	did it "do"	stinking (fruit)?
מַדּוּעַ	קִוֵּיתִי לַעֲשׂוֹת		עֲנָבִים	וַיַּעַשׂ	בְּאֻשִׁים (Isa 5:3–4)

48. Verbin, "Egyptian Viticultural Practices," 150–51.

49. Wildberger, *Isaiah 1–12*, 183, points to another parallel: in Song 7:8 the man wishes that his beloved's "breasts be like clusters of grapes on the vine." If the Song of the Vineyard has an undertone of conjugal imagery, then, the bride with "putrid grapes" is thoroughly unattractive.

50. Motyer, *Isaiah*, 68.

51. Williamson, *Isaiah 1–5*, 326, sets out at length the rhetorical effect of change in meter and pace across the poem.

The husbandman sets up his logic through his fourfold repetition of the verb "to do" (עשׂה), using a pair for his labors and pair for the outcome from the vines. There is nothing more he can *do* than he has *done*.[52] In return, the vineyard, instead of *doing* well, *did* unimaginably poorly. The watertight rhetoric of the case is presented as a matching pair of questions, asking "what" and "why." The answer to the first exonerates the plaintiff. The answer (or lack of it) to the second makes culpable the defendant.

Assuming that the silence incriminates the vineyard, the husbandman proceeds to pronounce a penalty:

Now I will tell you what I am going to do to my vineyard:

וְעַתָּה אוֹדִיעָה־נָּא אֶתְכֶם אֵת אֲשֶׁר־אֲנִי
עֹשֶׂה לְכַרְמִי

I will take away its hedge,	and it will be destroyed;	
הָסֵר מְשׂוּכָּתוֹ	וְהָיָה לְבָעֵר	
I will break down its wall,	and it will be trampled.	
פָּרֹץ גְּדֵרוֹ	וְהָיָה לְמִרְמָס	
I will make it a wasteland,	neither pruned nor cultivated,	and briers and thorns will grow there.
וַאֲשִׁיתֵהוּ בָתָה	לֹא יִזָּמֵר וְלֹא יֵעָדֵר	וְעָלָה שָׁמִיר וָשָׁיִת
I will command the clouds	not to rain upon it,	
וְעַל הֶעָבִים אֲצַוֶּה	מֵהַמְטִיר עָלָיו מָטָר (Isa 5:5–6)	

Now we have the last of the seven uses of the verb "to do" (עשׂה)—it has turned out to be the verb around which the song revolves.[53] It was used twice in 5:2 to describe the expected and actual yield of the vine; four times in 5:4 in accusation; and now, it is used to set out the farmer's decision on the vine: וְעַתָּה אוֹדִיעָה־נָּא; the hiphil cohortative with the

---

52. "The interrogative pronoun followed by the infinitive has gerundive force. . . . What is there yet to be done?" Young, *Isaiah 1–18*, 199. The LXX moves the question rhetorically into the future: "What more shall I do?" (τί ποιήσω ἔτι τῷ ἀμπελῶνί μου). The answer to both the MT and the LXX is: "Nothing."

53. Miscall, *Isaiah*, 31.

עַתָּה expresses the force of the speaker's feeling—"Now let me make you know."[54]

The man lists two tasks he will undertake against the vineyard, which he expresses in parallel ideas. He will begin by dismantling the fencing, or demolishing the wall. The result will be invasion by wild beasts and domestic animals, which will now destroy the vineyard by grazing and by trampling.[55] A similarly unprotected vineyard is described thus: "Why have you broken down its walls? . . . Boars from the forest ravage it, and insects from the field feed on it" (Ps 80:12–13). Second, the husbandman will lay it waste. This he will do by deliberate neglect. He will withhold his daily care for it. He will not prune it in season; he will not root out wild growth. Wildberger explains that two seasons of pruning were required for optimum yield. And since, in Israelite practice, vines would be allowed to grow along the ground rather than on trellises, there would be an even greater need for regular hoeing out of wild plants.[56] The final blow is that the husbandman will also not water the vineyard. Withholding of rain as punishment for default on covenant expectation is well-attested in the canon.[57] The ensuing result is a wasteland in which the vines will either dry up or be choked by the thistles that will overrun the parched land. In terms of the allegory, the intention to stop up the rain-bearing clouds may be understood as a curse of barrenness pronounced on the wife. It seems to be a reversal of the usual marriage blessing of Genesis 24:60 spoken on the bride: "may you increase to thousands upon thousands; may your offspring possess the cities of their enemies."[58]

Verbin explains how in the LXX, there is again the influence of Ptolemaic agricultural practice. Instead of declaring that he "will make it a wasteland," this husbandman says he will abandon his vineyard (καὶ ἀνήσω τὸν ἀμπελῶνά μου). To "abandon" was a technical term used in connection with land left untilled. The result of this action is a little different from the MT's "and briers and thorns will grow there." Rather, the LXX has, "and thorns will spring up on it as on a dry plot (χέρσος)." The word χέρσος is again drawn from the Egyptian agricultural context. It describes land once fertile but that has now turned unproductive. This would usually result from a collapse of the irrigation system or due to low levels of inundation by the Nile. This scenario is equivalent with the MT idea that the vineyard will not receive rain any further. But beyond

---

54. Oswalt, *Isaiah 1–39*, 154n20; Young, *Isaiah 1–18*, 117.
55. Wildberger, *Isaiah 1–12*, 183.
56. Wildberger, *Isaiah 1–12*, 183.
57. Deut 11:17; 28:24; cf. Lev 26:4; Amos 4:7; Isa 30:23; etc.
58. Willis, "Genre of Isa 5:1–7," 347–48.

simply indicating that the land was now a dry plot, the term meant that the land, being agriculturally unproductive, was exempt from taxes. Vineyards were particularly susceptible to such failures, owing to their high demand for water. The term χερσάμπελος was coined specifically to describe such vineyards, making them a specific class of unproductive agricultural land.[59] Thus, the LXX reflects well (in its own context) the extreme effect on the vineyard of the husbandman's decisions.

In both the MT and the LXX, the vineyard-keeper achieves the destruction of his vineyard by two means: first by actively working against it; and second, by withdrawing his care from it. By opening it up to invasion and by vacating it himself, the vineyard becomes doubly vulnerable. Dry and wild with brambles, it appears to fall into a state worse than before. It can no longer even be admired as fertile virgin ground with potential for cultivation. The verb sequences are telling: positive actions (dug, cleared, planted, built, hewed out) are replaced by a series of negative verbs (remove, break down, make waste, command drought), which in turn permit another series of passive verbs (be devoured, be trampled, not be pruned or hoed, be overgrown).[60] The audience, applying these back to the signified, understands that the cuckolded husband will henceforth cease to provide for and protect his wife, leaving her thoroughly vulnerable to those who might take advantage of her situation. The image of rain withheld may even point to a curse of barrenness pronounced over her (cf. Gen 24:60).[61]

The condition of the vineyard is in stark contrast with the garden of the Song. There, the woman summons the winds. She commands them to blow her garden's fragrance beyond its walls. So prodigious is its produce that it can attract the notice of those outside the garden boundaries. And that produce was possible because the garden responded vigorously to its water supply, as refreshing as rivulets "streaming down from Lebanon" (Song 4:15). In Isaiah 5, a different element of nature is addressed: the clouds. If the speaker now commands them to withhold their rain from the vineyard, we must assume that up to this point, the vineyard enjoyed its seasonal rain because the speaker bade the rain fall. Here is a piece of land that has responded poorly despite being well-watered. Instead of producing the sweet aroma of succulent grapes, it has presented odious fruit. No winds are needed to waft this stink abroad. Rather, the husbandman acts to stop the further production of such fruit by turning off the water source.

The singer makes clear the husbandman's displeasure. His "initial zeal

---

59. Verbin, "Egyptian Viticultural Practices," 151–52.
60. Brueggemann, *Isaiah 1–39*, 47–48.
61. Williams, "Frustrated Expectations," 462.

and energetic devotion" have "cooled completely." "The ardor is spent" and "the relationship is in deep jeopardy."[62] His audience may well have begun to catch the identity of the "beloved" on whose behalf he sings. Only God could command the clouds to rain or withhold rain, though the possibility also remains that humans can use such language (2 Sam 1:21).[63] At any rate, the singer now steps out again, and sets out the equivalences of the metaphor:

The vineyard of the Lord Almighty is the nation of Israel,

כִּי כֶרֶם יְהוָה צְבָאוֹת בֵּית יִשְׂרָאֵל

and the people of Judah are the vines he delighted in.

וְאִישׁ יְהוּדָה נְטַע שַׁעֲשׁוּעָיו

And he looked for justice, but saw bloodshed;

וַיְקַו לְמִשְׁפָּט וְהִנֵּה מִשְׂפָּח

for righteousness, but heard cries of distress.

(Isa 5:7) לִצְדָקָה וְהִנֵּה צְעָקָה

God is the husbandman and the vineyard is his people. They make up the vines in which he took pleasure—it was his delight (שַׁעֲשׁוּעִים). In Jeremiah 31:20, YHWH refers to Ephraim as "the child in whom I delight" (יֶלֶד שַׁעֲשׁוּעִים; cf. Prov 8:30). Along similar lines (though using a different noun), Ezekiel's wife is described as the "delight" (מַחְמַד) of his eyes (Ezek 24:16). That the vineyard was a "delight" is an indicator that this is a love song gone sour. The LXX describes the vineyard like this: "The plant that he loved" (νεόφυτον ἠγαπημένον). The term νεόφυτος, or "newly planted plant," is an Egyptian technical term for a freshly planted vineyard.[64] It was a new vine that he loved.

However, as Wildberger observes, "Yahweh is no 'impetuous lover' who tries to overpower his beloved like a whirlwind, but rather one who patiently surrounds her with his care and continuously tries to show new evidence of his affection."[65] But, as between the vineyard and the husbandman, in the relationship between YHWH and his new "wife," expectations have been severely thwarted. As the husbandman waited with anticipation, YHWH also waited eagerly (קוה). But the outcome is related just as tersely as before. He expected one thing and found its opposite. Instead of justice (מִשְׁפָּט), bloodshed (מִשְׂפָּח); instead of right-

---

62. Brueggemann, *Isaiah 1–39*, 47.
63. Wildberger, *Isaiah 1–12*, 184; Williamson, *Isaiah 1–5*, 341–42.
64. Verbin, "Egyptian Viticultural Practices," 152.
65. Wildberger, *Isaiah 1–12*, 187.

eousness (צְדָקָה), outcry (צְעָקָה). The similar-sounding pairs of words serve not just as wordplay. The second word in each pair feigns similarity to the first, bringing back images of grapes that on closer inspection turned out to be something quite different[66]—malodorous and loathsome berries.

The "Look!" (הִנֵּה) invites the audience to see the situation through the eyes of the subject, YHWH. As before—"Now you dwellers in Jerusalem and people of Judah, judge between me and my vineyard"—YHWH invites, or even forces, the hearer to enter into the discourse. Williams sets out how YHWH's deep frustration with his people is apparent right through the poem. The frustration comes through twice by way of the metaphor (5:2c, 4b) and then plainly in the concluding line (5:7b). Further, the plot of the poem "frustrates" the reader; by its reversal of a happy ending, and by its introduction of an unexpected speaker and theme, the reader is forced to pause to reinterpret that poem. "Our frustration at the interpretative process enables us to identify ourselves with Yahweh's frustration."[67]

Standing back from the detail, we can now see the parable's structure better:[68]

A[1]		The vineyard depicted (v. 1; four lines)
	B[1]	The vineyard cared for (v. 2ab; 5 verbs)
		C[1] The end hoped for and negated (v. 2c)
		C[2] The end invited (vv. 3–4)
		C[3] The end pronounced (v. 5)
	B[2]	The vineyard neglected (v. 6; 5 verbs)
A[2]		The vineyard explained (v. 7; four lines)

By the end of the poem, the love song becomes a bitter complaint against a wife, Israel, whose husband, YHWH, meets her every need and yet reaps a reward of disappointment. With this in mind we may compare Song 4 and Isaiah 5.

---

66. Mackay, *Isaiah 1–39*, 138.
67. Williams, "Frustrated Expectations," 459–65, esp. 459.
68. Lightly edited from Motyer, *Isaiah*, 68.

GARDENS: MAN AND WOMAN

In Song 4, the man consistently addresses the woman as his "bride." If the setting is the night of the wedding (cf. Song 4:6; 5:1), the groom woos his new bride so that the consummation of their relationship may be mutually pleasurable. Isaiah 5 could depict a rather similar situation. Spread over a longer timeframe than a single night, it is the husband's song about his (new) wife.

In the Song, the man sets up a make-believe scenario. The woman is a goddess situated in her abode on Lebanon. Lions and leopards keep her company, as they should a love goddess. He is a love-struck mortal who woos her to descend to him. One step at a time, he patiently courts her with his stirring poetry till finally he wins her completely. Within this world of make-believe, the mortal makes his suit against all odds, optimistic that he can secure the desire of his heart. In Isaiah, the man cares for his wife at expense to himself. In the language of the metaphor, he has secured a promising plot of land, and he does all that is within his capacity to realize its potential. He ploughs the ground, clears the stones, plants good vines, and fences the plot. He then goes beyond these basics to build the expensive tower and a winepress, anticipating the long-term productivity of the vineyard. Like the Song's bridegroom, the husband in Isaiah spares no effort. Both pay complete and devoted attention to the object of their affection, hoping for an outcome that will delight both parties in the relationship.

The women at whom these attentions are directed are both praise-worthily fertile. The Song's love goddess has a body like a lush garden. Canonically, the garden resonates with the language that describes the veritable cornucopia that Canaan is. Thus, the woman is variously described as a spring, a fountain, a well of flowing water streaming down from Lebanon, in language reminiscent of Canaan, which is "a land with brooks, streams, and deep springs gushing out into the valleys and hills." The garden's extravagantly fine stock recalls the "land with wheat and barley, vines and fig trees, pomegranates, olive oil, and honey" (Deut 8:7–8). Like Canaan, the garden has honeycombs dripping with honey, and trees bearing the pomegranate. If they are anything like their mythical counterparts, these pomegranates are the very elixir of life.

Isaiah's vineyard, when we are introduced to it, holds similar resonances with Canaan. Egypt is no match to its fertility: "The land you are entering to take over is not like the land of Egypt, from which you have come, where you planted your seed and irrigated it by foot as in a vegetable garden. But the land . . . is a land of mountains and valleys that drinks rain from heaven" (Deut 11:10–11). Isaiah's vineyard similarly enjoys the bounty of the clouds. In Deuteronomy, it is God who provides this seasonal rain: "It is a land that the Lord your God cares for; the eyes of the Lord your God are continually on it from the beginning of the year to its end, . . . So if you . . . love the Lord your God . . . then I will send rain on your land in its season, both autumn and spring rains, so that you may gather in your . . . new wine" (Deut 11:12–15; cf. Deut 28:23–24). The Isaian husbandman is no different in his careful tending of the vineyard. If only the vines had responded to that care, new wine was what the story could have ended with.

The difference between the garden and the vineyard lies in the nature of each. The Song's garden is eager to welcome the man who woos her as his bride: "Let my beloved come into his garden and taste its choice fruits" (Song 4:16). The vineyard, on the other hand, sullenly works against the husbandman who has lavished care on her. Rather than give him enjoyment, she brings his investment to ruin. When he enters his vineyard in the fruiting season, the fruit he receives is anything but "choice."

Just as much as Canaan is extravagantly generous—"a land where bread will not be scarce and you will lack nothing" (Deut 8:9)—the garden allows the man to feast to satiation. He comes, gathers, eats, and drinks. He gathers myrrh with spice, eats honeycomb with honey, and drinks wine with milk. The pairs seem to affirm the abundance available to him for the taking. His senses of smell and taste are satisfied—or perhaps even overwhelmed. Milk and honey are what Canaan proverbially overflows with (Deut 6:3; 11:9; etc.). Wine famously gladdens the heart (Ps 104:15). On the contrary, in Isaiah, the man's senses are revolted by the smell and taste of the grapes. Thus, while the Song ends with an exhortation to drink one's fill of love (5:1), the Song of the Vineyard ends with the husband's cessation of "delight" in his beloved.

One final point of comparison between the poems is the idea of the divine. In the Song, divinity is implicitly attributed to the woman, using make-believe. The effect of this device is to allow the woman to exercise her freewill in giving herself to the man. In fact, the man lays no claim on her for the larger part of the Songs of Lebanon. The exotica in her garden are all firmly "your"—that is, her—plants. It is only when she cedes her right over her garden to him that he dares own the garden and its delights. Then, he pronounces the garden "my garden." The point is that by giving herself to the man, the woman-as-goddess condescends in a way only a divine being can with a mortal.

In the Song of the Vineyard, the reverse happens. The divine being plays at being a human vineyard-keeper. When the mask finally drops, the human is revealed to be YHWH. In the make-believe world of the parable, he had taken ownership of, and responsibility for, a promising plot of land. His condescension as a divine entity lies in his willing service to the vineyard, the metaphorical representation of a human party. His gracious initiative in establishing the vineyard is affirmed in other texts that use this image: "You transplanted a vine from Egypt; you drove out the nations and planted it" (Ps 80:8). The vine is obligated to this husbandman for its very existence. It is "the root your right hand has planted" (Ps 80:15). As much as the Songs of Lebanon—if not more—the Song of the Vineyard is a show of gracious condescension.

The conversation between these two texts appears to end with this prescription: there is a place in human love relationships for willing service and a corresponding place for the expected returns for that service.

GARDENS: DEITY AND DEVOTEE

The garden metaphor lends itself to some intriguing allegorical exegesis. With Jewish exegetes, the equivalents fall into place rather predictably, centering largely around the theme of the exile.

The opening line—"With Me from Lebanon, O bride! With Me from Lebanon shall you come"—is the consolation God offers Israel as she goes into exile. "Lebanon" is the Temple, either because of its lavish use of cedar, or because of the traditional equation that arises from the paronomasia between לְבָנוֹן ("Lebanon") and לָבָן ("whiteness"),[69] which, for example, the Midrash Zuta explains: "Whoever brings his sacrifice there, and is sinful, does not depart from there until his sins become white as snow" (Isa 1:18).[70] So, when Israel is exiled from this "Lebanon," God assures her he goes with her, for as Isaiah 63:9 asserts: "In all their distress, he too was distressed."

The dangerous lions and leopards refer to the nations among whom Israel is exiled. They are wild beasts without the faculty of speech, unable to understand the tongue of the exiled Jews as foretold in Deuteronomy 28:49:[71] "The Lord will bring a nation against you from far away . . . a nation whose language you will not understand, a fierce-looking nation without respect for the old or pity for the young."

---

69. B. Yoma 39b; b. Gittin 56b; and Sifre, cited in Meir Zlotowitz, compiler, *Shir haShirim/ Song of Songs: An Allegorical Translation Based upon Rashi with a Commentary Anthologized from Talmudic, Midrashic and Rabbinic Sources* (New York: Mesorah, 1979), 134.

70. Midrash Zuta, cited in Zlotowitz, *Shir haShirim*, 134.

71. Shir Chadash, cited in Zlotowitz, *Shir haShirim*, 134.

Why does God call Israel both "sister" and "bride"? She is "sister" to him by being the inheritor of the merit of her ancestors, the patriarchs, with whom God had a special familial relationship. She is his "bride" because by her own merits she has earned his love. She is receptor of a dual love.[72] So great is this love that God says: "You have captured my heart with but one of your virtues, with but one of the precepts (מִצְוֹת) that adorn you like the beads of a necklace."[73]

God proceeds to extol Israel's beauty. The "fragrance of [her] oils" is her fine reputation. Her "lips drop sweetness" in her discourse of the Torah. This is the revealed portion of the Torah which is relayed publicly by the use of her "lips."[74] That "milk and honey are under [her] tongue" is a reference to the more hidden and more esoteric sections of the Torah. These are safeguarded from public discourse and saved for an exclusive audience.[75] The scent of her garments comes from her obedience to the regulations governing clothing: the fringes, the purple thread, the priestly garments, and the prohibition on wearing mixed wool and linen fabric.[76]

The walled garden, the locked-up spring, and the sealed fountain are expectedly read as a defense against sexual impurity. The Midrash explains it by connecting the patriarchs with the generation that went into exile: "Sarah went down to Egypt and guarded herself against immorality [Gen 12:14–20] and all the women [generations later, during the period of bondage] guarded themselves for her sake. Joseph went down to Egypt and guarded himself against immorality [Gen 39:7–12] and all the men guarded themselves for his sake."[77] As for the garden spring and the well of living waters, this is imagery in which God praises Jewish women for their faithful practice of ritual immersions and purifications.[78]

In response to Israel's virtues, God commands the winds to blow the fragrance of her piety far and wide to reach those still in dispersion, in preparation for the coming of the Messiah. The miracles that precede this final redemption will overwhelm the nations among whom the Jews live—so much so that they will escort the Jews to Israel as their homage

---

72. Divre Yedidah, cited in Zlotowitz, *Shir haShirim*, 136–37.

73. Rashi's translation, in Zlotowitz, *Shir haShirim*, 137. The equation between the precepts of the Torah and beads on a necklace comes from Prov 1:9: "They [instruction and teaching] are like . . . a chain to adorn your neck."

74. Rashi, cited in Zlotowitz, *Shir haShirim*, 138.

75. Divrei Yedidah, cited in Zlotowitz, *Shir haShirim*, 139.

76. Rashi, cited in Zlotowitz, *Shir haShirim*, 139.

77. Midrash, cited in Zlotowitz, *Shir haShirim*, 140.

78. Rashi, cited in Zlotowitz, *Shir haShirim*, 142.

to Israel's God (Isa 66:20).[79] Restored to her homeland and Temple, Israel will implore God to take up once again his dwelling in his Temple and "taste its choice fruits," that is, savor the sacrifices offered to him. The Targum sets out God's spirited response: "I have come into my Temple which you built for Me . . . I have caused My Presence to dwell among you. And I have favorably received your spice incense which you performed for My name. I have sent fire from heaven and it devoured the burnt offerings and the holy sacrifices. The libations of red wine and white wine, which the priests poured out on My altar, were favorably received." The final invitation to feast is to the priests: "Now come, O priests who love My precepts, and eat what is left of the offerings and delight yourselves with the bounty made ready for you."[80]

The Christian allegorical appropriation of the Songs of Lebanon is more detailed. The exegete labors to find equivalences at the verbal level, which can then be conceptualized. Thus, the mountain range that Christ calls his bride to leave is mined for deeper meaning. Amana (meaning "restless" or "agitated") refers to "people whom earthly delight overcomes," rendering them restless. Senir means "stench"—malodorous persons defiled by thought and act. Hermon (meaning "cursing") symbolizes the accursed, the ones excommunicated "on the ground of their manifest sins." The bride is to separate herself from these unsavory groups by way of Lebanon (meaning "making gleaming or white"), that is, through purification by devout prayer and by the mortification of carnality.[81] Christ calls his beloved "sister," an epithet that "excludes all suspicion of unhallowed love."[82]

Next, the parallelism drawn between "with one of your eyes" and "by one ornament of your neck" invites convoluted ingenuities. A typical straightforward treatment is that of Theodoret of Cyrus. "Your two eyes are wondrous. . . . But one of them affects me with unbounded wonder; it looks upon things divine . . . and contemplates hidden mysteries." Similarly, the bride's neck is adorned with many "ornaments of righteousness," and Christ marvels at even a single one of them.[83]

Similarly to Jewish allegory, the "honeycomb" signifies the divine

---

79. Rashi, cited in Zlotowitz, *Shir haShirim*, 143.

80. Targum to Song of Songs 5:1.

81. Richard of St.-Victor, *In Cantica Canticorum Explicatio*, cited in Richard A. Norris Jr., trans. and ed., *The Song of Songs: Interpreted by Early Christian and Medieval Commentators* (Grand Rapids: Eerdmans, 2003), 173–75.

82. Jerome, *Against Jovinianus* 1.30 and *Homilies on the Psalms* 42 (Psalm 127), cited in J. Robert Wright, ed., *Proverbs, Ecclesiastes, Song of Solomon*, ACCS, Old Testament 9 (Downers Grove, IL: InterVarsity, 2005), 336 and 342.

83. Theodoret of Cyrus, *Interpretatio in Canticum Canticorum*, cited in Norris, *Song of Songs*, 180.

Scriptures borne on the lips of the teachers of the church. They provide not only "honey" to the mature, but also "milk" to the infants.[84]

Making reference to her roots in Judaism, Christian exegetes understand the church's fragrance, which Christ praises, to be "the very sweet renown of the faith as it has been spread throughout the world, more widely than the law of the fathers [the Jews], which was confined to Judea alone."[85] Alternatively, her fragrant garments are Christ himself, for the church, by baptism into Christ, has "put on Christ."[86]

The bride is described as a garden enclosed, since the church is the garden of God. Varying from the regular allegorical theme of chastity,[87] this enclosure is read as protection. Like Eden (cf. Gen 3:24), it is "closed off on every side by a wall of fire and protected by angelic guards," "so that neither demons nor evil humans may be strong enough to harm her." The spring that refreshes this garden could have multiple equivalents. If it is Scripture, then this Scripture is sealed because its meaning is hidden to "unworthy persons." If it is the spring of baptism, it is "closed up for the heathen, opened and revealed for catechumens." If it is Christ, the "spring of life," then it is by him that the "filthy deeds of sinners" is washed away, and through him that those who "thirst for righteousness" (cf. Matt 5:6) are satisfied. "He was sealed up in that he was veiled with flesh," and at present "he is sealed up in that he is concealed from us by the glory of the Father . . ." If the spring is the church herself, she overflows with teaching that waters the plants in her garden, the believers.[88]

In the garden of God, that is, the church, grow the "orders of the elect." The many-seeded pomegranates are the martyrs, "full of red-hued blood."[89] The henna tree, since it is abundant in Egypt which is symbolic of the "darkness of this world," represents all spiritual persons who combat such darkness. The small nard tree is for the "humble and innocent saints, who in the presence of their neighbours make themselves small." Saffron, with its golden flower, represents those "who glow with a divine wisdom." The low-growing cassia "stands for those who suffer with

---

84. Theodoret of Cyrus, *Interpretatio in Canticum Canticorum* 4, cited in Wright, *Proverbs, Ecclesiastes, Song of Solomon*, 337.

85. The *Glossa Ordinaria*, cited in Norris, *Song of Songs*, 180.

86. Theodoret of Cyrus, *Interpretatio in Canticum Canticorum* 4, cited in Wright, *Proverbs, Ecclesiastes, Song of Solomon*, 338.

87. E.g., Ambrose and Gregory of Nyssa, cited in Wright, *Proverbs, Ecclesiastes, Song of Solomon*, 338.

88. Honorius of Autun, *Expositio in Cantica Canticorum*, cited in Norris, *Song of Songs*, 183–84.

89. Of the various plants in the Song's orchard, the pomegranate attracts the most elaborate treatment; e.g., Gregory of Nyssa and Theodoret of Cyrus, cited in Wright, *Proverbs, Ecclesiastes, Song of Solomon*, 339–40.

Christ and are ready to lay down their lives for their brethren." Cinnamon has multiple layers of skin. The outermost stand for the monks, "who separate themselves from the world out of love for Christ." Myrrh is preservative, and stands for the hermits who put their vices to death and preserve their flesh from the decay lust brings. Aloe, sometimes burned on altars in place of frankincense, represents the celibate, those who "suppress the wantonness of the flesh by the severity of their life."[90]

The call to the north and south wind to blow upon the garden has a curious Eurocentric bias. The harsh, cold north wind represents the "Prince of the power of darkness" (cf. Jer 1:14; 4:6; 10:22). The "warm and ever bright noontide" south wind is the Holy Spirit. So, in place of the usual rendering "Awake (ἐξεγέρθητι), north wind," the allegorist prefers "Up and out with you, O north wind" (cf. Luke 8:23–24).[91] A less contrived reading is that of Bede, who takes the winds to both represent the "twofold assault" of the world upon the church—the chill north wind being the world's "repellent harshness" and the balmy south wind its "deceptive charm" (cf. Matt 13:20–22). Christ calls upon these to blow on the church, so that she may use her freewill to choose how she should respond.[92]

Christ responds to the church's invitation to enter the garden, and "takes delight in the diversity of her fruit"[93]—"the fruits of true religion."[94]

In both samples of allegorical exegesis, we note that the woman is placed center-stage. Deity falls back into what we may call a supporting role. This well reflects the Songs of Lebanon, poems in celebration of the beauty of the bride.

CONCLUSION

Laying the Songs of Lebanon and the Song of the Vineyard side by side, we note that the influence of the Song on the traditional reading of Isaiah 5:1–7 is remarkable. Though the latter makes no reference to divine-human marriage, that metaphor has been read into it following

90. Honorius of Autun, *Expositio in Cantica Canticorum*, cited in Norris, *Song of Songs*, 185–86.

91. Gregory of Nyssa, *Homiliae XV in Canticum Canticorum* 10, cited in Norris, *Song of Songs*, 190–91. So also Theodoret of Cyrus, *Interpretatio in Canticum Canticorum*, and Rupert of Deutz, *Commentariorum Libri* 4, cited in Norris, *Song of Songs*, 189–90 and 192–93 respectively.

92. The Venerable Bede, *Expositio in Cantica Canticorum*, cited in Norris, *Song of Songs*, 192.

93. Ambrose, *Isaac, or the Soul* 5.49, cited in Wright, *Proverbs, Ecclesiastes, Song of Solomon*, 342.

94. Cyril of Alexandria, *In Joelem*, cited in Norris, *Song of Songs*, 194.

the vineyard and garden imagery in the Song of Songs. Isaiah 5 refers to the husband(man) YHWH in only one verse as "beloved," but that suffices to set up resonance with the Song's most used endearment. Thus, though we have submitted that Isaiah 5:1–7 is a juridical parable, we have attempted to show the validity of reading it also as a song composed by a disappointed husband about his wife.

If this is the case, then canonically, the woman of the Songs of Lebanon makes a perfect match for the man in the Song of the Vineyard. If he is the painstaking husbandman, she is the responsive garden. If he does all that could ever be done for a plot of land, she is the piece of land that puts out a yield guaranteed to satisfy the heart of any gardener. With her, he will never have to wait anxiously for a happy harvest. Rather, she will delight in inviting him in to gorge on her delectable fruit. Isaiah's unhappy parable is compensated by the picture in the Song. Together, the texts complete the picture of the ideal husband and wife.

When this prescription for human love is reconfigured to match deity and devotee, Jewish allegorists follow the predictable trajectory of transposing the Song onto their national history. The Songs of Lebanon provide the dialogue necessary for the rehearsal of the entire story of the exile: Israel goes into captivity, proves her faithfulness to YHWH in challenging circumstances, and is restored to the land. Christian allegorists lay the Songs of Lebanon over the salvation story, pausing to make detailed—and sometimes rather contrived—correlations. Christ calls his bride out of her undesirable environs, and she shows herself responsive to that invitation.

Deity, in both streams of exegesis, plays the lesser role. YHWH is the lover who remains by his beloved even when she endures the judgment he brings on her. Her distress is his. Christ successfully woos his bride to himself, casts a protective wall around her, and nourishes her with life-sustaining water. In both Jewish and Christian allegory, the devotee is foregrounded. Israel is the garden, and her willing yield is her obedience to the precepts of the Torah. Similarly, the church is a garden bursting with the ranks and orders of the elect, each displaying a particular virtue. In either case, deity responds with delight. YHWH is enthralled by the depth of his beloved's piety and returns to his garden to partake of the offerings Israel eagerly sets before him. Christ is ravished by his bride's many graces and responds to her invitation to enjoy them. If we were to look across the canon for a divine husbandman whose careful attentions this garden would well reward, we would find him in the Song of the Vineyard.

The Songs of Lebanon triptych is a paradise of arboreal ardor, an end for which the Song of the Vineyard hopes but fails to attain. Whether in human or in sacred romance, we understand, such a "paradise" results when one deeply cares and the other is vigorously responsive to that care.

PART IV

Love-and-Its-Jealousy

8.

The Unquenchable Love

At first rummage, the concluding section of the Song of Songs (8:5–14) is a mixed bag, an assortment on its way to a jumble sale. Without a noticeable thematic connector, the ten verses seem to be a mix of odds and ends whose owners we are unsure of—is this the voice of "he" or of "she" or of the "friends" or of the "brothers"?[1] We will argue that if there is a theme threading through this section, it is the theme of 8:6–7, exclusive love between a man and woman. Indeed, this theme may be suggested by the brackets around the section. It opens with "her beloved" (8:5a; דּוֹדָהּ) and finishes off with "my beloved" (8:14; דּוֹדִי).[2]

This idea breaks away from the proposal that, irrespective of who says what, the unit reprises *leitwörter* and leitmotifs played out over the earlier chapters.[3] This seems a plausible position, unless we consider 8:6–7. These two verses are dense with new vocabulary, some even at odds with the familiar: "seal" (חוֹתָם), "death" (מָוֶת), "cruel" (קָשָׁה), "Sheol," "jealousy" (קִנְאָה), "flame" (רֶשֶׁף), "fire" (אֵשׁ), "rivers" (נְהָרוֹת), "wealth" (הוֹן), and a *hapax* (שַׁלְהֶבֶתְיָה) that even Pope's massive commentary prefers to

---

1. Murphy comments that "if the word 'anthology' can be used for any part of the work, it is particularly suitable for 8:5–14" (Roland Murphy, *The Song of Songs*, Hermeneia [Minneapolis: Augsburg Fortress, 1990], 195).

2. Diane Bergant, *Song of Songs*, Berit Olam (Collegeville, MN: Liturgical, 2001), 95; Mary T. Elliott, *The Literary Unity of the Canticle* (Frankfurt: Lang, 1989), 191.

3. The "coming up from the wilderness"; the apple tree; the mother; the vineyard; the request to hear the voice of the loved one; the sending away of the beloved; the voices of all the characters.

Exum posits that this closing section takes the same shape as the opening section 1:2–2:7, that is, "a montage, with alternating voices expressing various aspects of love." Both have short pieces by the man, the woman, and the daughters of Jerusalem (Cheryl J. Exum, *Song of Songs: A Commentary* [Louisville: Westminster John Knox, 2005], 244).

leave untranslated.[4] Most agree that 8:6–7 is atypical of the Song's style, with the speaker unexpectedly trading her gauzy veil (4:3) for the gear of a sage,[5] her words addressed to an audience well beyond her usual world-of-two. This text is arguably the highpoint of the Song, and we will show how it functions as the center that holds together what looks like bits and pieces of revisited text.

INTRODUCTION: SONG 8:5

The first speakers in this concluding section of the Song are possibly the chorus, perhaps the daughters of Jerusalem addressed periodically in the book.[6] They draw our attention to the woman as she makes her entrance.

> Who is this coming up from the wilderness
> Leaning on her beloved? (8:5a)

The text echoes 3:6. Perhaps the scene is also identical and if so, we are to imagine a palanquin as in 3:7–10, in which the woman lies with her beloved, leaning against him.[7] Does this indicate dependency?[8] The lines that follow will establish the woman as remarkably independent—she will remind the man of a time when she "(a)roused" him; she will construct a universal definition of love, pronounce herself worthy of courtship, and invite her beloved to make haste to come enjoy her. Given these, her "leaning" on her lover seems more a public declaration

---

4. Marvin H. Pope, *Song of Songs: A New Translation with Introduction and Commentary*, Anchor Bible 7C (New Haven: Yale University Press, 1977), 653.

5. For elements of wisdom, see Edmee Kingsmill, *The Song of Songs and the Eros of God: A Study in Biblical Intertextuality* (Oxford: Oxford University Press, 2009), 71–72; M. Sadgrove, "The Song of Songs as Wisdom Literature," in *Studia Biblica 1978*, JSOTSup 11 (Sheffield: JSOT, 1978), 245–48, who identifies Song 8:6–7 as the introduction to a wisdom admonition; and Katharine J. Dell, "Does the Song of Songs have any Connections to Wisdom?," in *Perspectives on the Song of Songs*, ed. Anselm C. Hagedorn (Berlin: de Gruyter, 2005), 8–26, who argues that the couple in the Song are, figuratively, Solomon and his bride, the beautiful lady Wisdom.

6. Exum, *Song of Songs*, 248; Michael V. Fox, *The Song of Songs and the Ancient Egyptian Love Songs* (Madison: University of Wisconsin Press, 1985), 166; Elie Assis, *Flashes of Fire: A Literary Analysis of the Song of Songs* (New York: T&T Clark, 2009), 231; Gianni Barbiero, *Song of Songs: A Close Reading*, trans. Michael Tait, VTSS (Leiden: Brill, 2011), 440; Iain Provan, *Ecclesiastes, Song of Songs*, NIVAC (Grand Rapids: Zondervan, 2001), 366.

7. Pope, *Song of Songs*, 663; Exum, *Song of Songs*, 248; Fox, *Ancient Egyptian Love Songs*, 167.

8. E.g. Tremper Longman III, *Song of Songs* (Grand Rapids: Eerdmans, 2001), 208; Duane Garrett, "Song of Songs," in *Song of Songs, Lamentations*, ed. Duane Garrett and Paul R. House, WBC 23B (Nashville: Thomas Nelson, 2004), 252–53; Robert W. Jenson, *Song of Songs*, Interpretation (Louisville: John Knox, 2005), 87–88.

of her choice. As such, it may be a notice of possession.⁹ At least, the description conveys the woman's lack of reticence—which one would expect in an Eastern setting—in matters of romantic attachment.¹⁰ Next, we hear the woman speak:

Under the apple tree I roused you [עֹורַרְתִּיךָ];
There your mother conceived you [שָׁמָּה חִבְּלַתְךָ אִמֶּךָ],
There she who was in labor gave you birth [שָׁמָּה חִבְּלָה יְלָדַתְךָ].   (8:5b)

If her public display of affection is unconventional, her opening line is a bit of a shock to the system. "Under the apple tree I (a)roused [עוּר] you," the Shulammite reminisces. Given the use of the verb in the Song's refrain, "Do not arouse [עוּר] or awaken [עוּר] love until it so desires" (2:7; 3:5; 8:4), and given the apple tree—the Song's favorite aphrodisiac¹¹—we gather the woman is not talking about irritably nudging awake a snoring partner.¹² Yet, as Krinetzki puts it: "The claim by a woman that she has 'awakened' the man's love would . . . be extraordinary, particularly in an ancient Near Eastern poem."¹³ In line with this sentiment, and following the Syriac, some scholars prefer to amend the grammar of the MT here. By changing the pronoun suffixes in 8:5b from the masculine to the feminine, one could place the words in the mouth of the man rather the woman—allowing the man to be the agent of the verb "to arouse."¹⁴ But, unsettling as it may be to some readers ancient and modern that a woman should arouse a man, here is a woman who is bold both in public and in private to make the man hers. Indeed, as Keel rightly points out, the reader has seen glimpses of her initiative before (3:4; 4:9; 6:5): she goes looking for the man at night,

9. Tom Gledhill, *The Message of the Song of Songs: The Lyrics of Love*, Bible Speaks Today (Leicester: InterVarsity, 1994), 219.

10. Barbiero, *Song of Songs*, 447.

11. Othmar Keel, *The Song of Songs: A Continental Commentary*, trans. Frederick J. Gaiser (Minneapolis: Augsburg, 1994), 88, 82–83.

12. Contra Fox, *Ancient Egyptian Love Songs*, 168.

13. G. Krinetzki, *Kommentar zum Hohenlied: Bildsprache und Theologische Botschaft*, BBET 16 (Bern: Lang, 1981), cited in Keel, *Song of Songs*, 267.

14. Followed by a minority of scholars, Joüon holds that the woman has been unfaithful earlier (5:3), and the male lover here requires her fidelity (Paul Joüon, *Le Cantique Des Cantiques: Commentaire Philologique et Exégétique* [Paris: Beauchesne, 1909], 315). See also R. F. Littledale, *A Commentary on the Song of Songs from Ancient and Mediaeval Sources* (London: n.p., 1869), 355–57. Pope argues that the MT's masculine vocalization of the pronoun suffixes has endured through centuries of allegorical interpretation which would have had to allow that YHWH could be "(a)roused" by his bride Israel (*Song of Songs*, 663; also Murphy, *Song of Songs*, 191). See Keel, *Song of Songs*, 267–69, who refers to the initiative of ancient West Asian goddesses courting their admirers, and the Old Testament narratives of the bold Ruth and Tamar (Genesis 38).

and on finding him, she seizes him and leads him to her bedchamber; her beloved is helplessly smitten by "one glance of [her] eyes"; in fact, he must ask her to stop looking at him, so much do they "overwhelm" him.[15] What is more, in this book, the adjurations not to arouse love are repeatedly made not to men but to a group of women called the daughters of Jerusalem (2:7; 3:5; 8:4).

The recollection of arousing the man leads to talk of conception and childbearing. This is regularly noted as being the only reference to childbearing (ילד) in a book that clearly is a celebration of the physical aspects of romance. In fact, that the Song hardly mentions childbearing is odd in a canon that mentions sex mostly as a preamble to the business of begetting offspring—"and X made love to his wife, and she gave birth to Y."

Why does the woman invoke memories of the man's mother conceiving (חבל) and giving birth (ילד)?[16] In 3:4, she had similarly associated her intimacies with her beloved with the procreation of herself—she led the man into the bedroom of "the one who" conceived or became pregnant with (הרה) her.

In positioning her love life in tandem with that of a generation previous,[17] is the woman assuming a role of "keeper of the family tree"?[18] Or, is she reminding her beloved that their union also serves to "maintain and regenerate society"?[19] Or, could she be anticipating bearing her man's child? In Eastern societies, ancient and present-day, bearing a child traditionally legitimates the woman's claim on the man—she becomes the mother of the man's child. She expects that he owes her attachment for this reason alone, if not any other (Gen 29:32–34; 30:20). It is possible, then, that as the woman lies leaning on her beloved, her thoughts turn on possessing his affections to her satisfaction.

A quick aside here: The motif of love under the trees, specifically apple trees, is attested in ancient romantic poetry.[20] If we understand that the woman means to say that the man was also birthed under the apple tree,

15. Keel, *Song of Songs*, 268.

16. Cf. Ps 7:14 [EV 15]. While חבל is agreed to mean "to conceive," ילד is taken to mean "to be pregnant" (הרה) rather than the usual "to give birth to" (Ariel Bloch and Chana Bloch, *The Song of Songs: A New Translation with an Introduction and Commentary* [New York: Random House, 1995], 211; Keel, *Song of Songs*, 268) because of the improbability of doing so under a tree. Pope allows multiple possibilities (*Song of Songs*, 664).

17. Assis, *Flashes of Fire*, 233; Longman, *Song of Songs*, 209; Barbiero, *Song of Songs*, 452.

18. Keel, *Song of Songs*, 268–69.

19. Gledhill, *Message of the Song of Songs*, 223.

20. Pope, *Song of Songs*, 371–71; 663. The theme of love under apple trees is present in Sumerian love poems with lines such as "My sister, I would go with you to my apple tree" and "By an apple tree I knelt as is proper" (Samuel Noah Kramer, *The Sacred Marriage Rite: Aspects of Faith, Myth and Ritual in Ancient Sumer* [Bloomington: Indiana University Press, 1969], 100–101).

there is a whiff here of not just his apple-fragrance (7:8)[21] but also of the mythic. Pope furnishes a considerable list of gods birthed under trees.[22] Considering that allusions to the mythological are going to come thick and fast in this speech (8:5b–7), it should not surprise the reader that the poem makes a start here. Earlier, the woman cast her beloved in the role of the fabled Solomon (3:6–11) and described him as if he were a demigod (5:10–16). If here the man is being invested with shades of the mythological, it serves well as a poetic device to sweep this pair of lovers into the immortalization of Love in the lines to come. As such, they take their place amongst lovers whose names are forever intertwined in devotion to each other.

THE SEAL: SONG 8:6a

If we were right in reading the woman's public leaning upon her lover, her reference to conception, and even her possible elevation of themselves to the status of legendary lovers, as an implicit desire for exclusive love, then that desire is now explicitly expressed with an imperative:

Place me like a seal [שִׂימֵנִי כַחוֹתָם] over your heart [עַל־לִבֶּךָ];
Like a seal on your arm [כַּחוֹתָם עַל־זְרוֹעֶךָ]. (8:6aα)

Taking a cue from Egyptian love poems, and considering that seals were either worn on a cord around the neck or as a finger ring (Gen 38:18; Jer 22:24), some read this as a wish for nearness: "If only I were her little seal-ring, / the keeper of her finger! / I would see her love each and every day."[23]

A second alternative is that the woman is asking that she should identify with her beloved.[24] Seals were a man's "legal signature and

---

21. "'It seems to me that your mother could have conceived (חבלתך) you and gotten pregnant (ילדתך) with you under the apple tree, which is why your scent is like the apple among the trees of the wood'—just as she said to him earlier, when she wished and desired to sit in his shade and to have his left hand under her head." So Ibn-Ezra, cited in Fox, *Ancient Egyptian Love Songs*, 168–69.

22. Pope, *Song of Songs*, 663.

23. Cairo Love Songs, Group B: 21C, translated in Fox, *Ancient Egyptian Love Songs*, 38, 169. Similarly, William W. Hallo, "'As the Seal Upon Thine Arm': Glyptic Metaphors in the Biblical World," in *Ancient Seals and the Bible*, ed. Leonard Gorelick and Elizabeth Williams-Forte, Occasional Papers on the Near East 2/1 (Malibu, CA: Undena, 1983), 7–12.

24. Bergant, *Song of Songs*, 97; Bloch and Bloch, *Song of Songs*, 212; Assis, *Flashes of Fire*, 238; Exum, *Song of Songs*, 250–51; Richard S. Hess, *Song of Songs*, Baker Commentary on the Old Testament (Grand Rapids: Baker, 2005), 238; Elizabeth Huwiler, "Song of Songs," in Roland E. Murphy and Elizabeth Huwiler, *Proverbs, Ecclesiastes and Song of Songs*, NIBC (Peabody, MA:

identification" and, as such, among his most valuable possessions[25] (Gen 38:18–26; cf. Sir 17:22). This may be the sense in which YHWH speaks of Zerubbabel as his signet ring, bearing his identity: "I will make you like my signet ring, for I have chosen you" (Hag 2:23; cf. Gen 41:42; Jer 22:24). In this reading, the woman wishes to subsume her identity into that of the man, becoming part of him.

A third alternative is to understand the seal as a stamp seal that marks ownership, such as the engraved seals made of semi-precious stone used to stamp on the wet clay of a jar.[26] This reading also accentuates the idea of merging of identities, so that the owner and the owned are insepara-bly one. However, in reverse of the alternative above, the man takes his identity from the woman as one who belongs to her.

A fourth alternative is to understand the seal as a talisman, an amulet that protects the wearer.[27] Keel argues this at length, setting up women in this role. Anath and Isis, from Canaanite and Egyptian mythology respectively, each in their own way rescued their lovers from death. The Old Testament features a string of intrepid heroines who either used procreation as a means to outwit death—Lot's daughters (Gen 19:30–38), Tamar (Genesis 38), Ruth (Ruth 3)—or protected the life of those they loved: Michal (1 Sam 19:9–17), Abigail (1 Samuel 25), the wise woman of Maacah (2 Sam 20:14–22), Esther, and (in a way) Riz-pah (2 Sam 21:8–14). This reading is plausible if we read what follows as a כִּי clause:[28] "*Because* love is as strong as death, (its) jealousy unyield-ing as Sheol" (8:6aβ). The woman's love, worn on the man's heart and/or arm, will ward off at least an untimely descent into the underworld. An Indian reader would be reminded of the festival of *raksha bandhan*

Hendrickson, 1999), 290; Jill M. Munro, *Spikenard and Saffron: A Study in the Poetic Language of the Song of Songs*, JSOTSup 203 (Sheffield: Sheffield Academic, 1995), 65.

25. Pope, *Song of Songs*, 666.

26. Pope, *Song of Songs*, 666; see Keel, *Song of Songs*, 271–72; G. Lloyd Carr, *Song of Solomon: An Introduction and Commentary*, TOTC (Leicester: InterVarsity, 1984), 169; Longman, *Song of Songs*, 210.

27. Keel, *Song of Songs*, 272–75; Pope, *Song of Songs*, 666–67; Barbiero, *Song of Songs*, 459. Hallo, "A Seal Upon Thine Arm," 12–13, connects the seal and death to posit that the woman claims that her beloved will remain her beloved even beyond death. In "For Love Is as Strong as Death," *JANES* 22 (1993): 45–50, he provides detailed evidence of a funerary custom in which females were interred with jewelry pins mounted with the husbands' seals. A curious echo of four elements in Song 8:6–7 is in the pseudepigraphal *Testament of Solomon*, where the flaming demon Ornias, who dwells in the zodiacal sign of Aquarius ("the water-bearer who pours out a river"), is bound when the "seal of Solomon" is flung at his chest, and who offers "all the sil-ver and gold of the earth" to regain his freedom (Jesse Rainbow, "The Song of Songs and the *Testament of Solomon*: Solomon's Love Poetry and Christian Magic," *HTR* 100, no. 3 [2007]: 259–62).

28. The כִּי is more often read as asseverative rather than causal, and is better left untranslated (Murphy, *Song of Songs*, 191).

(the bond of protection) when a woman ties an amulet onto the wrist of a brother symbolizing her wish for his safety. In the cultural environment of ancient West Asia, the Song could well be expressing the same apotropaic sentiment.

Each of the four readings is an attractive option and has enough to commend it. The plea to be worn on the man so that the woman can find satisfaction in his nearness is a commonplace in romantic relationships. The desire that the woman should lose her identity in the man's is not merely plausible but culturally a given. Down to the present day, in Eastern communities, the bride leaves her maternal family to take on the name and identity of the man's family (e.g., Rebekah in Gen 24:61; Tamar in Gen 38:11; Ruth and Orpah in Ruth 1:7). However, this stereotypical woman is not the one we have experienced in the Song. If anything, she is startlingly countercultural. It is entirely possible that she is aggressively sealing her ownership of the man. Since there is no gram-matical indication of entreaty in her שִׂימֵנִי ("Set me!"), the imperative suggests insistence rather than plea. The woman has shown a keen sense of ownership so far: "My beloved is mine" (2:16; 6:3). Seals on heart and finger will thoroughly mark him as her territory.[29] In a culture in which polygamy and even infidelity on the part of the man are not unusual, she wishes to secure her claim on him and exclude rivals. What is more, in this role of aggressive owner, she may even see herself as his protection against danger and untimely death.

From here, the poem moves to the high point toward which the Song has been leading.[30]

LOVE AND ITS JEALOUSY: SONG 8:6a–7

So far, the Song has presented love in particular, that is, between a certain man and a certain woman. Now its scope suddenly opens up, and it presents love in broad universal language, "virtually personified." We had intimations of such personification in the adjurations to the daughters of Jerusalem, in which Love would wake when it chose to wake.[31] Now, Love is a force that takes its place among cosmic and chthonic deities.

29. It is pointed out that the "heart" and "arm" of Song 8:6 refer to thought and action respectively, which taken together make a synecdoche for the whole person (e.g., Longman, *Song of Songs*, 210).

30. E.g., Assis, *Flashes of Fire*, 236; Fox, *Ancient Egyptian Love Songs*, 168; Murphy, *Song of Songs*, 196; Munro, *Spikenard and Saffron*, 65; Exum, *Song of Songs*, 245; Hess, *Song of Songs*, 235; Pope, *Song of Songs*, 675.

31. Exum, *Song of Songs*, 249; Contra Gault, "A 'Do not Disturb' Sign? Reexamining the Adjuration Refrain in Song of Songs," *JSOT* 36, no. 1 (2011): 99–100, who rejects the idea of

For love is as strong/fierce as death [כִּי־עַזָּה כַמָּוֶת אַהֲבָה],
(Its) jealousy unyielding as Sheol [קָשָׁה כִשְׁאוֹל קִנְאָה]. (8:6aβ–γ)

The bicolon echoes with assonance in the first line, and swishes with sibilants in the second. Hard כ and ק sounds enmesh the two, perhaps to communicate the obdurate nature of the subject.[32] The parallelism arrests the imagination, being reinforced thrice over:

love	strong/fierce	death
jealousy	unyielding	Sheol/grave

We have here a pair of equations: Love with death, jealousy with Sheol. In making these equations, the woman starts with the default superlative for intense emotions, namely Death (Judg 16:16; Jonah 4:9; Matt 26:38).[33] In the Old Testament, Death is often paired with Sheol, the underworld, and is often translated "grave." The pair has a common distinctive—they are unassailable.[34] עַזָּה ("strong") helps to communicate this, allowing for a more nuanced meaning of "fierce."[35] קָשָׁה ("unyielding") does this even better. Exum translates קָשָׁה with "adamant," a force that cannot be resisted and is insurmountable, as in the combative contexts that use this adjective (Judg 4:24; 2 Sam 2:17; Isa 27:1, 8; Job 9:4).[36] In the equation, Love-and-jealousy are a match for Death-and-Sheol.[37]

Here we pause to consider the translation of קִנְאָה. The standard choice in English versions follows the LXX in its use of the basic sense:[38]

---

personification because of the definite article on אַהֲבָה (twice in 8:7), which he proposes suggests intensification.

32. Tod Linafelt, "Biblical Love Poetry (. . . and God)," *JAAR* 70 (2002): 331.

33. D. W. Thomas, "A Consideration of Some Unusual Ways of Expressing the Superlative in Hebrew," *VT* 3 (1953): 220–21.

34. Ps 89:49 [EV 48]; Hab 2:5; Ps 49:14.

35. Bloch and Bloch, *Song of Songs*, 213, cf. Deut 28:50; Judg 14:18; Prov 30:30.

36. Exum, *Song of Songs*, 252.

37. See Watson's note for a quick summary of views on love vis-à-vis death, and for his further contribution from the Epic of Gilgamesh: Wilfred G. E. Watson, "Love and Death Once More (Song of Songs VIII 6)," *VT* 47, no. 3 (1997): 385–96.

38. קִנְאָה has a spectrum of meanings, all of them circling around the sense of deep emotion. (The cognate roots in Akkadian and Arabic mean "to become intensely red" or "become red with passion.") Thus, with reference to the context, קִנְאָה has been rendered "jealousy" (Prov 6:34; 14:30; 27:4), "competitiveness" (Qoh 4:4; 9:6), "anger" (Num 5:14, 30), and "zeal" (2 Kgs 10:16; Ps 69:10; 119:139; Job 5:2; Sir 30:24). See *HALOT*, קִנְאָה. The analogy between divine and human jealousy lies in the demand for exclusive possession or devotion, and the central meaning of קִנְאָה relates to jealousy as applicable to a marriage relationship, this relationship being used metaphorically to describe the bond between Israel and their God. Though most strongly developed in Hosea 1–3, Jeremiah 3, and Ezekiel 16 and 23, the language of conjugal

"to be jealous" (e.g., KJV, NAS, NLT, NIV).[39] Those translations that are either uncomfortable with the negative baggage this word carries, or wish to keep קִנְאָה strictly parallel to אַהֲבָה ("love") use "passion" (e.g., NET, NRSV, NJPS)[40] or suggest "ardor" (NIV).[41]

But is jealousy improper in a love relationship? Garrett explains it well: "Those who passionately love are passionately possessive. . . . Exclusivity is not of itself corrupt or oppressive . . . the term [jealousy] refers to a proper possessiveness in the setting of a wholesome relationship. Rightly experienced by healthy souls, this exclusivity is part of the glory of love and further indicates the seriousness of entering this relationship."[42] Similarly, Longman shows how jealousy is appropriate in two relationships:

> Humans can have only one God. If they worship another, it triggers God's jealousy. God's jealousy is an energy that tries to rescue the relationship. Similarly, a man and a woman can have only one spouse. If there is a threat to that relationship, then jealousy is a proper emotion. All this is because so much hangs on the integrity of the relationship. It is so basic, so deep, that it stirs up strong emotions and passions.[43]

The woman's stance and speech so far (8:5–6aα) indicate her desire for exclusive rights to the man. Fidelity being a non-negotiable demand in a relationship such as the woman describes, Walsh uses it to nail down the difference between אַהֲבָה ("love") and קִנְאָה ("jealousy"): "Fidelity is clearly honed in the term [jealousy] in a way that is not the case for 'love,'" and so communicates the inability of one partner to "tolerate receiving divided loyalties."[44] As such, jealousy is seen as an aspect of the subject, love.[45]

Exum, who argues strongly for the rendering of קִנְאָה as "jealousy," makes no bones about its dangers. It is a "violent emotion, usually aroused when a rival . . . is felt to threaten an exclusive relationship."[46]

jealousy sometimes describes God's feelings for Israel in Pentateuchal texts (e.g., Deut 4:24; 5:9; 6:15).

39. So Francis Landy, *Paradoxes of Paradise: Identity and Difference in the Song of Songs*, 2nd ed. (Sheffield: Phoenix, 2011), 119–20; Fox, *Ancient Egyptian Love Songs*, 169.

40. Pope, *Song of Songs*, 669; Robert Gordis, *Song of Songs: A Study, Modern Translation and Commentary*, Text and Studies of the Jewish Theological Seminary of America 20 (New York: Jewish Theological Seminary of America, 1954), 74.

41. Murphy, *Song of Songs*, 191.

42. Garrett, "Song of Songs," 256–57.

43. Longman, *Song of Songs*, 211–12.

44. Carey Ellen Walsh, *Exquisite Desire: Religion, the Erotic, and the Song of Songs* (Minneapolis: Fortress Press, 2000), 165.

45. Bloch and Bloch, *Song of Songs*, 213; Exum, *Song of Songs*, 251. Contra Landy, *Paradoxes of Paradise*, 119–21, who sees them as polarities.

46. Exum, *Song of Songs*, 251.

It can stir up ferocious anger, which may be turned against the rival[47] or even against the beloved partner, who is seen as a possession.[48] Exum supports her case with Proverbs 27:4, which, like the Song, describes jealousy as a force that cannot be withstood: "Anger is cruel and fury overwhelming, but who can stand before jealousy [קִנְאָה]?"[49]

It appears, then, that the woman's emotional state accommodates starry-eyed אַהֲבָה ("love") just as much as green-eyed קִנְאָה ("jealousy"). Hers is a passion that is best not betrayed! Barbiero rightly points out that this is unique in a canon where jealousy within man-woman relationships is invariably a male emotion, the classic case of which is the suspicious husband who makes the "jealousy offering" (Num 5:11–31).[50]

The woman returns to describe Love further, going without warning from the icy cold of Death and Sheol to the heat of blazing fire:[51]

> It burns like blazing fire [רְשָׁפֶיהָ רִשְׁפֵּי אֵשׁ],
> Like a mighty flame [שַׁלְהֶבֶתְיָה]
> Many waters cannot quench love [מַיִם רַבִּים לֹא יוּכְלוּ לְכַבּוֹת אֶת־הָאַהֲבָה];
> Rivers cannot sweep it away [וּנְהָרוֹת לֹא יִשְׁטְפוּהָ]. (8:6b–7a)

Here, the שׁ of the previous line (קָשָׁה כִשְׁאוֹל קִנְאָה) continues its lyrical sweep,[52] now onomatopoeic with the hiss of flames.[53] There is רשׁף twice followed by אשׁ, slowing down at the unfamiliar noun שַׁלְהֶבֶתְיָה.[54] Derived from the verb להב ("to blaze"), the word has an unusual שׁ prefix, a feminine ת ending, and a debated יָה suffix. This last is read in three ways.

First, יָה may be read literally as an abbreviated form of the tetragrammaton functioning as genitive of source ("the flame of YH").[55] Second, it may be read idiomatically as the divine name expressing the superlative or intensive in the same way that אֱלֹהִים and אֵל are sometimes used:

47. Prov 6:34; Ezek 36:5–6; 38:19; Zech 1:14; 8:2.

48. Numbers 5; Ezek 16:38, 42; 32:25.

49. Exum, *Song of Songs*, 251–52. Similarly, e.g., Longman, *Song of Songs*, 211.

50. Barbiero, *Song of Songs*, 461.

51. Gledhill, *Message of the Song of Songs*, 232.

52. Elliott, *Literary Unity*, 197.

53. Assis, *Flashes of Fire*, 240.

54. D. W. Thomas, "A Consideration of Some Unusual Ways of Expressing the Superlative in Hebrew," *VT* 3 (1953): 209–24. Examples of אֱלֹהִים: "a mighty wind" (Gen 1:2), "a mighty prince" (Gen 23:6), "a great struggle" (Gen 30:8), "a great fire" (Job 1:16), "an exceedingly great city" (Jonah 3:3). Examples of אֵל: "the mighty mountains" (Ps 36:7) and "the mighty cedars" (Ps 80:11). Examples of יָה suffixed: "darkest gloom" (Jer 2:31), "mighty deeds" (Jer 32:19), and "mighty deeds" (Ps 77:12).

55. See Murphy, *Song of Songs*, 191–92; Keel, *Song of Songs*, 275–76; Elliott, *Literary Unity*, 197.

"a most vehement flame" (KJV), "a mighty flame" (RSV, NIV), "a blazing flame" (NJPS).[56] However, both these possibilities are weakened by the absence of the expected *maqqef* and *mappiq*, which occurs only in the Ben Naphtali tradition: שַׁלְהֶבֶת־יָה ("the flame of YH").[57]

That leaves us with the third possibility: the יָה is just an intensive adjectival suffix as in some cognate languages.[58] This gives us the same reading as the second option ("a blazing flame") but is disappointingly mundane, stripped as it is of any association with the sacred name.[59] In translation, the furthest we can go toward the divine is along the lines of "almighty flame"[60] or "god-awful flame."[61]

Two considerations soften our disappointment. First is the common observation that the woman's description of אַהֲבָה ("love"; 8:6–7) tingles with allusions to chthonic and cosmic powers. Mot, the god of death; Death and Sheol, which are sometimes twinned personifications;[62] Resheph, the god who shoots arrows (רְשָׁפִים) of plague and pestilence;[63] the מַיִם רַבִּים ("many waters") reminding of Marduk's triumph over Tiamat, goddess of the chaotic deep; and Yam, also called Prince River (נָהָר), the god of the Sea.[64] Why should not the poet have smuggled in an echo of his national deity, YH?[65]

The unmistakable allusions to gods and personified forces lead to a further inference. Scholars sometimes understand that in this text, Love

56. Cf. Jer 2:31; 32:19.

57. See Magne Sæbø, "On the Canonicity of the Song of Songs," in *Texts, Temples, and Traditions*, ed. Michael V. Fox et al. (Winona Lake, IN: Eisenbrauns, 1996), 275. Also Exum, *Song of Songs*, 253; Fox, *Ancient Egyptian Love Songs*, 170–71.

58. *-iy*, *-ay*, and *-awi* are intensive adjectival suffixes in Aramaic, Akkadian, and Arabic respectively. יָה read as such best explains both Song 8:6 and Jer 2:31 ("darkest gloom") and 32:19 ("mighty deeds"). See Sabatino Moscati et al., *An Introduction to the Comparative Grammar of the Semitic Languages* (Wiesbaden: Harrassowitz, 1969), §§ 12.18 and 12.23. See also Bloch and Bloch, *Song of Songs*, 213.

59. Pope's (*Song of Songs*, 653) voluminous commentary concedes the difficulty of choosing between options by leaving the phrase untranslated!

60. Exum, *Song of Songs*, 254.

61. Longman, *Song of Songs*, 213.

62. Judg 16:16; Jonah 4:9.

63. See Pope, *Song of Songs*, 670.

64. See Longman, *Song of Songs*, 214, and Herbert G. May, "Some Cosmic Connotations of *Mayyim Rabbim*, 'Many Waters,'" *JBL* 74, no. 1 (1955): 9–21.

65. Exum, *Song of Songs*, 254; Hess, *Song of Songs*, 240; R. M. Davidson, "Is God Present in the Song of Songs?," *JATS* 16 (2005): 143–54. Walsh (*Exquisite Desire*, 203–10) lists six themes "that hint at the possibility of God's presence in a text that never names him": the ambiguous identity of the male lover; phrases that recall theophanies, such as fire and the phrases "cleft of the rock" and "column of smoke"; the metaphoric use of "vineyard"; imagery that evokes the Temple.

is locked in combat with these powers.[66] That the great waters should attempt to quench Love may suggest this. The sea parallels the chaotic deep (Ps 77:19 [EV 20]; 93:4; Isa 17:13), and the rivers are the dragon-like rivers of the underworld (cf. Ps 24:2; 93:3; Hab 3:9), both of which seem to threaten love and life.[67] However, a more plausible reading is to understand that while personified Love may be caught up in the usual cosmic power struggles, the poet's point is to show that it too may not be resisted by humans.[68]

To explain: these entities are powerful in relation to humans—humans stand defenseless before them. Deathly Mot takes even the young and virile Baal prisoner. How much more so humankind! Death and the underworld Sheol are the inexorable destination of all humans. Resheph consumes lives with the diseases he sends. Yam is the unmerciful, untamable sea that may be subdued only by Baal—as Tiamat only by Marduk. By being equated with them, Love becomes as much to be dreaded as these fearsome powers. Humans stand equally helpless before Love.[69] Indeed, humans remember that even Mot was foiled by Anath's love for her brother-husband Baal, a love that empowered her to retrieve her beloved from the very belly of Death:

> As the heart of an ewe for her lamb,
> So was Anat's heart toward Baal.
> She seized divine Mot—
> With sword she split him,
> With sieve she scattered him,
> With fire she burned him,
> With millstones she ground him,
> In the field she sowed him.
> His flesh the birds did eat,
> His parts the sparrows consumed;
> Flesh to flesh did cry.[70]

This is the reach of Love, a reach that encompasses the worlds above and below, as celebrated beyond West Asian mythology. The Greeks had their story of Orpheus who braved the underworld with his flute to rescue his beloved Eurydice. The Hindu epic *Mahabharata* sings of the widowed Savithri who outwitted the god of death Yama to win back

66. Exum, *Song of Songs*, 251–54; Jenson, *Song of Songs*, 91–92; Keel, *Song of Songs*, 270–76; Longman, *Song of Songs*, 210–14; Pope, *Song of Songs*, 668–69.

67. Keel, *Song of Songs*, 276; Pope, *Song of Songs*, 672–73.

68. Murphy, *Song of Songs*, 197. He allows that the fire of love and the great waters are in contest; 192, 198.

69. Similarly, Gledhill, *Message of the Song of Songs*, 231.

70. From the Ugaritic Baal myth (*CAT* 6.2.6–37), cited in Pope, *Song of Songs*, 668.

her husband Satyavan. If Love can triumph over its heavenly rivals, then Love trumps all things material.

Back to the Song:

If one were to give all the wealth of one's house for love [אִם־יִתֵּן אִישׁ אֶת־כָּל־הוֹן בֵּיתוֹ בָּאַהֲבָה],
It/he would be utterly scorned [בּוֹז יָבוּזוּ לוֹ]. (8:7b)

If the poet is still speaking within the context of death and Sheol, then Keel suggests he means that buying love would be just as absurd as attempting to buy off Death (Ps 49:7–8).[71] Perhaps speaking within the context of bride price, the poet dismisses the hope that love can be bought, even with all the wealth a man owns (cf. Prov 6:30–35). The wealth (or perhaps the man himself[72]) would be "utterly scorned." The Hebrew uses the emphatic to makes its thrust.[73] Who does the scorning? Love, or more accurately, Love-and-its-jealousy: "Who can stand before jealousy [קִנְאָה]?" (Prov 27:4).

To sum up this lyrical piece of text: Dipping her brush in three paint-pots, the woman portrays Love with the elemental colors of Death, Fire, and Water. On her canvas, אַהֲבָה ("love") and קִנְאָה ("jealousy") dissolve into each other. Indeed, we appreciate that it is from קִנְאָה ("jealousy") that the portrayal of אַהֲבָה ("love") gains its depth. Together, they form a substance as unyielding as the underworld, and an emotion like a raging fire barely under control, whose red-hot blaze cannot be doused by floodwaters. It is beyond price.

Within the canon it is unprecedented that a woman should speak of a jealous love,[74] unrelenting and fiery. Exum reminds us that there are no biblical examples of women displaying jealous wrath.[75] In a social environment in which exclusive rights were a male prerogative, women limited themselves to backstage bickering (Gen 30:14–16). It is highly counter-cultural that the woman, with her talk of seals on sundry body parts, should demand full reciprocation of her love. Rather than cause jealousy, it appears she can exercise it. Therein lays her demand for exclusive love.

71. Keel, *Song of Songs*, 276.

72. So, Bloch and Bloch, *Song of Songs*, 214; Gordis, *Song of Songs*, 74. Murphy, *Song of Songs*, 192, allows both antecedents. Most English versions render the object of scorn as "it," the wealth (KJV, NRSV, NAB, HCSB) or the offer of wealth (NET, NLT). A few render the object of scorn as the man making the offer (ESV, NJPS). NIV allows both.

73. The infinitive absolute form of the verb is followed by the 3ms imperfect of the same verb.

74. See Garrett, "Song of Songs," 257, who equates the woman's unusual demand for exclusive love with that of Lady Wisdom's in Prov 1:20–33 (cf. Prov 5:7–23).

75. Exum, *Song of Songs*, 252–53.

THE WALL: SONG 8:8–10

From this stirring eulogy to Love the section moves into seemingly disconnected fragments of verse. Our interest is to see if the idea of dedicated, exclusive love continues into these texts.

Song 8:8–10 could be spoken by a single voice, the woman's.[76] More often, it is considered as a speech made by the brothers (8:8–9),[77] with a response from the woman (8:10).[78] If it is the woman's speech entirely, then the understanding is that the brothers' speech is embedded in hers[79]—she is quoting them and then making her response, a device used more explicitly in some other parts of the Song (2:10–14; 5:2).

Exum persuasively outlines a coherent shape to 8:8–12. She takes 8:8–10 as the woman's speech and 8:11–12 as the man's matching speech. Both have marriage as the general background. Both begin with a "story"—the story of the little sister and the story of Solomon's vineyard. Unlike the little sister who has yet to reach puberty and whose marriage prospects are still under discussion, the woman is nubile and has decided whom she will marry. Unlike Solomon, whose vineyard benefits many, the man has a vineyard he alone enjoys. Her story is cultural—a woman's concern, arising from a world in which the men of the household arranged marriages. His story comes from the economic sphere, and uses the metaphors of share-cropping and dividends. In both cases the stories are an introit to declarations of mutual belonging.[80]

> We have a little sister,
> And her breasts are not yet grown.
> What shall we do for our sister
> On the day she is spoken for?
> If she is a wall [אִם חוֹמָה הִיא],

76. Exum, *Song of Songs*, 254–55.

77. Assis, *Flashes of Fire*, 243–44; Bloch and Bloch, *Song of Songs*, 214; Daniel J. Estes, "The Song of Songs," in *Ecclesiastes and the Song of Songs*, ed. Daniel C. Fredericks and Daniel J. Estes, AOTC 16 (Downers Grove, IL: InterVarsity, 2010), 411; Elliott, *Literary Unity*, 201; Fox, *Ancient Egyptian Love Songs*, 171; Murphy, *Song of Songs*, 198; Huwiler, "Song of Songs," 288; Jenson, *Song of Songs*, 96; Bergant, "Song of Songs," 100; Barbiero, *Song of Songs*, 474–75.

78. This view is supported by the mention of the brothers in 1:6. Since this closing section reprises significant vocabulary from earlier parts of the Song to the point of reusing some lines almost verbatim, the motif of the brothers forms an inclusio. See Assis, *Flashes of Fire*, 248; Hess, *Song of Songs*, 243; Elliott, *Literary Unity*, 201; Murphy, *Song of Songs*, 198.

If the view is that the closing section revisits its dramatis personae, then the speakers of 8:8–9 are probably the daughters of Jerusalem (Exum, *Song of Songs*, 257; Garrett, "Song of Songs," 259). For a host of alternative options for speakers see Exum, *Song of Songs*, 256–57.

79. Murphy, *Song of Songs*, 192, 198; Munro, *Spikenard and Saffron*, 33–34, 77; Gledhill, *Message of the Song of Songs*, 235; Hess, *Song of Songs*, 242; Longman, *Song of Songs*, 215.

80. Exum, *Song of Songs*, 255.

We will build a turret/battlement of silver on her [נִבְנֶה עָלֶיהָ טִירַת כָּסֶף].
If she is a door [וְאִם־דֶּלֶת הִיא],
We will enclose her with panels of cedar [נָצוּר עָלֶיהָ לוּחַ אָרֶז].

I am a wall,
And my breasts are like towers.
Thus I have become in his eyes [אָז הָיִיתִי בְעֵינָיו]
Like one bringing contentment [כְּמוֹצְאֵת שָׁלוֹם]. (8:8–10)

The brothers are conferring about a girl whose marriage prospects are their concern and who is very likely to be their responsibility (cf. Rebekah in Gen 24:29–60; Dinah in Gen 34:6–17; the daughters of Shiloh in Judg 21:22; Tamar in 1 Kgs 13:21). The girl's body has yet to show signs of puberty (cf. Ezek 16:7), but talk has already begun of the day she will become eligible to be given in marriage. In India, when the girl child first menstruates, it often becomes a ceremonial event, so that the community is given notice of her availability for a future marriage "alliance."

In the Song, the speakers agree among themselves that they must enhance, and perhaps protect, the girl's prospects. Scholars disagree on whether the lines are in synonymous[81] or antithetical parallelism.[82] If synonymous, both lines express the speakers' desire to safeguard the girl's virginity while enhancing her attractiveness as a marriage prospect. They express themselves using the metaphors of a wall and a (closed) door, both of which evoke the idea of inaccessibility. The Hebrew here is דֶּלֶת rather than פֶּתַח, and some read the former as referring to a closed door while the latter refers to an opening.[83] The Song has sufficiently confirmed that inaccessibility is culturally desirable in a maiden. A woman who made herself available to a man before marriage would be considered damaged goods. Indeed, even if the woman had been taken against her will, her marriageability would be forfeit.[84] Thus, the girl in

81. Gordis, *Song of Songs*, 97; Fox, *Ancient Egyptian Love Songs*, 172; Elliott, *Literary Unity*, 202; Keel, *Song of Songs*, 278–79; Bergant, *Song of Songs*, 101; Assis, *Flashes of Fire*, 246; Garrett, "Song of Songs," 260; Huwiler, "Song of Songs," 288; Carr, *Song of Solomon*, 172.

82. Murphy, *Song of Songs*, 193, 198–99; Bloch and Bloch, *Song of Songs*, 215–17; Estes, "Song of Songs," 412; Hess, *Song of Songs*, 243; Longman, *Song of Songs*, 216–17; Barbiero, *Song of Songs*, 476–77. R. Lansing Hicks, "The Door of Love," in *Love and Death in the Ancient Near East: Essays in Honour of Marvin H. Pope*, ed. John H Marks and Robert M Good (Guildford, CT: Four Quarters, 1987), 153–58, makes a detailed argument from ancient sources for antithetical parallelism between "wall" and "door."

83. Fox, *Ancient Egyptian Love Songs*, 172; Keel, *Song of Songs*, 279; Garrett, "Song of Songs," 260.

84. Thus a man who forcibly takes a maiden must himself marry her, presumably because no one else might. A further clause protects her by preempting any unscrupulous behavior—he must never divorce her (Deut 22:28–29). An Indian proverb well describes the vulnerability of

this text is to keep her chastity safe as behind an impregnable wall or a closed door. While this is what the girl does to keep herself desirable, those who have her interests at heart will do the best they can to enhance that desirability. They will decorate the wall with a silver טִירָה—a battlement (or turret);[85] they will panel the door with cedar. When added to the architectural imagery, the verbs sound aggressively military: they will build (בנה), they will barricade (צוּר). However, the materials that these verbs act on soften the sense. Silver and cedar are precious. We will hear of silver again in the next vignette, in fantastic amounts. As for cedar, it was a measure of affluence in its use in David's palace (2 Sam 5:11) and in the Temple (1 Kgs 6:10), and the symbol of irresponsible luxury in Jehoiakim's palace (Jer 22:14–15).[86] Neither silver nor cedar do anything to reinforce the inaccessibility. Rather, they ornament and increase the value of the already inaccessible wall and door in anticipation of a fat bride price and a good catch.

If the lines are understood antithetically, then the wall and door are to be read as opposites. The wall prevents entry while the door allows it. Thus, if the girl is taking care to preserve her chastity, the speakers will cooperate with her, helping to increase her attractiveness. If she displays sexual misconduct, they will forcibly restrict her availability (cf. Hos 2:5–6). Both readings carry the same emphasis: dedication to an exclusive sexual relationship. And, in either case, the girl is, in a sense, family property—linking the idea of the wealth of one's house in 8:7 to the personally owned vineyard in 8:12.

If we read this as a quote from a conversation the woman recalls from childhood, then her response immediately makes sense. She has since grown into womanhood. Reworking the same metaphor, she describes herself as a wall—chaste—with embellishments that make her well-wishers' assistance unnecessary. Indeed, her towers stand proud against any advances.[87] The woman's self-description as a high wall brings with it the idea of seclusion. What is on the other side of the wall? A passer-by can never know. The wall recalls similar images of inaccessibility earlier in the book.[88] The woman is the dove in the high ledges of the cliffside, now visible, now retreating out of sight (2:14). She is the "garden locked up," the "spring enclosed," the "sealed fountain" (4:12) whose refreshing delights can only be enjoyed on invitation (4:16). She is the one who

the woman in matters sexual: "Whether the leaf falls on the thorn or the thorn on the leaf, it is the leaf that is torn."

85. See discussion of טִירָה in Pope, *Song of Songs*, 680–81.

86. Fox, *Ancient Egyptian Love Songs*, 173.

87. Garrett, "Song of Songs," 261.

88. See Bloch and Bloch, *Song of Songs*, 217.

waits behind windows (2:9) and in the private space of her bedchamber (3:1). Her door is bolted from the inside, and one who wishes to enter must entreat and then wait till she undoes the bolt (3:1–5). Even her own beloved has had to endure waiting and separation till she deigns to let him into her private space. He hasn't received a spare key by which he can let himself in.

Having declared herself as impregnable as a wall, the woman takes the metaphor a step further to make a disclosure that must have startled her brothers. Yes, she is a city immune to siege with towers unassailable. However, as such a city might decide to do,[89] she has decided to bring/find[90] *shalom*, that is, to surrender.

Here, following Exum, the door in the wall makes sense as one that could be either open or shut. It has thus far been firmly shut, but now has been opened willingly to her beloved[91] in surrender. In the act of surrender, she brings peace. The one besieging accepts her offer, and thus she simultaneously finds peace.[92] Her breasts, which she described as defensive towers, become the conqueror's possession and pleasure (1:13; 4:5; 7:3 [EV 4]; 7:7–8 [EV 8–9]).[93]

The entire exchange, as we can see, has brilliantly played the military metaphor, applying it to all the stages of this girl's journey. From a flat-chested child, she flowers into a nubile virgin, and intentionally surrenders her maidenhood to the man of her choice. This is in remarkable contrast to the usual journey that young women make in other parts of the canon, where a woman becomes attached to a man when she finds grace (חֵן) in his eyes.[94] In the Song, the woman speaks of bringing

---

89. Garrett, "Song of Songs," 258n10d.

90. מוֹצֵאת may be read as the *hiphil* active participle of יצא ("one who brings"): Hess, *Song of Songs*, 245; Longman, *Song of Songs*, 218; Bergant, *Song of Songs*, 102; John G. Snaith, *The Song of Songs*, NCB (Grand Rapids: Eerdmans, 1993), 126. Or, it may be read as the *qal* of מצא ("one who finds"): Assis, *Flashes of Fire*, 247; Bloch and Bloch, *Song of Songs*, 217–18; Estes, "Song of Songs," 412–13; Garrett, "Song of Songs," 258n10d; Murphy, *Song of Songs*, 193; Fox, *Ancient Egyptian Love Songs*, 173; Barbiero, *Song of Songs*, 479–82; Carr, *Song of Solomon*, 172–73; Elliott, *Literary Unity*, 204–5; Gordis, *Song of Songs*, 98. Some allow both: Exum, *Song of Songs*, 258–60; Edward M. Curtis, *Ecclesiastes and Song of Songs*, Teach the Text Commentary (Grand Rapids: Baker, 2013), 158. See Landy for four possible meanings (find or bring peace; surrender; be the "evening star"): Francis Landy, "Beauty and the Enigma: An Inquiry into Some Interrelated Episodes of the Song of Songs," *JSOT* 17 (1980): 81–83.

91. See Fox, *Ancient Egyptian Love Songs*, 173, for emendation to establish the identity of this person (3ms).

92. Exum, *Song of Songs*, 258.

93. Hess, *Song of Songs*, 245.

94. Ruth 2:2, 10, 13; Deut 24:1. For parallels to this bold characterization in Greek literature (by which the Song may have been influenced), see Joan B. Burton, "Themes of Female Desire and Self-Assertion in the Song of Songs and Hellenistic Poetry," in *Perspectives on the Song of Songs*, ed. Anselm C Hagedorn (Berlin: de Gruyter, 2005), 181–205.

and finding *shalom*, appropriating and perpetuating the brothers' military language[95] in a way they might never have imagined. She is not one to wait for a man's grace, letting him choose her. She rather chooses one, and brings him *shalom*. Unlike the woman of easy virtue whose door is open to all who wish to enter, she is exclusive in whom she will permit entry.[96]

THE VINEYARD: SONG 8:11–12

Now, either the woman continues, or the man begins to speak.[97]

> Solomon [שְׁלֹמֹה] had a vineyard in Baal-Hamon;
> He let out his vineyard to tenants.
> Each was to bring for its fruit
> A thousand shekels of silver.
> But my own vineyard is mine to give [כַּרְמִי שֶׁלִּי לְפָנָי];
> The thousand are for you, Solomon [הָאֶלֶף לְךָ שְׁלֹמֹה],
> And two hundred are for those who tend its fruit. (8:11–12)

The line previous to this speech ended with the word *shalom* (8:10). The speaker picks up the word in his/her opening line: "Solomon (*Šelōmōh*) had a vineyard." It appears to be a lexical signal that the speaker intends to continue the theme of the previous stanza—the idea of love given exclusively to one's beloved—and we must investigate to see if this is so.

The metaphor of buildings and cities switches to the metaphor of the vineyard. From the military, we move to the agricultural. The reader well knows that the vineyard is a circumlocution for the female body (1:6; 2:15; 6:11; 7:12 [EV 13]) and begins to read the text at two levels—as both vineyard-tending and amorous pursuit.

Without pressing the parallels too hard, the metaphor serves to con-

---

95. Bloch and Bloch, *Song of Songs*, 218; Marcia Falk, *The Song of Songs: A New Translation and Interpretation* (New York: HarperCollins, 1973), 195.

96. See Kathryn Imray, who uses Proverbs 1–9 as a hermeneutical starting point to argue that the Song's female protagonist is both dangerously uncontrollable and eminently domesticated; the book holds the two images in tension suggesting "dual-aspect misogyny" ("Love Is [Strong as] Death: Reading the Song of Songs through Proverbs 1–9," *CBQ* 75, no. 4 [2013]: 649–65).

97. In favor of the woman as speaker are: Assis, *Flashes of Fire*, 250–51; Estes, "Song of Songs," 414; Garrett, "Song of Songs," 259; Murphy, *Song of Songs*, 199–200; Hess, *Song of Songs*, 246–47; Longman, *Song of Songs*, 218–19. Preferring the man as speaker are: Exum, *Song of Songs*, 255–56, 259–61; Elliott, *Literary Unity*, 206; Munro, *Spikenard and Saffron*, 41–42; Fox, *Ancient Egyptian Love Songs*, 174; Bloch and Bloch, *Song of Songs*, 218; Jenson, *Song of Songs*, 99; Bergant, *Song of Songs*, 102; Keel attributes the critical text 8:12 to the man (*Song of Songs*, 282). For a summary of views, see Robert L. Alden, "Song of Songs 8:12a: Who Said It?," *JETS* 31, no. 3 (1988): 274–76.

trast the speaker with Solomon. Both possess vineyards, but vastly different in size. Solomon's is so vast that he must let it out to sharecroppers. We have heard of Solomon's magnificent wealth earlier (1:5; 3:7, 9, 11). Tenancy does not permit the "fruit" of the vineyard to be entirely Solomon's. Part of the proceeds goes to his tenants. Is the allusion here to the keepers of Solomon's fabled harem (1 Kgs 11:3; Song 6:8) who may help themselves to its delights? If so, in contrast to Solomon, the speaker has a vineyard that is exclusively his. In the Hebrew, he accentuates this exclusive possession with a redundant three-word sentence, each ending with a first-person singular pronoun. The NET nicely tracks this emphasis: "*My* vineyard, which belongs to *me*, is at *my* disposal alone"[98] (italics added). Solomon is lord of Baal-Hamon, a (probably fictitious[99]) place-name suggesting at once both an abundance of wealth and women. *Hāmôn* (הָמוֹן "abundance") is a phonetic reminder of *hôn* (הוֹן "wealth") in 8:7. The "lord of abundance," *Băʿal-Hāmôn*, is no better than the fool who thinks his money, *hôn*, can buy love.[100] The speaker can scornfully dismiss Solomon and his money and his women in three words: הָאֶלֶף לְךָ שְׁלֹמֹה ("Keep your thousand, Solomon!").

Contrary to the intimate world-of-two of the lover and beloved, Solomon is removed from the possibility of love by intermediaries and by distance.[101] Love eludes Solomon.[102] The paradox is that his having so much is precisely the reason he has nothing. The point, then, is that love is best sought in exclusive relationships.[103] Certainly, neither polygamy nor promiscuity can achieve it.[104]

If the speaker is the man, his words reiterate his earlier claims—also

---

98. The Hebrew לְפָנַי may be read either literally as "before me" / "in front of me" (Exum, *Song of Songs*, 260; Huwiler, "Song of Songs," 290), or as more often, idiomatically. If the latter, it could mean "at my disposal" (cf. Gen 13:9, 20:15; so Murphy, *Song of Songs*, 194, 200; Garrett, "Song of Songs," 258n12a; Gledhill, *Message of the Song of Songs*, 240: Keel, *Song of Songs*, 282; Pope, *Song of Songs*, 690; Barbiero, *Song of Songs*, 490; Elliott, *Literary Unity*, 207–8; Provan, *Ecclesiastes, Song of Songs*, 370) or "near at hand" (cf. Prov 4:3; Isa 53:2; so Bloch and Bloch, *Song of Songs*, 219; Fox, *Ancient Egyptian Love Songs*, 175, suggesting an extended meaning of "in my care"). Alden points out a textual parallel in Judg 11:9 in which Jephthah speaks about defeating the Ammonites: וְנָתַן יְהוָה אוֹתָם לְפָנַי; lit. "[if] the Lord gives them before me . . ." The sense here is clearly idiomatic. Jephthah is entertaining the possibility that Ammon will be handed over *to* him as his prize in war "to dispose of, exploit, enslave." Thus, if the man is speaking, the vineyard is his "to hold, to enjoy, or to use." If it is the woman who speaks, she is claiming she "controls" or "owns" the vineyard. "Song of Songs 8:12a," 274.

99. Bloch and Bloch, *Song of Songs*, 219; Fox, *Ancient Egyptian Love Songs*, 174. Contra those who seek to identify it with an actual place: e.g., Pope, *Song of Songs*, 687–88.

100. Bloch and Bloch, *Song of Songs*, 219.

101. Garrett, "Song of Songs," 263.

102. Assis, *Flashes of Fire*, 255.

103. Longman, *Song of Songs*, 219.

104. Hess, *Song of Songs*, 247; Longman, *Song of Songs*, 220.

made with plant imagery—that his beloved is solely his. "I have come into *my* garden . . . gathered *my* myrrh with *my* spice . . . eaten *my* honeycomb and *my* honey . . . drunk *my* wine and *my* milk" (5:1; italics added). And again: "Your stature is like that of the palm, and your breasts like clusters of fruit. I said, '*I* will climb the palm tree; *I* will take hold of its fruit'" (7:7–8; italics added).

If the speaker is the woman, she expresses her right to give herself to the one she has set her heart on. "My own vineyard is mine to give," she asserts, echoing other places in the Song when she has offered herself to her beloved with similar eagerness: "Let my beloved come into his garden and taste its choice fruits" (4:16); "Let us go early to the vineyards . . . there I will give you my love" (7:12); "I would give you spiced wine to drink, the nectar of my pomegranates" (8:2).

The woman can make these offers because she is confident of their reception. Earlier, she asserted the man's ownership of her, and deployed it within an equation of mutual belonging: "My beloved is mine and I am his" (2:16); "I am my beloved's and my beloved is mine" (6:3). The third repetition of this sentiment is significant to the offer of herself: "I am my beloved's, and his desire [תְּשׁוּקָה] is for me" (7:10). She gives in the confidence that she satisfies his desire. The word is the same as in Genesis 4:7, where sin crouches at the door, waiting single-mindedly for the one who will emerge. Its evil desire (תְּשׁוּקָה) is to master Cain. The word is also the same as in Genesis 3:16. When sin shatters the harmony between man and wife, the woman displays the desire (תְּשׁוּקָה) to dominate her husband, but he resists her and wins the struggle.[105] The Song reverses the violent use of the word in these other two instances. Here in the Song, the one desired need not resist the one who desires. More than that, the one desired deliberately chooses to give. In fact, she bestows upon the other all that he desires.

Pope seems to have missed this idea of joyful, mutual belonging when he deliberates on the identity of the speaker of 8:11–12: "If the groom speaks, declaring dominion over his spouse's body, it is classic male chauvinism. If the female here asserts autonomy, this verse becomes the golden text for women's liberation."[106] Rather than each taking what is theirs, the Song has showed the man and woman in happy ownership of each other. The term "my garden" appears on the lips of both, while referring to the woman's body (4:16; 5:1). Similarly, the phrase

105. Gordon J. Wenham, *Genesis 1–15*, WBC 1 (Waco, TX: Word, 1994), 105–6.
106. Pope, *Song of Songs*, 690. Contra Alden, "Song of Songs 8:12a," 277–78.

"my vineyard" is a dual claim bracketing the book (1:6; 8:12).[107] There is no competition in exclusive love.

LAST WORDS: SONG 8:13–14

Now there is a final exchange, and from the familiar words, we readily identify the speakers.

> You who dwell in the gardens
> With friends in attendance,
> Let me hear your voice!
> Come away, my beloved,
> And be like a gazelle
> Or like a young stag
> On the spice-laden mountains. (8:13–14)

Once more the man asks to hear his beloved's voice. And once more, she replies with a double entendre. She sends him away and yet calls him to herself.[108] Indeed, she borrows from the חבר ("companion") in his line to create the ברח ("flee") in her invitation. He must flee from his companions to be with her.[109]

THE IDEA OF EXCLUSIVE LOVE

We have attempted to show that the closing section of the Song (8:5–14) is more than curtain calls by all its leading actors reprising snatches from earlier poems. It would be an odd choice for the poet to embed his literary masterpiece on the nature of Love (8:5b–7) in a flurry of bows and goodbyes. Rather, we have demonstrated that within the section bracketed off with "her beloved" (8:5) and "my beloved" (8:14), each

---

107. Bloch and Bloch, *Song of Songs*, 220.

108. Exum, *Song of Songs*, 245, and 11–13 for the theme of resistance to closure; Murphy, *Song of Songs*, 194, 200; Estes, "Song of Songs," 417; Gledhill, *Message of the Song of Songs*, 243–44; Huwiler, "Song of Songs," 289–90; Jenson, *Song of Songs*, 102; Longman, *Song of Songs*, 222; Pope, *Song of Songs*, 698–99; Barbiero, *Song of Songs,* 498–501; Carr, *Song of Solomon*, 175; Provan, *Ecclesiastes, Song of Songs*, 372. A further nuance is that the woman is asking the man to "flee" his companions to come to her: Fox, *Ancient Egyptian Love Songs*, 177; Hess, *Song of Songs*, 248–49; Garrett, "Song of Songs," 265; Keel, *Song of Songs*, 285; Bergant, *Song of Songs*, 105. A few hold that the woman is genuinely sending the man away in anticipation of a future rendezvous: Assis, *Flashes of Fire*, 259–60; Elliott, *Literary Unity*, 210; Munro, *Spikenard and Saffron*, 89; Andre LaCocque, *Romance She Wrote: A Hermeneutical Essay on Song of Songs* (Harrisburg: Trinity, 1998), 189–90; Bloch and Bloch, *Song of Songs*, 221.

109. Hess, *Song of Songs*, 249.

speech resonates with the rest in its praise of love between a devoted couple. We can go a step further and see if the reprises of earlier vocabulary, phrasing, and themes are not merely repetitions, but repetitions with increment—that is, incremented by the idea of exclusive love.

At the level of vocabulary and phrasing, we could begin with the verb עוּר ("arouse"; 8:5a). The woman has used it in her periodic adjurations to the daughters of Jerusalem, creating a threefold refrain. In this refrain, each using the verb twice, the woman cautions other women that they should "not arouse or awaken Love until it so desires." In this closing section, the verb is used not as a caution but as a recollection of past intimacies. The woman has aroused love, and to all appearances, she has followed her own advice in timing it right. What is more, she has been selective about the setting—as evidenced by the twice repeated locative "there" (שָׁמָּה)—and placed herself within a tradition, within a family. She not only waits till the time is right for love, but respects that it must be given and taken within cultural and familial boundaries. This seems to be the sentiment expressed in earlier poems as well, when she places the consummation of their love within the generational flow on both sides, his and hers. She brings (or longs to bring) her beloved into her mother's house (3:4; 8:2); she expresses excitement that her beloved is adorned by his mother for his wedding day (3:11). Clearly, there is no room in the Song for "free love."

Second, there is the motif of the apple tree. When attempting to place her "beloved among the young men," the woman had likened him to "an apple tree among the trees of the forest" (2:3). In a poem where he is the initiator, she takes "delight to sit in his shade," eats his fruit, lets him lead her to a banquet hall, and urges him to "strengthen me . . . refresh me" (2:3–5). Any reciprocal imagery was only a quick simile in which the man admired how "the fragrance of [her] breath" is "like apples" (7:8 [EV 9]). Now, we have a satisfying match for the imagery, and for the initiative in matters amorous. Under that figurative apple tree, the woman had willingly submitted to the man's embraces: "His left arm is under my head, and his right arm embraces me" while she lies "faint with love" (2:5–6). At the other end of the book, perhaps under a literal apple tree, the woman matches the man's earlier initiative. Boldly, she awakens his desire, and no doubt, reduces him to being faint with love. By way of subtle bookends, the Song advocates its ideal of reciprocal and exclusive love.

Third, the section reprises building imagery. So far it had been used in praise poems to describe the woman's physical assets. Her neck is "like the tower of David, built with courses of stone" with warrior shields strung out in display (4:4), much like an "ivory tower" (7:4). She is "as beautiful as Tirzah," "as lovely as Jerusalem" (6:4). Her eyes "are the pools of Heshbon by the gate of Bath Rabbim" (7:4), while her nose is like "the tower of Lebanon looking towards Damascus" (7:4). All this beauty, we assume, belongs to the man, since in these poems he speaks of the object of his admiration as his—his darling, his bride, his sister, his love. It is in the closing section, however, that these assumptions of exclusive ownership are affirmed to be true. When the imagery of building is reprised, it is with increment. If she is Tirzah or Jerusalem, then her conqueror is her beloved. Since the woman speaks within the context of marriage arrangements, we understand that the door does not open to just anyone who fancies entering.

Fourth, there is the metaphor of the vineyard. The earlier text that best speaks to 8:12 is the piece of folk song in 2:15: "Catch for us the foxes, the little foxes that ruin the vineyards, our vineyards that are in bloom." Here is a picture of a free-for-all. Young men pumped up with a springtime hormone rush are cavorting in the vineyards, rooting up now this vine and now that. It is a game, where maidens are really only pretending resistance to the foxes' advances. However, this is not the case with the woman of the Song. She immediately contrasts the foxes in the vineyards with her experience of love: "My beloved is mine and I am his" (2:16). Hers is not a roll in the hay with any fox that catches her fancy in springtime. The man expresses the dedication of the relationship with a confidence that matches hers: "My vineyard, which belongs to me, is at my disposal alone." It is not the equation of one to a thousand, as with Solomon and his harem. It is not one with multiple options, as with foxes running wild in vineyards. It is just one person and another.

Fifth, we have the two almost verbatim repetitions from earlier in the Song. First is the question מִי זֹאת עֹלָה מִן־הַמִּדְבָּר ("Who is this coming up from the wilderness?"), identical to both 3:6 and 8:5a. In the earlier instance it started off a praise poem. The woman described her beloved from a distance, calling out to the daughters of Jerusalem to come share her enjoyment of his approach. Though the poem made a hopeful beginning with describing the beloved, it quickly let itself be distracted by the entourage, the palanquin, and even by what the beloved was wearing. In 8:5, the question has a different focus. The couple have closed the distance. They travel together, publicly declaring their mutual affection. The repetition of the question is incremented by movement of the relationship toward union.

The other verbatim repetition is the man's plea to hear his beloved's voice. Here is a long-range inclusio across the breadth of the book:

Song 2:14:   הַשְׁמִיעִנִי אֶת־קוֹלֵךְ

Song 8:13:   לְקוֹלֵךְ הַשְׁמִיעִנִי

The answer is as before, but with differences at the start and end of the lines.

Song 2:17:

Turn, my beloved and be like a gazelle or like a young stag on the **rugged** hills.

סֹב דְּמֵה־לְךָ דוֹדִי לִצְבִי אוֹ
לְעֹפֶר הָאַיָּלִים עַל־הָרֵי בָתֶר

Song 8:14:

Come away, my beloved, and be like a gazelle or like a young stag on the **spice-laden** mountains.

בְּרַח דּוֹדִי וּדְמֵה־לְךָ לִצְבִי אוֹ
לְעֹפֶר הָאַיָּלִים עַל־הָרֵי בְשָׂמִים

For the second time, the woman's response balances on the knife-edge between two opposing meanings:[110] the man should depart from her; the man should come to her. The increment in the repetition is that "(re)turn" is replaced with "flee." The imperative is more urgent than before. As to the destination, "hills of Bether" is replaced with "hills of spices." In an earlier praise poem, where the man outdid himself in adoration of the woman's assets, he said: אֵלֶךְ לִי אֶל־הַר הַמּוֹר וְאֶל־גִּבְעַת הַלְּבוֹנָה ("I will go to the mountain of myrrh and to the hill of incense"; 4:6b). He went on to an impressive catalogue of what grows in her "garden"—"henna and nard, nard and saffron, calamus and cinnamon, with every kind of incense tree, with myrrh and aloes and all the finest spices" (4:13–14). On her invitation, he let himself into her garden and "gathered" myrrh and spice (5:1). We hardly need persuasion that with the repetition the woman speaks an even more urgent invitation than before—he must make haste and come! The mountains of spice he well knows are impatiently waiting for him.

We have seen, then, that the vocabulary in the closing section of the Song is more than a series of repetitions. The riff of dedicated love played out over seven chapters is gathered up and foregrounded through these reprises.

110. For discussion, see chapter 2, p. 31.

CONCLUSION

The Song ends with a celebration of mutual devoted love—even endorsing a jealous love that demands stamping the beloved with a mark of ownership. If our toes instinctively curl at what might seem to us to be an excess, we should remember that the vocabulary and intent of the central poem of Song 8:5–14 resonates with that of Deuteronomy 6:6–8. YHWH requires that his instructions to Israel figuratively "be on your hearts" (cf. Deut 11:18; Prov 3:3; 7:3) and, as physical symbols, be worn on hands and foreheads. The wearers are to be reminded of who commands their devotion, and the world is to know to whom they owe their allegiance. The requirement is made in the context of the creed that declares Israel's exclusive relationship with YHWH—"YHWH is our God, YHWH alone"—and demands Israel's whole-hearted devotion:[111] "Love YHWH your God with all your heart and with all your soul and with all your strength" (Deut 6:4–5). On the other hand, the same Deuteronomy text warns Israel not to "follow other gods" for YHWH "is a jealous God" (Deut 6:14–15). Jealousy is given its proper place within the equation of belonging, and the canon's ancient readers would have seen this divine demand reflecting their social reality of marital dynamics. However, the shift—of tectonic proportions!—is the validation of *mutual* jealous love, where the woman may claim her man as equally as the man can claim her.

The theme ripples through the whole section, sometimes riding on another motif, that of wealth. Set in the cultural context of her day, the woman herself is, in a sense, valuable property. Her brothers are willing to invest silver and cedar to enhance the value of her virginity—as a marriageable maiden she commands a bride price. To the man, she is even more precious. In fact, he can despise even Solomon's legendary wealth and women for the love of this one woman. She herself is aware of her worth in the eyes of her beloved. She is myrrh and incense, items of indulgence. What is more, she is a whole mountain of such spices! She brings him *shalom*, that state of being prized over all else. Her prodigious worth makes irresistible her plea that the man should wear her as his most prized possession, his signet. Indeed, an enduring love such as she declares for him, directed uniquely at him alone, is worth "all the wealth of [his] house" and more.

Some readers express a sense of disappointment and even surprise that the Song should not make consummation its high point. But, what is the

---

111. David M. Carr, *The Erotic Word: Sexuality, Spirituality and the Bible* (Oxford: Oxford University Press, 2003), 135–36.

closing section if not a hymn to two becoming one? She leans on him in intimate nearness. She surrenders to him like a city to a conqueror. He exults that his vineyard is his alone, his to possess as he will. She urgently calls him to take her body and delight in it. But well beyond all this playful double entendre is the consummation that indwells her description of love. Bound to him forever and as inextricably as the imprint of a seal upon an object, she declares a love as inexorable as Death and Sheol, whose blaze not even the chaotic waters of the great deep or the dragon-rivers of the underworld can extinguish. Herein is the consummation of a woman and her beloved that elevates them into the echelons of lovers remembered for all time—as those who loved none else but each other.

9.

The Insatiable Lust

Among the texts that are sometimes called pornoprophetic literature, Ezekiel 23 is arguably the low point. Unredeemed by the poetic luminescence of its sister passage in Ezekiel 16, and doubled by featuring a pair of siblings, this is a sordid account of promiscuity. Its coarseness of language means to shock the sensibilities. Its uninhibited narrative is intentionally graphic, perhaps even pornographic.

Our interest in Ezekiel 23 is as a conversation partner with Song 8:5–14. If the latter ascends the heights of unquenchable love, does the former plumb the depths of insatiable lust? If so, these texts are well matched, especially since the speaker in Ezekiel 23 is the man. His musings upon and reactions to marital infidelity make his speech the canonical counterpart to that of the woman's in Song 8. We study Ezekiel 23 to see what it says about love and its jealousy. Germane to this intertextual conversation are Ezekiel 23:1–21 and 23:40–44. These are descriptions of the infidelity that arouses the husband's passions. We will make only brief reference to the rest of the chapter, which deals with the punishment on the unfaithful wives.

THE SISTERS IN EGYPT: EZEKIEL 23:1–4

The story begins by introducing the reader to a pair of sisters. It is not a promising start.

> The word of the Lord came to me: "Son of man, there were two women, daughters of the same mother. They became prostitutes in Egypt, engaging in prostitution from their youth [וַתִּזְנֶינָה בְמִצְרַיִם בִּנְעוּרֵיהֶן זָנוּ]. In that land their breasts were fondled [שָׁמָּה מֹעֲכוּ שְׁדֵיהֶן] and their virgin bosoms

caressed [וְשָׁם עִשּׂוּ דַּדֵּי בְּתוּלֵיהֶן]. The older was named Oholah, and the sister was Oholibah. They were mine [וַתִּהְיֶינָה לִי] and gave birth to sons and daughters. Oholah is Samaria, and Oholibah is Jerusalem. (Ezek 23:1–4)

The flashback takes the reader to a time when the girls were "young" (נְעוּרִים). This is a period when girls are of marriageable age, but as yet in the premarital state.[1]

In contrast to the text that will follow, the speaker narrates the fact of the whoring in the passive and in past tense without any description of the recipients of the services. Their breasts were fondled (מעך; *pual* pf. 3cp) and their virgin nipples were caressed (עשׂה; *piel* pf. 3cp). These are faceless, anonymous clients—too unremarkable to waste time on. The fact of their promiscuity (זנה) is more important and is emphasized by a chiasm:[2]

they whored	in Egypt	in their youth	they whored
וַתִּזְנֶינָה	בְּמִצְרָיִם	בִּנְעוּרֵיהֶן	זָנוּ

In conversation with Song 8, there is a double locative in this text as well: "there" (שָׁמָּה and שָׁם in 23:3; שָׁמָּה twice in Song 8:5b). Just as much as the Song's woman recalls the event under the apple tree, the husband in Ezekiel remembers the details of his wives' experiences "there" in Egypt. Both are memories of the sexual act,[3] but the contrast could not be greater. The Song looks back to an act of love between a man and woman devoted to each other, in which the woman may take the liberty to express herself in a way that was unusual for a woman—she arouses her beloved. In Ezekiel, the woman is the object of the lust of multiple clients (cf. 23:8). Their comings and goings are a blur of wantonness. The locatives in both texts emphasize how carefully the lover in each stores up memories of or about the object of affection. Throughout Ezekiel 23, the husband never expresses his love for his wives, but the fact that he married these sisters suggests it.

The woman in Song 8 can hark back to her maiden days, even back

---

1. Daniel I. Block, *The Book of Ezekiel: Chapters 1–24*, NICOT (Grand Rapids: Eerdmans, 1997), 734.

2. Lawrence Boadt, "The A:B:B:A Chiasm of Identical Roots in Ezekiel," *VT* 25, no. 4 (1975): 699.

3. Contra Moshe Greenberg, *Ezekiel 21–37: A New Translation with Introduction and Commentary*, Anchor Bible 22A (New York: Doubleday, 1997), 474. Based on a similar description of squeezed breasts in Mishnaic Hebrew, his view is that the Egyptian experience was seduction that began the tendency to prostitution, and excluded the sexual act. To consider the sisters as prostitutes while still in Egypt is to "miss the gradation."

to the time when she was a flat-chested girl on the other side of puberty. Her brothers worried about her marriage prospects, hoping that she would remain a "wall"—in other words, retain her virginity. Chastity, valued above all else in a maiden, is the very thing the sisters in Ezekiel do not have. They have, on the contrary, been an open and inviting "door." The initiative seems clearly theirs, since they are twice the subjects of the verb "to whore." They appear to have chosen promiscuity as a way of life. In contrast to the Song, there is no experience of a "day she is spoken for" (Song 8:8) as these grow from girls into young women. There are no arrangements for marriage. Indeed, in an Eastern community chances of marriage would be slim, if not nonexistent.

Why then would a man marry them? We may reasonably assume some feeling—at least compassion, if not affection. And so, by marriage, they become his: "they were mine."[4] The declaration of possession calls to a skidding halt the procession of clients, each claiming their piece of the sisters' bodies. Now the women are called to direct their attentions to one man who is legally entitled to them. In place of a series of partners, they are called to loyalty to their husband.

What is more, mutual belonging is sealed by children, as "sons and daughters" are born of the union. Given that bearing children further legitimated a wife, here is every requisite for a happy domestic life. This is what the Song's woman seems to have wished for too. Between leaning on her beloved and urging him to let her be a seal upon him, her thoughts turned to childbearing. While childbearing offers evidence that a marriage has been consummated,[5] the emphasis here seems to be on exclusive belonging to a man, bearing his children. Certainly, these are what secure the existence of the Eastern woman, even to the present day.

If the husband gave them new names, then "Oholah" and "Oholibah" might indicate their new status. The latter possibly means "my tent is in her" with "Oholah" being a variation.[6] It is a claim with sexual

4. Block, *Ezekiel 1–24*, 736, rightly reads this as shorthand for the details of marriage ritual acts in the parallel story in Ezekiel 16, esp. vv. 8–13. This marriage to two sisters may be a convenient rhetorical construct rather than a reflection of practice (Christopher J. H. Wright, *The Message of Ezekiel: A New Heart and a New Spirit*, Bible Speaks Today (Leicester: InterVarsity, 2001], 147). Though such marriages may have been acceptable in some contexts or circles—cf. Jacob (Genesis 29) and Elkanah (1 Sam 1:2)—Ezekiel, being a priest, would be well aware of the injunction against marriage to two living sisters (Lev 18:18).

5. Block, *Ezekiel 1–24*, 736.

6. See the elaborate treatment in Walther Zimmerli, *Ezekiel 1: A Commentary on the Book of the Prophet Ezekiel Chapters 1–24*, trans. Ronald E Clements, Hermeneia (Philadelphia: Fortress Press, 1979), 483–84. See Block, *Ezekiel 1–24*, 735–36, who after discussing the possible meaning and significance of the names concludes: "It is not their meaning that is most significant but their similarity. Like Hasan and Husein, the two sons of Ali, the son-in-law of Muhammad, these names match, highlighting the women's sibling relationship." Or cf. Tweedledum and

overtones, one that overrides the sordid past. It recalls the Song's man boastfully declaring that his beloved is "my own vineyard" which is "at my disposal" (Song 8:12). The sisters have been taken from society's unsavory edges into its mainstream, where a woman belongs to a given man. They are respectable women now, or at least, have every opportunity to be so.

OHOLAH: EZEKIEL 23:5–8

Oholah engaged in prostitution while she was still mine [וַתִּזֶן אָהֳלָה תַּחְתִּי]; and she lusted after her lovers [וַתַּעְגַּב עַל־מְאַהֲבֶיהָ], the Assyrians—warriors [קְרוֹבִים] clothed in blue [תְּכֵלֶת], governors [פַּחוֹת] and commanders [סְגָנִים], all of them handsome young men [בַּחוּרֵי חֶמֶד כֻּלָּם], and mounted horsemen [פָּרָשִׁים רֹכְבֵי סוּסִים]. She gave herself as a prostitute to all [וַתִּתֵּן תַּזְנוּתֶיהָ עֲלֵיהֶם] the elite of the Assyrians [מִבְחַר בְּנֵי־אַשּׁוּר כֻּלָּם] and defiled herself with all the idols of everyone she lusted after [וּבְכֹל אֲשֶׁר־עָגְבָה בְּכָל־גִּלּוּלֵיהֶם נִטְמָאָה]. She did not give up the prostitution she began in Egypt [וְאֶת־תַּזְנוּתֶיהָ מִמִּצְרַיִם לֹא עָזָבָה], when during her youth men slept with her [כִּי אוֹתָהּ שָׁכְבוּ בִנְעוּרֶיהָ], caressed her virgin bosom [וְהֵמָּה עִשּׂוּ דַּדֵּי בְתוּלֶיהָ] and poured out their lust on her [וַיִּשְׁפְּכוּ תַזְנוּתָם עָלֶיהָ]. (Ezek 23:5–8)

We are taken aback that the description of Oholah's life as a wife commences with the same verb that introduced her life in Egypt: she whored (זנה). The husband's pain at her return to her former depravity resonates in the word תחת. תַּחְתִּי could mean being under someone's authority and thus belonging to that person[7] ("while she was still mine") and also mean "instead of" ("lusted after other lovers instead of me").[8] Both meanings are possible here, and each carries its own note of poignant regret. The husband grieves that she cares nothing about her loyalty to him, the one to whom she belongs. Just as great is the hurt that she prefers other men to him. The verb "to love" (אהב) applies not to him, but to a whole string of Assyrians lumped together in the phrase "her lovers." But we note that her emotion for these Assyrians is not love but lust (עגב).[9]

Tweedledee (Leslie C. Allen, *Ezekiel 20–48*, WBC 29 [Waco, TX: Word, 1990], 48). Both follow A. B. Davidson, *The Book of the Prophet Ezekiel* (Cambridge: Cambridge University Press, 1892), 181.

I am reminded of Indian movies with titles such as *Sita aur [and] Gita* or *Ram aur Shyam* in which the rhyming names immediately suggest a pair of siblings, if not twins.

7. So most English versions.

8. So NLT; Zimmerli, *Ezekiel 1–24*, 471; John W. Wevers, ed., *Ezekiel*, NCB (London: Thomas Nelson, 1969), 180.

9. עגב is a rare verb and means "to be driven by lust, by inordinate passion/affection." Other than here, it occurs only in Jer 4:30 (Block, *Ezekiel 1–24*, 738).

The lovers form an impressive and long list. The קְרוֹבִים are probably generals in the army, the פַּחוֹת are either governors or ambassadors, and the סְגָנִים are prefects or provincial governors, while the פָּרָשִׁים רֹכְבֵי סוּסִים are (not cavalry, but) "drivers of horses." They are fashionably dressed in blue-dyed fabric, an expensive commodity.[10] Together, they comprise the elite (מִבְחַר) of the Assyrians, and perhaps, this is a listing in descending order of rank.[11] To Oholah, however, they are in a single category—"all" (כֹּל) of them are handsome young men (בַּחוּרֵי חֶמֶד כֻּלָּם). Even the narrator-husband seems to admit that there is no lack of looks here, and unlike him, perhaps, they have the appeal of youth.

Two "alls" (כֹּל) sweep together the astounding scope of Oholah's sexual activity. She willingly (נתן) prostitutes (זנה; qal) herself with all; she defiles (טמא; niphal) herself with all—the first verb is active, the second is reflexive. In both, she is the eager subject, hurling herself headlong into promiscuity the magnitude of which staggers the imagination. We need hardly be taken aback, though, the husband reminds us, because of the history Oholah brings with her. Her past was a haze of prostitution anyway, he says—summing it up with three graphic images. Men had intercourse (שכב) with her, fondling (עשׂה) her breasts, and ejaculating (שפך) into her. Indeed, their lust (תַזְנוּתָם) reciprocates her whoring (תַזְנוּתֶיהָ). That the vocabulary is a perfect match is fearful—she has the sexual energy to match the energies of an unspecified and clearly enormous number of customers!

The three images link back to the past: to a time in Egypt, when she was young, when her breasts were still virginal. The man seems almost to berate himself that he was a fool to expect anything better from a woman with such a past. But again, the hope had been that she might "give up" this past. עזב is a weighty verb,[12] meaning "to forsake" or "to abandon." How ironic that the man's hope turns around and strikes him a crushing blow. Rather than forsake her habits, she chooses to forsake him. Meanwhile, what of her sibling Oholibah?

---

10. Greenberg, *Ezekiel 21–37*, 475–76, explains that the dye was produced from a mollusk, and used in the royal palace of Persia (Esth 8:15; cf. Exod 26:1). He cites y. Berakot 1.5 [3a] to describe the hue of the blue (תְּכֵלֶת): "*Tekhelet* resembles the sea, the sea resembles grass, and grass resembles the heavens."

11. Block, *Ezekiel 1–24*, 738–39. Contra Block, Greenberg, *Ezekiel 21–37*, 475–76, proposes that the קְרוֹבִים are those "near to" (קרב) the king, and therefore, royal bodyguards; and that פָּרָשִׁים רֹכְבֵי סוּסִים are cavalry.

12. Consider, e.g., the theological weight of the verb עזב in Deuteronomy in the context of the YHWH-Israel relationship. Havilah Dharamraj, *A Prophet Like Moses? A Narrative-Theological Reading of the Elijah Stories*, PBM (Milton Keynes: Paternoster, 2011), 94–96.

OHOLIBAH: EZEKIEL 23:11–21

Her sister Oholibah saw this, yet in her lust and prostitution she was more depraved than her sister [וַתַּשְׁחֵת עַגְבָתָהּ מִמֶּנָּה וְאֶת־תַּזְנוּתֶיהָ מִזְּנוּנֵי אֲחוֹתָהּ]. She too lusted after the Assyrians—governors and commanders, warriors in full dress, mounted horsemen, all handsome young men. I saw that she too defiled herself [וָאֵרֶא כִּי נִטְמָאָה]; both of them went the same way [דֶּרֶךְ אֶחָד לִשְׁתֵּיהֶן]. (Ezek 23:11–13)

The story moves on to its second half, to Oholibah. Again, the summary that opens the account leaves the reader with no positive expectations. The twice-repeated מִן comparative within the two parallel lines of the preview anticipates a doubling of Oholah's excesses:

And she was depraved	in her lust	more than her
וַתַּשְׁחֵת	עַגְבָתָהּ	מִמֶּנָּה
And her whoring	greater than the whoring	of her sister
וְאֶת־תַּזְנוּתֶיהָ	מִזְּנוּנֵי	אֲחוֹתָהּ

The list of Assyrian goods follows much the same pattern as in the Oholah story, reinforcing the similarity in the siblings' tastes. Oholibah has kept her eyes on Oholah ("Oholibah saw") but has seen selectively. She has taken note only of the free love and found that desirable, and remained completely blind to the consequences (23:9–10). While Oholibah has been looking at her sister, the husband has been looking too—at her. "I saw" is another of the insights—so easy to overlook—to his state of mind. Here is an expression of hope-turned-sour. He had been watching carefully to see if the second sister would learn a lesson—after all, Oholah has become "a byword among women," notorious (וַתְּהִי־שֵׁם לַנָּשִׁים; 23:10). Now, the husband's disappointment echoes through the three words that baldly report the fact of the case: דֶּרֶךְ אֶחָד לִשְׁתֵּיהֶן ("both of them went the same way"). It is a statement of resignation, even helplessness. Both pairs of feet have chosen the same road. If the anticipatory summary is an indicator, then in the story that follows, we should see Oholibah overtaking her sister on that road.

But she carried her prostitution still further [וַתּוֹסֶף אֶל־תַּזְנוּתֶיהָ]. She saw [וַתֵּרֶא] men portrayed on a wall, figures of Chaldeans portrayed in red, with belts around their waists and flowing turbans on their heads; all of them looked like Babylonian chariot officers [שָׁלִשִׁים], natives of Chaldea. As soon as she saw them, she lusted after them [וַתַּעְגַּב עֲלֵיהֶם לְמַרְאֵה]

[עִינֶיהָ] and sent messengers to them in Chaldea [אֲלֵיהֶם מַלְאָכִים וַתִּשְׁלַח]. Then the Babylonians came to her [בְנֵי־בָבֶל אֵלֶיהָ וַיָּבֹאוּ], to [כַשְׂדִּימָה] the bed of love [דֹּדִים לְמִשְׁכַּב], and in their lust they defiled her [וַיְטַמְּאוּ] [אוֹתָה בְּתַזְנוּתָם]. After she had been defiled by them [וַתִּטְמָא־בָם], she turned away from them in disgust [מֵהֶם נַפְשָׁהּ וַתֵּקַע]. When she carried on her prostitution openly and exposed her naked body [וַתִּגַל תַּזְנוּתֶיהָ וַתְּגַל] [אֶת־עֶרְוָתָהּ], I turned away from her in disgust [מֵעָלֶיהָ נַפְשִׁי וַתֵּקַע], just as I turned away from her sister [אֲחוֹתָהּ מֵעַל נַפְשִׁי נָקְעָה כַּאֲשֶׁר]. Yet she became more and more promiscuous [אֶת־תַּזְנוּתֶיהָ וַתַּרְבֶּה] as she recalled the days of her youth [נְעוּרֶיהָ אֶת־יְמֵי לִזְכֹּר], when she was a prostitute in Egypt [מִצְרָיִם בְּאֶרֶץ זָנְתָה אֲשֶׁר]. There she lusted after her lovers [פִּלַגְשֵׁיהֶם עַל וַתַּעְגְּבָה], whose genitals were like those of donkeys [אֲשֶׁר] and whose emission was like that of horses [בְשָׂרָם בְּשַׂר־חֲמוֹרִים] and whose emission was like that of horses [וְזִרְמַת] [סוּסִים זִרְמָתָם]. So you longed for the lewdness of your youth [אֵת וַתִּפְקְדִי] [נְעוּרָיִךְ זִמַּת], when in Egypt your bosom was caressed [מִמִּצְרַיִם בַּעְשׂוֹת] and your young breasts fondled/squeezed[13] [נְעוּרָיִךְ שְׁדֵי לְמַעַן]. [דַּדָּיִךְ] (Ezek 23:14–21)

Oholibah's lack of insight continues to be her downfall. She does not perceive (ראה) that her fate will be as inglorious as her sister's. Rather, her eyes (עינים) are enraptured by the looks (מַרְאֶה) of Chaldeans in their "broad and probably embroidered military girdle[s]" and their conspicuous military headwear.[14] As one might flip through a catalogue and end up splurging, Oholibah runs her eyes over the images of Chaldean maleness,[15] and impulsively places a bulk order for the שָׁלִשִׁים, probably knights or royal adjutants. At any rate, these are the nobility of the court of Babylon.[16] She's done with Assyrians, and the Chaldeans are the flavor of the season—must-haves. Her depravity is indeed proving greater. Whereas Oholah's lust (עגב; 23:5) was aroused by flesh-and-blood persons, pictures suffice to inflame Oholibah (עגב; 23:16).[17] And if Oholah gave herself to available Assyrians, Oholibah goes one step further in sending for the Babylonians. Unlike a prostitute who gets propositioned

13. Following the Syriac and Vulgate, לְמַעַן is better read as לִמְעֹךְ ("to squeeze").

14. Walther Eichrodt, *Ezekiel*, trans. Cosslett Quin, OTL (London: SCM, 1970), 325.

15. These are exclusively male forms, sculptured in relief on walls or fresco-like, and enhanced by outlines in red lead; cf. the unsavory drawings on the walls of the Jerusalem temple (Ezek 8:10) (Block, *Ezekiel 1–24*, 744; Eichrodt, *Ezekiel*, 325; Greenberg, *Ezekiel 21–37*, 478–79).

16. Block, *Ezekiel 1–24*, 745; C. F. Keil, *Ezekiel, Daniel*, trans. James Martin and M. G. Easton, Commentary on the Old Testament 9 (Peabody, MA: Hendrickson, 1996), 187; see Zimmerli, *Ezekiel 1–24*, 473, who thinks these are the "third man" in a war chariot.

17. Greenberg, *Ezekiel 21–37*, 478. For an interesting study on the sexual aesthetics of these ancient depictions of violence in war, see Cynthia R. Chapman, "Sculpted Warriors: Sexuality and the Sacred in the Depiction of Warfare in the Assyrian Palace Reliefs and in Ezekiel 23:14–17," in *The Aesthetics of Violence in the Prophets*, ed. Claudia V. Camp and Andrew Mein, LHBOTS 517 (New York: T&T Clark, 2010), 1–17.

by her clients, this woman propositions potential clients. She is her own pimp.[18]

So the Babylonians come and do as invited. The sentence deploys a sexual word at every turn, saturating itself with the act. The Babylonians came (בּוֹא; in the Old Testament the verb is a euphemism for intercourse); they came to the bed of lovemaking (דֹּדִים); they expended their lust on her (תַּזְנוּת). Inexplicably, the orgy leaves a bad taste in her mouth. It may have been the *love* couch that she entertained them on, but it was *lust* that drove their acts and hers. So lust evaporates, leaving no residue except a sudden deflation, a sense of estrangement (יקע) as might happen in a one-night stand with a perfect stranger. The revulsion she feels toward her lovers is expressed by a curious phrase: וַתֵּקַע נַפְשָׁהּ מֵהֶם, "her soul was dislocated" (cf. Gen 32:25).[19] How different this is from how the woman of the Song of Songs feels toward her lover: he is one whom her soul loves (שֶׁאָהֲבָה נַפְשִׁי; Song 3:1–4) and one in whose absence her soul expires (נַפְשִׁי יָצְאָה; Song 5:6).

The man interrupts the flow of the narrative to make his response. The text repetitiously circles on itself to make its point (23:17–18):

she	became estranged	from them
נַפְשָׁהּ	(יקע)	מֵהֶם
I	became estranged	from her
נַפְשִׁי	(יקע)	מֵעָלֶיהָ
(Just as) I	became estranged	from her sister
נַפְשִׁי (כַּאֲשֶׁר)	(יקע)[20]	מֵעַל אֲחוֹתָהּ

Oholibah turns her back on her infatuation with the Babylonians, but she does not turn to her husband. She hurls herself headlong, instead, into the embrace of a third round of lovers. With this third party her behavior becomes unspeakable. There are no love nests set in the privacy of bedrooms. Rather, the orgies move into the open, making for even easier access to customers. Now, any passersby will do, perhaps.

---

18. A parallel picture of such lack of sexual restraint is Jer 2:23–24, which uses the (less offensive) imagery of female animals in heat: "You are a swift she-camel running here and there, a wild donkey . . . sniffing the wind in her craving—in her heat who can restrain her? Any males that pursue her need not tire themselves; at mating time they will find her."

19. Nancy R. Bowen, *Ezekiel*, AOTC (Nashville: Abingdon, 2010), 141.

20. יקע occurs as the biform נקע. See Zimmerli, *Ezekiel 1–24*, 473.

and she exposed (וַתְּגַל) her lewdness (תַּזְנוּתֶיהָ)

and she exposed (וַתְּגַל) her nakedness (אֶת־עֶרְוָתָהּ).

"Ezekiel couples the imagery of human fondling with the sights and sounds of a stable."[21] At this point, the husband severs his association with her. With Oholah he had dissociated himself after one round of infidelities with the Assyrians (and perhaps a return to the Egyptians). With Oholibah he has waited out three cycles: the Assyrians, the Babylonians, and the Egyptians.[22]

However, is this a permanent severance of the ties of marriage, ties that have suffered unimaginable stress? It may not be so. The husband separates himself from Oholibah so as to shock her into reconsidering her behavior. Thus, English versions regularly render the sentence following with the *waw* adversative: "*Yet* (or *but*) she became more and more promiscuous" (23:19). For the second time, Oholibah is cautioned, and for the second time she willfully ignores it (cf. 23:11).

From this point on, the husband can see clearly that the road she (like her sister) has chosen is looping back to Egypt. Before we comment further, we should compare the stories of the siblings.

Oholah	Oholibah
23:5–7	*23:12–13*
"lusted after (עגב) . . . the Assyrians"	"lusted after (עגב) the Assyrians"
warriors clothed in blue	warriors in full dress
governors and commanders	governors and commanders
all handsome young men	all handsome young men
mounted horsemen	mounted horsemen

21. Margaret S. Odell, *Ezekiel*, Smyth and Helwys Bible Commentary Series (Macon, GA: Smyth & Helwys, 2005), 303.

22. Zimmerli makes a detailed attempt to connect the oracle with the political history of the northern and southern kingdoms (*Ezekiel 1–24*, 483–87). Most posit three cycles of political mésalliances for Judah. See, e.g., Ronald M. Hals, *Ezekiel*, FOTL 19 (Grand Rapids: Eerdmans, 1989), 170; Allen, *Ezekiel 20–48*, 46, 49; Joseph Blenkinsopp, *Ezekiel*, Interpretation (Louisville: John Knox, 1990), 100; Jenson, *Ezekiel*, 190–91; Ralph W. Klein, *Ezekiel: The Prophet and His Message* (Columbia: University of South Carolina Press, 1988), 88; Millard C. Lind, *Ezekiel*, Believers Church Bible Commentary (Scottdale, PA: Herald, 1996), 194; Wevers, *Ezekiel*, 179; Steven Tuell, *Ezekiel*, NIBC (Peabody, MA: Hendrickson, 2009), 155; Odell, *Ezekiel*, 302. Greenberg, *Ezekiel 21–37*, 489, reads in the stories of both sisters their reverting back to—rather than simply recollecting—prostitution with Egypt (23:8, 19–21) and posits that what angers YHWH the most is that they return to their "original sin." That is why the oracle ends with the specter of Oholibah tearing out the breasts that were seduced in Egypt (23:34).

defiled herself (טמא)	defiled herself (טמא)[23]
	23:14–18
	saw figures of Chaldeans
	lusted (עגב) after them
	Babylonians came to her, defiled her (טמא)
	turned away in disgust (יקע)
	continued prostitution (תַזְנוּת)
	I turned away in disgust (יקע)
	yet increased prostitution (תַזְנוּת)
23:8	*23:19–21*
did not give up (עזב) Egypt	remembered (זכר) . . . Egypt (23:19)
recalled (פקד) . . . Egyptians (23:21)	
whoring (זנה) . . . during her youth (נְעוּרִים)	the whoring (זנה) of her youth (נְעוּרִים) (23:19) the wantonness (זִמָּה) of her youth (נְעוּרִים) (23:21)
they slept (שכב) with her	lusted after (עגב) her "concubines" (פִלַגְשִׁים) (23:20)
fondled (עשה) her virgin breasts (דַדֵּי בְתוּלִים)	fondled (עשה) her breasts (דַדַּיִם) and squeezed (מעך) her young bosom (שַׁדֵי נְעוּרִים)
ejaculated (שפך) their lust (זנה) on her	with genitals like donkeys and emission like horses

The narratives of both sisters end where they began, in Egypt. While Oholah let her body be used, Oholibah seems to have outdone her clients in their appetite for the sexual, so much so that they are called "her concubines" (פִלַגְשֵׁיהֶם).[24] The text seems to assign to her the role of the male when it comes to measuring her performance alongside that of her men! Reprising the start of the stories (23:3), Oholah's experience is described with one item: her virgin breasts were fondled. Oholibah's is reprised in full, but remarkably the adjective "virgin" is missing (and replaced with "young"). In the face of Oholibah's extraordinary and repeated cycles of whoring, it is perhaps impossible to remember that there was ever a time when she was virginal. It seems oxymoronic to juxtapose chastity with this uncontrollably inflamed woman. The final

23. Block, *Ezekiel 1–24*, 743–44, makes a similar table comparing Ezek 23:5–6 and 12.

24. Elsewhere in the OT, the noun describes female concubines, used by men for sexual gratification. Block, *Ezekiel 1–24*, 746–47; Zimmerli, *Ezekiel 1–24*, 474; see Greenberg, *Ezekiel 21–37*, 480, who cites with dissatisfaction sources that suggest that Oholibah consorted with the male servants ("concubines") of the Egyptians.

point of comparison between the sisters' Egyptian experiences is the description of the sexual act(s). Oholah is the object (even if willingly) of the promiscuity (זנה) of the Egyptians. They pour out "on" (עַל) her body, the preposition perhaps being an indicator of their aggressive position in intercourse. When it comes to describing Oholibah in the same situation, hers are not anonymous customers but seemingly handpicked "concubines." They are selected for size and volume,[25] criteria that so distract the speaker that he describes the act solely in reference to them.

At the end of the two stories, Oholah is barely in the competition. The effect of this piling-on of gross marital infidelity is to direct the reader to the one who relates the stories. He has married them against the most basic cultural expectations as regards marriageable women. He watches their unrepentant sexual license. He refuses to take the usual recourse available to him, to either have them stoned with their lovers, or to divorce them on grounds of adultery. Implicit in the narrative is the shame such a man must bear for not exercising his legal privileges, and standing by passively while his wives pleasure whom they will. We will return to comment on the response he finally makes, but before that, we should visit the cameo which features these two siblings together and with which the narrative closes.

THE SISTERS TOGETHER: EZEKIEL 23:40–44

They even sent messengers for men who came from far away [וְאַף כִּי תִשְׁלַחְנָה לַאֲנָשִׁים בָּאִים מִמֶּרְחָק], and when they arrived you bathed yourself for them, applied eye makeup and put on your jewelry. You sat on an elegant couch [מִטָּה כְבוּדָּה], with a table spread before it on which you placed the incense and olive oil that belonged to me [וּקְטָרְתִּי וְשַׁמְנִי שַׂמְתְּ עָלֶיהָ]. (Ezek 23:40–41)

In this text, both Oholah and Oholibah are acting in concert. This appears to be a device on the part of the husband to arraign both by presenting one single case.[26] However, the description of the men is so

---

25. In comparison to Assyria and Babylonia whose males are warlike, the Egyptians are depicted as merely lewd (Greenberg, *Ezekiel 21–37*, 479). Further, there is a coalescence of ideas here: Egypt was known for its horses (Deut 17:16; 1 Kgs 10:28) and horses were associated with virility (cf. Jer 5:8) (Paul M. Joyce, *Ezekiel: A Commentary*, LHBOTS 482 [London: T&T Clark, 2007], 162).

26. E.g., Block, *Ezekiel 1–24*, 759; Eichrodt, *Ezekiel*, 333; Blenkinsopp, *Ezekiel*, 101; Klein, *Ezekiel*, 91; Tuell, *Ezekiel*, 152; Odell, *Ezekiel*, 297. Greenberg, *Ezekiel 21–37*, 490–91, and Wevers, *Ezekiel*, 178–79, provide a redaction-critical explanation proposing this text (23:34–49) to be a preliminary version of the separate and sequential careers of the two sisters that this chapter narrates. So also, e.g., Allen, *Ezekiel 20–48*, 47–48; Zimmerli, *Ezekiel 1–24*, 480, 492.

different from the depiction of the Assyrian and Babylonian lovers that
we must read them either as the same men re-described[27] or as a generic
depiction of their waywardness.

The sisters conduct themselves much like prostitutes would, making
themselves ready for their clientele.[28] At first glance, this appears like
classy prostitution. They lounge on luxurious couches, bathed and beautified and suitably accessorized. On the table would be laid out the different items for the meal. The oil is meant for anointing at mealtime.[29] The
room is scented with clouds of incense. The difference, however, is that,
atypically for prostitutes, these women have sent for their customers.

The noise of a carefree crowd was around her [וְקוֹל הָמוֹן שָׁלֵו בָהּ]; drunkards were brought from the desert along with men from the rabble
[וְאֶל־אֲנָשִׁים מֵרֹב אָדָם מוּבָאִים סוֹבָאִים מִמִּדְבָּר], and they put bracelets on
the wrists of the woman and her sister [וַיִּתְּנוּ צְמִידִים אֶל־יְדֵיהֶן] and beautiful crowns on their heads [וַעֲטֶרֶת תִּפְאֶרֶת עַל־רָאשֵׁיהֶן]. Then I said about
the one worn out by adultery [וָאֹמַר לַבָּלָה נִאוּפִים], "Now let them use
her as a prostitute, for that is all she is" [עַתָּ יִזְנֶה תַזְנוּתֶהָ וָהִיא]. And they
slept with her [וַיָּבוֹא אֵלֶיהָ]. As men sleep with a prostitute [כְּבוֹא אֶל־אִשָּׁה
זוֹנָה], so they slept with those lewd women, Oholah and Oholibah [כֵּן בָּאוּ
אֶל־אָהֳלָה וְאֶל־אָהֳלִיבָה אִשֹׁת הַזִּמָּה]. (Ezek 23:42–44)

How different from the earlier description of the "wealthy, powerful,
good-looking and sexually potent"[30] Assyrian elite (23:6, 8)! These are
drunkards and rabble,[31] swirling around the sisters in a multitude
(הָמוֹן).[32] They confidently bring their hosts gifts of jewelry, and feel
free to slip them on with their own hands. The description of the harlot
siblings is similarly sleazy. "Though her lovers come bearing gifts, one
senses . . . an image of harlots with fading beauty, whose toilets are of

---

27. Block, *Ezekiel 1–24*, 761, thinks these might be the Assyrians, since they are common to
both sisters.

28. Cf. Ezek 16:11–12, 18; 23:17; Prov 7:15–16.

29. Keil, *Ezekiel*, 191.

30. Bowen, *Ezekiel*, 141.

31. John B. Taylor, *Ezekiel: An Introduction and Commentary* (Leicester: InterVarsity, 1969),
176. Alternatively, סבאים (*qere*) is rendered "Sabeans." Since Saba does not feature elsewhere
in Ezekiel (unless this word is related to שְׁבָא "Sheba," which occurs in Ezek 27:22, 23; 38:13),
"drunkards" (סובאים, *ketiv*) may be the better fit, despite the suggestion of a dittographic error
from the previous word, מובאים (Tuell, *Ezekiel*, 159; Block, *Ezekiel 1–24*, 761; Allen, *Ezekiel
20–48*, 45; Greenberg, *Ezekiel 21–37*, 486; Zimmerli, *Ezekiel 1–24*, 478–79).

32. This is a textually difficult verse. Block, *Ezekiel 1–24*, 761, thinks that the "carefree
crowd" are the general public, who have been permitted access to the licentious goings-on; and
that the "noise" could include musical instruments. See Zimmerli, *Ezekiel 1–24*, 478, for possibility of loud singing.

necessity more elaborate, whose level of clientele has degenerated, whose day has nearly passed."[33]

The speaker interrupts the orgy to pass judgment on the "one worn out by adultery." "Worn out" (בלה) is used in another context to describe worn out sacks, wineskins, sandals, and garments (Josh 9:4–5) and, in a closer context, to a woman who is past the age of childbearing (Gen 18:12).[34] We cannot say whether this worn-out woman is Oholah or Oholibah or the two addressed collectively,[35] but the remarkable detail is that for the first time in these narratives, she is charged with adultery (נאף). This raises the gravity of the charge.[36] However, she is, he says, not simply a wife indulging in an illicit affair. It is much worse—drunkards and rabble "go in" to her, just as men would "go into" women of pleasure.

With this the narrative is neatly bracketed by comparable vignettes of the sibling whores:

23:2–4	*23:42–44*
Two women (שְׁתַּיִם נָשִׁים), daughters (בָּנוֹת) (23:2)	
(unidentified men) (23:3)	drunkards, men from the rabble (23:42)
breasts and nipples (23:3)	bracelets and beautiful crowns (23:42)
prostitutes (זנה) in Egypt engaging in prostitution (זנה) (23:3)	as men enter a prostitute (אִשָּׁה זוֹנָה) so they entered [them] (23:44)
from their youth (23:3)	worn out by adultery (23:43)
"They were mine" (23:4)	"I said . . . 'Now let them use her'" (23:43)
Oholah and Oholibah (23:4)	Oholah and Oholibah (23:44)
	lewd women (אִשֹׁת הַזִּמָּה) (23:44)

The sisters, when we first met them, were "two women." When the narrative ends, they are "lewd women." In the interim between these bookends, the customers they service have gone from the unremarkable to

---

33. Katheryn Pfisterer Darr, "Ezekiel's Justifications of God: Teaching Troubled Texts," *JSOT* 55 (1992): 108.

34. Block, *Ezekiel 1–24*, 762; Greenberg, *Ezekiel 21–37*, 486, renders בלה as "old (= worn out) whore."

35. 23:43 is fraught with textual difficulties to the point of being "unintelligible" (Zimmerli, *Ezekiel 1–24*, 492). The solutions need not concern us here; our interest is in the use of the term נאף, "adultery." See Zimmerli, *Ezekiel 1–24*, 491 and Wevers, *Ezekiel*, 186–88, for the swings between singular and plural in 23:36–49.

36. Block, *Ezekiel 1–24*, 759.

the remarkable—but in the worst sense. They indiscriminately entertain rabble. They are older now, and considering the wear over the years, their physical assets may not be as attractive as they once were. Instead, if there is anything beautiful on them, it is the jewelry. The trade remains the same as before, but if they were youthful tarts once, they are jades now. The tragedy is not that age and their choice of lifestyle have taken their toll. It is that they once belonged to someone who cared. Now, the husband relinquishes his charge of them. From now on they belong to many, and in that condition, belong to none.

The story finishes off a little like the Song does. The women in both are last seen surrounded by companions, the center of attention. In the Song, the woman has "friends in attendance" (Song 8:13). In Ezekiel 32, there is a multitude (הָמוֹן) of admirers. The Song's woman wishes to move from public into private space, from the company of friends to the company of her beloved. She urges him to make haste to come to her (Song 8:14). For Ezekiel's siblings, there is no difference between the public and the private. And as for exclusive love—it does not offer the variety their bodies crave. They would rather have a multitude than one man.

In both texts, there are indications of expensive ornamentation. In the Song, there was talk of silver and cedar. These were metaphors for the girl's rites of passage into nubility. They would increase her desirability. The sibling sisters in Ezekiel hardly need brothers to enhance their assets. They have their own tried and tested routine of bathing, prettying their eyes with *kohl* and accentuating their charms with jewelry. If there is a counterpart to the brothers, it is the suitors themselves, who bring the women bracelets and tiaras. But unlike the silver and cedar wood that enhance the marriage prospects of a virgin adolescent, these are a prostitute's hire—and that for a pair of jaded whores. When the Song's woman gives herself, it is a gift of immeasurable value. All the wealth a man possesses would not suffice to buy him her love. Ezekiel's sisters, on the other hand, send for men to come and freely avail of them. They perfume the room with incense in preparation for their lovers. The Song's woman, in contrast, needs no such expensive stimulants. Unlike the sisters, whose bodies have been plundered and stripped of every charm, she can invite her beloved to delight in her spice-laden mountains (Song 8:14).

COMPARING SONG 8 AND EZEKIEL 23

The women in the Song and in Ezekiel are each the antithesis of the other.

When the curtain rises on each text, the women are engaged in activity that summarizes their difference. The Song's woman is nestled against "her beloved" (Song 8:5), the sole focus of her attention. The sisters are intimate too, but with who knows whom? They have multiple partners, all lumped together into a gray masculine pronoun, "they." They do not even merit the common noun "men." The sisters appear not to care who these persons are who come and go, as long as they are male and gratify their licentious urges.

In both texts there is mention of breasts (שָׁדַיִם). In the Song, they are "towers" that are surrendered just as a city might capitulate to a conqueror. This is a mutual victory. The woman is just as pleased to offer her "towers" as the conqueror is to accept them. The word that links the giver and the recipient is *shalom*, contentment. Breasts are a refrain in Ezekiel 23. First mentioned in the Egypt phase, the story of each sister will circle back to reprise them. These breasts are hardly defensive towers rising above city walls. In fact, if the sisters are cities, they are cities without walls. If there were any walls at all, indifference has brought about their collapse. The sisters care naught for chastity, cannot be bothered with careful consideration of whom to let in. On the contrary, they are eager to let men in, as many as are pleased to come. And so they come, scrambling over the ruined walls and pillaging the towers. Their breasts are fondled (מִעֵךְ), their nipples caressed (עִשָּׂה) by anonymous hands. The verbs have a range of meaning—to press, to squeeze, to crush[37]—that moves beyond the erotic into the sadistic-masochistic. What happens to these breasts is metonymic with what happens to the rest of the body. There is lust here, raw and unrestrained—not the *shalom* that love brings.

The Assyrians and the Babylonians are swoon-worthy men, the finest samplings of the male of the human species. They are young and handsome, accomplished and rich, elite and chic. Here is Solomon's fabulous harem in reverse, if one could obtain them all. And Oholah and Oholibah do. To the watching husband, however, his wives are Lady

---

37. Thus, מִעֵךְ is used to describe an act more violent than fondling, such as the crushing of testicles (Lev 22:24) or the thrusting of a spear into the ground (2 Sam 26:7). Greenberg, *Ezekiel 21–37*, 474, posits that the sense of עִשָּׂה to mean "crush" is related to the verb עָסַס, which is used to mean "trample" (Mal 3:21 [4:3]) and for (pressed out) wine (Amos 9:13).

The Hebrew of 23:21 is difficult, but is illuminated by the parallel phrases in 23:3, 8, and the rendering in Syriac and the Vulgate. See Block, *Ezekiel 1–24*, 743nn74–75; Greenberg, *Ezekiel 21–37*, 480.

Chatterleys hosting a mob bacchanalia. The word multitude (הָמוֹן) reminds us of Solomon, who owned real estate in Baal-Hamon (Song 8:11). We inferred that this is a fictitious place name, whose function in the poem was to invoke Solomon's "abundance" both in terms of his wealth and his women. Comparatively, the Ezekiel sisters behave like potentates. They select their men in a binge of self-indulgence, without any cultural inhibitions, without having to care about cost. However, one round of debauchery only whets their appetite for the next round, leaving them in a constant state of dissatisfaction. There is no shortage of lust, but there is not the satisfaction of love. The Song dismisses these liaisons with scorn, liaisons that the common man would slaver over as exotic and delectable, but liaisons that can turn to ashes in one's mouth: "Keep your thousand, Solomon!" (Song 8:12). The Song would dismiss these playboy lovers as it would Solomon's "sixty queens," "eighty concubines," and "virgins without number"; it would despise these lecherous sisters even more than it does Solomon.

Indeed, Oholibah experiences the taste of ashes with the second phase of reprobate living. While painted images were sufficient to incite lust, the real thing barely slakes it. On the contrary, the "bed of love" is very soon something she jerks away (יקע) from. Love turns to loathing, proving the point that lust has nothing to do with love.[38] It is a stirring of the loins that can dissipate as quickly as it comes. Love, meanwhile, is as tenacious as death itself, not letting go its hold on the human heart. If Oholibah's lust reminds us at all of love, it may be her determination to obtain the objects of her desire. She sets her mind on making them hers, just as much as the Song's woman wishes to seal her beloved as hers alone. But, unlike the latter who seeks the contentment of the one she desires (Song 8:10), Oholibah craves self-gratification. Her lust is a fire too, one that moves restlessly and even ravenously from one lover to another. It is an insanely insatiable conflagration, one that is unquenchable by any stirrings of conscience. It barely notices when her husband, who has borne her perversions this long, dissociates himself from her. He may hope that it will bring her to her right mind, but she is caught up in the roaring blaze, insensible to all but the passions of her flesh. Unlike the almighty flame of love, which warms and enlivens, the fire of lust devours the one who ignites it. Oholibah emerges from the Babylonian experience disgusted, worse off than before.

From lust to disgust to more lust, Oholibah reaps ever-diminishing

---

38. Note the clever repetition with increment that makes the point of love-turned-to-loathing: "I will stir up your lovers (מְאַהֲבַיִךְ) against you, those you turned away from in disgust" (23:22); "I am about to deliver you into the hands of those you hate (שָׂנֵאת), to those you turned away from in disgust" (23:28) (Block, *Ezekiel 1–24*, 754).

returns. The "more and more promiscuous" she becomes (23:19), the higher her threshold for pleasure rises. Arguably, the description of sexual experiences shows a steady deterioration. The Egyptian experience is rough sex, which, in its own way, is titillating. Indeed, Oholibah will yearn for it in later years. With the Assyrians, both sisters are depicted as subjects of the verbs of prostitution (23:7, 13): Oholah gives (נתן) herself; both defile themselves (טמא). The Babylonians, interestingly, enact defilement upon Oholibah (טמא; 23:17). In fact, for the first time, the clients' lust (תַּזְנוּת) is mentioned. In the generic description, the males are even more clearly the subjects of the intercourse. Using a verb that is revoltingly crude if read literally in this context, the text says these men "entered into" her as men "enter into a whore" (בּוֹא; 23:43–44). There is no mention here of her lust, the usual preamble to a cycle of debauchery. Neither is there mention of defilement; it is as if the idea of defilement is ridiculously redundant. The tragedy is that the sisters' search for satisfaction was a chasing after the wind. So futile is the present that solace lies in recalling days long gone (and perhaps returning to them). Everything was better then. Even male organs came in larger sizes. The reader wonders if Oholibah might even be so dissolute as to prefer bestiality. She would sample, if she could, it appears, anything male, from mounted horsemen (23:12) to the stallions they sit upon (cf. 23:20).

As the stories circle back to the starting point in Egypt, a long-range chiasm brings closure.

23:3   breasts (שָׁדַיִם) were fondled (מִעֲךְ)   bosoms (דַּדַּיִם) were caressed (עשׂה)

23:21   bosom (דַּדַּיִם) was caressed (עשׂה)   breasts (שָׁדַיִם) were fondled (מִעֲךְ implied)

In the Song, the theme of love is played out in one long cycle, the ending anticipating the start of the book. But this is a cycle that moves into the future, shining with the promise of past joy. When the Song ends with a familiar refrain, "Come away, my beloved" (Song 8:14; cf. 2:17), it anticipates the next rendezvous, which will be every bit the romp on the hills that the last was, and another opportunity for the woman to ask that her beloved should "kiss [her] with the kisses of his mouth" (Song 1:2).

We have set out that the women in Ezekiel 23 are the antithesis of the woman in the Song. What can we say about the husband of Oholah and Oholibah?

LOVE AND ITS JEALOUSY: THE HUSBAND IN EZEKIEL 23

This is a bleak narration of the story of a pair of reprobate sisters told from the point of view of the husband, who presents himself as the victim.[39] He notes the stages of the journey from when they were virgins

39. Texts such as Hosea 2, Ezekiel 16 and 23, Jeremiah 2–5, and Isaiah 47 are categorized as "pornoprophetic literature," and attract a lively ongoing debate, especially from feminist scholars. Three key samples are: Fokkelien van Dijk-Hemmes, "The Metaphorization of Woman in Prophetic Speech: An Analysis of Ezekiel 23," *VT* 4, no. 2 (1993): 162–70; Athalya Brenner, *The Intercourse of Knowledge: On Gendering Desire and "Sexuality" in the Hebrew Bible* (Leiden: Brill, 1997); Athalya Brenner and Fokkelien van Dijk-Hemmes, *On Gendering Texts: Female and Male Voices in the Hebrew Bible* (Leiden: Brill, 1993).

Andrew Sloane, "Aberrant Textuality? The Case of Ezekiel the (Porno) Prophet," *TynBul* 59, no. 1 (2008): 54, presents a longer bibliography of scholars who question the ethics of these prophets, accusing them of being oppressive, violent, misogynistic, and abusive.

In response, a sample of scholars who refute such a reading, especially with respect to Ezekiel 16 and 23, are:

Corrine L. Paton, "'Should Our Sister be Treated Like a Whore?': A Response to Feminist Critiques of Ezekiel 23," in *The Book of Ezekiel: Theological and Anthropological Perspectives*, ed. Margaret S. Odell and John T. Strong (Atlanta: SBL, 2000), 221–45. She shows the function the metaphor takes on in a primarily male population "emasculated" by the horrors of defeat in war. Related to this theme is Pamela Gordon and Harold C. Washington, "Rape as a Military Metaphor in the Hebrew Bible," in *A Feminist Companion to the Latter Prophets*, ed. Athalya Brenner, FCB (Sheffield: Sheffield Academic, 1995), 308–25.

Gerlinde Baumann, "Prophetic Objections to Yahweh as the Violent Husband of Israel: Reinterpretations of the Prophetic Marriage Metaphor in Second Isaiah (Isaiah 40–55)," in *Prophets and Daniel*, ed. Athalya Brenner, FCB Series 2 (Sheffield: Sheffield Academic, 2001), 88–120. She shows how the metaphor of the violent husband is an older pattern that gets rewritten more positively in Second Isaiah.

Darr, "Ezekiel's Justifications of God," 97–117, offers an author-centered point of view on why Ezekiel used the violent female sexual imagery that he did. Michael Fishbane, "Sin and Judgment in the Prophecies of Ezekiel," *Int* 38, no. 2 (1984): 131–50, reads the metaphor in terms of the theme of the book, "knowing YHWH." Amy Kalmanofsky, "The Dangerous Sisters of Jeremiah and Ezekiel," *JBL* 130, no. 2 (2011): 299–312, considers how "the portrayal of Israel and Judah as sisters introduces a particular set of anxieties into the metaphor of the wayward wife that are an essential part of the prophets' rhetoric of horror designed to terrify their audience into reform" (300). Jaqueline E. Lapsley, "Shame and Self-Knowledge: The Positive Role of Shame in Ezekiel's View of the Moral Self," in *The Book of Ezekiel: Theological and Anthropological Perspectives*, ed. Margaret S. Odell and John T. Strong (Atlanta: SBL, 2000), 143–73, argues that Ezekiel constructs shame as a positive value that the target audience should embrace, by identifying with the sisters in the metaphor. Sloane, "Aberrant Textuality," 53–76, rebuts the arguments of the feminist critics Athalya Brenner and Fokkelien van Dijk-Hemmes, who reject Ezekiel's use of the metaphor as gender-asymmetric pornography, and argues that the purpose of these offensive texts is to confront the hearers with the "horror of their sin and its consequences." A brief explanation of religious "pansexuality" in ancient West Asia that could have prompted Ezekiel's choice of imagery is given by Jenson, *Ezekiel*, 192–93. Julie Galambush, *Jerusalem in the Book of Ezekiel: City as Yahweh's Wife*, SBLDS 130 (Atlanta: Scholars, 1992), approaches the Ezekiel texts from two perspectives: the covenantal demand for exclusive loyalty and the tradition of marriage between personified capital cities and their patron deities.

A summary of ways scholars appropriate these difficult texts is listed in Athalya Brenner, "Pornoprophetics Revisited: Some Additional Reflections," *JSOT* 70 (1996): 63–86, esp. 85–86.

newly entering prostitution to their end as a pair of professional hookers. Within this narrative, the sisters have been associated with verbs indicating their loose morals: "to whore" (זנה) and "to lust after" (עגב) dominated the earlier sections; "to commit adultery" (נאף) came toward the end (23:45; cf. 23:37). As we pointed out earlier, the last is the most serious and is, in fact, the only one that is legally punishable. It warrants the death penalty.[40]

The rest of the chapter, outside the narrative we have examined, concerns the penalty that falls on Oholah (23:9–10) and Oholibah (23:22–35) and a final address to the two (23:36–49). If the husband is to put his finger on the point at which their sin began, it is this: "you have forgotten me and turned your back on me" (23:35). From here on, their eyes strayed without control. If they were not ogling potential lovers of exotic extraction, they were gazing back with longing at lovers past. This estrangement between husband and wives is implicit in that never once are the two parties in direct conversation. The husband speaks "about" the wife (23:43), making his remark to an unseen audience; he speaks to a third party (23:1, 36); he directs an imperative concerning them to an unidentified party (23:46). His wives set themselves on a road (23:13) and crossed the boundary within which he could claim them to be "mine" (23:4).

Ezekiel 23 has the undertone of a legal proceeding, the formal features of a *rib*, suggesting that the husband arraigns them before judges (23:45). What moves him to this? It is his jealousy (23:25, קִנְאָה), the same emotion that Song 8 had spoken about—the jealousy that is as unrelenting as Sheol. Oholah and Oholibah face the jealousy of love, a jealousy that properly belongs in the marriage relationship that binds them to their husband. The penalty for adultery being death, death is served out to the sisters in an enactment of the *lex talionis*. They are handed over to the same men for whom they turned their backs on him (23:9, 28), men who will now "punish you according to their standards" (23:24). There is the

40. Block, *Ezekiel 1–24*, 732, notes the similarities and the difference between Ezekiel 23 and its parallel text in Jer 3:6–11: In Jeremiah, as in Ezekiel, YHWH has two wives, the senior being Israel, whose lewd behavior the junior wife Judah observes and imitates. The significant difference is that while in Jeremiah the penalty is a certificate of divorce, in Ezekiel, the penalty is death.

cutting off of their noses,[41] the removal of children from their custody, the stripping naked,[42] the confiscation of goods.[43]

The most gruesome is that they must drink from the cup (23:32–34),[44] a custom detailed in Numbers 5 as the "law for [cases of] jealousy" in marriage (תּוֹרַת הַקְּנָאֹת; Num 5:29). Oholibah drinks it, as her sister has, and must drink it to its dregs. Its equivalent in the legal code is "bitter water that brings a curse . . . and causes bitter suffering" (Num 5:24). The tradition is that if the husband's jealousy is legitimate, that is, if she has "made herself impure and been unfaithful to her husband" (Num 5:27), her belly will swell. As Oholibah gulps down the bitterness and suffering, the "drunkenness and sorrow," "the ruin and the desolation" (23:33), she is brought to the brink of insanity. Perhaps it is the unbearable pain that causes her to smash the drained cup,[45] and then chew on its shards in an effort to contain her paroxysms of agony.[46] Driven beyond human limits, she tears at her flesh, perhaps with the sharp pieces of the broken cup, not knowing how else to relieve her suffering. The same erogenous breasts that once her lovers caressed, she mangles. The loathing she feels for her lovers, she turns upon herself.

The sisters have invited on themselves (23:30, 49) the jealousy of love. As one stands helpless before Sheol, they stand helpless before its fury. Rather than swear by a love that will outdo death, they become recipients of death themselves. Rather than offer and find *shalom* in the eyes of their husband, they look into the face of war and its devastations. Instead of gazelles upon the mountains, armies march against them with their

41. See Greenberg, *Ezekiel 21–37*, 482, for a series of offenses that could attract the penalty of mutilation of the face. Under Middle Assyrian law, the nose of an adulterous wife could be cut off if the husband so required.

42. See S. M. Olyan, "In the Sight of Her Lovers: The Interpretation of *nablūt* in Hosea 2:12," *BZ* 36 (1992): 255–61; Peggy L. Day, "Adulterous Jerusalem's Imagined Demise: Death of a Metaphor in Ezekiel XVI," *VT* 50, no. 3 (2000): 287–309.

43. This is a listing of the atrocities Assyrians and Babylonians notoriously inflicted on defeated populations. Block, *Ezekiel 1–24*, 751–52; Zimmerli, *Ezekiel 1–24*, 489.

44. Block, *Ezekiel 1–24*, 755, lists how drinking from a cup (כּוֹס) is a common OT metaphor for either the reward or the retribution God metes out. Reward: Ps 16:5; 23:5; 116:13; Retribution: Isa 51:17, 22; cf. Jer 49:12; Lam 4:21; Ps 75:9 [EV 8]. Jer 25:15–29 particularly resonates with this Ezekiel text. See also Greenberg, *Ezekiel 21–37*, 492–93; W. McKane, "Poison, Trial by Ordeal and the Cup of Wrath," *VT* 30 (1980): 487–92.

45. 23:34 is textually difficult. Whether there is a "gnawing" (the rare verb גרם) is debatable. What we can be sure of is violence done to the cup and self-mutilation performed on the breasts. See Block, *Ezekiel 1–24*, 754n137; Allen, *Ezekiel 20–48*, 44; Wevers, *Ezekiel*, 185–86.

46. Peter Naylor, *Ezekiel* (Darlington, UK: Evangelical Press, 2011), 360; Odell, *Ezekiel*, 304. Perhaps it is her uncontrollable thirst for more that drives her to suck at the shards (Block, *Ezekiel 1–24*, 756; Bowen, *Ezekiel*, 142). Or perhaps she is "deranged by the contents of the cup" (Greenberg, *Ezekiel 21–37*, 484).

weapons of destruction (23:24).[47] They do not "rouse" (עוּר) the man to the act of love; rather, their actions cause him to "rouse" (23:22; עוּר) against them the engines of war. Instead of lovers gamboling on their bodies, the same lovers lay them bare and mutilated and waste (23:10, 25–26, 29, 46–47).

Whereas the Song finishes off its examination of the phenomenon of love and its jealousy with a prescription for human lovers (Song 8:6–7), Ezekiel 23 also ends in a prescription, but in exactly the opposite direction. The husband pronounces Oholah and Oholibah to be examples women must never follow (23:48).

LOVE AND ITS JEALOUSY: DEITY AND DEVOTEE

Out of the various themes that make up the warp and weft of the Song of Songs, allegorical sentiment is at its most passionate with the theme of exclusive love. That the various speakers of Song 8 are mostly anybody's guess comes as a bonus in interpretation.

So for Jewish exegetes, the opening words are those of God and his heavenly tribunal. (When next they speak, we will hear the plural "we"; 8:8.) They admire Israel as she travels through the desert after her liberation from the Egyptian bondage. Bearing the just-given Torah, she comes "leaning on her beloved," that is, professing her love for her God.[48] Israel replies to the heavenly observation: "Under Sinai suspended above me, there I roused Your love, there was Your people born a mother to other nations, there she endured the travail of her birth."[49] The suspended mountain is what the "apple tree" refers to, a mountain uprooted and miraculously held over Israel (for Deut 4:11 says that the people "stood beneath the mountain"). Why should Sinai be likened to an apple tree? This is because just as an apple tree produces its fruit in Sivan, so did the Sinai bear its fruit—the Torah—in Sivan.[50] The "travail" endured is the enmity of the nations,[51] or perhaps the anxiety at the experience of standing under a hanging mountain.[52] Because of her love for God, Israel asks God to love her in return by

---

47. See Block, *Ezekiel 1–24*, 750–51, for the list in Ezek 23:24, which depicts the Assyrians armed to the teeth.

48. Rashi, cited in Meir Zlotowitz, compiler, *Shir haShirim/Song of Songs: An Allegorical Translation based upon Rashi with a Commentary Anthologized from Talmudic, Midrashic and Rabbinic Sources* (New York: Mesorah, 1979), 193.

49. Rashi, cited in Zlotowitz, *Shir haShirim*, 193–95.

50. Midrash, cited in Zlotowitz, *Shir haShirim*, 194.

51. Rashi, cited in Zlotowitz, *Shir haShirim*, 194.

52. *Torah Temimah*, cited in Zlotowitz, *Shir haShirim*, 194.

setting her as a seal upon his heart and arm—the former assures her that he will always love her, and the latter signifies that he will manifest that love in deeds on her behalf.[53] The seal(s) are her guarantee that she "shall never again be exiled." And why should she not be exiled? It is because her love for God is like "coals which keep glowing," or a "roaring blaze which not even the strongest waters can extinguish."[54] Indeed, because of this love for God, Israel's life is constantly under threat: "For your sake we face death all day long; we are considered as sheep to be slaughtered" (Ps 44:23 [EV 22]).[55] The Targum takes the fire and water to symbolize the hostile heathens. Their enmity blazes like Gehinnom, and when they gather together (to blot God out), they are like the waters of the Great Sea.[56] Of course, their labors would be futile.

Now God and his divine council speak of a "little sister" whose "breasts are not yet grown." The "breasts" might refer to the condition of exiled Israel, who has no great leaders such as the brothers Moses and Aaron.[57] Or, they may refer to the twin tablets of the covenant, in which case, the insufficiency is that the Second Temple lacks the repository of the tablets—the ark.[58] The "little sister" may also be the ten northern tribes in diaspora. Judahites wonder what will happen to them when the day of restoration comes.

In either case, the result depends on how the people comport themselves. If Israel behaves like a wall fortified (with brass; cf. Jer 1:18) that the heathen cannot infiltrate, that is, if she refrains from intermarrying and intermingling, then God will reward her with adornments—a rebuilt Temple. If, however, she behaves like a door "which revolves on its hinges and opens whenever someone knocks," that is, if "she is open to all blandishments," then, God will barricade her with cedar panels—letting her remain in exile.[59]

To this, Israel makes confident reply: "I am as strong as a wall in the words of the Law and my children are as sturdy as a tower." Because of this, she is sure that she will "find favor in the eyes of her Lord."[60]

Israel continues to speak, recalling her worth in God's sight. Solomon's vineyard in Baal-Hamon ("the owner of the multitude") is a metaphor for God's vineyard Israel that was located in "populous

53. Alshich, cited in Zlotowitz, *Shir haShirim*, 195.
54. *Metzudas David*, cited in Zlotowitz, *Shir haShirim*, 196.
55. Alshich, cited in Zlotowitz, *Shir haShirim*, 195–96.
56. Targum to Song of Songs 8:6–7.
57. *Tz'ror haMor*, cited in Zlotowitz, *Shir haShirim*, 198.
58. Ramban, cited in Zlotowitz, *Shir haShirim*, 198.
59. See Rashi and *Metzudas David*, cited in Zlotowitz, *Shir haShirim*, 199.
60. Targum to Song of Songs 8:10.

Jerusalem." Because of her disobedience, he gave over the vineyard to cruel "keepers"—successively Babylon, Media, Greece, and Rome, who extracted from her exorbitant taxes, figuratively the "thousand shekels of silver." God calls these "keepers" to account for their exploitation. Rebuked, the nations hurry to make amends. They say that they will return not only the "thousand," but also pay an additional "two hundred" (cf. Isa 60:17). This follows the *halachah* that anyone who derives unjust gain from consecrated property must repay not only the principal but the penalty of an added fifth.[61]

God then takes the turn to say the words he will speak to Israel at the end of days: "You, O Assembly of Israel (like a little garden among the nations), sitting in the House of Study with the members of the Sanhedrin, and the rest of the people who listen to the voice of the head of the academy and learn from his mouth words of the Law: make me hear the sound of your words at the time when you sit to acquit or convict and I will be agreeable to all you do."[62]

To this, the elders of the assembly of Israel will reply: "Flee, my Beloved, Lord of the world, from this polluted earth, and let your Presence dwell in heaven above. But in times of trouble, when we pray to you, be like a gazelle which sleeps with one eye closed and one eye open, or like an antelope fawn which looks behind as it runs away. Just so, look on us and regard our pain and affliction from heaven above, until the time when you will be pleased with us and redeem us and bring us up to the mountains of Jerusalem and there the priests will burn before you the incense of spices."[63]

Like the Jewish allegorists, Christian exegetes also make use of the uncertainty of the speakers in the concluding section of the Song to construct a passionate conversation between Christ and his church. If the Jewish idiosyncrasies follow the Targum, the Christian reading gets its peculiarities from the Vulgate.

The woman who comes up "all whitened"[64] is, of course, the church. Here, she is on an "ascent into the heavens," led by her beloved.[65] Just as John the beloved did, she reclines on the bosom of Christ.[66] In contrast to the Jewish reading, the opening lines are placed—with patriarchal

61. Rashi, cited in Zlotowitz, *Shir haShirim*, 201–2.

62. Targum to Song of Songs 5:13.

63. Targum to Song of Songs 8:14.

64. From the LXX's λελευκανθισμένη.

65. Theodoret of Cyrus, *Interpretatio in Canticum Canticorum*, cited in Richard A. Norris Jr., trans. and ed., *The Song of Songs: Interpreted by Early Christian and Medieval Commentators* (Grand Rapids: Eerdmans, 2003), 281.

66. Ambrose, *Isaac, or the Soul* 8.72, cited in J. Robert Wright, ed., *Proverbs, Ecclesiastes, Song of Solomon*, ACCS, Old Testament 9 (Downers Grove, IL: InterVarsity, 2005), 363.

propriety!—in the mouth of the heavenly bridegroom. "I raised you up under an evil tree," he says. "There your mother was corrupted, there she who bore you was violated." The evil tree is one reading of the Vulgate's *sub arbore malo*. It turns the interpretation into a rehearsal of the fall and restoration. The corrupted "mother" is human nature. Once incorruptible, impassible, and immortal, it was degraded by the craft of the Devil into the passible and mortal. As for "she who bore you," that is, of course, Eve "the mother of all," who was "violated by the serpent's suasions." Christ "raised" both. Eve he restored by preserving Mary—the one who bore him—inviolate. Human nature he restored under another tree, the "tree of the cross."[67]

Because of what he has done for the church, he asks that she seal herself with him. The "seal is the humanity of Christ," and "the wax is the human soul, shaped to the image of God" (cf. Col 1:15; 2 Cor 4:16; Gen 1:26–27). The bride is to place this seal upon her heart so that she may remember him in reciprocal love, and as a seal upon her arm so that she may imitate him in her actions. He goes on to describe this love: "Just as death overpowers all the mighty, and is therefore mightier than all, so too love is mightier than all, which has overpowered me who am the mightiest, and brought me to death for your sake. And just as hell is stronger than all bitter things, and therefore not to be broken down, so jealousy is unconquerable—I mean my own envy, by which I envy the Devil because he possesses you, my Bride. . . . Therefore, it is fair that you should love me to the point of . . . undergoing death for my sake."[68]

For the bride, this death-like love "renders one whom it has perfectly taken hold of insensible to earthly desires."[69] "If death releases you from the desire for everything, how much more appropriate is it that the love of God should release you from the desire for everything."[70] For Honorius of Autun, this love is like a "great fire that neither rains nor floods can put out." "Waters" are "flattery" and "floods" are "temptations."[71] Augustine of Hippo points to the martyrs, "on fire with this love" (cf. 1 Cor 13:3). The "many waters," then, are the tears of those who tried to restrain them from death. "But when," he asks with moving eloquence, "did tears—however abundant and with however much force

67. Honorius of Autun, *Expositio in Cantica Canticorum*, cited in Norris, *Song of Songs*, 284–85.

68. Honorius of Autun, *Expositio in Cantica Canticorum*, cited in Norris, *Song of Songs*, 285–86.

69. Gregory the Great, *Forty Gospel Homilies* 9 (11), cited in Wright, *Proverbs, Ecclesiastes, Song of Solomon*, 365.

70. John of Apamea, *Letter* 45, *To Hesychius*, cited in Wright, *Proverbs, Ecclesiastes, Song of Solomon*, 366.

71. Honorius of Autun, *Expositio in Cantica Canticorum*, cited in Norris, *Song of Songs*, 286.

they poured out—put out the fire of love?"[72] If a man gave "all the property of his household in exchange for love, he would despise [what was given away] as if it were nothing." Jesus illustrated this with the parable of the treasure discovered hidden in a field, and with the parable of the pearl of great price (Matt 13:44–46). In line with this, the early church gave up all possessions, and yet "to themselves seemed to lack nothing."[73]

Christ now speaks of a "little sister." This is taken to refer to the gentile church in its infancy.[74] Bede sees Christ conferring with the "synagogue" asking what they can jointly do for her. Christ answers his question by proposing to confer upon the gentile church his own properties of being a wall and a gate. He is a wall around his church, defending it against enemies, and he is the door in that wall by which those who believe enter in (John 10:9; 14:6). The gentile church acquires the double gift. Its teachers become the "wall" against heresies, and its preachers the "gate" by which the willing enter the kingdom. The gentile church replies with alacrity: "Rightly am I named a wall: I have been put together out of 'living stones' (1 Pet 2:5); I have been unified by the bond of love; I have been set upon an immoveable foundation; I cannot be cast down by any blow of a heretical battering ram."[75] Within this wall are the towers, those who are gifted by graces and virtues. While they can withstand the attack of the false teachings, they also, like breasts, provide the needed nourishment to the weaker in the faith. And thus the gentile church rests content in that she has found peace through the work of the bridegroom.[76]

The bride finishes the dialogue. She refers to the "peaceful one,"[77] who had a vineyard "which contains people."[78] This refers, in Christian exegesis, to the "catholic church throughout the world," which is served unwearyingly by its "keepers": the prophets, the apostles, the successors of the prophets and apostles, the heavenly armies—all those who, age after age, guard the church against "malicious agents, whether human beings or spirits." A man bringing a thousand pieces of silver for the fruit of this vineyard signifies one who gives up all for the sake of Christ. Indeed, the perfect number "thousand" indicates the whole world. The bridegroom breaks in to express his appreciation of such sacrifice: "My

72. Augustine of Hippo, cited in Norris, *Song of Songs*, 287.

73. The Venerable Bede, *Expositio in Cantica Canticorum*, cited in Norris, *Song of Songs*, 288.

74. On the other hand, the "little sister" can be taken to be the Jewish people (Aponius, *Exposition of the Song of Songs* 12.29, cited in Wright, *Proverbs, Ecclesiastes, Song of Solomon*, 366–67).

75. The Venerable Bede, *Expositio in Cantica Canticorum*, cited in Norris, *Song of Songs*, 291.

76. The Venerable Bede, *Expositio in Cantica Canticorum*, cited in Norris, *Song of Songs*, 289–91.

77. The Vulgate translates "Solomon" with a common noun: *pacifico*.

78. The Vulgate: *Vinea fuit pacifico in ea quae habet populous*.

vineyard is in my presence . . . [cf. Matt 28:20]; the thousand belong to [me], and two hundred to those who guard its fruits."[79]

The vineyard now makes way for the "gardens"—paradise, in which Christ sits conversing with his heavenly company. Humans have no part in this, having been expelled from Eden through disobedience; but restored humanity, that is, the church, expresses her desire once again to hear his voice.[80] But, in the interim—similar to the Targum—the bride bids the departing bridegroom farewell as he goes (cf. John 16:7) to the higher realms, higher even than the "mountains of spices," that is, the angelic spirits.[81]

CONCLUSION

We saw that Song 8 and Ezekiel 23 speak in unison in the demand both make for exclusive, devoted love. While Song 8 plays out the tenacity of love, Ezekiel 23 plays out the inevitability of its jealousy. Together, they complete the description of love and its jealousy. We understand better what that awful flame (Song 8:6) is capable of. It is a flame that can both sustain life and destroy it. In Ezekiel, the man exhibits this jealousy within marriage. In the Song, the woman weaves it aggressively into her definition of devoted love. If there are two characters who understand love and its jealousy, they are the woman in Song 8 and the husband in Ezekiel 23. They understand well the love that reaches its fullest depth by its complete and non-negotiable custody of the other's loyalty. If not for Song 8, the man of Ezekiel 23 could never be canonically matched by a woman like him. And we would be the poorer for being left holding a lopsided paradigm of love, one in which we only know what the woman must never be, one which echoes the patriarchal power dynamic that defined marriage. It is the text and intertext taken together that shape for us the contours of love characterized by mutual demand and mutual surrender, the only kind of love by which lovers live on in the memories of mortals.

When speaking of the love that should operate between deity and devotee, the same pattern recurs. While Jewish exegesis of the Song shows a God passionately committed to his human wife, Christian allegory sets out a deity who offers love that is steadfast unto death. The Song presents the idealized bride of God—whether she is Israel or the

---

79. The Venerable Bede, *Expositio in Cantica Canticorum*, cited in Norris, *Song of Songs*, 293–94.

80. Ambrose of Milan, cited in Norris, *Song of Songs*, 295.

81. John of Ford, *CXX Sermones*, cited in Norris, *Song of Songs*, 296–97.

church—as equally devoted. She is insensible to competing allurements and unflinching in the face of threat. However, it is when we move beyond the pages of the Song, to pair the Song's devotee with the divine husband of Ezekiel 23, that we can best conceive the consummation of the demand for exclusive love that God makes of his people.

Both human and divine love, the canon helps us understand, are imperfect if love is not exclusive. The definition of this emotion is complete only when we speak of love *and* its jealousy.

10.

Conclusion

"He is altogether lovely!" That is how the female protagonist of the Song of Songs concludes her part-by-part description of her lover (Song 5:16). What we have sought to show is that when texts that make up the prophetic marriage metaphor are juxtaposed with the Song, the texts, *all* taken *together*, make up something *lovely*. They sketch for us the ideal pair of lovers in human-human and divine-human romance. All together, lovely.

The starting point for the intertextual reading was identifying shared iconicity between the Song and prophetic marriage metaphor texts. We settled on four common icons: love-in-separation, beauty, gardens, and love and its jealousy. Engaging each pair of parallel texts resulted in the emergence of a "third" text, that is, the transcript of the "reciprocal reading."[1]

For the icon of love-in-separation, we studied the characterization of the Song's woman in its poems of separation (Song 2:8–3:5 and 5:2–6:3). She began as the "woman at the window," an equivalent of Sisera's mother or Jezebel, all senses alert for sound or sight of her beloved. However, by the end of the rendezvous, the reader was left dissatisfied, unsure whether she had signaled an end to the separation or not. The uncertainty was more than compensated in a nighttime episode. Shrugging off the encumbrances of social strictures, she roamed the city's streets and squares till she chanced upon her lover, whereupon she seized him and brought him back to her house. In a parallel poem, she pays

---

1. Stefan Alkier, "Intertextuality and the Semiotics of Biblical Texts," in *Reading the Bible Intertextually*, ed. Richard B. Hays, Stefan Alkier, and Leroy A. Huizenga (Waco, TX: Baylor University Press, 2009), 12.

dearly for hesitating to open the door to the man and plunges frantically into another nighttime excursion, only to fall into the rough hands of other men. But again, she will not give up seeking until she has brought to closure the state of separation.

We set these poems alongside an isomorphic text, Hosea 2. This is the inner speech of a husband who has lost his wife to her many lovers. His solutions for an end to separation span the full range of human emotions from murderous rage to besotted (re-)wooing. One way is to subject his wayward wife to containment; another is to brutally employ the power marriage allows the man and make a public show of her; a third route is to compete with her lovers by a second round of courtship, perhaps even more tender than the first, with the hope that he can permanently end their long separation. Either the husband proceeds from one strategy to the next, or he thinks them through and rejects the first two before choosing the third.

The Song's woman and Hosea's man match each other in anguished persistence—a persistence that requires them to elbow social and cultural constraints recklessly out of the way till they reach and regain the lost beloved. While the end is laudable and even prescriptive to human romantic relationship, the twenty-first-century reader hesitates to applaud the actual or potential use of male power as a means to that end.

The second theme was that of beauty. If the three poems in admiration of the Song's woman are to be given any credit, she is unbelievably fair of face and full in form. Our endeavor, however, was not to find her a canonical match for bodily beauty. Rather, we noted her uncanny ability to create beauty. She conjures up her lover from memory, piece by breathtaking piece, into a godlike construct (Song 5:10–16). "This is my beloved!" she declares to a smitten audience. A match for this woman, then, would be a man who can similarly bestow beauty on the one he loves. Such a man is located in Ezekiel 16:3–14, a man whose affectionate care turns a newborn abandoned in her birth-blood into a woman whose beauty gains international acclaim. If the Song's woman and Ezekiel's man are meant for each other, it is in the capacity to establish as beautiful the object of their affection. Indeed, it is their affection that energizes the creation of the beautiful beloved. But again, our admiration for the man is restricted by the turn the story takes. The foundling-wife turns dissolute, and the furious husband turns upon her his "jealous anger" (Ezek 16:38).

The third section examined the icons of gardens and vineyards, used as images of the female beloved. Here we studied side-by-side the Songs of Lebanon (Song 4:8–5:1) with the Song of the Vineyard in Isaiah 5:1–7.

The resonance across the intertexts was of garden and gardener. The Song of the Vineyard featured a husbandman who invested extraordinary energy into a plot of land. It lay on a sunny hillside, its soil dripping with promise of yield. So optimistic is the owner that, besides the usual labor of clearing and plowing the ground, he invests well into the future. Looking toward a day when the returns will overtake the investment, he has permanent structures erected both for guarding what he expects will be a high-value property, and for harvesting the looked-for bumper yields. After this unusual capital investment, how deep his frustration when he finds that his carefully chosen stock of vines bears diseased, putrid grapes!

Meanwhile, the Songs of Lebanon describe a garden that would delight the heart of Isaiah's gardener with a reward befitting his labors. It is at once an orchard and a spice garden. Its herbs and trees are dense in leaf and turgid with sap drawn from the fountain that waters them. They droop with "choice" fruit and are heavy with the "finest" spices. The air is redolent with ripeness, and should the wind stir up the clouds of sweetness, the heady scents would pour over the enclosing walls to the world outside. It is a garden that eagerly waits for its owner to come in and revel in its yield. Here is the idyll of "arboreal ardor," where the lover deeply cares for his beloved and the beloved responds vigorously to that care.

The fourth section studied love and its jealousy. From the intertexts of Song 8:5–14 and Ezekiel 23 emerged the profile of lovers who demand exclusive affection. The Song's woman speaks of sealing her beloved to establish her inalienable ownership of him. Her love gains depth from jealousy—a jealousy that requires that her beloved's devotion be undividedly hers. Her Ezekielian counterpart has exactly such an expectation, directed at a pair of wives who share out their attentions and their bodies with an appalling lack of restraint. We inferred that lovers who insist on each other's loyalty have discerned the rightful function of jealousy. Yet, while we appreciate exclusivity in human romance, we are horrified at the outcome of the failed marriages in Ezekiel 23. As in other instances of the prophetic marriage metaphor, the betrayed husband takes into his hands the vicious privileges patriarchy allows him. The brutality visited on the wanton wife seems to exceed the violence she perpetrated on the marriage.

When readers confine themselves to the world-of-two created by the Song of Songs, they come away with prescriptions for what human love relationships can be. These are ideals for seeking and finding, for discerning beauty in the object of affection, for devoted care that yields the hoped-for reward, and for mutuality of exclusive loyalty. The Song's male and female protagonists demonstrate these, though perhaps not equally. To the delight of most feminist critics, the female dominates. In the parallel texts in Hosea, Ezekiel, and Isaiah, the Song's exuberant female meets an equally red-blooded male. Whether in the ardor of love or in the agony of separation, they can match each other measure for measure. Reading across the isomorphic intertexts, the ideals for human romantic love gain a richness and depth that well surpasses what is possible within the boundaries of the Song of Songs.

On the other hand, the reciprocal reading creates an intracanonical critique. If the world of the Song of Songs is a return to the paradisiac conditions of pre-fall Eden, it functions as a magnifying glass held over the tragedy of marriage in the prophetic texts. Here are marriages governed by power relations rather than by love; here are wives who breathlessly chase after other men; here are livid husbands authorized by patriarchy to evict the errant wife with a certificate of divorce, to strip and shame her publicly, to terrorize her with death threats, to make her body the location of their vicious vengefulness. The Song of Songs reproachfully reminds the reader of what can and *should* be in human marriage. It returns us to Paradise, a world in which—to use Carr's terms—hierarchy is replaced by mutuality; terror by tenderness; and betrayal by trust.[2]

When read within the canonical metaphor for divine-human relationship, the Song of Songs continues its critique. It rues the sad fact that Israel's wrongdoing can most effectively be communicated to her through the savage rhetoric of gendered power dynamics. The Song throws into relief the catastrophic scope of divine-human estrangement—an estrangement that requires the dramatizing of a human marriage gone so horrifically wrong that the telling of the details becomes pornography. The Song, in its conversations with the prophetic texts, regrets that the language of "gender terror"[3] (whether applied to the situation of marriage or of war) may be the only words that sinful Israel will understand and respond to. The Song critiques the *manner* in which the divine-human crisis must be articulated.

Within the allegorical world of the Song of Songs that Jewish and Christian traditions have created with painstaking attention to detail, the deep fissures of alienation—between YHWH and Israel, between Christ and his church—close. Here is a devotee for whom deity is "the one my

---

2. David M. Carr, *The Erotic Word: Sexuality, Spirituality and the Bible* (Oxford: Oxford University Press, 2003), 83–84.

3. David M. Carr, "Ancient Sexuality and Divine Eros: Rereading the Bible Through the Lens of the Song of Songs," *USQR* 54, no. 3–4 (2000): 14.

soul loves." She pursues him till she finds him; she recites the praise of his beauty; she will give herself to none but him; and she reminds herself with confident delight that he belongs to her and she to him. Her love for him inhabits its full human potential.

This divine-human ideal in the Song of Songs amplifies to assume canonical proportions when it is read intertextually with the prophetic marriage texts. In each of the pairs of intertexts, the woman reflects faithfully the many-splendored love of the divine husband. In this, the Israel of the Song of Songs compensates canonically for the persistently licentious Israel of prophetic literature. Without the Song's contribution to the marital metaphor, the reader-devotee would have no starting point from which to launch their imagination for what can and *should* be between God and his people.

That is why, when the cringeworthy marital metaphor texts are read alongside the embarrassingly uninhibited lyrics of the Song of Songs as prescriptions for human and divine-human affective dynamics, these texts become—all together—lovely.

Bibliography

Abernethy, Andrew T. *Eating in Isaiah: Approaching the Role of Food and Drink in Isaiah's Structure and Message.* Biblical Interpretation Series. Leiden: Brill, 2014.

Abma, R. *Bonds of Love: Methodic Studies of Prophetic Texts with Marriage Imagery (Isaiah 50:1–3 and 54:1–10, Hosea 1–3, Jeremiah 2–3).* Assen: Van Gorcum, 1999.

Albright, W. F. "Some Canaanite-Phoenician Sources of Hebrew Wisdom." In *Wisdom in Israel and in the Ancient Near East,* edited by M. Noth and D. Winton Thomas, 1–15. Leiden: Brill, 1960.

Alden, Robert L. "Song of Songs 8:12a: Who Said It?" *JETS* 31, no. 3 (1988): 271–78.

Alexander, Philip S. "The Song of Songs as Historical Allegory: Notes on the Development of an Exegetical Tradition." In *Targumic and Cognate Studies in Honour of Martin McNamara,* edited by Kevin J. Cathcart and Michael Maher, 14–29. JSOTSup 230. Sheffield: Sheffield Academic, 1996.

Alkier, Stefan. "Intertextuality and the Semiotics of Biblical Texts." In *Reading the Bible Intertextually,* edited by Richard B. Hays, Stefan Alkier, and Leroy A. Huizenga, 3–21. Waco, TX: Baylor University Press, 2009.

Allen, Leslie C. *Ezekiel 20–48.* Word Bible Commentary 29. Waco, TX: Word, 1990.

Alter, Robert. "Afterword." In *The Song of Songs: A New Translation with an Introduction and Commentary,* edited by Ariel Bloch and Chana Bloch, 119–31. New York: Random House, 1995.

———. *The Art of Biblical Poetry.* New York: Basic Books, 2011.

Andersen, Francis I., and David Noel Freedman. *Hosea: A New Translation with Introduction and Commentary.* Anchor Bible 24. New Haven: Yale University Press, 1980.

Aramaic Targum to Song of Songs. Hebrew text compiled from *Mikraot Gedolot* and Raphael Hai Melamed. *The Targum to Canticles according to Six Yemen MSS*. Philadelphia: Dropsie College, 1921. English translation by Jay Treat. https://tinyurl.com/yb37vrk4.

Arbel, Daphna V. "'My Vineyard, My Very Own, Is for Myself.'" In *The Song of Songs*, edited by Athalya Brenner and Carole R. Fontaine, 90–101. A Feminist Companion to the Bible, Series 2. Sheffield: Sheffield Academic, 2000.

Assis, Elie. *Flashes of Fire: A Literary Analysis of the Song of* Songs. New York: T&T Clark, 2009.

Bakhtin, M. *The Bakhtin Reader: Selected Writings of Bakhtin, Medvedev and Voloshmov*. Edited by P. Morris. London: Edward Arnold, 1994.

———. *The Dialogic Imagination*. Edited by M. Holquist. Translated by C. Emerson and M. Holquist. Austin: University of Texas Press, 1981.

———. *The Formal Method in Literary Scholarship*. Translated by A. Wehrle. Baltimore: Johns Hopkins University Press, 1978.

———. *Problems of Dostoevsky's Poetics*. Translated and edited by C. Emerson. Manchester: Manchester University Press, 1963.

Barbiero, Gianni. *Song of Songs: A Close Reading*. Translated by Michael Tait. Supplements to Vetus Testamentum 144. Leiden: Brill, 2011.

Barton, John. "*Déjà Lu*: Intertextuality, Method or Theory?" In *Reading Job Intertextually*, edited by Katharine Dell and Will Kynes, 1–16. New York: Bloomsbury, 2013.

Baumann, Gerlinde. *Love and Violence: Marriage as Metaphor for the Relationship between YHWH and Israel in the Prophetic Books*. Translated by Linda M. Maloney. Collegeville, MN: Liturgical, 2003.

———. "Prophetic Objections to Yahweh as the Violent Husband of Israel: Reinterpretations of the Prophetic Marriage Metaphor in Second Isaiah (Isaiah 40–55)." In *Prophets and Daniel*, edited by Athalya Brenner, 88–120. A Feminist Companion to the Bible, Series 2. Sheffield: Sheffield Academic, 2001.

Baumgartner, Walter, Ludwig Koehler, and Johann Stamm. *The Hebrew and Aramaic Lexicon of the Old Testament*. Leiden: Brill, 2000.

Beale, Timothy K. "Intertextuality." In *Handbook of Postmodern Biblical Interpretation*, edited by A. Adams, 128–29. St. Louis: Chalice, 2000.

Beeby, H. D. *Grace Abounding: A Commentary on the Book of Hosea*. Grand Rapids: Eerdmans, 1989.

Bekkenkamp, Jonneke, and Fokkelien van Dijk-Hemmes. "Canon and Cultural Traditions." In *A Feminist Companion to the Song of Songs*, edited by Athalya Brenner, 67–85. A Feminist Companion to the Bible. Sheffield: Sheffield Academic, 1993.

Ben Zvi, Ehud. "Observations on the Marital Metaphor of YHWH and Israel in

Its Ancient Israelite Context: General Considerations and Particular Images in Hosea 1.2." *JSOT* 28, no. 3 (2004): 363–84.

Bergant, Diane. *The Song of Songs.* Berit Olam. Collegeville, MN: Liturgical, 2001.

Bernat, David. "Biblical *Wasfs* beyond Song of Songs." *JSOT* 28, no. 3 (2004): 327–49.

Bird, Phyllis. "The Harlot as Heroine: Narrative Art and Social Presupposition in Three Old Testament Texts." *Semeia* 46 (1989): 119–39.

———. "'To Play the Harlot': An Inquiry into Old Testament Metaphor." In *Gender and Difference in Ancient Israel*, edited by Peggy L. Day, 75–94. Minneapolis: Fortress Press, 1989.

Birch, Bruce C. *Hosea, Joel, and Amos.* Westminster Bible Companion. Louisville: Westminster John Knox, 1997.

Black, Fiona C. "Beauty or the Beast? The Grotesque Body in the Song of Songs." *Biblical Interpretation* 8, no. 3 (2000): 302–23.

Blenkinsopp, Joseph. *Ezekiel.* Interpretation. Louisville: John Knox, 1990.

Bloch, Ariel, and Chana Bloch. *The Song of Songs: A New Translation with an Introduction and Commentary.* New York: Random House, 1995.

Block, Daniel I. *The Book of Ezekiel: Chapters 1–24.* NICOT. Grand Rapids: Eerdmans, 1997.

Boadt, Lawrence. "The A:B:B:A Chiasm of Identical Roots in Ezekiel." *VT* 25, no. 4 (1975): 693–99.

Boersma, Matthew. "Scent in Song: Exploring Scented Symbols in the Song of Songs." *Conversations with the Biblical World* 31 (2011): 80–94.

Bolle, Kees W. "Hieros gamos." *Encyclopaedia of Religion* 6:317–22.

Bowen, Nancy R. *Ezekiel.* Abingdon Old Testament Commentaries. Nashville: Abingdon, 2010.

Brenner, Athalya. "Come Back, Come Back the Shulammite." In *On Humour and the Comic in the Hebrew Bible*, edited by Y. T. Radday and Athalya Brenner, 251–76. Sheffield: JSOT/Almond, 1990.

———, ed. *A Feminist Companion to the Song of Songs.* A Feminist Companion to the Bible. Sheffield: Sheffield Academic, 1993.

———. *The Intercourse of Knowledge: On Gendering Desire and "Sexuality" in the Hebrew Bible.* Leiden: Brill, 1997.

———. "Pornoprophetics Revisited: Some Additional Reflections." *JSOT* 70 (1996): 63–86.

———. "On Prophetic Propaganda and the Politics of 'Love': The Case of Jeremiah." In *A Feminist Companion to the Latter Prophets*, edited by Athalya Brenner, 256–74. A Feminist Companion to the Bible. Sheffield: Sheffield Academic, 1995.

————. "To See Is to Assume: Whose Love Is Celebrated in the Song of Songs?" *Biblical Interpretation* 1, no. 3 (1993): 265–84.

Brenner, Athalya, and Fokkelien van Dijk-Hemmes. *On Gendering Texts: Female and Male Voices in the Hebrew Bible*. Leiden: Brill, 1993.

Brownlee, William H. *Ezekiel 1–19*. WBC 28. Waco, TX: Word, 1986.

Brueggemann, Walter. *Isaiah 1–39*. Westminster Bible Companion. Louisville: Westminster John Knox, 1998.

Burton, Joan B. "Themes of Female Desire and Self-Assertion in the Song of Songs and Hellenistic Poetry." In *Perspectives on the Song of Songs*, edited by Anselm C. Hagedorn, 181–205. Berlin: de Gruyter, 2005.

Carmy, Shalom. "Perfect Harmony." *First Things*, December 2010, 34–36.

Carr, David M. "Ancient Sexuality and Divine Eros: Rereading the Bible Through the Lens of the Song of Songs." *Union Seminary Quarterly Review* 54, no. 3–4 (2000): 1–18.

————. *The Erotic Word: Sexuality, Spirituality and the Bible*. Oxford: Oxford University Press, 2003.

————. "Gender and the Shaping of Desire in the Song of Songs and its Interpretation." *JBL* 119, no. 2 (2000): 233–48.

————. "Passion for God: A Center in Biblical Theology." *Horizons in Biblical Theology* 23 (2001): 1–24.

Carr, David M., and Colleen M. Conway. "The Divine-Human Marriage Matrix and Construction of Gender and 'Bodies' in the Christian Bible." In *Sacred Marriages: The Divine-Human Sexual Metaphor from Sumer to Early Christianity*, edited by Martti Nissinen and Risto Uro, 275–303. Winona Lake, IN: Eisenbrauns, 2008.

Carr, G. Lloyd. *The Song of Solomon: An Introduction and Commentary*. Tyndale Old Testament Commentary. Leicester: InterVarsity, 1984.

Chapman, Cynthia R. "Sculpted Warriors: Sexuality and the Sacred in the Depiction of Warfare in the Assyrian Palace Reliefs and in Ezekiel 23:14–17." In *The Aesthetics of Violence in the Prophets*, edited by Claudia V. Camp and Andrew Mein, 1–17. Library of Hebrew Bible, Old Testament Studies 517. New York: T&T Clark, 2010.

Childs, Brevard S. *Isaiah: A Commentary*. Old Testament Library. Louisville: Westminster John Knox, 2001.

Clements, Ronald E. *Isaiah 1–39*. New Century Bible Commentary. Grand Rapids: Eerdmans, 1980.

Clines, David J. A. "Hosea 2: Structure and Interpretation." In *On the Way to the Postmodern: Old Testament Essays, 1967–1988*, edited by David J. A. Clines, 293–313. Vol. 1 of JSOTSup 292. Sheffield: Sheffield Academic, 1998.

————. "Why Is There a Song of Songs and What Does It Do to You If You

Read It?" In *Interested Parties: The Ideology of Writers and Readers of the Hebrew Bible*, edited by David J. A. Clines, 94–121. JSOTSup 205. Sheffield: Sheffield Academic, 1995.

Cogan, Mordechai. "A Technical Term for Exposure." *JNES* 27 (1968): 133–35.

Cohen, Gerson D. "The Song of Songs and the Jewish Religious Mentality." In *Studies in the Variety of Rabbinic Cultures*, 3–17. Philadelphia: Jewish Publication Society, 1991.

Cohen, Martin S. *The Shi'ur Qomah: Liturgy and Theurgy in Pre-Kabbalistic Jewish Mysticism*. Lanham, NY: University Press of America, 1983.

Cook, Albert. *The Root of the Thing: A Study of Job and the Song of Songs*. Bloomington: Indiana University Press, 1968.

Cooper, Jerrold S. "New Cuneiform Parallels to the Song of Songs." *JBL* 90 (1971): 157–62.

———. "Sacred Marriage and Popular Cult in Early Mesopotamia." In *Official Cult and Popular Religion in the Ancient Near East: Papers of the First Colloquium on the Ancient Near East—The City and Its Life, Held at the Middle Eastern Culture Centre in Japan (Mitaya, Tokyo), March 20–22, 1992*, edited by Eiko Matsushima, 81–96. Heidelberg: Carl Winter, 1993.

Corney, Richard W. "What Does 'Literal Meaning' Mean? Some Commentaries on the Song of Songs," *Anglican Theological Review* 4 (1998): 494–516.

Craigie, Peter C. *Ezekiel*. Philadelphia: Westminster, 1983.

———. "The Poetry of Ugarit and Israel." *TynBul* 22 (1971): 3–31.

Curtis, Edward M. *Ecclesiastes and Song of Songs*. Teach the Text Commentary Series. Grand Rapids: Baker, 2013.

Dalman, Gustaf H. *Palästinischer Diwan: Als Beitrag zur Volkskunde Palästinas*. Leipzig: Hinrichs, 1901.

Darr, Katheryn Pfisterer. "Ezekiel's Justifications of God: Teaching Troubled Texts." *JSOT* 55 (1992): 97–117.

Dass, M. "Divorce (?) Formula in Hos 2:4a." *Indian Theological Studies* 34 (1997): 56–88.

Davidson, A. B. *The Book of the Prophet Ezekiel*. Cambridge: Cambridge University Press, 1892.

Davidson, R. M. "Is God Present in the Song of Songs?" *Journal of the Adventist Theological Society* 16 (2005): 143–54.

Davies, G. I. *Hosea*. New Century Bible Commentary. Grand Rapids: Eerdmans, 1992.

Davis, Ellen F. *Getting Involved with God: Rediscovering the Old Testament*. Cambridge, MA: Cowley, 2001.

Day, Linda. "Rhetoric and Domestic Violence in Ezekiel 16." *Biblical Interpretation* 8, no. 3 (2000): 205–30.

Day, Peggy L. "Adulterous Jerusalem's Imagined Demise: Death of a Metaphor in Ezekiel XVI." *VT* 50, no. 3 (2000): 287–309.

Dearman, J. Andrew. *The Book of Hosea*. NICOT. Grand Rapids: Eerdmans, 2010.

Dell, Katharine J. "Does the Song of Songs have any Connections to Wisdom?" In *Perspectives on the Song of Songs*, edited by Anselm C. Hagedorn, 8–26. Berlin: de Gruyter, 2005.

———. "Introduction." In *Reading Job Intertextually*, edited by Katharine Dell and Will Kynes, xv–xxiii. New York: Bloomsbury, 2013.

Dharamraj, Havilah. *A Prophet Like Moses? A Narrative-Theological Reading of the Elijah Stories*. Paternoster Biblical Monographs. Milton Keynes: Paternoster, 2011.

Dijk-Hemmes, Fokkelien van. "The Imagination of Power and the Power of Imagination: An Intertextual Analysis of Two Biblical Love Songs: The Song of Songs and Hosea 2." *JSOT* 44 (1989): 75–88.

———. "The Metaphorization of Woman in Prophetic Speech: An Analysis of Ezekiel 23." *VT* 4, no. 2 (1993): 162–70.

———. "Traces of Women's Texts in the Hebrew Bible." In *On Gendering Texts: Female and Male Voices in the Hebrew Bible*, edited by Athalya Brenner and Fokkelien van Dijk-Hemmes, 17–109. Leiden: Brill, 1993.

Driver, G. R. "Difficult Words in the Hebrew Prophets." In *Studies in Old Testament Prophecy Presented to Professor Theodore H. Robinson*, edited by H. H. Rowley, 52–72. Edinburgh: T&T Clark, 1950.

Eichrodt, Walther. *Ezekiel*. Translated by Cosslett Quin. Old Testament Library. London: SCM, 1970.

Elliott, Mary T. *The Literary Unity of the Canticle*. Frankfurt: Peter Lang, 1989.

Emerton, J. A. "The Translation of Isaiah 5,1." In *The Scriptures and the Scrolls: Studies in Honour of A. S. van der Woude*, edited by F. Garcia Martinez, A. Hilhorst, and C. J. Labuschagne, 18–30. Supplements to Vetus Testamentum 49. Leiden: Brill, 1992.

Eslinger, Lyle. "The Case of an Immodest Lady Wrestler in Deuteronomy XXV 11–12." *VT* 31 (1981): 269–81.

———. "Inner-Biblical Exegesis and Inner-Biblical Allusion: The Question of Category." *VT* 1 (1992): 47–58.

Estes, Daniel J. "The Song of Songs." In *Ecclesiastes and the Song of Songs*. Edited by Daniel C. Fredericks and Daniel J. Estes. Apollos Old Testament Commentary 16. Downers Grove, IL: InterVarsity, 2010.

Exum, J. Cheryl. *Plotted, Shot and Painted: Cultural Representations of Biblical Women*. JSOTSup 215. Sheffield: Sheffield Academic, 1996.

———. *Song of Songs: A Commentary*. Louisville: Westminster John Knox, 2005.

Falk, Marcia. *The Song of Songs: A New Translation and Interpretation.* New York: HarperCollins, 1973.

Fewell, Donna Nolan. "Introduction: Writing, Reading and Relating." In *Reading between Texts: Intertextuality and the Hebrew Bible,* edited by Donna Nolan Fewell, 11–20. Literary Currents in Biblical Interpretation. Louisville: Westminster John Knox, 1992.

Fishbane, Michael. *Biblical Interpretation in Ancient Israel.* Oxford: Clarendon, 1985.

———. "Sin and Judgment in the Prophecies of Ezekiel." *Interpretation* 38, no. 2 (1984): 131–50.

———. "Types of Biblical Intertextuality." In *Congress Volume: Oslo 1998,* edited by André Lemaire and Magne Sæbø, 39–44. Supplements to Vetus Testamentum 80. Leiden: Brill, 2000.

Fitzmyer, Joseph A. *The Genesis Apocryphon of Qumran Cave I.* Rome: Pontifical Institute Press, 1971.

Fox, Michael V. "The Entertainment Song Genre in Egyptian Literature." In *Egyptological Studies,* edited by Sarah Israelit Groll, 268–316. ScrHier 28. Jerusalem: Magnes, 1982.

———. "Love, Passion and Perception in Israelite and Egyptian Love Poetry." *JBL* 102, no. 2 (1983): 219–28.

———. "Scholia to Canticles." *VT* 33, no. 2 (1983): 199–206.

———. *The Song of Songs and the Ancient Egyptian Love Songs.* Madison: University of Wisconsin Press, 1985.

Friedman, Mordechai A. "Israel's Response in Hosea 2:17b: 'You are my Husband.'" *JBL* 99, no. 2 (1980): 199–204.

Frymer-Kensky, Tikvah. "The Ideology of Gender in the Bible and the Ancient Near East." In *DUMU-E2-DUB-BA-A: Studies in Honour of Åke W Sköberg,* edited by Herman Behrens, Darlene Loding, Martha T. Roth, 185–91. Philadelphia: Samuel Noah Kramer Fund, 1989.

Galambush, Julie. *Jerusalem in the Book of Ezekiel: City as Yahweh's Wife.* SBLDS 130. Atlanta: Scholars, 1992.

Garrett, Duane. "Song of Songs." In *Song of Songs, Lamentations,* by Duane Garrett and Paul R. House, 1–265. Word Biblical Commentary 23B. Nashville: Thomas Nelson, 2004.

Gault, Brian P. "An Admonition against 'Rousing Love': The Meaning of the Enigmatic Refrain in Song of Songs." *Bulletin for Biblical Research* 20, no. 2 (2010): 161–84.

———. "A 'Do Not Disturb' Sign? Reexamining the Adjuration Refrain in Song of Songs." *JSOT* 36, no. 1 (2011): 93–104.

Geller, Markham J. "The Elephantine Papyri and Hosea 2,3: Evidence for the

Form of the Early Jewish Divorce Writ." *Journal for the Study of Judaism in the Persian, Hellenistic and Roman Period* 8, no. 2 (1977): 139–48.

Gerleman, G. *Ruth, Das Hohelied.* BKAT 18. Neukirchen-Vluyn: Neukirchener, 1965.

Gile, Jason. "Ezekiel 16 and the Song of Moses: A Prophetic Transformation?" *JBL* 130, no. 1 (2011): 87–108.

Gledhill, Tom. *The Message of the Song of Songs: The Lyrics of Love.* Bible Speaks Today. Leicester: InterVarsity, 1994.

Gordis, Robert. "The Root דגל in the Song of Songs." *JBL* 88, no. 2 (1969): 203–4.

———. *The Song of Songs: A Study, Modern Translation and Commentary.* Text and Studies of the Jewish Theological Seminary of America 20. New York: Jewish Theological Seminary of America, 1954.

Gordon, Cyrus H. "New Directions." *Bulletin of the American Society of Papyrologists* 15 (1978): 59–66.

Gordon, Pamela, and Harold C. Washington. "Rape as a Military Metaphor in the Hebrew Bible." In *A Feminist Companion to the Latter Prophets*, edited by Athalya Brenner, 308–25. A Feminist Companion to the Bible. Sheffield: Sheffield Academic, 1995.

Goshen-Gottstein, M. H. "Philologisch e Miszellen zu den Qumrantexten." *RevQ* 2 (1959–60): 43–51.

Goulder, Michael D. *The Song of Fourteen Songs.* JSOTSup 36. Sheffield: JSOT Press, 1986.

Gray, John Buchanan. *Isaiah 1–39.* ICC 1. Edinburgh: T&T Clark, 1912.

Greenberg, Moshe. *Ezekiel 1–20: A New Translation with Introduction and Commentary.* Anchor Bible 22. Garden City, NY: Doubleday, 1983.

———. *Ezekiel 21–37: A New Translation with Introduction and Commentary.* Anchor Bible 22A. New York: Doubleday, 1997.

Greer, Rowan A. *Theodore of Mopsuestia: Exegete and Theologian.* Westminster, UK: Faith, 1961.

Grossberg, Daniel. *Centripetal and Centrifugal Structures in Biblical Poetry.* Atlanta: Scholars, 1989.

———. "Nature, Humanity, and Love in Song of Songs." *Interpretation* 59, no. 3 (2005): 229–42.

———. "Two Kinds of Sexual Relationships in the Bible." *Hebrew Studies* 35, no. 1 (1994): 7–25.

Hagedorn, Anselm C. "Jealousy and Desire at Night: *Fragmentum Grenfellianum* and Song of Songs." In *Perspectives on the Song of Songs*, edited by Anselm C. Hagedorn, 206–27. Berlin: de Gruyter, 2005.

————. "Of Foxes and Vineyards: Greek Perspectives on the Song of Songs." *VT* 53, no. 3 (2003): 337–52.

Hallo, William W. "For Love Is as Strong as Death." *JANES* 22 (1993): 45–50.

————. "'As the Seal Upon Thine Arm': Glyptic Metaphors in the Biblical World." In *Ancient Seals and the Bible*, edited by Leonard Gorelick and Elizabeth Williams-Forte, 7–17. Occasional Papers on the Near East 2/1. Malibu, CA: Undena, 1983.

Halperin, David J. *The Faces of the Chariot: Early Jewish Responses to Ezekiel's Vision.* Tübingen: Mohr Siebeck, 1988.

————. *Seeking Ezekiel: Text and Psychology.* University Park: Pennsylvania State University Press, 1993.

Hals, Ronald M. *Ezekiel.* Forms of Old Testament Literature 19. Grand Rapids: Eerdmans, 1989.

Harding, Kathryn. "'I Sought Him but I Did Not Find Him': The Elusive Lover in the Song of Songs." *Biblical Interpretation* 16 (2008): 43–59.

Harris, Rivkah. "Inanna-Ishtar as Paradox and a Coincidence of Opposites." *HR* 30 (1991): 261–78.

Hess, Richard S. *Song of Songs.* Baker Commentary on the Old Testament. Grand Rapids: Baker, 2005.

Hicks, R. Lansing. "The Door of Love." In *Love and Death in the Ancient Near East: Essays in Honour of Marvin H Pope*, edited by John H. Marks and Robert M. Good, 153–58. Guildford, CT: Four Quarters, 1987.

Hillers, Delbert. *Treaty Curses and the Old Testament Prophets.* Rome: Pontifical Biblical Institute, 1964.

Hoffner, Harry H. "Symbols for Masculinity and Feminity," *JBL* 85 (1966): 326–34.

House, Paul R. *Lamentations.* Word Biblical Commentary 23B. Nashville: Thomas Nelson, 2004.

Hubbard, David Allan. *Hosea: An Introduction and Commentary.* Tyndale Old Testament Commentaries. Leicester: InterVarsity, 1989.

Hunt, Patrick. *Poetry in the Song of Songs: A Literary Analysis.* SBL 96. New York: Peter Lang, 2008.

Hunter, Richard. "'Sweet Talk': *Song of Songs* and the Traditions of Greek Poetry." In *Perspectives on the Song of Songs*, edited by Anselm C. Hagedorn, 228–44. Berlin: de Gruyter, 2005.

Huwiler, Elizabeth. "Song of Songs." In *Proverbs, Ecclesiastes and Song of Songs*, edited by Roland E. Murphy and Elizabeth Huwiler, 221–90. New International Bible Commentary. Peabody, MA: Hendrickson, 1999.

Imray, Kathryn. "Love Is (Strong as) Death: Reading the Song of Songs through Proverbs 1–9." *CBQ* 75, no. 4 (2013): 649–65.

Jacobson, Diane. "Hosea 2: A Case Study on Biblical Authority." *Currents in Theology and Mission* 23, no. 3 (1996): 165–72.

Jacobsen, Thorkild. *Toward the Image of Tammuz and Other Essays on Mesopotamian History and Culture.* Cambridge, MA: Harvard University Press, 1970.

———. *The Treasures of Darkness: A History of Mesopotamian Religion.* New Haven: Yale University Press, 1976.

Jenson, Robert W. *Ezekiel.* London: SCM, 2009.

———. *Song of Songs.* Interpretation. Louisville: John Knox, 2005.

Josephus. *The New Complete Works of Josephus.* Translated by William Whiston and with commentary by Paul L. Maier. Revised and expanded. Grand Rapids: Kregel, 1999.

Joüon, Paul. *Le Cantique Des Cantiques: Commentaire Philologique Et Exegetique.* Paris: Beauchesne, 1909.

Joüon, Paul, and T. Muraoka. *A Grammar of Biblical Hebrew.* Vol 2, *Subsidia Biblica 14/II.* Rome: Pontifical Biblical Institute, 2005.

Joyce, Paul M. *Ezekiel: A Commentary.* Library of Hebrew Bible, Old Testament Studies 482. London: T&T Clark, 2007.

Kaiser, Otto. *Isaiah 1–12.* Translated by R. A. Wilson. London: SCM, 1972.

Kalmanofsky, Amy. "The Dangerous Sisters of Jeremiah and Ezekiel." *JBL* 130, no. 2 (2011): 299–312.

Kamionkowski, S. Tamar. *Gender Reversal and Cosmic Chaos: A Study on the Book of Ezekiel.* JSOTSup 368. Sheffield: Sheffield Academic, 2003.

———. "Gender Reversal in Ezekiel 16." In *A Feminist Companion to Prophets and Daniel,* edited by Athalya Brenner, 170–85. A Feminist Companion to the Bible, Series 2. Sheffield: Sheffield Academic, 2001.

———. "'In Your Blood, Live' (Ezekiel 16:6): A Reconsideration of Meir Malul's Adoption Formula." In *Bringing the Hidden to Light: Studies in Honor of Stephen A. Geller,* edited by Kathryn F. Kravitz and Diane M. Sharon, 103–13. Winona Lake, IN: Eisenbrauns, 2007.

Keefe, Alice A. *Woman's Body and the Social Body in Hosea.* JSOTSup 338. Gender, Culture, Theory 10. Sheffield: Sheffield Academic, 2001.

Keel, Othmar. *The Song of Songs: A Continental Commentary.* Translated by Frederick J. Gaiser. Minneapolis: Augsburg Fortress, 1994.

Keene, Frederick W. "Anger and Pain in Hosea." *Continuum* 3 (1994): 204–17.

Keil, C. F. *Ezekiel, Daniel.* Translated by James Martin and M. G. Easton. Commentary on the Old Testament 9. Peabody, MA: Hendrickson, 1996.

Kidner, Derek. *Love to the Loveless: The Story and Message of Hosea.* Bible Speaks Today. Leicester: InterVarsity, 1981.

Kingsmill, Edmee. *The Song of Songs and the Eros of God: A Study in Biblical Intertextuality*. Oxford: Oxford University Press, 2009.

Kissane, Edward J. *The Book of Isaiah 1–39*. Vol. 1. Rev. ed. Dublin: Browne and Nolan, 1960.

Klein, Ralph W. *Ezekiel: The Prophet and His Message*. Columbia: University of South Carolina Press, 1988.

Korpel, Marjo C. A. "The Literary Genre of the Song of the Vineyard (Isa. 5:1–7)." In *The Structural Analysis of Biblical and Canaanite Poetry*, edited by Willem van der Meer and Johannes C. de Moor, 119–55. JSOTSup 74. Sheffield: Sheffield Academic, 1988.

Kramer, Samuel Noah. *The Sacred Marriage Rite: Aspects of Faith, Myth and Ritual in Ancient Sumer*. Bloomington: Indiana University Press, 1969.

Krinetzki, G. *Kommentar zum Hohenlied: Bildsprache und Theologische Botschaft*. BBET 16. Bern: Peter D. Lang, 1981.

Kristeva, Julia. *The Kristeva Reader*. Edited by Toril Moi. New York: Columbia University Press, 1986.

———. "Word, Dialogue and Novel." In *Desire in Language: A Semiotic Approach to Language and Art*, 64–91. Translated by T. Gora and A. Jardine. Edited by L. S. Roudiez. New York: Columbia University Press, 1980.

Kruger, P. A. "The Hem of the Garment in Marriage: The Meaning of the Symbolic Gesture in Ruth 3:9 and Ezek 16:8." *JSNL* 12 (1984): 79–86.

———. "Israel, the Harlot." *JSNL* 11 (1987): 107–17.

LaCocque, Andre. *Romance She Wrote: A Hermeneutical Essay on Song of Songs*. Harrisburg, PA: Trinity, 1998.

Landy, Francis. "Beauty and the Enigma: An Inquiry into Some Interrelated Episodes of the Song of Songs." *JSOT* 17 (1980): 55–106.

———. *Hosea*. 2nd ed. Sheffield: Sheffield Phoenix, 2011.

———. *Paradoxes of Paradise: Identity and Difference in the Song of Songs*. 2nd ed. Sheffield: Phoenix, 2011.

———. "The Song of Songs and the Garden of Eden." *JBL* 98, no. 4 (1979): 513–28.

———. "In the Wilderness of Speech: Problems of Metaphor in Hosea." *Biblical Interpretation* 3, no. 1 (1995): 35–59.

Loprieno, Antonio. "Searching for a Common Background: Egyptian Love Poetry and the Biblical Song of Songs." In *Perspectives on the Song of Songs*, edited by Anselm C. Hagedorn, 105–35. Berlin: de Gruyter, 2005.

Lapinkivi, Pirjo. "The Adorning of the Bride: Providing Her with Wisdom." In *Sex and Gender in the Ancient Near East: Proceedings of the 47th Rencontre Assyriologique Internationale, Helsinki, July 2–6, 2001*, part 1, edited by S. Parpola and R. M. Whiting, 327–35. Helsinki: Neo-Assyrian Text Corpus Project, 2002.

———. "The Sumerian Sacred Marriage and Its Aftermath in Later Sources." In *Sacred Marriages: The Divine-Human Sexual Metaphor from Sumer to Early Christianity*, edited by Martti Nissinen and Risto Uro, 7–41. Winona Lake, IN: Eisenbrauns, 2008.

Lapsley, Jaqueline E. "Shame and Self-Knowledge: The Positive Role of Shame in Ezekiel's View of the Moral Self." In *The Book of Ezekiel: Theological and Anthropological Perspectives*, edited by Margaret S. Odell and John T. Strong, 143–73. Atlanta: SBL, 2000.

Levinson, Bernard M. *Deuteronomy and the Hermeneutics of Legal Innovation.* Oxford: Oxford University Press, 1997.

Lieberman, Saul. "Mishnat Shir ha-Shirim." In *Jewish Gnosticism, Merkabah Mysticism, and Talmudic Tradition*, edited by Gershom Scholem, 118–26. 2nd ed. New York: Jewish Theological Seminary, 1965.

Linafelt, Tod. "Biblical Love Poetry (. . . and God)." *JAAR* 70 (2002): 323–45.

Lind, Millard C. *Ezekiel.* Believers Church Bible Commentary. Scottdale, PA: Herald, 1996.

Littledale, R. F. *A Commentary on the Song of Songs from Ancient and Mediaeval Sources.* London: n.p., 1869.

Loewe, Raphael. "Apologetic Motifs in the Targum to the Song of Songs." In *Biblical Motifs: Origins and Transformations*, edited by Alexander Altmann, 173–93. Cambridge, MA: Harvard University Press, 1966.

Longman, Tremper, III. *Song of Songs.* Grand Rapids: Eerdmans, 2001.

Loring, Richard Tuttle. "The Christian Historical Exegesis of the Song of Songs and Its Possible Jewish Antecedents." PhD dissertation, General Theological Seminary, New York, 1967.

Löw, Immanuel. *Die Flora der Juden.* Vol. 1, *Kryptogamae, Acanthacae, Graminaceae.* Leipzig: Wien, 1928.

Macintosh, A. A. *Hosea: A Critical and Exegetical Commentary.* International Critical Commentary. Edinburgh: T&T Clark, 1997.

Mackay, John L. *Hosea.* Mentor. Fearn, UK: Christian Focus, 2012.

———. *Isaiah 1–39.* Vol. 1. Darlington, UK: Evangelical Press, 2008.

Magdalene, F. Rachel. "Ancient Near Eastern Treaty-Curses and the Ultimate Texts of Terror: A Study of the Language of Divine Sexual Abuse in the Prophetic Corpus." In *A Feminist Companion to the Latter Prophets*, edited by Athalya Brenner, 326–52. A Feminist Companion to the Bible. Sheffield: Sheffield Academic, 1995.

Malul, Meir. "Adoption of Foundlings in the Bible and Mesopotamian Documents: A Study of Legal Metaphors in Ezekiel 16:1–7." *JSOT* 46 (1990): 97–126.

———. "Janus Parallelism in Biblical Hebrew: Two More Cases." *Biblische Zeitschrift* 41 (1997): 246–49.

Martindale, C. *Romantic Progression.* New York: Hemisphere, 1975.

May, Herbert G. "Some Cosmic Connotations of *Mayyim Rabbim,* 'Many Waters.'" *JBL* 74, no. 1 (1955): 9–21.

Mays, James Luther. *Hosea.* Old Testament Library. London: SCM, 1969.

McKane, W. "Poison, Trial by Ordeal and the Cup of Wrath." *VT* 30 (1980): 487–92.

McKeating, Henry. "Sanctions against Adultery in Ancient Israelite Society: With Some Reflections on Methodology in the Study of OT Ethics." *JSOT* 11 (1979): 57–72.

Meek, Theophile James. "Babylonian Parallels to the Song of Songs." *JBL* 43 (1924): 245–52.

———. "The Song of Songs and the Fertility Cult." In *A Symposium on the Song of Songs,* edited by Wilfred H. Schoff, 48–79. Philadelphia: Commercial Museum, 1924.

Meredith, Christopher. "The Lattice and the Looking Glass: Gendered Space in Song of Songs 2:8–14." *Journal of the American Academy of Religion* 80, no. 2 (2012): 365–86.

Meyers, C. "Gender Imagery in the Song of Songs." *Hebrew Annual Review* 10 (1986): 209–23.

———. "To Her Mother's House: Considering a Counterpart to the Israelite *Bet 'ab.*" In *The Bible and Politics of Exegesis: Essays in Honour of Norman K. Gottwald on His Sixty Fifth Birthday,* edited by David Jobling, Peggy L. Day, and Gerald T. Sheppard, 39–51. Cleveland: Pilgrim, 1991.

Miscall, Peter D. *Isaiah.* Sheffield: Sheffield Academic, 1993.

Mitchell, Matthew W. "Finding the Naked Woman in Hosea ii 11." *VT* 57 (2007): 114–23.

———. "Hosea 1–2 and the Search for Unity." *JSOT* 29, no. 1 (2004): 115–27.

Moran, William. "The Ancient Near Eastern Background for the Love of God in Deuteronomy." *CBQ* 25 (1963): 77–87.

Moor, Johannes C. de. "The Love of God in the Targum to the Prophets." *Journal for the Study of Judaism* 24, no. 2 (1993): 257–65.

Moore, Stephen D. "The Song of Songs in the History of Sexuality." *Church History* 69, no. 2 (2000): 328–49.

Morgenstern, J. *Rites of Birth, Marriage, Death, and Kindred Occasions among the Semites.* Cincinnati: Hebrew Union College Press, 1966.

Moscati, Sabatino, et al. *An Introduction to the Comparative Grammar of the Semitic Languages.* Wiesbaden: Harrassowitz, 1969.

Motyer, J. A. *The Prophecy of Isaiah.* Leicester: InterVarsity, 1993.

Muller, H.-P. "Das Hohelied." In *Das Hohelied, Klagelieder, Das Buch Ester*, edited by H.-P. Muller, O. Kaiser, and J. A. Loader, 1–90. Alte Testament Deutsch 16/2. Göttingen: Vandenhoeck & Ruprecht, 1992.

Munro, Jill M. *Spikenard and Saffron: A Study in the Poetic Language of the Song of Songs.* JSOTSup 203. Sheffield: Sheffield Academic, 1995.

Murphy, Roland E. "Patristic and Medieval Exegesis—Help or Hindrance?" *CBQ* 43 (1981): 505–16.

———. *The Song of Songs.* Hermeneia. Minneapolis: Augsburg Fortress, 1990.

Murphy, Roland E., and Elizabeth Huwiler. *Proverbs, Ecclesiastes and Song of Songs.* New International Bible Commentary. Peabody, MA: Hendrickson, 1999.

Naylor, Peter. *Ezekiel.* Darlington, UK: Evangelical Press, 2011.

Nissinen, Martti. "Love Lyrics of Nabû and Tašmetu: An Assyrian Song of Songs?" In *"Und Mose schrieb dieses Lied auf": Studien zum Alten Testamentum und zum Alten Orient—Festschrift für Oswald Loretz*, edited by Manfried Dietrich and Ingo Kottsieper, 285–634. AOAT 250. Münster: Ugarit-Verlag, 1998.

———. "Song of Songs and Sacred Marriage." In *Sacred Marriages: The Divine-Human Sexual Metaphor from Sumer to Early Christianity*, edited by Martti Nissinen and Risto Uro, 173–218. Winona Lake, IN: Eisenbrauns, 2008.

Nissinen, Martti, and Risto Uro, eds. *Sacred Marriages: The Divine-Human Sexual Metaphor from Sumer to Early Christianity.* Winona Lake, IN: Eisenbrauns, 2008.

Norris, Richard A., Jr., trans. and ed. *The Song of Songs: Interpreted by Early Christian and Medieval Commentators.* Grand Rapids: Eerdmans, 2003.

Odell, Margaret S. *Ezekiel.* Smyth and Helwys Bible Commentary Series. Macon, GA: Smyth & Helwys, 2005.

Olyan, S. M. "In the Sight of Her Lovers: The Interpretation of *nablūt* in Hos 2:12." *Biblische Zeitschrift* 36 (1992): 255–61.

Origen. *The Song of Songs: Commentaries and Homilies.* Translated by R. P. Lawson. Ancient Christian Writers 26. Westminster, MD: Newman, 1947.

Oropeza, B. J. "Intertextuality." In *The Oxford Encyclopedia of Biblical Interpretation*, edited by Steven L. McKenzie, 1:453–63. Oxford: Oxford University Press, 2013.

Oropeza, B. J., and Steve Moyise. *Exploring Intertextuality: Diverse Strategies for New Testament Interpretation of Texts.* Eugene, OR: Cascade, 2016.

Ortlund, Raymond C., Jr., *Whoredom: God's Unfaithful Wife in Biblical Theology.* Grand Rapids: Eerdmans, 1996.

Oswalt, John N. *The Book of Isaiah: Chapters 1–39.* NICOT. Grand Rapids: Eerdmans, 1986.

Patai, R. *Family, Love and the Bible.* Garden City, NY: Doubleday, 1960.

———. *Sex and Family in the Bible and the Middle East.* Garden City, NY: Doubleday, 1959.

Patmore, Hector. "'The Plain and Literal Sense': On Contemporary Assumptions about the Song of Songs." *Vetus Testamentum* 56, no. 2 (2006): 239–50.

Paton, Corrine L. "'Should Our Sister Be Treated Like a Whore?': A Response to Feminist Critiques of Ezekiel 23." In *The Book of Ezekiel: Theological and Anthropological Perspectives,* edited by Margaret S. Odell and John T. Strong, 221–45. Atlanta: SBL, 2000.

Paul, S. M. "A Lover's Garden of Verse: Literal and Metaphorical Imagery in Ancient Near Eastern Love Poetry." In *Tehillah le-Moshe: Biblical and Judaic Studies in Honour of Moshe Greenberg,* edited by M. Cogan, B. A. Eichler, and J. H. Tigay, 99–110. Winona Lake, IN: Eisenbrauns, 1997.

Phillips, Anthony. "Another Look at Adultery." *JSOT* 20 (1981): 3–25.

Polaski, Donald C. "What Will Ye See in the Shulammite? Women, Power and Panopticism in the Song of Songs." *Biblical Interpretation* 5, no. 1 (1997): 64–81.

Pongratz-Leisten, Beate. "Sacred Marriage and the Transfer of Divine Knowledge: Alliances between the Gods and Kings in Ancient Mesopotamia." In *Sacred Marriages: The Divine-Human Sexual Metaphor from Sumer to Early Christianity,* edited by Martti Nissinen and Risto Uro, 43–73. Winona Lake, IN: Eisenbrauns, 2008.

Pope, Marvin H. *Song of Songs: A New Translation with Introduction and Commentary.* Anchor Bible 7C. New Haven: Yale University Press, 1977.

Pritchard, James B. *Ancient Near Eastern Texts: An Anthology of Texts and Pictures.* Princeton: Princeton University Press, 2011.

Provan, Iain. *Ecclesiastes, Song of Songs.* NIVAC. Grand Rapids: Zondervan, 2001.

Rainbow, Jesse. "The Song of Songs and the *Testament of Solomon*: Solomon's Love Poetry and Christian Magic." *Harvard Theological Review* 100, no. 3 (2007): 249–74.

Reiner, Erica. "A Sumero-Akkadian Hymn of Nanā." *JNES* 33 (1974): 221–36.

Riegner, Irene E. *The Vanishing Hebrew Harlot: The Adventures of the Hebrew Stem ZNH.* SBL 73. New York: Peter Lang, 2003.

Roberts, D. Philip. *Let Me See Your Form: Seeking Poetic Structure in the Song of Songs.* Lanham, MD: University Press of America, 2007.

Sadgrove, M. "The Song of Songs as Wisdom Literature." In *Studia Biblica*, 245–48. JSOTSup 11. Sheffield: JSOT, 1978.

Sæbø, Magne. "On the Canonicity of the Song of Songs." In *Texts, Temples, and Traditions: A Tribute to Menachem Haran*, edited by Michael V. Fox et al., 267–77. Winona Lake, IN: Eisenbrauns, 1996.

Sarna, Nahum. "Psalm 89: A Study in Inner Biblical Exegesis." In *Biblical and Other Studies*, edited by Alexander Altmann, 29–46. Cambridge: Harvard University Press, 1963.

Sasson, Jack M. "A Further Cuneiform Parallel to the Song of Songs?" *ZAW* 85 (1973): 359–60.

Saussure, Ferdinand de. *Course in General Linguistics*. Chicago: Open Court, 1983.

Sawyer, John F. A. *Isaiah*. Vol. 1. Philadelphia: Westminster, 1984.

Schafer, P. *Synopse zur Hekhalot Literatur*. Tübingen: Mohr, 1981.

Sherwood, Yvonne. *The Prostitute and the Prophet: Hosea's Marriage in Literary-Theoretical Perspective*. JSOTSup 212; Gender, Culture, Theory 2. Sheffield: Sheffield Academic, 1996.

Schulz-Rauch, Martin. *Hosea und Jeremia: Zur Wirkungsgeschichte des Hoseabuchs*. CThM 16. Stuttgart: Calver, 1996.

Schultz, Richard L. "Intertextuality, Canon, and 'Undecidability': Understanding Isaiah's 'New Heavens and New Earth' (Isaiah 65:17–25)." *Bulletin for Biblical Research* 20, no. 1 (2010): 19–38.

Seifert, Brigitte. *Metaphorisches Reden von Gott in Hoseabuch*, FRLANT 166. Göttingen: Vandenhoeck & Ruprecht, 1996.

Setel, T. Drorah. "Prophets and Pornography: Female Sexual Imagery in Hosea." In *Feminist Interpretation of the Bible*, edited by Letty M. Russell, 86–95. Oxford: Blackwell, 1985.

Sheppard, G. T. "More on Isaiah 5:1–7 as a Juridical Parable." *CBQ* 44 (1982): 45–47.

Shields, Mary E. "Multiple Exposures: Body Rhetoric and Gender Characterization in Ezekiel 16." *Journal of Feminist Studies in Religion*, 14, no. 1 (1998): 5–18.

———. "Self-response to 'Multiple Exposures.'" In *A Feminist Companion to Prophets and Daniel*, edited by Athalya Brenner, 160–63. A Feminist Companion to the Bible, Series 2. Sheffield: Sheffield Academic, 2001.

Silva, Charles H. "Literary Features in the Book of Hosea." *Bib Sacra* 164 (2007): 34–48.

———. "The Literary Structure of Hosea 1–3." *Bib Sacra* 164 (2007): 181–97.

Simon, Uriel. "The Poor Man's Ewe Lamb: An Example of a Juridical Parable." *Biblica* 48 (1967): 207–42.

Sjöerg, Åke W. "in.nin šà.gur4.ra: A Hymn to the Goddess Innana by the en-Priestess Enḫeduanna." *ZA* 65 (1975): 161–253.

Sloane, Andrew. "Aberrant Textuality? The Case of Ezekiel the (Porno) Prophet." *Tyndale Bulletin* 59, no. 1 (2008): 53–76.

Smith, Mark S. "Sacred Marriage in the Ugaritic Texts? The Case of KTU/CAT 1.23 (Rituals and Myths of the Goodly Gods)." In *Sacred Marriages: The Divine-Human Sexual Metaphor from Sumer to Early Christianity*, edited by Martti Nissinen and Risto Uro, 93–113. Winona Lake, IN: Eisenbrauns, 2008.

Smith, Ralph L. "Major Motifs of Hosea." *Southwestern Journal of Theology* 18, no. 1 (1975): 22–32.

Snaith, John G. *The Song of Songs*. New Century Bible Commentary. Grand Rapids: Eerdmans, 1993.

Sommer, Benjamin D. "Exegesis, Allusion and Intertextuality in the Hebrew Bible: A Response to Lyle Eslinger." *VT* 46, no. 4 (1996): 479–89.

———. *A Prophet Reads Scripture: Allusion in Isaiah 40–66.* Stanford, CA: Stanford University Press, 1998.

Soulen, Richard D. "The *Wasfs* of Song of Songs and Hermeneutic." *Journal of Biblical Literature* 86 (1967): 183–90.

Stacey, David. *Isaiah 1–39*. Epworth Commentaries. London: Epworth, 1993.

Stephan, H. *Modern Palestinian Parallels to the Song of Songs*. Studies in Palestinian Customs and Folklore 3. Jerusalem: Palestine Oriental Society, 192.

Stienstra, Nelly. *YHWH Is the Husband of His People: Analysis of a Biblical Metaphor with Special Reference to Translation*. Kampen: Pharos, 1993.

Stuart, Douglas. *Hosea-Jonah*. WBC 31. Waco, TX: Word, 1987.

Swanpoel, M. G. "Ezekiel 16: Abandoned Child, Bride Adorned or Unfaithful Wife?" In *Among the Prophets: Language, Image and Structure in the Prophetic Writings*, edited by Philip R. Davies and David J. A. Clines, 84–104. JSOT-Sup 144. Sheffield: Sheffield Academic, 1993.

Sweeney, Marvin A. *Isaiah 1–39*. Forms of Old Testament Literature 16. Grand Rapids: Eerdmans, 1996.

Tangberg, K. A. "A Note on *Pisti* in Hosea II 7, 11." *VT* 27, no. 2 (1977): 222–24.

Tanner, J. Paul, "The History of Interpretation of the Song of Songs." *Bibliotheca Sacra* 154 (1997): 23–46.

Taylor, John B. *Ezekiel: An Introduction and Commentary*. Leicester: InterVarsity, 1969.

Teppo, Saana. "Sacred Marriage and the Devotees of Ištar." In *Sacred Marriages: The Divine-Human Sexual Metaphor from Sumer to Early Christianity*, edited by Martti Nissinen and Risto Uro, 75–92. Winona Lake, IN: Eisenbrauns, 2008.

Thomas, D. W. "A Consideration of Some Unusual Ways of Expressing the Superlative in Hebrew." *VT* 3 (1953): 209–24.

Thompson, John L. *Reading the Bible with the Dead.* Grand Rapids: Eerdmans, 2007.

Toeg, Aryeh. "Num 15.22–31 Midrash Halacha." *Tarbiẓ* 43 (1973–74): 1–20.

Törnkvist, Rut. *The Use and Abuse of Female Sexual Imagery in the Book of Hosea: A Feminist Critical Approach to Hos 1–3.* Uppsala Women's Studies: Women in Religion 7. Uppsala: Uppsala University Press, 1998.

Trible, Phyllis. *God and the Rhetoric of Sexuality.* Philadelphia: Fortress Press, 1978.

Tuell, Steven. *Ezekiel.* NIBC. Peabody, MA: Hendrickson, 2009.

Underhill, Evelyn. *Mysticism.* New York: Dutton, 1961.

Vang, Carsten. "God's Love According to Hosea and Deuteronomy: A Prophetic Re-working of a Deuteronomic Concept?" *Tyndale Bulletin* 62, no. 2 (2011): 173–94.

Verbin, John S. Kloppenborg. "Egyptian Viticultural Practices and the Citation of Isa 5:1–7 in Mark 12:1–9." *NT* 44, no. 2 (2002): 134–59.

Wacker, Marie-Theres. *Figurationen des Weiblichen im Hosea-Buch*, HBS 8. Freiberg: Herder, 1996.

Walsh, Carey Ellen. *Exquisite Desire: Religion, the Erotic, and the Song of Songs.* Minneapolis: Fortress Press, 2000.

Waltke, Bruce K., and M. O'Connor. *An Introduction to Biblical Hebrew Syntax.* Winona Lake, IN: Eisenbrauns, 1990.

Watson, Wilfred G. E. *Classical Hebrew Poetry: A Guide to Its Techniques.* 2nd ed. JSOTSup 26. Sheffield: Sheffield Academic, 1995.

———. "Love and Death Once More (Song of Songs VIII 6)." *VT* 47, no. 3 (1997): 385–96.

Watts, John D. W. *Isaiah 1–33.* WBC 24. Waco, TX: Word, 1985.

Weems, Renita J. *Battered Love: Marriage, Sex and Violence in the Hebrew Prophets.* Minneapolis: Fortress Press, 1995.

———. "Gomer: Victim of Violence or Victim of Metaphor?" *Semeia* 47 (1989): 87–104.

Weinfeld, Moshe. *Deuteronomy and the Deuteronomic School.* Oxford: Clarendon, 1972.

Weider, Andreas. *Ehemetaphorik in prophetischer Verkündigung: Hos 1–3 und seine Wirkungsgeschichte im Jeremiabuch: Ein Beitrag zum alttestamentlichen Gottes-Bild.* FzB 71. Würzburg: Echter, 1993.

Wenham, Gordon J. *Genesis 1–15.* WBC 1. Waco, TX: Word, 1994.

Wertheimer, S. A., ed. *Batte Misrashot*. Vol. 1. 2nd ed. Jerusalem: Ktav Vasefer, 1968.

Wevers, John W., ed. *Ezekiel*. Century Bible New Series. London: Thomas Nelson, 1969.

Whedbee, J. William. "Paradox and Parody in the Song of Solomon: Towards a Comic Reading of the Most Sublime Song." In *A Feminist Companion to the Song of Songs*, edited by Athalya Brenner, 266–78. A Feminist Companion to the Bible. Sheffield: Sheffield Academic, 1993.

White, John Bradley. *A Study of the Language of Love in the Song of Songs and Ancient Egyptian Poetry*. SBLDS 38. Missoula, MT: Scholars, 1978.

Wildberger, Hans. *Isaiah 1–12: A Commentary*. Translated by Thomas H. Trapp. Continental Commentaries. Minneapolis: Augsburg Fortress, 1991.

Williams, Gary Roye. "Frustrated Expectations in Isaiah V 1–7: A Literary Interpretation." *VT* 35, no. 4 (1985): 459–65.

Williamson, H. G. M. *Isaiah 1–5*. ICC. Edinburgh: T&T Clark, 2006.

Willis, J. T. "The Genre of Isa 5:1–7." *Journal of Biblical Literature* 96 (1977): 337–62.

———. "On the Text of Micah 2:1aα–β." *Biblica* 48 (1967): 534–41.

Wolde, Ellen van. "Texts in Dialogue with Texts: Intertextuality in the Ruth and Tamar Narratives." *Biblical Interpretation* 5, no. 1 (1997): 1–28.

Wolff, Hans Walter. *Hosea*. Translated by Gary Stansell. Hermeneia. Philadelphia: Fortress Press, 1974.

Wright, J. Robert, ed. *Proverbs, Ecclesiastes, Song of Solomon*. Ancient Christian Commentary on Scripture, Old Testament 9. Downers Grove, IL: InterVarsity, 2005.

Wright, Christopher J. H. *The Message of Ezekiel: A New Heart and a New Spirit*. Bible Speaks Today. Leicester: InterVarsity, 2001.

Wyrtzen, David B. "The Theological Centre of the Book of Hosea." *Bib Sacra* 141, no. 564 (1984): 315–29.

Young, Edward J. *The Book of Isaiah 1–18*. Vol. 1. Grand Rapids: Eerdmans, 1965.

Yee, Gale A. "The Form-Critical Study of Isaiah 5:1–7 as a Song and a Juridical Parable." *CBQ* 43 (1981): 30–40.

———. "'She Is Not My Wife and I Am Not Her Husband': A Materialist Analysis of Hosea 1–2." *Biblical Interpretation* 9, no. 4 (2001): 345–83.

Zakovitch, Y. *Das Hohelied*. HThKAT. Freiburg: Herder, 2004.

———. *An Introduction to Inner-Biblical Interpretation*. Even-Yehuda: Reches, 1992.

Zimmerli, Walther. *Ezekiel 1: A Commentary on the Book of the Prophet Ezekiel,*

Chapters 1–24. Translated by Ronald E Clements. Hermeneia. Philadelphia: Fortress Press, 1979.

Zlotowitz, Meir, compiler. *Shir haShirim/Song of Songs: An Allegorical Translation Based upon Rashi with a Commentary Anthologized from Talmudic, Midrashic and Rabbinic Sources*. New York: Mesorah, 1979.

Author Index

ANCIENT AND MEDIEVAL AUTHORS AND SOURCES

Scripture Index